The Evolution of the British Welfare State

Related Palgrave Macmillan titles:

Helen Fawcett and Rodney Lowe (eds), *Welfare Policy in Britain: The Road from 1945*

David Gladstone, *The Twentieth-Century Welfare State*

Rodney Lowe, *The Welfare State in Britain since 1945*, 2nd edition

Robert Page and Richard Silburn (eds), *British Social Welfare in the Twentieth Century*

The Evolution of the British Welfare State

A History of Social Policy since the Industrial Revolution

Third Edition

Derek Fraser

First edition published 1973
Reprinted seven times
Second edition 1984
Third edition 2003
Published by
PALGRAVE MACMILLAN
Houndmills, Basingstoke, Hampshire RG21 6XS and
175 Fifth Avenue, New York, N.Y. 10010
Companies and representatives throughout the world

PALGRAVE MACMILLAN is the global academic imprint of the Palgrave
Macmillan division of St. Martin's Press, LLC and of Palgrave Macmillan Ltd.
Macmillan® is a registered trademark in the United States, United Kingdom
and other countries. Palgrave is a registered trademark in the European
Union and other countries.

ISBN 1–4039–0469–3 hardback
ISBN 0–333–94659–6 paperback

This book is printed on paper suitable for recycling and made from fully
managed and sustained forest sources.

A catalogue record for this book is available from the British Library.

Library of Congress Cataloging-in-Publication Data
Fraser, Derek.
    The evolution of the British welfare state: a history of social policy since the
    Industrial Revolution / Derek Fraser — 3rd ed.
        p.   cm.
    Includes bibliographical references and index.
    ISBN 1–4039–0469–3 (cloth)
    1. Great Britain—Social policy.   2. Welfare state.   I. Title.

    HN385 .F66 2003
    361.6′1′0941—dc21

                                                        2002028673

10   9   8   7   6   5   4   3   2   1
12   11   10   09   08   07   06   05   04   03

Printed and bound in Great Britain by
Creative Print and Design, Wales

For Ruth

Contents

List of Tables

Preface

This book has grown out of my years of teaching and research in the field of British social history. Its precise origins lay in a course on 'The Historical Background to Social Policy' which was launched in 1965 for the University of Bradford's School of Applied Social Studies. Elements of this original scheme (much amended since) also figured strongly in the university's history courses. I owe a great deal to the seven cohorts of history and applied social studies undergraduates at Bradford University who have passed through my hands. They helped me, by perceptive criticism, by intelligent discussion and sometimes by perverse misunderstanding, to formulate, clarify and refine my ideas on social policy.

All of us who are interested in the history of social policy face the difficulty of pulling together the separate elements in social administration and its study. It has often been the province of experts in social work searching for the origins of present-day services. The awareness of the professional casework issues involved elevates the value of such studies, but they are written almost invariably in isolation from the ever-growing army of administrative historians working, for instance, on the Victorian administrative state. Such a concept itself involves explicitly the whole field of the history of ideas, political, economic and social. Similarly, the historian of social policy looks to economists working on the impact of the old Poor Law on wages or the nature and consequences of inter-war unemployment. The urban and regional historians are providing evidence of the practical workings of social administration at the local level. Social policy equally flits in and out of the national political story, with greater frequency as time goes on. The list could be extended.

Considerable difficulties are posed when trying to bring such variegated shafts of light into focus. The present book aims to provide a context in which the many different strands in social policy can be woven together. It also seeks to integrate into a coherent analysis the disparate academic researches involved in this subject. Such a synthesis naturally builds on the work of many researchers, who have thus aided in the writing of this book unawares. The references and the bibliography identify the scholars who have made this book the work of many hands. I hope I have done justice to the ideas of others, who are in no way responsible for my particular selection, arrangement or assessment of the evidence. While incorporating the results of the recent research of others, the book also draws on my own researches into the history of the press and nineteenth-century cities. Something, too, derives from my work on the Lloyd George, Beveridge and Braithwaite papers.

Colleagues at Bradford in both history and applied social studies have been sympathetic and helpful. In particular, Chris Little has been a stimulating mentor in the field of contemporary social policy. He was kind enough to lend me his much-annotated and now tattered copy of the Beveridge Report, and he made some useful suggestions on the last two chapters of the book. My close friend and history colleague Ken Clayton read the whole book at both typescript and proof stage. He painstakingly corrected the text and made many useful stylistic and grammatical improvements. He was always generous with his advice, though unsparing in his criticism. For both I thank him. I must also thank Barbara Dalby, who made light work of a difficult manuscript and worked exceptionally hard under pressure to produce a final typescript.

At the publishers my contacts were always kind and encouraging, and I am grateful to Alastair Maclean, who first recruited me; T. M. Farmiloe, who nursed me through a difficult intermediary stage and bore well the perennial author's plea for the book to be 'later and longer'; and Derick Mirfin, who acted as godfather and saw the book through the press. At home, Philip, Clio and Adam ensured that I retained a due sense of perspective by frequently converting my study into a playroom and by displaying an irresistible attraction for all forms of writing instruments, which mysteriously disappeared from my desk. Fellow-authors will know how much I owe to my wife, who acted as sounding-board, proof-reader, grammarian, dictionary, comforter and confessor. The book has been a joint burden.

D. F.

University of Bradford

Preface to the Second Edition

The opportunity to revise a book ten years after its first publication provides a temptation to go right back to the drawing board and start again. I have resisted this temptation partly because the original structure still seems to be reasonable and partly because of the advice I received from colleagues elsewhere who counselled a cautious revision. The organisation of the chapters is therefore unchanged, though one chapter has been retitled to clarify its contents. All chapters have been revised in the light of recent research and of the changing perceptions of welfare during the past decade. Several new documents have been introduced into the appendices and the bibliography has been substantially extended, now including a much fuller survey of articles and essays. The original introductory and concluding chapters are left to stand intact as an indication of what it seemed appropriate to say in 1973, a year which has since been identified as an important turning-point in British social and political history. A new foreword is provided to elucidate the variety of perspectives from which welfare history may be considered. These perspectives are both clearer to me and more explicitly represented in current research and writing than they were ten years ago. In a new postscript I offer a brief comment on the developments of the last decade which seemed likely to make the Welfare State of the last quarter of the century a very different institution from that established in the mid-century.

I am very pleased to record my gratitude to my colleague Jack Morrell who made many valuable suggestions for improving the original text and to Alan Deacon who shared with me his unrivalled knowledge of the recent history of British social policy. My main thanks are due to those many teachers at all levels (as I understand, from O-level through to postgraduate) whose support for the book has seen it through seven reprints and has extended its life beyond my expectations. I hope that they and their students will find this second edition of some help as an introduction to a fascinating field of historical studies.

D. F.

University of Bradford
February 1983

Preface to the Third Edition

To revise a book first written thirty years ago (and revised nearly twenty years ago) poses a particular challenge. What author would deny that the passage of time really demands a wholly new book? However, an established and well-used text is familiar to those who find it still of value and I again have followed their advice that the book's essential structure should be retained intact. Yet this has not prevented me from making some important changes. The Conclusion of the first edition and the Postscript of the second are now replaced by a wholly new chapter on the Welfare State's first half century. This now permits an analysis of what is increasingly being referred to as 'the classic Welfare State' and its partial disintegration through Thatcherite and Blairite policies. I have revised each chapter in the light of the massive amount of research which has been published since 1984 and over 200 items have been added to what, I hope, is a comprehensive bibliography.

I am pleased to record my thanks to several people without whose assistance I would never have reached this point. Maureen Nicholl, a mature research student, did sterling work in bibliographical searches and ensured that I was apprised of the latest literature. Again, I thank Alan Deacon for advice and guidance on contemporary welfare issues. At Palgrave Macmillan I have been treated with great patience, as successive deadlines were missed. I am grateful to Terka Acton for retaining faith in me and for seeing the book through the process. Finally, and most important of all, my sincere thanks are due to my personal assistant, Karen Alexander, who made light work of the complex task of producing the revised typescript.

D. F.

University of Teesside
March 2002

Acknowledgements

The author wishes to acknowledge with thanks that access was granted to source material by the following institutions: the Public Record Office; the Beaverbrook Library; the University of London Library; the British Library of Political and Economic Science; the Thoresby Society, Leeds.

Permission to quote from Crown copyright material was given by the Director of Publications at Her Majesty's Stationery Office; from the Lloyd George papers by the First Beaverbrook Foundation; from the Beveridge and Braithwaite papers by Mr C. G. Allen for the British Library of Political and Economic Science; from *The Times* by Times Newspapers Ltd; from the Leeds Waterworks pamphlets by the Thoresby Society; from his unpublished MA thesis 'Newspapers and Opinion in Cambridge, 1790–1850' (University of Kent, 1971) by Mr M. J. Murphy; from the Pilgrim Trust studies by the Cambridge University Press; rom W. H. Beveridge's *Unemployment a Problem of Industry* by Mr Philip Mair; and from B. Seebohm Rowntree's *Poverty and Progress* by the Joseph Rowntree Charitable Trust. The author and publisher express their thanks for the granting of such permission.

Select time chart, 1801–2002

POLITICS		SOCIAL POLICY	
		1801	First census
1802	Peace of Amiens	1802	Health and Morals of Apprentices Act
		1808	National Vaccine Establishment
1812	Lord Liverpool Tory PM		
1815	Peace; Corn Law	1816	Peel's Factory Inquiry
1819	Peterloo; Six Acts		
1824	Repeal of Combination Acts		
1828	Wellington Tory PM	1828	Madhouses Act; first Asylum Inspector
1829	Catholic Emancipation	1829	Metropolitan Police Force
1830	Grey Whig PM	1830	Oastler's letters on 'Yorkshire Slavery'
		1831	Central Board of Health (Cholera)
1832	Reform Act	1832	Sadler Committee; Royal Commission on the Poor Law
		1833	Althorp's Factory Act; grant to education
1834	Melbourne Whig PM	1834	Poor Law Amendment Act
1835	Municipal Corporations Act		
1837	Accession of Queen Victoria	1837	Civil registration
1838	People's Charter	1839	Police Act; Committee of the Council for Education
		1840	Free vaccination

1841	Peel Conservative PM		
1842	Peel's first free trade budget	1842	Mines Act; Chadwick Report
		1843	Factory Bill withdrawn
1844	Bank Charter Act	1844	Factory Act; Health of Towns Commission
		1845	Lunacy Act
1846	Repeal of Corn Laws; Conservatives split – Russell Whig PM	1846	Liverpool Sanitary Act; Minutes of the Committee of the Council
		1847	Ten Hours Act; Poor Law Board
1848	Revolutions in Europe; Chartist Kennington Common fiasco	1848	Public Health Act
1851	Great Exhibition	1851	Shaftesbury Acts – Common Lodging Houses
		1853	Compulsory vaccination
1854	Crimean War	1854	Youthful Offenders Act
1855	Palmerston Whig PM	1856	County and Borough Police Act
		1858	Medical Act – General Medical Council; Local Government Act; Medical Department of Privy Council
		1858–61	Newcastle Commission

		1862	Revised Code for Education
1865	Death of Palmerston	1866	Sanitary Act
1867	Second Reform Act	1867	Metropolitan Poor Act; Factory Act; Hours of Labour Regulation Act
1868	Gladstone Liberal PM	1868	Torrens Act
		1869	Sanitary Commission; Charity Organisation Society
		1870	Forster's Education Act
		1871	Local Government Board
		1872	Public Health Act
1874	Disraeli Conservative PM	1874	Factory Act
		1875	Public Health Act; Artisans' Dwellings Act (Cross)
		1876	Sandon's Education Act
		1878	Factories and Workshops Act
1880	Gladstone Liberal PM	1880	Mundella's Education Act
1884	Third Reform Act	1882–5	Koch and Pasteur – germ theory of disease
1885	Redistribution of seats; Medical Relief (Disqualifications Removal) Act	1885	Royal Commission on Housing of the Working Classes; Housing of the Working Classes Act

1918	'Coupon election'	1918	Fisher's Education Act
		1919	Addison's Housing Act; Ministry of Health
		1920	Unemployment Insurance Act
1922	Fall of Lloyd George; Bonar Law Conservative PM		
1923	Baldwin Conservative PM	1923	Chamberlain's Housing Act
1924	Ramsay MacDonald PM; Baldwin Conservative PM	1924	Wheatley's Housing Act
		1925	Contributory pensions
		1925–7	Blanesburgh Committee
1926	General Strike	1926	Hadow Report
1929	MacDonald Labour PM	1929	Local Government Act
		1930	Greenwood's Housing Act
1931	May Committee Report; fall of Labour Government; MacDonald PM of National Government	1931	Dole cut – family means test
		1932	Holman Gregory Report
		1933	Children and Young Persons Act
		1934	Unemployment Act
1935	Baldwin National PM	1935	Unemployment Assistance Board; Housing Act
		1936	Public Health Act

1937	Chamberlain National PM	1937	Factory Act
		1938	Spens Report
1939	Second World War	1939	Emergency medical service
1940	Churchill Coalition PM	1940	National milk scheme; supplementary pensions
		1941	Determination of Needs Act
		1942	Beveridge Report
		1943	White Paper on Education
		1944	White Papers on Insurance, Health and Full Employment; Butler's Education Act
1945	Attlee Labour PM	1945	Family Allowances Act
		1946	National Insurance Act; National Insurance (Industrial Injuries) Act; National Health Service Act
		1948	National Assistance Act
		5 July 1948	Appointed day
1950	Korean War		

1951	Churchill PM	1951	Bevan resigns over NHS charges
		1952	Prescription charges introduced
		1953	300,000 new houses built
1955	Eden PM	1955	Guillebaud Report on NHS
1956	Suez Crisis		
1957	Macmillan PM	1957	Rent Act – deregulation of rents
		1958	Thorneycroft (Chancellor) resigns over welfare cuts
1959	Macmillan 'never had it so good' election		
1964	Wilson Labour PM		
		1965	Prescription Charges Abolished Circular 10/65 – End of selection at 11 +
		1966	Supplementary Benefit introduced (replaced National Assistance), Ministry of Social Security
1967	Sterling crisis: pound devalued		
		1968	Seebohm Report on Social Services
1970	Heath Conservative PM		
		1971	Family Income Supplement
		1972	Housing Finance Act
		1972	*Framework for Expansion* White Paper

1974	2 Elections, Wilson PM	1974	Joseph, local government and NHS structural reform
		1975	SERPS – earnings related pensions
1976	Callaghan PM	1976	'Great Debate' on education
1976	Financial crisis	1976	Child Benefit Reform postponed
1978–79	'Winter of discontent'	1978	30th Anniversary of Welfare State
1979	Thatcher Conservative PM		
		1980	Social expenditure cuts
1982	Falklands War	1982	Social Security and Housing Benefit Act
1983	Conservatives win election		
		1986	Fowler Review of Social Security Social Security Act
1987	Thatcher wins third election		
		1988	Education Reform Act (National Curriculum)
		1989	*Working for Patients* White Paper
1990	Thatcher resigns, Major PM	1990	NHS and Community Care Act
		1991	Citizens Charter, *The Health of the Nation* White Paper
1992	Major wins election		
		1993	Portillo/Lilley review of Welfare State
		1994	Labour 'National Commission' report
1997	Blair Labour PM	1997	'Welfare to Work' – New Deal

		1998	*A New Contract for Welfare* Green Paper
		1999	Income guarantee for pensioners
		2000	Brown budget – increases NHS expenditure, promotes work for unemployed
2001	Blair wins second landslide victory	2001	Stakeholder pensions
		2002	Brown budget – further major increase in NHS expenditure

Foreword: Perspectives on the history of welfare

The Welfare State is a concept which historians and sociologists alike have found difficult to define. Like socialism, it has meant different things to different people. As the distinguished social scientist W. A. Robson has remarked, it is not easy 'to discover what is the nature of the Welfare State...there is no positive or comprehensive philosophy, no ideology that underlies the Welfare State...the term...does not designate a definite system'.[1] Some features of the Welfare State in practice are clear, however. It is a system of social organisation which restricts free market operations in three principal ways: by the designation of certain groups, such as children or factory workers, whose rights are guaranteed and whose welfare is protected by the community; by the delivery of services such as medical care or education, so that no citizen shall be deprived of access to them; and by transfer payments which maintain income in times of exceptional need, such as parenthood, or of interruption of earnings caused by such things as sickness or unemployment. The history of social policy is concerned with these three areas and we shall find that it was not always believed that the protection of vulnerable groups, the provision of social services or the maintenance of income were the responsibility of the state. What the historian notices most about the place of the Welfare State in the history of social policy is that it is very much a time-bound concept. The term itself did not become commonly used until the 1940s, and it is in that decade that we can, with unusual chronological specificity, pinpoint the beginning of the Welfare State. On 5 July 1948 the connected schemes of insurance, assistance and medical care first came into operation in Britain. It was, indeed, a very important day, as the *Daily Mirror* explained: 'The great day has arrived. You wanted the State to assume greater responsibility for individual citizens. You wanted social security. From today you have it.'[2]

This stress on a specific beginning does not mean that the Welfare State was, like the conjuror's rabbit, plucked out of thin air. It was the end product of a very long historical process. The Beveridge Report of 1942 was the nearest thing to a blueprint for a Welfare

State which Britain had and that confirmed that though a Welfare State would be a revolution, 'in more important ways it is a natural development from the past. It is a British revolution.'[3] When James Griffiths, a Labour minister in 1946, introduced the insurance legislation on which the Welfare State is based, he said it was the result of at least fifty years of development of the social services. An American scholar, comparing the emergence of 'social programs' in different countries, has concluded that 'between 50 and 80 years is the likely diffusion time for all such programs'.[4] This diffusion time, perhaps in the British case a century and a half, is the subject of this study of the history of social policy. How should that history be characterised and in what context may it be understood? The research and writing on welfare history have revealed eight broad perspectives of study. The list is not exhaustive nor the categories exclusive but they cover the main frames of reference which have been employed. For convenience we may call the eight perspectives whig, pragmatic, bureaucratic, ideological, conspiratorial, capitalistic, democratic and mixed economy. Each perspective will be examined in turn.

The **whig** model of welfare history is so called because of its affinity with the 'whig interpretation of history'.[5] This was an English school of historical interpretation, established by certain whig historians such as Macaulay in the mid-nineteenth century. Believing themselves to be the possessors of a near-perfect liberal constitution, these historians wished to demonstrate the historical evolution of that constitution by stressing the forward-looking people and developments which had brought it about. It was a view of history characterised by a belief in progress and by an assessment of the past in terms of its relevance to the present. Similarly, in the whig interpretation of welfare history, developments in social policy are viewed as elements of progress on a path from intellectual darkness to enlightenment. As society became more sensitive to social need so the harsh excesses of the free market were curbed. Compassion and concern outweighed cruelty and indifference, and progressive reform resulted. As one social work scholar has expressed it, 'if reform is good then the social welfare policies which have been the elements of reform are also good. Social welfare thus basks in the warm reflection of its own historical rectitude.'[6] That moral rectitude was imparted by humanitarian reformers who opened people's eyes to the evils around them and who with untiring zeal pressurised the state to do the just thing by its citizens.

The whig model has many features to commend it. It appeals very much to the popular view of the Welfare State as a boon and therefore the product of a benevolent process. Understandably such a view found widespread acceptance during the years after 1948, reinforced by media accounts of foreigners flocking to Britain to take advantage of the benefits not available elsewhere. The whig view also satisfies a general desire to relate present to past in a clear and simple lineage and this interpretation pictures a strong line of development onward and upward to the Welfare State. The dangers of the model are equally clear. It encourages a mode of analysis which judges past social policy not on its own terms but by reference to some later, often unanticipated, development. It is a frame of reference which all too easily disseminates a condescending attitude in the present–past dialogue. The past is often judged by the moral standards of the present and usually found wanting. Thus in 1949 one scholar wrote with reference to the children of the 'perishing classes', 'Looking backward at the past from the vantage point of the mid-twentieth century, it is remarkable how slowly obvious needs came to be appreciated and how inadequate in quantity and quality were the services instituted.'[7] It may be thought more valuable to enquire why 'obvious needs' were not so regarded earlier, than to assert present enlightenment by describing the lack of awareness as 'remarkable'. As one historian warned, we do not study history to score points off the past but to try to understand it.

The **pragmatic** model perhaps surmounts some of these difficulties by considering present social policy not so much as better but different from that of the past. As the novelist L. P. Hartley put it, 'the past is a foreign country, they do things differently there'. The pragmatic view is much closer to the German school of history personified by von Ranke, who wanted to tell history 'as it really was', than to Macaulay's whig story of progress. Social policy is seen as evolving under the practical necessity of solving problems in the wake of industrialisation. In this model, developments tend to be *ad hoc* and unplanned, producing more incremental and less radical, more erratic and less direct paths than in the whig view. In the 1950s the American political scientist E. M. Burns described this model as typical of the way in which social policy responded to a changing society. Starting from a narrow base, *ad hoc* and incremental expansion, often responding to immediate pressures, alternated with short-term periodic reviews necessitated by inconsistencies and inadequacies within the system. After each review, in which ideological inputs might be important, *ad hoc* incrementalism took over again, and so policy developed along disparate routes, covering some terrain yet leaving other areas as virgin territory. As the British welfare historian Rodney Lowe explains, the only realistic view is the incrementalist approach comprising 'a series of small adjustments, often governed by expedience and by limited objectives which have unforeseen consequences'.[8] British experience can be explained on the Burns model. The practical problems caused by industrial change were so serious that they demanded immediate attention. With little thought for the ideological implications, governments utilised policy expedients to solve these problems which themselves revealed the need for further action. The shortfalls or misdirections of policy led to major reiews which may be identified in the 1830s, the Edwardian years and the 1940s, but there were no obvious or necessary linear connections between them and it is only hindsight which provides such connections. The pragmatic model is the dominant interpretative framework of this present study, though it is not intended to be the only one. Because it seeks to explore social policy within its historical and political context, this model tends to stress the practical against the theoretical, the short-term decision-making process rather than long-term policy evolution, and the significance of policy within its contemporary society in preference to its relevance to subsequent developments. It gives to the humanitarian reformer not the role of saint leading the people to moral truth, but that of propagandist in defining what problems were on the political agenda. When informed opinion was convinced that certain social evils were 'intolerable' then governments were required to respond. Social problems were on the agenda by being perceived as such. But the pragmatic model reveals that the agenda was never a complete guide to the worst of the social problems, for some unnoticed disadvantaged groups, such as handicapped children, were only belatedly added to it.

In carrying out whatever policy pragmatic political expediency demanded, governments increasingly came to use officials to enforce it and it is their importance which has led to the **bureaucratic** mode of interpretation. As before, humanitarians were the prime movers but they soon disappeared from the scene, as officials at all levels implemented policy, defined its future goals and became progenitors of further policy initiatives with an almost self-perpetuating momentum. This model requires us to explore in detail the specific legislation introduced, and above all its administration. Social policy changes are here best understood by analysing the role of the institutions of welfare and the officials who staffed them. Whether at local or national level these officials became professional experts, immune from political pressures and vested interests, and thus endowed with an impartial objectivity which gave their judgements great authority. They became 'statesmen in disguise' initiating, maturing and implementing new policies, so that the historian must uncover the private manoeuvres deep within the administrative system as well as narrating the public events such as parliamentary debates or protest meetings. There is a very important historiographical reason why the bureaucratic perspective should have acquired an important hold over scholars. Many of the source materials relevant to the history of social policy originated in official institutions and are preserved in essentially bureaucratic archives. Since they have survived in considerable bulk their study perforce has to be the central thrust of most research in welfare history. This not only means that bureaucratic activities are given a prominent place, it also means that there is a tendency to reconstruct the past through bureaucratic eyes. The problems are the problems as defined by the bureaucratic mentality, and the explanations of policy development may thus be unduly distorted by the workings of the official mind. Despite this the bureaucratic model has, in Roy Hay's words, 'been very important in conditioning the way in which the development of social policy has been conceived and interpreted by historians... who...have found it difficult to break out of the framework for the analysis of social policy which has been created'.[9]

One of the major criticisms of both the pragmatic and the bureaucratic models is that they undervalue the importance of ideas. How did some issues gain a place on the agenda of reform and how did bureaucrats decide on their policy goals? An understanding of the values, attitudes and mores of a society can place policy within its contemporary intellectual context so that an

ideological model may be fruitfully employed. The ideological perspective makes it possible to relate social policy to the prevailing cultural climate. It requires a much broader canvas than other models because the cultural ideology will express itself in a whole *gestalt*, not merely within the context of social questions. Out of that intellectual milieu a contemporary sense of values will emerge to justify particular policies. As any general historical survey demonstrates, profound ideological changes accompanied the equally profound social, economic and political thrust of that 'modernisation' which has characterised recent centuries. We should not underestimate how important these intellectual changes were in influencing the course of a social policy. In the mid-nineteenth century the prevailing philosophy decreed that provision for old age and sickness were the province of the individual: in the mid-twentieth they were reclassified as the responsibility of the state. In the early nineteenth century British 'classical economists' confidently asserted that the state could not possibly determine the level of employment. By the end of the Second World War the socialist writer G. D. H. Cole could record as a commonplace, 'the view that special measures, for which the Government must make itself responsible, are necessary in times of peace in order to ensure an adequate total demand for labour is now not only held by most economists but officially accepted as the Government's own policy'.[10] Naturally the proper role of government was perceived differently in different ideologies and it was the prevailing intellectual orthodoxy which to a great degree endowed certain social policy objectives with the necessary 'legitimacy' to justify state intervention.[11]

Thus the history of social policy may be conceived as the history of changes in what Robert Pinker has called 'the idea of welfare'.[12] Social policy at a particular time was the product of the social ethos of that time, and when in subtle ways and for complex reasons the ethos changed, the policy changed in conformity. So Cole, himself an ideologue, could describe the history of social policy as essentially a conflict between the ideas of *laissez-faire* and the ideas of state intervention, between the ideology of capitalism and the ideology of socialism.[13] A more recent analysis identified four ideological perspectives wherein social policy contends – the anti-collectivist, the reluctant collectivist, the Fabian socialist and the Marxist.[14] Another suggests that social policy evolves under the impact of changing theoretical ideology of law in relation to social welfare.[15] The labels will differ: the essential point remains the same – social policies reflect the contemporary ideological culture. We shall find much evidence of this truism. Nineteenth-century classical economics underlay the apparently harsh provisions of the 1830s just as twentieth-century collectivism underlay the apparently more generous provisions of the 1940s. Yet it remains obscure just how ideas spread and come to influence policy, and it is at least arguable that social policy influenced ideas as much as the other way round.

A more compelling criticism is that a simple contest of ideas, in which a more rational or appropriate theory succeeds by pure intellectual merit, takes too little account of the social basis of ideology. Class societies produce class ideologies and a prevailing contemporary culture is likely to represent the imposition of the values of a society's dominant class. Hence a policy apparently in conformity with a current ideology may in fact be geared to the hegemony of the class whose interests it benefits. An ideology may have a compelling attraction wherein intellectual conviction is buttressed by the rationalisation of self-interest. It is to take account of such possibilities that what is termed here the **conspiratorial** model has been widely utilised. On this model social policy is viewed as an aid to further some coercive social or political objective, whose identity is by no means clear from the terms in which the policy may be publicly discussed. The ulterior motive has to be probed. In this perspective welfare is far from benevolent, for its main attraction to those who espouse it is as an instrument of social control.[16] Welfare is therefore characterised as one of the means by which order and authority are preserved, social revolution avoided, and political stability maintained.

The conspiratorial model has found favour particularly with radical scholars who have been much impressed by the structuralism of Foucault. Michel Foucault, a French sociologist, identified the growing institutionalisation of treatment for the sick, the mentally ill and the criminal as a sign of a more subtle and disciplined attack upon all sorts of deviant or marginal behaviour. An example will illustrate how such a view may radically alter our interpretation and assessment of the historical record. During the first half of the nineteenth century much effort and money was expended in designing and building hospitals, asylums, prisons, workhouses and like institutions on a more rational plan. The whig perspective might see this as evidence of a more enlightened humane treatment and the bureaucratic as evidence of the growing specialisation and professionalisation of treatment. But the structuralist conspiratorial model finds here evidence of a desire to rule the populace more effectively through the behavioural controls of life in total institutions. As Foucault said of the great scheme of Jeremy Bentham modelled on these lines, it could 'constrain the convict to good behaviour, the madman to calm, the worker to work, the schoolboy to application, the patient to the observation of the regulations'.[17] The conspiratorial model has been further reinforced by American sociologists who stress the role of welfare in 'regulating the poor' or 'controlling the dangerous classes'.[18] Nor should we think that the Welfare State itself is free of these influences. A recent writer examining the nature of freedom in the Welfare State reminds us of 'the extent to which institutions of the Welfare State attempt to control society's most potentially dissident members, the people who are not sharing in the benefits of prosperity, the deviants and the unconformists'.[19]

Whether or not we find the conspiratorial perspective acceptable as an explanatory package, it should at the very least induce a healthy scepticism about the overt justification of the authority of rulers over the ruled. We are inclined to view nineteenth-century paternalism as an example of a benevolent sense of community. A historian reminds us, however, that an authoritarian society was an essential belief of paternalism and that the first duty of the paternalist was to rule.[20] Therefore a harsh system of poor relief might be attractive because it would bring the poor's 'tempers as well as their stomachs into subjection and make them feel the power of the village squire'.[21] Similarly a dominant social élite might support educational establishments so that the appropriate deferential values could be implanted among the poor. Continental experience suggested that it was not politic to allow the poor no hope at all and from Europe came the eponymous means of avoiding social revolution. Bismarckianism was overtly a policy of killing socialism by kindness through the adoption of social welfare measures. This was social insurance not just in the actuarial sense but literally as an insurance for society against revolution. A generous housing programme might thus be promoted as a reward to war heroes whereas its true function was as an antidote to Bolshevism.

The idea of social policy as an alternative to socialism runs counter, of course, to that view which regards welfare as a form of socialism in conflict with capitalism. Cole has already been quoted in this vein, echoed in the unequivocal assertion that 'the ethic of welfare and the ethic of capitalism are in basic opposition'.[22] Conversely, however, a Dutch writer has claimed that the very survival of capitalism depends upon welfare[23] and this is the essence of the **capitalistic** perspective. In this model welfare measures are seen as serving the economic interests of a modernising society by bearing the social costs of industrialisation and by promoting a social organisation geared to the needs of business. This view has been much encouraged by international comparisons which suggest that, despite some differences, all developed industrialised societies move towards common welfare systems.[24] This perspective, sometimes thought of as convergence theory,[25] has led a distinguished German historian to posit the idea of an international welfare system, since 'there seems to be not a single highly developed country in the world that is not a Welfare State'.[26] It is this international perspective which has promoted the term 'welfare capitalism'. What might be considered in a narrow British context as socialistic appears internationally as ingrained within capitalism. With this theme in mind the labour historian John Saville took issue with the idea that somehow the Welfare State lay on the road that led to socialism: 'both in Western Europe and the United States social security schemes are placed firmly within the framework of a free enterprise economy and no-one suggests that what is a natural development within a mature capitalist society should be given new names'.[27]

This conceptual framework is posited upon the assumption that welfare must offer real economic advantages to industry, that at a particular stage of capitalist development welfare served industry's needs. Recent research does indeed suggest that businessmen at times could conceive of welfare as sound economic sense.[28] Increased educational provision could provide a more highly trained workforce just as measures to promote medical care could produce a healthier, hence more productive, workforce. Such awareness, which perceived welfare as conducive to 'national efficiency', was likely to be enhanced in times of war. A nation in competition for survival needed all the military advantages which welfare could offer, or, rather, needed welfare to remedy the deficiencies which military weakness had revealed. It is perhaps no coincidence that Britain's twentieth-century 'road to welfare' has been punctuated by three wars. And Donnison raises the chilling thought that the needs of war may not in the future be that stimulus to welfare they have been in the past:

> in the last resort the nation depended for its survival on the capacity of ordinary people to bear and raise healthy sons who could be willing to fight for king and country. From time to time that knowledge led to real advances in social policy....But with the spread of nuclear weapons...sheer cannon fodder has been devalued and one more motive for building a healthy and united nation has been lost.[29]

Hence, the capitalistic model interprets social policy by reference to the economic or military needs of the country and this firmly roots social welfare within capitalism, rather than as an alternative to it. This conclusion has been put in the following uncompromising terms: 'the functioning and managing of state welfare suggests that it remains part of a **capitalist** state which is fundamentally concerned with...reproducing a reserve army of labour, the patriarchal family and the disciplining of the labour force'.[30] Such a model, here applied to modern welfare, is equally appropriate to earlier periods where a relief system might be tuned to keep down wages or to provide a pool of available labour, as and when required.

If both the conspiratorial and the capitalistic models suggest that welfare was conducive to the interests of the governing or employing classes, it is likely that a model will be needed as a counterweight which places central importance upon the working class. The **democratic** perspective views social welfare as fundamentally a response to democratic consumer demand. As working-class consciousness developed and as institutions of working-class cohesion, such as trade unions, formulated labour demands so it became increasingly likely that governments would respond, if only for reasons of public order already cited. There was a ratio between the degree of democracy at a particular time and the centrality of social policy questions. The more the poor acquired votes in the wake of suffrage reform, the more bread and butter issues dominated the political arena, for the poor could no longer be weaned on social paternalism, they had to be wooed by electoral promises. As Ian Gough puts it, 'once universal suffrage and the other major liberal rights are established, this provides a crucial channel through which to obtain welfare improvements'.[31] As democracy broadened, a notion of citizenship emerged which legitimised working-class aspirations for social betterment.[32] Such a belief in democratic citizenship was incompatible with the patronising spirit intrinsic to those philanthropic endeavours which had previously organised social provision. Charity presupposed a hierarchical society with a superior class of dispensers and an inferior class of receivers. This class-based division was reinforced by the behavioural objectives of so much charitable effort, to make the poor sober or clean or industrious or respectable. Democratic society called for a quite different mode of social provision – 'a citizen service...which the individual utilizes without loss of dignity...free from any taint of patronage'.[33] Thus a changed political climate demanded a changed system of welfare which had to reflect the egalitarianism of modern society. As Robson argued, 'a Welfare State must be democratic...political and social freedom are essential ingredients'.[34]

It is perhaps one of the difficulties of the democratic model that often working-class opinion has been hostile to the growth of state intervention which regulated working-class lives from above. This was neatly illustrated in a polemical tract published in 1911:

> We wants more money and...they pass laws how us shall behave...an' how to keep our health, so's us shall work better to their profit. What we want is proper pay,...to work out our own life according to our own ideas, not their's...New Acts, with new penalties attached, come tumbling upon his [the workman's] head from on high...He is treated like a child badly brought up by its parents; a child very wronged and very naughty.[35]

On the other hand, the history of social policy is characterised by strong protest movements and 'pressure from without' which often forced the government's hand. If the democratic rights of citizenship decreed the legitimacy of social justice, it would still have to be forcibly squeezed out of the political system by a barrage of persuasion. Concessions to working-class welfare were rarely made through altruism; more often than not it was for fear of something worse. When protectors became voters then the support for social improvement was correspondingly strengthened. It is indeed true that in a very general sense the growth in democracy has been accompanied by a growth in welfare.

More recently all of these approaches have been challenged to a greater or lesser extent by what may be termed a **mixed economy** model. Rejecting some earlier versions which allegedly portrayed a technological welfare escalator which carried Britain from the basement of the Poor Law to the penthouse of the Welfare Sate, some now prefer to think of a 'moving frontier' between state, voluntary and other stakeholders.[36] On this view the provision of social security has always been a flexible partnership between the individual, the family, employers, voluntary bodies and the state. The challenge for the historian, on this model, is not to look for sequence, trend or causal relationship in policy development, but to identify why at a particular historical moment the specific balance of provision was sustained. As one of the main proponents of this view, Jane Lewis, explains:

> Rather than seeing the story of the modern Welfare State as a simple movement from individualism to collectivism... it is more accurate to see Britain as always having had a mixed economy of welfare, in which the state, the voluntary sector, the family and the market have played different parts at different points in time.[37]

In this approach the idea of the Welfare State itself becomes a much more problematic and contested concept.

In this mixed economy model it is important to identify the components in the social risk 'basket' at any period and the relationship between them. Clearly the state is never, even in a modern Welfare State, the sole provider of social support. Indeed at some stages of historical development employers or voluntary groups saw themselves as alternatives to the state provider and sometimes one of the explicit motivators for social action was to make state action less likely. For example, charitable activity in the mid-nineteenth century was seen as an alternative or substitute for state action, by the mid-twentieth century voluntarism had become incorporated into state provision and by the end of the twentieth century had become a partner and agent for state delivery.

Neither the mixed economy thesis nor any of the other approaches will provide a satisfactory single conceptual model and in this book, as in others, a variety of perspectives are discussed and evaluated. The complex story of British social policy since the industrial revolution is not amenable to oversimplified analysis. The comments by Jose Harris on the late Victorian period are equally apposite for the two centuries covered in this study:

> The practical process by which change occurred was a largely piece-meal and unsystematic one involving many ambiguities and inconsistencies in public policy and many attempts to harness together and reconcile social principles that were seemingly in tension...such ambiguities...accurately reflect the many counter-vailing social forces in a highly complex and diverse society.[38]

Notes

1. W. A. Robson, *Welfare State and Welfare Society* (1976), pp. 11–12.
2. *Daily Mirror*, 5 July 1948.
3. W. H. Beveridge, *Social Insurance and Allied Services* (1942), p. 17.
4. H. Heclo, *Modern Social Politics in Britain and Sweden* (1974), p. 11.
5. For which see H. Butterfield, *The Whig Interpretation of History* (1931) and J. W. Burrow, *A Liberal Descent* (1980).
6. M. E. Gettleman, 'The Whig Interpretation of Social Welfare History', *Smith College Studies in Social Work*, 44 (1974), pp. 152–3.
7. E. W. Cohen, *English Social Services* (1949), p. 19.
8. E. M. Burns, *Social Security and Public Policy* (New York, 1956) and R. Lowe, *The Welfare State in Britain Since 1945* (2nd edn, 1999), pp. 50–1.
9. J. R. Hay, *The Development of the British Welfare State, 1880–1975* (1978), pp. 103–5.
10. M. P. Fogarty, *Prospects of the Industrial Areas of Great Britain* (1945), p. xxix.
11. For a discussion of the importance of 'legitimacy' see P. Hall, H. Land, R. Parker and A. Webb, *Change, Choice and Conflict in Social Policy* (1975).
12. R. Pinker, *The Idea of Welfare* (1979).
13. G. D. H. Cole, 'A Retrospect of the History of Voluntary Social Service', in A. F. C. Bourdillon (ed.), *Voluntary Social Services: Their Place in the Modern State* (1945), pp. 11–30.
14. V. George and P. Wilding, *Ideology and Social Welfare* (1976).
15. A. I. Ogus, 'Great Britain', in P. A. Kohler and H. F. Zacher (eds), *The Evolution of Social Insurance, 1881–1981* (1982).
16. For a discussion of this concept and its application to nineteenth-century developments see A. P. Donajgrodzki (ed.), *Social Control in Nineteenth-Century Britain* (1977).

17. M. Foucault, *Discipline and Punish* (1977), p. 202; cf. also his other books, *Madness and Civilisation* (1971), and *The Birth of the Clinic* (1973).

18. F. Piven and R. Cloward, *Regulating the Poor: The Function of Public Welfare* (New York, 1971); B. R. Mandell, *Welfare in America: Controlling the 'dangerous classes' – The Handout as a Form of Social Control* (Englewood Cliffs, 1975).

19. B. Jordan, *Freedom and the Welfare State* (1976), p. 3.

20. D. Roberts, *Paternalism in Early Victorian England* (1979).

21. J. Glyde, *Suffolk in the Nineteenth Century* (1865), p. 165.

22. George and Wilding, *Ideology*, p. ix.

23. P. Thoenes, *The Elite in the Welfare State* (1966), p. 143.

24. For the clearest statement of this view see C. Kerr, J. T. Dunlop, F. H. Harbison and C. F. Myers, *Industrialism and Industrial Man* (Cambridge, MA, 1960). For an international comparison which makes more of the differences see G. V. Rimlinger, *Welfare Policy and Industrialisation in Europe, America and Russia* (New York, 1971).

25. This theory is discussed in R. Mishra, *Society and Social Policy: Theoretical Perspectives on Welfare* (1977) and, with reference to Britain and the Soviet Union, in the same author's paper 'Convergence Theory and Social Change', *Comparative Studies in Society and History*, 18 (1976), pp. 28–56.

26. K. W. Deutsch, 'From the National Welfare State to the International Welfare System', in W. Mommsen (ed.), *The Emergence of the Welfare State in Britain and Germany* (1981), p. 426.

27. J. Saville, 'The Welfare State: an historical approach', *New Reasoner* (1957), reprinted in M. Fitzgerald *et al.*, *Welfare in Action* (1977), p. 8.

28. See, for example, J. R. Hay, 'Employers and Social Policy in Britain: the evolution of Welfare Legislation in Britain, 1905–14', *Social History*, 4 (1977), pp. 435–55.

29. D. Donnison, *The Politics of Poverty* (1982), p. 24.

30. N. Ginsburg, *Class, Capital and Social Policy* (1979), p. 2.

31. I. Gough, *The Political Economy of the Welfare State* (1979), p. 60.

32. T. H. Marshall, *Social Policy* (various edns, 1970–5).

33. Cohen, *English Social Services*, p. 150.

34. Robson, *Welfare State*, p. 16.

35. *Seems So! A Working-Class View of Politics*, quoted by S. Yeo, in N. Parry, M. Rustin and C. Satyamurti (eds), *Social Work, Welfare and the State* (1979), p. 71.

36. G. Finlayson, 'A Moving Frontier: Voluntarism and the State in British Social Welfare', *Twentieth-century British History*, 1 (1990). See

also D. Gladstone (ed.), *Before Beveridge: Welfare Before the Welfare State* (1999).

37. J. Lewis, *The Voluntary Sector, the State and Social Work in Britain*, (1995), p. 3
38. J. Harris, *Private Lives, Public Spirit* (1994), p. 218.

Introduction

The purpose of this book is somewhat better explained by the subtitle than by the title. The attempt to chart the course of British social policy since the Industrial Revolution is its main aim, and it is only from such a study that the evolution of the Welfare State emerges. The evolution of the British Welfare State is not seen as an example of the whig interpretation of history, the unfolding of some great scheme of progress as increasingly enlightened men approached ever onward and upward a future promised land. Rather it is seen as an erratic and pragmatic response of government and people to the practical individual and community problems of an industrialised society. We are not so much searching for the origins of a specific set of social truths as tracing the route British social policy followed during a specific period.

The period under review is that from the late eighteenth to the mid-twentieth century, with some retrospective glances at earlier developments within the Poor Law. The starting-point has been taken as the Industrial Revolution because its profound impact upon English society totally transformed social policy. Facing unprecedented problems, nineteenth-century Britain had no obvious markers to steer by and a pragmatic, inconsistent complex of policy responses ensued. A history thus begun at the very centre of social change ends with that synthesis of social security, universal health and welfare services, education, housing and full employment which came to be called the British Welfare State. The substance of the book explains how that synthesis was arrived at.

Since the Industrial Revolution was so great a turning-point in modern British history, it is as well to have in mind what industrialisation comprised. A host of theories have been suggested to explain it: some mono-causal, others multi-causal; some propounding a leading sector, others identifying society-wide

1

impulses; some building the stages of economic growth, others postulating prerequisites for growth. The Industrial Revolution admits of no simple explanation and was a complex socio-economic process involving a variety of forces. Indeed the origins of the Industrial Revolution may lie in the conjunction of these forces, combining by the accident of time in mutual interaction within the matrix of the unique fabric of English society. It was perhaps the coincidental occurrence of agrarian, demographic, techno-logical, commercial and transport changes fructifying in the ideal forcing-ground of English attitude and social structure which produced the Industrial Revolution.

Industrialisation presupposes a contemporaneous agrarian revolution, if for no other reason than the shift in human resources from rural to urban which gives a smaller proportion of the population the task of feeding a larger proportion. If in the course of an industrial revolution the majority are to become consumers rather than producers of food, then the remaining agrarian minority must make the land yield more. In eighteenth-century England this was achieved not so much by the imple-mentation of a new rural technology dominated by the seed-drill, but by a revolution in land use. Enclosures increased the acreage (exploiting hitherto under-utilised resources), and new forms of husbandry (notably leguminous root-crop rotation and convert-ibility between arable and pasture) increased productivity per acre. That vast increase in production *per capita* which was the definitive characteristic of the Industrial Revolution appeared first in agriculture rather than in industry.

The stimulus to agrarian innovation was primarily the increased demand for food from a growing population. Population growth was at once cause and consequence of industrialisation. As a demand-inducing agent for both agricultural and industrial products, increased population was a dynamic force promoting economic change. Yet that very economic change led to even greater popu-lation growth in the fast-growing cities, whose improved employment prospects and enlarged social contacts produced a natural rate of increase higher than that of the countryside. The first census was not until 1801, civil registry was not introduced until 1837, and prior statistics derived from parish registers are not wholly reliable, so that the lack of firm evidence has hampered the search for an explanation of eighteenth-century population growth. A lowering of the marriage age, with its consequent extension of the child-bearing years, together with the cumulative effects of even a marginal decline in infant mortality (perhaps due to improved food, clothing and housing), would have been sufficient to cause the spurt in population in the third quarter of the eighteenth century. This sparked the process of economic growth which, added to a boom in the trade cycle, provoked in turn a great leap in population in the 1780s and 1790s. The crucial factor in England was that population growth was not accompanied by a sharp decline in purchasing power (compare eighteenth-century Ireland or twentieth-century India) so that an increased population enlarged the aggregate demand for consumption.

It was this elastic demand which persuaded industry to search for more efficient methods of production, and at the heart of the Industrial Revolution lay the technical innovation which mechanised the process of manufacture. Population growth did not swamp the labour market and a manufacturer had to do more than simply enlarge his workforce. Bottlenecks in production and a shortage of enough labour to meet increased demand stimulated the process of invention and technical innovation. Every industry had its own crucial technological breakthrough, but central to all was the steam engine, supplying, in Matthew Boulton's phrase, what all the world wants: power. A mobile, self-regulating source of motive power transformed British industry and elevated the productive capacity of the economy to undreamt-of levels. Historians have long discounted the view of the Industrial Revolution as merely a series of inventions centred on a kettle boiling over, and we rightly acknowledge that technology was as much a response to market forces as a prime mover. However, we should not stray so far from reality in our theoretical analysis of the Industrial Revolution as to forget that the mechanisation of production was its most obvious feature. It was the machine which created a new world.

We oversimplify if, like Samuel Smiles, we look to the great inventors and engineers as the sole heroes of the Industrial Revolution. For every James Watt there had to be a Matthew Boulton, for every inventor an entrepreneur with the capital to exploit innovation. Without capital, businessmen would not have been able to buy machinery or build great factories, and the commercial origins of industrialisation were of great importance. British industrialisation was financed mainly by domestic capital, and the accumulation of reserves of capital from land and trade had been a long-term process in which the propensity to save was a crucial factor. Eighteenth-century England was not in the position of a modern underdeveloped country with a chronic shortage of capital for investment; she had the capital available to be exploited. Entrepreneurs probably relied mainly on family and friends for their initial capital, and to these sources was added an efficient banking system which oiled the wheels of trade and helped to convert circulating into fixed capital. Interest rates were low in the eighteenth century and overseas trade was growing. While the main demand was domestic, the growth in overseas trade tended to buoy up demand when there was a domestic slump and acted as the extra fillip to growth in times of boom, as at the end of the American War of Independence.

To satisfy the domestic market, which from the time of the union with Scotland in 1707 was the largest free-trade area in Europe, improved communications were required. Again this was an essential part of the process of industrialisation, for raw materials had to be brought to the place of manufacture and finished goods had to reach the market. Turnpike trusts which transferred the cost of the roads from local inhabitants to road users enabled professional engineers to be employed on the first major road-building programme since Roman times. More spectacularly, the canals quartered the cost of transporting goods and provided a new communications network specifically geared to industrial needs. Having enabled the market economy to work smoothly at a crucial period in the country's economic development, the canals were themselves overtaken in the mid-nineteenth century by the railways. The building of the railways not only further enlarged the market and enhanced mobility, but also acted as an enormous stimulus to further economic growth. Transport changes were an essential feature of industrialisation.

The various changes taking place in the late eighteenth century, continually acting and reacting on each other, were given their generating momentum by contemporary English society. It was the particular features of English society which enabled the separate developments mentioned above to get together into the process of industrialisation. There was clearly something about the atmosphere of eighteenth-century Britain which encouraged inventiveness, a spirit of innovation, a willingness to take risks, a capacity to visualise change, in short the entrepreneurial qualities which were apparently so generalised at the time. It has long been thought to have something to do with Protestant Nonconformity, since a large proportion of the new industrialists were Dissenters. From Puritanism Britain perhaps derived a sober, hard-working attitude and a propensity to save, and some have identified in a Nonconformist upbringing the youthful repression which was likely to produce strong psychological drives for success later in life. Other factors suggested include the prior settlement of the great constitutional and religious questions which persisted in other countries, and the impact of the scientific revolution of the seventeenth century, permeating though the ruling élite via scientific societies and universities. The open social structure, in which the vertical loyalties of family, interest or connection established a chain of cohesion and an avenue for upward mobility, provided the context in which success could be rewarded by social status. The doctrine of individual liberty originating with Locke encouraged the free pursuit of self-interest long before this was elevated into an economic doctrine by Adam Smith. There was a crucial yet intangible connection between English attitude and social structure and the Industrial Revolution.

The Industrial Revolution was a complete change in society, replacing a rural by an urban industrial society. The problems posed by that profound social transformation figure largely in the story of nineteenth-century social policy. Where the causes of the Industrial Revolution were disputed the consequences were less so, for they were more easily identifiable in the artefacts of the new society. The main economic changes were a growing specialisation of labour, a new occupational and industrial structure and the uneven progress towards mechanisation and the factory system. Underlying all was a phenomenal growth in production with its consequent enlargement of the national wealth. Every production and trade index recorded soaring productivity as machinery came to the aid of human labour. Even allowing for population growth, the gross national product increased fourfold in real terms during the nineteenth century. Indeed some have argued that the definition of an industrial revolution is an increase in production *per capita* that was revolutionary compared to previous experience. Through industrialisation increased wealth was generated beyond belief, and this achievement underpinned much of the faith in individualism and *laissez-faire*: these were the virtues which had made it possible.

In a simple cost–benefit analysis we might say that England paid for the economic benefits of increased production with the social costs of urbanisation. The social consequences of industrialisation provided the fieldwork with which social policy had to deal, and they were broadly of three sorts, affecting the individual, his work and his environment. Urban industrial society placed the individual in a new relationship with his fellow-man and the symbols of social authority. In place of the security of a cohesive *vertical* social structure in which every individual had a formal or informal connection with those above and below, there was the uncertainty of a mass society in which a *horizontal* class structure gradually emerged. It was during the process of change, when the first-generation migrant had forsaken his niche in the old world yet was without the security of a stable position in the evolving new one, that alienation and anomie permeated English society. The factory owner had the privilege of the old lord of the manor but none of the responsibilities. The cash nexus of employment had replaced the paternalism of connection or interest group.

Most historians now feel that people were drawn to the cities by the magnet of work and higher wages rather than driven off the soil by enclosures. However, the nature of industrial work had perhaps unanticipated effects. Probably a large proportion of rural workers had long been used to manufacturing through their own part-time employment within the domestic system. Two things were different in factory labour. First, there was the relentless discipline of mechanisation. Here was the origin of the conveyor-belt mentality where man, the creator of the machine, was made its servant. The discipline of the machine was reinforced by the authority of master or overlooker and the sombre instructions of the factory bell, summoning hands, not people. Second, the decision of whether and when to work was taken out of the hands of the individual and placed at the whim of impersonal market forces. An independent handworker worked when he pleased; a factory operative could only work when required to do so by the demands of the market.

The nature of factory production had other important results. It debased and rendered obsolete certain craft skills which had often taken years of experience to perfect, and while in the long term industrialisation created more work, in the short there was inevitably technological unemployment. Mechanisation created routine unskilled jobs, some of which could be better and more cheaply performed by women and children, who were also subjected to the rigours of factory discipline. The problem of work became, within the context of the factory question, an issue of social policy. Men were not necessarily compensated for their changed economic status by higher wages. Wages were rising before about 1790 and after about 1840, but in the intervening period some workers, especially depressed handworkers, experienced falling wages. This has given rise to a historical debate over the standard of living, between the 'pessimists' who believe the workers' position worsened and the 'optimists' who believe it improved during the Industrial Revolution.

Any discussion of the standard of living must encompass more than mere money wages, and so the quality of urban industrial life has to be weighed in the balance. The quality of life revolves primarily around the physical environment which people experience. The absence of modes of public transport forced workers to live cheek by jowl with the factories in the smoke and dirt of industrial life. Middle-class wealth made suburban residence possible, giving rise to a residential zoning based on economic class, which produced a diverse rather than uniform experience for different classes. Overcrowding, minimum building standards and insanitation provided workers with a physical environment which the middle classes could buy themselves out of. Though the housing of the industrial workers may have compared favourably with that of previous rural labourers, the urban environment put the health of the working class at risk. Smoke and cesspools, lack of drainage and open sewers, bred environmentally caused diseases to which all were subject. It was impossible for a family to insulate itself from the ravages of epidemic or endemic disease, and so private health became a matter of public health. The concentration of population in rapidly growing cities created a new area of social policy.

In responding to the problems and needs of the new industrial society, men both within and outside it could find few precedents to guide them in the treatment of an unprecedented social condition. Issues like poverty, public health, employment and education cut right across normal party lines, and governments had to establish the boundaries and the terms of reference on which state action would be admitted. In the effort to understand the workings of industrial society, many were continually reminded by their everyday experience that the great changes which had come about were the creation of free individuals unaided by the state. Their initial reaction was to feel that somehow people should find their own salvation and that the common good was really the sum of the self-interest of every member of society.

Common sense and common experience elevated individualism into a great tenet of social conduct and, as an anonymous pamphleteer explained:

> The great duties of social life must be thoroughly taught and expounded, not to a few, but to all, without exception, the habits and dispositions being trained in conformity. These duties are: – to strive to the utmost to be self-supporting – not to be a burden upon any other man or upon society ... to make such use of all superior advantages whether of knowledge, skill or wealth, as to promote, on all occasions, the general happiness of mankind.[1]

Self-help and the greatest happiness of the greatest number were twin principles in the credo of the new industrial age. Some felt that they were incompatible, for the general welfare could not always be secured by individuals and hence there was a case established for the state to be the guardian of the common weal. Thus when the Government proposed to assume greater responsibility for education, one journal supported this since 'a great and intelligible principle will be thus established – a principle which will have a vast influence on future legislation and on the welfare of the people of England'.[2] The principle was that the state existed for the welfare of the people. Not all agreed, and therein lay the origin of the nineteenth-century debate over the proper role of social policy.

Contemporaneously with that debate over social policy the British political system underwent a process of adjustment to the new industrial age. The change in social structure had to be reflected in parallel changes in the power structure, and an oligarchy became a virtual democracy in little over half a century. England avoided the social revolution which so many forecast by a programme of political concession which first defused middle-class discontent; later, the combination of prosperity and political gain side-tracked potential working-class rebellion. When a working-class mass franchise became a reality, then social policy itself was used as a means of avoiding social revolution.

Social policy must be seen in its political context, and so the history of social policy must be closely related to the political history of the period under examination. Much of the nineteenth century was taken up with the problems of the new society and its painful emergence. In the 1815–20 period post-war dislocation added to the problems of economic change, and mass distress produced a period of political uncertainty most famously symbolised by Peterloo in 1819. In the 1820s a more liberal approach was adopted by Lord Liverpool's Tory Government, which in its commercial policy made some attempt to satisfy middle-class opinion. When right-wing critics of Wellington's Catholic Emancipation policy took their revenge, a Whig Cabinet under Earl Grey was appointed with a commitment to a reform of Parliament. The Reform Act, which was passed at the third attempt in 1832, was an attempt to relate the distribution of political power to the realities of the new society. What the Whigs called the rational, intelligent and safe portion of the community (i.e. the propertied middle class) was brought into partnership with the governing class of landed gentlemen. It required a further massive propaganda campaign by the Anti-Corn Law League, the most professional and efficient extra-Parliamentary pressure group of the period, to establish the symbol of parity between land and industry in the repeal of the Corn Laws in 1846. Peel, himself the son of a Lancashire cotton magnate, has been described as the first statesman of the Industrial Revolution because he acknowledged that social changes had taken place and also recognised the need to adjust policy accordingly.

The new industrial bourgeoisie achieved political power because it was deemed safe enough to be enfranchised, and in the longer term the same was true of the working class. Driven by acute economic distress and the desperate condition of the depressed handworkers, the Chartist movement of the period 1838–48 could achieve nothing of its programme while the propertied classes feared spoliation from a discontented mass.

Working-class activities in fields like the Poor Law or the factory question or trade unionism were more successful in the short term, though Chartism did play a major role in forging a strong working-class consciousness. It was during the mid-Victorian years of prosperity that the urban working class established its bona fides as a sound, property-respecting social class. In 1867 the urban workers got the vote and they were joined in 1884 by rural workers, while in 1885 a major redistribution of seats gave population something like its proportionate weight over mere property.

No doubt there is a close link between the extension of the suffrage and the widening concerns of social policy, which were expressed mainly in ideas in the last quarter of the nineteenth century and in legislative action during the twentieth. This helps to explain the structure of this book, which is thematic for the period up to about 1880 and adopts a chronological approach thereafter. The first four chapters are devoted to case studies of social policy on specific issues which were pragmatically dealt with and were not part of a coherent overall policy. Guidelines were established and cases made out for each issue on its own merits, always with a reluctance to stray far from the correct path of individualism. The fifth chapter explores the theoretical orthodoxy of the age and the practical evolution of an administrative state which was already undermining it. From the late nineteenth century the persistence of poverty encouraged a growing awareness of the need for a more extensive and comprehensive social policy, whose course is then followed through the work of the last Liberal Government, the events of the inter-war years and the final Welfare State synthesis of the 1940s. Reference is made in each chapter to the series of key documents which appear in the Appendix and which should be used in conjunction with the text.

1 The factory question

I   The factory child

Child labour was not the creation of the Industrial Revolution. Many a medieval tapestry, depicting children at work, gives the lie to the idea of a 'Merrie England' of feudal times when children laboured not at all. Behind closed doors the domestic system hid much unseen exploitation of children, for in many ways parents were the severest taskmasters of all. There is no real case to support the hostile anti-industrial view in the early nineteenth century which invented, most notably in the words of Engels, a golden age of rural bliss in pre-industrial society: 'The workers enjoyed a comfortable and peaceful existence ... they were not forced to work excessive hours. ... Children grew up in the open air of the countryside and if they were old enough to help their parents work this was only an occasional employment and there was no question of an 8 or 12 hour day'.[1]

The vision of children whiling away the hours in idyllic surroundings and doing nothing more strenuous than dancing round the maypole is certainly not supported by the recollections of men who had themselves grown up in the eighteenth century. They recalled arduous employment in cramped conditions and inevitable long walks in the early hours to the nearest market.

Yet, as with so many other social problems, the Industrial Revolution concentrated and multiplied what had previously been diffuse and remote from the public gaze. A visit to one large mill in industrial Lancashire or Yorkshire could furnish the evidence of child labour which would have taken a large-scale investigation into private dwellings in the age of the domestic system. The excessive labour of children could be ignored when scattered across the Pennine hamlets, but not for long would it remain unnoticed and unremarked in a smoky industrial city. Apart from this concentration, the Industrial Revolution added two main strands to the prevailing pattern, those of discipline and danger which were the creation of the new factory system.

Many of the abuses to which children were subjected stemmed from the discipline imposed by the very nature of factory labour. Excessive hours produced tiredness, and the overlookers or foremen were motivated as much by the need to keep children awake and alert as by the proverbial sadism for which they were pilloried. Factory discipline was most easily administered by the strap and, as one former child operative reported later in life, 'The confinement and the labour were no burden but the severity was intolerable, the marks of which I yet carry and shall carry to the grave.' The relentless process of mechanised production led to a monotonous but demanding routine from which, like the tread-mill, there was no escape: 'For 12 mortal hours does the leviathan of machinery toil on with vigour undiminished and with pace unslackened and the human machines must keep pace with him. What signify languor, sickness, disease? The pulsations of the physical monster continue and his human agents must drag after him.'[2] The rigorous demands and the dehumanising effects of the discipline of the factory system were galling to adults and even more pernicious for children.

The second new factor was the danger, both physical and moral, which was an apparently inevitable feature of the factory system. Perhaps English society was slow to react to the dangers of factory employment, but there had to be a generation of adults who had literally 'been through the mill' before the long-term effects of child labour could be visibly observed. Unfenced machinery took its toll of fingers, hair and loose clothes which, often because of fatigue, were allowed to fall into what the novelist Frances Trollope called 'the ceaseless whirring of a million hissing wheels', and the long hours of standing and bending produced the characteristic weak legs and arched back of the former child operative. In addition to these orthopaedic conditions consequent upon factory labour there were a whole range of respiratory diseases due to the high temperature and humidity in which children worked. As early as 1795 a Manchester doctor had drawn attention to 'the debilitating effects of hot and impure air' and had cited factories in general as particularly injurious to the health of all who worked in them. Factories, and especially mines, were corrupting influences upon young children, who soon adopted the licentious morals of their adult colleagues. Children in factories were clearly at risk physically and morally.

The long hours, discipline and dangers comprise an apparently unanswerable indictment of the factory system, and yet these are not the whole picture. Both contemporaries and historians have doubted whether the situation was *universally* as black as has been described. This was a controversial subject and propagandists were often inclined to exaggerate conditions and to generalise from particular incidents. Much of the verbal evidence taken in the many inquiries was the personal memories of adults who may have embroidered some of their most painful recollections. Not all factories were dens of capitalist avarice and exploitation, and some children were given an education in a factory school which would otherwise have been denied to them. Medical opinion was divided, and while one doctor could say in 1816 that 'there was no age, no time of life whatever' when thirteen hours' labour could be healthy, others two years later testified that there were no harmful effects for a ten-year-old who stood for twelve hours or worked all through the night. Where some eyes saw debilitated and deformed children, others saw alert and lively youngsters doing useful, healthy work. In an age when few children could expect a full formal education there were many who supported the contention that there was a moral education provided by 'early subordination, industry and regularity' and that 'there can be no training of the volatile mind of youth equal to that which is maintained at the factories'.[3] Above all, child labour kept children out of mischief: it avoided the idleness which so many believed would lead to dissipation, since 'the devil finds work for idle hands'.

Even allowing that there was some exaggeration and that there were some compensating advantages, it still remained true that a high proportion of the child labour force worked a twelve- to fourteen-hour day from about the age of eight onwards. Men had to face up to these facts without the advantage of precedent and had to consider on how best to ameliorate factory conditions. It was not a black-and-white question, good against evil, as some have portrayed. Indeed many of the simplifications used to understand the movement for factory reform have violated the truth so much as to defeat understanding. It has been portrayed as Tory philanthropy fighting against Whig political economy, or Anglican evangelicanism against selfish capitalism, or landed aristocracy against urban bourgeoisie. The element of truth in all these does not justify the blanket treatment for a movement which was intensely complex and which exposed the social and political ambiguities of early industrial England. Not all Tories were factory reformers and not all factory owners were opposed to legislation. The essential point about a movement which had a hybrid Tory–Radical base was that it cut right across normal party lines. It was never exclusively the property of one class or interest; it was always a patchwork of outlooks and opinions.

Prior to 1830 there was no organised factory movement but a slowly rising tide of protest coming from various unconnected individuals and groups. Skilled handworkers, themselves on the verge of losing the battle with machinery, were incensed at the debasement of their skill by the artificial apprenticeships which were being used to indent large numbers of pauper children into the early riverside textile mills. Many doctors, seeing the effects of child labour, accumulated evidence which was later to be the substance of much propaganda. Anglican clergymen took up the cause of factory children and established a tradition of priestly concern which was to persist throughout the whole movement. Although some Methodists too joined in, the main body of Dissenting ministers were not publicly identified with the cause of factory reform but were often associated both denominationally and politically with factory owners, and so there was always an undercurrent of Church versus Dissent. A whole range of sentimental traditionalists also protested (often as part of a wider protest against industrialism itself), and these included poets such as Coleridge, Southey and Wordsworth as well as Radical leaders such as Cobbett.

Although paternalistic Tudor Governments had been prepared to legislate in matters of trade and industry, in the early nineteenth century the first steps towards legislative control over child labour were the result of the efforts of individuals. The first Sir Robert Peel, father of the future Prime Minister and himself a cotton spinner, introduced the Health and Morals of Apprentices Act in 1802. This referred exclusively to pauper children who were being widely used in textile mills, especially water-driven mills in remote areas with a labour shortage. The Act restricted cotton apprentices to twelve hours but was rarely enforced and, as Peel himself later admitted, the increased use of steam power and consequent wider use of non-pauper children rendered the Act a 'dead letter'. Robert Owen, the pioneering social reformer, claimed to have proved at his model mill in New Lanark that reduced hours and decent conditions did not destroy the economic viability of his business, and he began a campaign in 1813 to protect factory children. Peel chaired a Commons Committee in 1816 and Lord Kenyon chaired one in the Lords in 1818 and 1819. From the maze of conflicting evidence Peel's Act of 1819 emerged. This forbade children under nine from working in cotton mills and restricted children over nine to a twelve-hour day.

In the mid-1820s John Cam Hobhouse, the Whig–Radical MP for Westminster, took up the question in Parliament, but his proposals for further legislation were considerably watered down and the main effect of the 1825 Act was to prohibit night work for children. In 1829 Hobhouse secured further provisions which increased the efficiency of the 1825 Act. Already a group of Lancashire cotton spinners led by John Doherty had formed the nucleus of a proletarian agitation, and a handful of Bradford worsted manufacturers had attempted to promote voluntary limitations on hours. In 1830 those worried about child labour were lacking in organisation, direction and leadership: their needs were about to be met in a dramatic way.

II The state steps in, 1830–3

Traditionally the process of factory reform has been viewed as a triumph for the humanitarian efforts of Lord Ashley, seventh Earl of Shaftesbury, whose Parliamentary endeavours especially in the 1840s pushed an unwilling Government towards interventionist legislation. Of late, however, historians have devoted more attention to the extra-Parliamentary agitation for factory reform which antedated Ashley's concern inside Parliament. One of the key themes of the second quarter of the nineteenth century was the pressure brought to bear by a changing society upon the political system. Parliament was composed mostly of men who represented the traditional landed classes, who knew little of the problems of the newer industrial areas. Hence ignorance had to be removed by making legislators aware of the problems. Protest from without was a prerequisite of Parliamentary concern, and popular movements required inspiring leaders. When the precedents were being made and crucial pioneering decisions taken about state and society in the early 1830s, the leader of the factory movement, 'the factory King', was not Shaftesbury but Richard Oastler. Oastler, an Evangelical Anglican with a sincere concern for suffering, was an agent for a great landowner at Fixby Hall near Huddersfield. Born in Leeds in 1789, he had been educated at the Moravian school at Fulneck and had spent several years as a merchant before following his father as steward at Fixby. Though for ten years his residence panoramically surveyed the multiplying chimneys of Huddersfield, his rural life insulated him from the realities of the factory system which was growing up around him in the West Riding. Suddenly a mind which had been filled with boundary fences, rent rolls and tithe disputes was invaded by righteous indignation about little factory children. In September 1830, on a visit to a wealthy Bradford manufacturer, Oastler was told about conditions prevailing in the Bradford worsted industry and was urged to do something about them. Scarcely believing that such abuses could exist unnoticed on his own doorstep, Oastler set down in vivid prose the horror he felt about 'Yorkshire Slavery'. His first letter to the *Leeds Mercury*, where he contrasts concern over Negro slavery with indifference over a worse form of exploitation in Yorkshire itself, may be taken as the starting-point of the factory movement. Justifiably famous, its words still impart the religious zeal which Oastler was always to demonstrate. (Document 1A.)*

Oastler did not anticipate the consequences his letter would have, transforming him from an unknown into a popular hero of the masses. He stirred consciences in the West Riding and a fierce argument developed in the local press which anticipated the division of political opinion on the factory question. Oastler's material became too controversial for the Nonconformist, middle-class, Liberal *Leeds Mercury*, whose readership included the very employers Oastler was castigating, and so his later letters were published in the Tory *Leeds Intelligencer*. Oastler's campaign was also supported by the

---

*For this and subsequent references to documents, see Documentary Appendix, pp. 296–341.

Radical *Leeds Patriot* and so the nucleus of the Tory–Radical alliance was created. This was further nurtured by the most significant development of all, the formation in the spring of 1831 of Short Time Committees, first in the West Riding and then in Lancashire and Scotland. These were the storm-troops of the factory campaign and were composed mostly of operatives themselves, together with sympathetic tradesmen. Oastler still saw his contribution as that of an individual working through his pen, but in the decisive 'Fixby Hall Compact' of June 1831 a deputation of operatives persuaded Oastler to join with them and indeed lead the movement. From different social groups, and fundamentally disagreeing on politics, the signatories to the compact agreed to forget all but the factory question and 'work together totally irrespective of political or party considerations'. Oastler now discovered a talent as a popular orator and became the head of a mass movement which organised meetings, demonstrations, petitions and pamphlets in favour of factory reform. Thus at the very height of the Reform Bill crisis there was in the north a competing agitation with its own chronology, programme and supporters.

While Oastler dominated the extra-Parliamentary movement, the case for factory reform was put inside the House of Commons by Michael Thomas Sadler, like Oastler an Evangelical Tory from a devout Methodist background. Sadler was an even more extreme Church-and-King Tory than Oastler, and his strong denunciation of Catholic Emancipation in 1829 had earned him the patronage of the Duke of Newcastle, who provided Sadler with a seat in Parliament via the pocket borough of Newark. Once in Parliament, Sadler took up the cause of three groups, the Irish peasants, the depressed agricultural workers of England and the factory children. He at once adopted Oastler's cry for a ten-hour day when Hobhouse's bill of 1831 was effectively emasculated, even though Hobhouse denounced this demand as a vain, unrealistic and unattainable aspiration. It is a sobering thought that a ten-hour day for children of nine was the ultimate *reform* which was being sought: even a ten-hour day, to twenty-first-century eyes excessive, was deemed impracticable idealism by sympathisers such as Hobhouse.

The extent and nature of the opposition to a ten-hour day must be understood to realise the difficulties which Oastler and Sadler faced. Many people, when confronted with the evidence of child labour and proposals for reform, expressed sympathy but ignorance and therefore wished for the advice of 'practical men' familiar with industry. In effect, practical men came to mean the employers themselves, who were hardly an unbiased authority. It may be assumed that almost all the mitigatory claims, about the exaggeration, the healthy children, the benevolence of masters and the lack of any need for reform, were an expression of special pleading motivated by self-interest. Less specious was the widely publicised belief that substantial restriction of hours would have serious economic repercussions. Much was made of foreign competition, of Nassau Senior's dogma that profits were made in the last hour, of reduced output and increased unemployment.

'Practical men' rationalised what their own judgement deemed commercially profitable by resort to the current ideology of the day. Many who had no financial interest in factories were philosophically and ideologically hostile to state intervention in what was deemed to be the free exercise of capital. They believed that it was not in the province of government to interfere between masters and men, and that all restraints on trade were unconducive to the national wealth and general welfare. Free market forces must be allowed to determine the price of labour. The corollary, which was to be increasingly used in the 1840s, was that there was not a free-market economy because of such restrictions as the Corn Laws, hence the way to tackle child labour was to allow labour to be sold at a rate which would remove the *necessity* of children working to supplement the family income. This was the most persuasive argument of all. In the conditions prevailing in England in the early 1830s working-class families were in the grip of 'cruel necessity' which demanded that they send their children to work to avoid starvation. When working people had only the sale of their labour to produce the family income, was it really a reform in the best interests of those concerned to restrict the earning potential of the family by limiting the hours of work? All agreed, both masters and reformers, that to reduce children's hours would inevitably reduce adult hours as well, which in turn would reduce wages. Even Oastler admitted that there could be no justice in demanding twelve hours' wages for eight hours' work.

To this contorted intellectual argument Oastler and Sadler offered a relatively simple and unsophisticated antidote – revulsion, horror and moral indignation at what so-called free people were doing to their children. This is not to say that Oastler and Sadler were not politically aware. Both were hostile to Whiggism and in many ways factory reform was 'a Tory stick to beat the Whigs'. Oastler once wrote, 'I hate Whig politics with a most perfect hatred', and there was no more strenuous opponent of the Whig Reform Bill than Sadler. Basically, however, their approach was that of a moral or religious crusade against an intolerable evil. Such evil undermined the basic tenets of family life and Oastler was determined to restore 'woman in her right place on her own hearthstone, making it ready to be comfortable for her industrious husband when he returns to his house'. Social historians have recently taken up the 'gendering' dimension of the factory move-ment and the subsequent legislation in promoting both a gendered workforce and a male-dominated family. Such views also influ-enced Tory philanthropist medical men who were concerned with the malevolent health effects of industrial labour upon women and girls.[4] Sophisticated economic theory was irrelevant as far as they were concerned. It simply could not be right for these things to persist, and if England's wealth really did depend on the slavery of little children, then 'sink your commerce and rise Humanity, Benevolence and Christianity'.[5]

This was the tone of the campaign Oastler led throughout the north in support of the ten-hour bill introduced by Sadler in March 1832. The most memorable demonstration of public support for the bill was the mass pilgrimage to York on Easter Monday which produced a petition signed by over 130,000 people. Parlia-ment remained unmoved and appointed Sadler to chair a Select Committee to take evidence in connection with his bill. Before the committee could submit its report, Parliament was dissolved and Sadler faced an election under the new Reform Act with his own seat, then at Aldborough, swept away.

To examine the Leeds election of 1832 is not to follow a meander-ing by-way remote from the main story of factory reform; it is to concentrate on the central issue, for the Leeds election was seen by all factory reformers as a test case for their cause. It was natural that Sadler, a Leeds linen merchant himself and a member of Leeds Corporation, should be invited to stand, but this did not itself make it a 'factory election'. All three candidates for the two-member seat were involved in some way with the factory question. Indeed the three candidates personified the three key issues: commercial self-interest in the person of John Marshall, Jr, heir to the great flax-spinning empire created by his father and employer of large numbers of children; individualist philosophy in the person of the great Whig orator T. B. Macaulay; and humanitarian concern for suffering in the person of Sadler. As Hobhouse remarked, 'The factory question is mixed up with party politics in Yorkshire and more especially in the town of Leeds',[6] and the personality of the candidates ensured that it remained so. Sadler became the symbolic torch for the factory reformers as a whole and he received unprecedented addresses from Short Time Committees all over the north.

The cross-party identification on factory reform was illustrated by the support Sadler got from working-class Radicals who ignored his views on the Reform Bill and judged him solely on his concern for the poor. Perhaps the terminology of a Tory–Radical alliance is wrong, for party divisions were irrelevant to the factory issue, which was decided on its own merits without reference to normal party labels. As one imaginary workman put it: 'Why talk about Toaries and Redigals and such like while Oastler and Sadler and them'll stand up for us, I care nowt about what colour they wear; it's not blue nor yellow at makes 'em either better or warse.'[7]

Sadler's supporters did not have to generalise about factory conditions, for they could highlight Marshall's own mill practice. Marshall remained adamantly hostile to a ten-hour day. From Macaulay the Leeds electors got a concise summary of the nature and function of government according to the new *laissez-faire* philosophy of the classical economists:

> The best government cannot act directly and suddenly and violently on the comforts of the people; it cannot rain down provisions into their houses; it cannot give them bread, meat and wine; these things they can only obtain by their own honest industry and to protect them in that honesty industry and secure to them its fruits is the end of all honest government.[8]

Macaulay admitted the case for legislation on child labour but would not be drawn on a ten-hour day.

As far as the new electoral system was concerned, the classes represented by Marshall and Macaulay had a built-in advantage over those represented by Sadler. While the latter had the support of the crowds, these crowds by and large did not have votes.

Sadler was defeated, never again to be in Parliament, and the factory movement had lost its spokesman. As Oastler put it, the electors of Leeds were much more under the influence of the factory lords than the factory children, for quite simply '*the people* do not live in £10 houses'. To have lost Sadler was bad enough; to ponder the balance of forces in the new system which had thus excluded the champion of the factory children was even more demoralising. It was in this somewhat chastened atmosphere that Ashley agreed to replace Sadler as Parliamentary leader in February 1833. He was to find, like Oastler, that the factory children had altered the whole course of his life.

In March 1833, Ashley reintroduced Sadler's bill for a ten-hour day, and hopes were raised because of the reception of the Sadler Report two months earlier. Though Sadler was out of the lime-light, his name was etched already on the tablet of history because of the report of his committee, which was one of the most significant social documents of the nineteenth century. (Document 1B.) With great skill and organisation Oastler and the Short Time Committees marshalled suitable witnesses and prepared the ground. The committee heard the evidence of more than eighty witnesses, mostly operatives, and when the dissolution cut short the sittings it was decided to publish the evidence without comment. The stark mountain of evidence shattered illusions about freedom and political economy: it was widely hailed as an epoch-making compendium and the evidence was regarded as a disgrace to the nation. Sadler, Oastler and the Short Time Committees had not achieved a ten-hour day, but they had, through the report, made some form of legislation inevitable. The state was being pushed inexorably into action.

Despite almost universal sympathy for the suffering revealed, the Whig Government decided on grounds of equity that the employers, who had not submitted evidence to Sadler, must be heard, and so Ashley was forced to delay his bill pending the report of a Factory Commission. Led by Southwood Smith and Edwin Chadwick, the Commissioners worked efficiently and swiftly to produce a definitive statement about the factory question. Cool, detached and clinical, these men had none of Oastler's paternalistic sympathy and he clashed violently with the two Commissioners who visited Yorkshire. Regarding them as the employers' stooges bent on delay, he refused to co-operate and began to show signs of the irrational extremism which was to grow in him during the later 1830s. It was a matter of remark in the report that Ashley's supporters had been hostile to the inquiry, for Oastler had said 'Let them dread the dagger and the torch...I have ceased to reason'. The Factory Commission Report of June 1833 produced unoriginal but authoritative conclusions. In addition, in recommending effective enforcement and education the report went beyond the provisions of Ashley's bill. In effect the Commission had been set up to provide some impartial justification to act: to reconcile legislation for children with the individualism so dear to the ethos of the new industrial society. Chadwick and his friends stamped the Benthamite approval on the notion of a free agent which had been widely discussed in the three previous years. Perhaps Macaulay had best summed it up in his 1832 election campaign:

> The general rule – a rule not more beneficial to the capitalist than to the labourer -is that contracts shall be free and that the state shall not interfere between the master and the workman. To this general rule there is an exception. Children cannot protect themselves and are therefore entitled to the protection of the public.[9]

This conclusion the Commission fully endorsed. Adults were free to leave their employment if they did not like conditions; children were clearly not free agents and so legislation was justified. (Document 1C.)

Events moved quickly following this decisive report. Ashley's ten-hour bill was lost in July and, during August 1833, Althorp, the Whig Chancellor, introduced his own bill which quickly became law. Applying to all textile mills except silk and lace, the Act forbade the employment of children under nine. Children from nine to thirteen were limited to an eight-hour day, while young persons under eighteen were restricted to a twelve-hour day. Two hours a day were to be set aside for education and, most important of all, four factory inspectors were designated to enforce the Act.

Though four was a woefully inadequate establishment which gave each inspector a vast region to supervise, there was also to be a corps of resident superintendents authorised to initiate prosecutions. The inspectors were given extremely wide powers including the right to issue legally enforceable regulations and the right to sit as magistrates and fine immediately 'on view' when an offence was discovered. These 'judicial' powers were, however, used sparingly and were rescinded in 1844. The inspectorate was also granted access to all information, including business records, relating to the condition of factory workers, especially children, whose age was to be medically certified (civil registration did not commence until 1837). There is some evidence that the 1833 Act may have accelerated an already established trend away from child employment in textile factories, that it was perhaps dealing with a problem already on the wane. By the end of the 1840s, for instance, only 6 per cent of offences prosecuted by the factory inspector for the Lancashire textile region were for children working illegal hours. Despite this, the 1833 Factory Act clearly marks a great turning-point in the history of social policy.

The Act acknowledged the right of the state to intervene where there was an overwhelming need to protect exploited sections of the community. The ultimate responsibility for ensuring the welfare of children at work was centred not on parent or employer but on the community at large. Not only were these developments in principle, but, for the first time, provision was made for effective implementation. Previously Factory Acts had been the work of individuals applying only to the cotton industry; now the pattern was set for more general Acts introduced by the Government with administrative machinery for enforcement. Yet such was the ambivalence of this issue that it is possible to regard Althorp's Act as at once an exception to and a confirmation of *laissez-faire*. In defining a social category for whom the philosophy of total freedom was inappropriate, the keepers of the Benthamite conscience imposed the disciplines of individualism all the more rigorously upon adult workers. The exception proves the rule, and the elevation into orthodox dogma of the concept of the adult as a free agent meant that the ten-hour day *for adults* could only come via the limitations upon the hours of young persons. The children had been saved; the adults still worked on without legal protection.

III   The achievement of a ten-hour day

While the 1833 Factory Act may be viewed in the long term as a decisive extension of the state's social policy, the immediate aftermath for the factory reformers was intense deflation. Oastler felt that they had been tricked and outmanoeuvred by the

Government's provision for children to have less than a ten-hour day. Young persons would still work long hours and adults would still be the victims of the Whig political economy he despised so much. Inevitably there would be little point in campaigning once more so soon after the passage of such an important Act, and the working-class movement was being drawn away from the factory question to trade unionism, the anti-Poor Law movement and then Chartism. Indeed the factory movement itself virtually became swallowed by the protests against the Poor Law and by the wider working-class agitation for the People's Charter. Oastler, though never deserting the factory cause, joined in the clamour against the 'inhuman' new Poor Law and became increasingly troubled by financial problems which ended in his imprisonment in the Fleet debtors' prison in 1840.

The ebb and flow of the tides of the factory movement may be traced through the years, but there was never to be the concerted strength and vitality of the formative years of Oastler's baptism between 1830 and 1833. This was partly due to competing causes and the difficulties and decline of Oastler himself. Yet in many ways the main task had been achieved, for now that the precedent had been established, now that Parliament had deemed factory reform an appropriate area for social legislation, there would be a built-in self-perpetuating momentum. If for no other reason than the need to review the novel administrative machinery, there was bound to be future consideration of the factory question. The great achievement of Oastler, Sadler and the Short Time Committees was to build up so great a public pressure that Parliament was forced to take action. (Document 1D.) To continue the reforming process required Parliamentary rather than extra-Parliamentary pressure, and this is where Ashley's efforts were so decisive. It by no means belittles Ashley's contribution to understand that he did not create the demand for factory reform but carried it forward in Parliament to provide more extensive legislation. As Ashley himself admitted in 1833, the credit belonged to Oastler and Sadler, who had 'borne the real toil, encountered the real opposition, roused the sluggish public'.

The aim of the movement was still a ten-hour day, and Ashley persistently attempted to graft a ten-hour clause on to any factory bill under consideration, such as the unsuccessful bills of 1838, 1839 and 1841. He was more successful in 1840 in getting a committee under his chairmanship appointed to examine the workings of the 1833 Act. Over half the report of Ashley's Committee on the Factory Act comprised the comments of the inspectors themselves, who highlighted defects in administration which reduced the efficacy of the Act. Above all, the report confirmed the principle of intervention and the need for further legislation. One of the most famous inspectors, Leonard Horner, an authority quoted on all sides, re-emphasised in a pamphlet the nature of the social legislation involved: 'Parliament must tell the masters that they must accommodate themselves the best way they can to the conditions upon which alone the State will allow them to purchase infant labour... the interposition of the Legislature in behalf of children was justified by the most cold and severe principle of political economy.'[10] Experience as a factory inspector gradually eroded Horner's belief in the free agent, so that by the 1840s he was one of the most powerful influences in support of a ten-hour day.

Indeed, to some extent Horner ignored the evidence of his own prosecutions in order to make propaganda for further reform. So, for example, he quoted to Ashley's committee remarks made in his annual reports on the matter of inadequate fines:

Instead of visiting offences with such a penalty as would at once be a punishment of the offender and a warning to others, the magistrates in several places have availed themselves to such an extent of their power... to mitigate the penalties that their lenity will, I fear, rather encourage than check future violations. ... It seems to be an established rule in some courts of petty sessions that mill owners may violate any provision... for once at least on payment of 20s.[11]

Yet a comparison of fines levied by Halifax magistrates (severely criticised by Oastler) with those levied by Horner himself, when fining 'on view', shows no discrepancy between the two. Though fines per offence seem rather low, fines per offender (the sum of fines levied for separate offences on the same employer) were much higher. The level of fines was of course limited by what Parliament laid down, intended more to educate than to punish offenders.

Ashley's report did not produce the hoped-for legislation in the last year of an ailing Whig administration, but the 1842 Report of the Royal Commission on the Employment of Children, appointed on Ashley's insistence, was more fruitful. As with the Sadler Committee, the public conscience was shocked into action by the

Children's Employment Commission's revelations about child labour in coal mines. The conditions, which Ashley described as 'disgusting and intolerable', were vividly revealed not only by detailed appendices but also by the now famous woodcut illustrations depicting near-naked children labouring in cramped passages. This was an affront to civilisation and humanitarian sentiment was aroused on the grounds of decency. There was also in Ashley's promotion of a subsequent Coal Mines Bill a desire to release children from this grinding labour so that they could be subject to the influence of moral education in the interests of social order. As in 1833, the Commission rehearsed the 'free agent' argument and one of its members asserted that there was 'no case for any interference with the mode of labour of persons who are of an age of discretion, and capable of making their own contracts'.[12] The question was at what age a child became a free agent. In Ashley's bill, which because of public outrage passed the Commons easily, children would have begun work only at thirteen. The House of Lords, under pressure from powerful aristocratic mine owners, reduced this to ten. Though apprentices were removed from the provisions, women were admitted as unfree agents and were barred from working underground.

Ashley was bitterly disappointed, but the Commons passed the amended bill, again with provision for enforcement by inspectors. Not all Tories were of Ashley's opinions, and the new Peel Government quietly accepted the Lords' amendments to the mines bill and positively refused Ashley's pleas on behalf of a ten-hour day. When Sir James Graham, the Home Secretary, did introduce a new factory bill in 1843 he was mainly motivated by a desire to implement effective education for factory children. Such was the hostility of Dissenters to these educational provisions that the bill had to be dropped. (This is further discussed in Chapter 4.)

When Graham reintroduced the bill in 1844 without its offensive clauses there was much confusion of parties during its passage. At one stage Ashley got a ten-hour amendment accepted, and yet later the House rejected both a ten- and a twelve-hour day. By the mid-1840s the Anti-Corn Law League was very active and the middle-class liberal case against Ashley was that factory legislation was not the way to solve the problem, which was essentially the result of protection. John Bright, a supporter of practically every reform movement in the nineteenth century, opposed factory reform because he saw the end of child labour in free trade. Factory legislation was like 'applying lotions to pimples when a dose of medicine for the whole system is required', or, put another way, 'We demand of the legislature not to interfere between masters and men but to remove all the impediments to commerce and let the operative have fair play and the value of his labour will be his best and surest protection'.[13] Paternalistic social legislation was the kingpin of the traditional Toryism of Sadler, Oastler, Ashley and the new firebrand, Busfeild Ferrand. New Conservatives like Peel and Graham were much more sympathetic to the ideology of the industrial middle class.

Peel would not support a ten-hour day and made the twelve-hour provision an issue of confidence which, to the consternation of Ashley, defeated the ten-hour proposal decisively. The 1844 Factory Act was a significant step forward. Children were allowed to start work younger, at eight, but worked half-time, no more than six and a half hours daily. Graham incorporated Horner's suggestions for the tightening of administration, and machinery was to be fenced. Above all, the unfree agent definition was enlarged to include women, following the precedent of the 1842 Mines Act. Women, like young persons, were to work a twelve-hour day.

During the following campaign which began with Ashley's presentation of the ten-hour bill in January 1846, the movement had once more to seek a new Parliamentary leader as Ashley resigned over Peel's change of policy on the Corn Laws. All issues were subservient to this during the 1846 session, which was not an auspicious time for John Fielden, a Liberal Todmorden factory owner, to take over from Ashley. Fielden's support for the factory movement had always undermined the theory that all factory owners were hostile to legislation. His bill was lost in May 1846, but the confusion at Westminster following Peel's defeat and the decline in trade made 1847 a more promising year, since a ten-hour day was in practice being worked and there was much unemployment. Employers could hardly complain about restrictions on output while the mills were idle.

Fielden reintroduced his bill in 1847 supported by a massive agitation in the north, with Oastler once more in the field. The Parliamentary situation was much more conducive to a ten-hour bill than it had been when Ashley had campaigned in 1844. The widespread support given to Fielden by the Protectionist Tories, now split from Peel over the Corn Laws, has been traditionally explained as revenge on the Anti-Corn Law League. There had been a running rural versus urban battle throughout Ashley's campaign, with the accusation that he ignored the destitution of the agricultural labourers on his own estates while exuding sympathy for mill workers hundreds of miles away. Marx saw the agricultural interest, wounded by the repeal of the Corn Laws, fighting back at the manufacturers by supporting a ten-hour day. It was much more likely that the removal of Peel's whip allowed Protectionists to follow their natural inclinations and support paternalistic protection for the industrial poor. Many of the Protectionists would have voted with Ashley in 1844 had Peel not made the twelve-hour day an issue of confidence. It was therefore perfectly natural to find the Protectionists behind Fielden, but the Peelites, with their belief in economic liberalism, opposed him. Russell, the Prime Minister, was cool on the factory issue but did not press the point and so the ten-hour bill was accepted by Parliament in 1847.

The provisions of the 1847 Factory Act envisaged that young persons and women would be restricted to eleven hours in the first year and ten in the second. The widespread rejoicing at the ultimate success of the movement was, however, premature, for not only did the 1847–8 depression reduce its impact, but as trade revived employers found loopholes in the legislation. By using relays of children and varying meal breaks it was possible to continue to work adult males more than twelve hours. Horner found, like some twenty-first-century Inland Revenue tax inspector, that smart operators will always evade Parliament's intentions. Horner pursued the issue through the courts so that the illegality of relays could be confirmed, or so he thought. When a test case went to the Exchequer in February 1850, relays were found to be legal. Baron Parke, the presiding judge, was reported to have commented privately that while the framers of the Act had intended to exclude relays, 'as it is a law to restrain the exercise of capital and property it must be construed stringently'.[14] Even the judiciary was imbued with *laissez-faire* and so the employers got the benefit of the doubt.

The impact of this decision may be gauged from Ashley's diary comment: 'great remedial measure, the Ten Hours Act, nullified. The work to be done all over again; and I am seventeen years older than when I began'.[15] Parliament now needed to amend the law to restore its original intention and the factory lobby used this opportunity to secure a ten-and-a-half-hour day in the hastily drafted 1850 Factory Act. This was a compromise to which Ashley agreed, much to the disgust of many of his former friends in the factory movement. Poor craftsmanship had omitted to make clear that children could not work beyond 6 p.m., and it was not until Palmerston introduced the 1853 bill, carefully prepared by Horner, that the normal day of 6 a.m. to 6 p.m. was established. Children could not work their six-and-a-half hours beyond these limits; young persons and women were restricted to a ten-and-a-half-hour day; as a corollary the adult male free agent also worked a ten-and-a-half-hour day even though Parliament had not mentioned adult males at all.

The factory movement as such disappeared in the 1850s with great success to its credit. As yet the legislation applied only to textiles, and Ashley, who in 1851 became seventh Earl of Shaftesbury, continued the battle in Parliament to extend legislation to unprotected trades. The damaging consequences which factory owners anticipated never materialised in the mid-Victorian prosperity, so that by the 1860s many of the former opponents, motivated by self-interest or ideology, had come round to the view that factory legislation was both necessary and beneficial. In 1862 Shaftesbury suggested the establishment of the Children's Employment Commission to inquire into the conditions in unregulated trades. By 1866 the Commission had published five reports which the Russell Government was preparing to act on. The minority Conservative Government took up these plans and produced two measures in 1867: the Factory Act Extension Act applying to premises with more than fifty employees, and the Hours of Labour Regulation Act for those, including private houses, with fewer. The former Act applied to industries such as metalworking, printing, paper and glassworks, while the main effects of the latter were felt in clothing. Children under eight were forbidden to work and older children were required to have ten hours' schooling a week. Young persons and women were also protected, and in all the measures affected 1.4 million people – a great triumph for Shaftesbury.

In the early 1870s A. J. Mundella, a Radical MP, introduced a nine-hour bill several times, and factory hours were an issue, especially in Lancashire, during the 1874 election. R. A. Cross, Disraeli's Home Secretary, finally achieved the ten-hour day by the

1874 Factory Act which raised the age for half-time employment from eight (which it had been since 1844) to ten, and for full-time from thirteen (which it had been since 1833) to fourteen. Women and young persons were given a ten-hour day and so consequentially were adult males. Still, Cross felt he must pay lip-service to the old Chadwick doctrine of the free agent: 'So far as adult males were concerned there could be no question that freedom of contract must be maintained and men must be left to take care of themselves.'[16] Despite this, the 1874 Act was the most paternalistic of all Disraeli's social legislation. The 1878 Factory Act, though more comprehensive and rounding off Cross's work, was essentially a consolidating Act which pulled together all the provisions into one scheme. The depression of the 1870s inclined some to argue that factory legislation had gone too far and indeed was the main cause of the country's failure to keep up with her new industrial competitors. By that time, however, the principle of state intervention was so well-established that it could not be reversed. Children, young persons and women at work were the responsibility of the state, secured by legal provision enforceable through a bureaucratic machinery. The effectiveness of the provision of course depended upon the effectiveness of the bureaucracy itself.

In this context, it should be noted that the inspectorate was always likely to be too deficient in size to secure comprehensive coverage. In coal-mining only one inspector was appointed under the 1842 Act and it was not until the Coal Mines Inspection Act of 1850 that officials were empowered to make underground inspections. The number of inspectors was raised to four in 1850, six in 1852 and twelve in 1855. Even this figure gave each inspector an impossibly large district to administer and this was equally true of the factory inspectorate where a reorganisation in the later 1830s left each inspector some 1,500 mills to supervise with the assistance of four superintendents. The total establishment for the factory inspectorate was raised to about twenty in 1839, at which level it remained for some thirty years. The inspectors were also hampered by inadequate budgets: in the mid-1860s the mines inspectorate had a budget of only £10,000 while that of the factory inspectorate was about a third more.

Nevertheless, inspectors, even today, complain of overstretched resources and it was never intended that this industrial police force should supervise industry's every move. They were intended to create a moral climate of observance by the principle of inspection. Indeed, it was strongly believed that inspectors should not take from employers the ultimate responsibility for running decent industrial establishments. Inspectors existed to facilitate good industrial practice, not to become surrogate employers. Thus a mines' inspector was advised by the Home Office:

> While you will afford to any parties who may solicit it, such advice or suggestion as your knowledge or experience may enable you to offer, you will abstain from dictation or any unauthorised interference.... You will not fail to act with courtesy and forbearance in your official intercourse with all persons, and you will encourage a good feeling and understanding between the miners and their employers.[17]

But if inspectors were to tread warily and not offend, how effective could they be? Much depended on the individual official, for the inspectors did not act in concert as a unified service. There were considerable differences in background and personality both between and within the inspectorates. Mines' inspectors tended to be technically qualified and experienced in that industry, whereas factory inspectors were more likely to be men of liberal education. Leonard Horner, the most famous, was inclined to act rather inflexibly on matters of principle while his colleague, Robert Saunders, was much more pragmatic. Differences of approach in the 1860s and 1870s between the joint senior factory inspectors, Alexander Redgrave and Robert Baker, led a Royal Commission in 1876 to question whether a unified policy existed. It was therefore common for inspectors to have different prosecution rates and to concentrate on different sorts of offences.

Much research remains to be done on the administration of factory and coal mines legislation and what has been done suggests conflicting conclusions. It has recently been argued that in the matter of fencing and safety at work, the inspectorate was quite ineffectual in raising standards.[18] However, in other areas of factory regulation much greater success appears to have been registered. The analysis of the success rate of prosecutions tends to undermine the widely held view, often encouraged by the inspectors themselves, that magistrates frequently acquitted on flimsy grounds. One recent estimate calculates that well over three-quarters of prosecutions were successful and at times the success rate was over 90 per cent. Manchester magistrates dismissed only 4 per cent of cases, those at Leeds only 7 per cent.[19] This evidence is echoed in subsequent analysis which confirms that magistrates generally co-operated with inspectors and that most prosecutions were successful. However, it is also true that prosecutions were sometimes withdrawn or not even commenced where a negotiated agreement was reached between employers and inspector. It may also be true that magistrates represented large-scale industrialists and that most offenders were running smaller establishments.[20]

The opposition of industrialists to what was sometimes seen as unreasonable intervention by individual inspectors does suggest that it was not only through prosecution that improvements could be effected. For example, the interpretation of fencing requirements was regarded by employers as:

> a mere arbitrary capricious regulation . . . contrived by inspectors themselves of their own mere motion and conceived in a spirit of vexatious interference with the 'rights of capital' in the conduct of private establishments.[21]

It is almost impossible to discover how far the law was being observed because of the inspectors' inability to monitor practice comprehensively. Conclusions also depend on how the evidence is interpreted. Acquittals have usually been taken to indicate connivance and self-interest of magistrates but some were based on humanitarian grounds where impecunious parents were prosecuted for their children's offences. The relatively low number of prosecutions may indicate the inadequacy of the establishment but may equally suggest widespread observance and enforcement through persuasion rather than legal process. Albeit erratically, inspection and regulation gradually became a normal feature of Victorian industrial life.

2 The Poor Law

I The 43rd of Elizabeth

Hark, hark, the dogs do bark,
The beggars are coming to town.

It was undoubtedly fear of social disorder in the two and a half centuries following the Black Death which gradually converted the maintenance of the poor from an aspect of personal Christian charity into a prime function of the state. With approximately one-third of her population removed by plague, England's fourteenth-century economy had a chronic labour shortage and a paternalistic state attempted to introduce wage control by the Statute of Labourers of 1351. This was reinforced by the Poor Law Act of 1388 which not only tried to fix wages but also to prevent that mobility of labour which would cause wages to rise. Laws against vagrancy were thus the origins of poor relief, and whenever economic conditions prevailed which encouraged men to wander the country in search of employment, the late medieval and early modern English state sought to restrict this mobility for fear of its social consequences.

Initially, Tudor legislation was just as repressive (and ineffective) as earlier vagrant laws had been, but the stocks and the beatings did not deter men whose economic plight forced them to uproot themselves. Gradually a more constructive attitude towards vagrancy began to emerge. Like so much in the Tudor period, this process began in the reign of Henry VIII in the 1530s. In 1536 parishes were authorised to collect money in order to support the impotent poor who would therefore no longer need to beg. The state was thus acknowledging some minimal community responsibility for those who were unable to work. For the able-bodied poor, in modern terminology the unemployed but in contemporary eyes rogues, vagabonds and criminals, there was still the harsh treatment of earlier vagrant legislation. Indeed in 1547, after the death of Henry VIII, Parliament ordered that slavery was to be the punishment for vagrancy.

Elizabethan legislation showed itself more aware of the underlying causes of vagrancy which so frightened many in authority. Historians are now of the opinion that the numbers of vagrants who roamed the countryside in bands in Tudor times have been greatly exaggerated. Nevertheless persistent vagrancy was sufficient to prompt the state to evolve from experience a viable system of poor relief. Two economic processes occurred during the sixteenth century which swelled the numbers of those without subsistence (and neither had much to do with the dissolution of the monasteries which was traditionally cited as the cause of increased vagrancy). First, there was the process of enclosure which largely involved the conversion of arable to pasture and produced widespread depopulation, the extent of which is a matter of debate. Second, there was the massive inflation, the so-called 'price revolution', consequent upon the import of precious metals from the New World.

Clearly, Elizabethan Governments did not understand this inflation or the economic fluctuations in the growing wool trade, but the effects of enclosures were known to all and were the subject of propaganda in some circles. It may well be that the worst effects of enclosures had been felt much earlier in the century, but the important thing was that those in authority were prepared to acknowledge causes of unemployment beyond the idle whim of the vagrant. If nothing more, it encouraged in poor-relief legislation the notion of distinguishing between those who would work and could not and those who could work but would not – between the genuinely unemployed and the idler. Much earlier, of course, the impotent poor had been identified as a distinct group requiring special treatment.

In 1576 the concept of 'setting the poor on work' was enshrined in statute law where it was to remain for something like three and a half centuries. If the able-bodied required assistance they had to work for it, and in the 1576 Poor Relief Act JPs were instructed to provide a stock of raw materials on which beggars could work in return for the relief they received. This clearly owed much to the practice already prevailing in London, where the City authorities had converted the great unused palace of Bridewell in Blackfriars into a poor-house, accommodating both the impotent and the able-bodied poor. Parishes and magistrates were reluctant to lay out more money than was absolutely necessary, and the new system had not spread widely before the great codifying legislation of 1598 and 1601 superseded all earlier regulations.

The Poor Law Act of 1601 was in effect a reissuing of that of 1598, yet the whole Elizabethan system is known by the later measure, the much-beloved though much-abused 43rd of Elizabeth. Once again fears of social disorder prompted action, as a series of bad harvests combined with returning soldiers to heighten the tension of vagrancy which was a near-permanent feature of Tudor times. Learning from the experience of a century, the 43rd of Elizabeth abandoned mere repression in favour of a logical solution soundly administered. The key was what later came to be called 'classification', finding the appropriate remedy for the particular group.

Essentially the Elizabethan Poor Law identified three main groups to be dealt with. The impotent poor (the aged, the chronic sick, the blind, the lunatic), who really needed institutional relief, were to be accommodated in 'poor-houses' or 'almshouses'. The able-bodied were to be set to work on hemp or some other appropriate material and for this a 'house of correction' (really a workhouse), not at first residential, was to be established. As a corollary to this, children in need of relief were to be apprenticed to a trade so that they would become useful, self-supporting citizens. Finally, the able-bodied who absconded and preferred the open road or the persistent idler who refused to work were to be punished in this 'house of correction'. In other words the ideal was for three different sorts of treatment for three different sorts of pauper.

Whereas earlier legislation had been somewhat vague in administrative detail, the Acts of 1598 and 1601 firmly rooted the scheme in the only effective local government system available, that of the JPs. Each parish was to administer its own poor relief via overseers (a name first used in 1572) who were to be appointed by the magistrates. Overseers were empowered to levy poor rates on property which the magistrates were to enforce, and the whole system was to be supervised by the Privy Council.

Harsh but effective, it was typical of the paternalistic Tudor state, and if ability to survive was a sign of efficacy then this was certainly efficient, for more than two hundred years later men were swearing loyalty to and searching for the original pristine 43rd of Elizabeth.

Perhaps its greatest strength was that it was firmly rooted in the localities, yet this contributed to the diffuseness which the 43rd of Elizabeth was to acquire over the years. The very men whom Parliament correctly deemed knew most about the specific problems of their own localities were the men who continually adapted statute law to meet their own local difficulties. With each parish a sort of petty kingdom with its own sovereign will, the Poor Law became nationally the combined rationalisation of accumulated local custom. Indeed the student of Poor Law history is well advised to accept as a first premise that the story of poor relief is but dimly (and often not at all) told through the pages of national legislation.

Since each parish was required to look after its 'own' poor, there evolved a national pattern of dispute and litigation over where responsibility lay for individual paupers whose real place of residence was doubtful. At the heart of all anti-vagrancy legislation from the fourteenth century onwards had been the desire to return wanderers to their proper and rightful parish, but the location of this was often difficult to determine. The Elizabethan formula was that a vagrant should be returned to his place of birth or, if that was not known, a place where he had resided for one year, or to the last parish through which he had passed without punishment. Overseers, conscious that ratepayers wished to keep poor rates down, did all they could to prevent paupers becoming chargeable on their particular parish, and the courts were full of rival overseers disputing settlement. Indeed one suspects that often more time and money were spent on litigation than the sustenance of the pauper would have involved. Poor Law archives are full of stories of wretched families being shuttled about the country in search of a haven or of expectant mothers hurried on to the next village for fear of the offspring becoming natives and hence dependants of the parish.

The famous Act of Settlement of 1662 attempted to clarify a situation confused by mountains of legal decisions, though in time further judicial interpretations in turn complicated the intention of this legislation. By the 1662 Act a legal settlement was gained by birth, marriage, apprenticeship and, later in practice, inheritance. A stranger could be removed within forty days of his arrival in a parish unless he occupied freehold land, but essentially men who did not require relief were left alone. The parish overseers feared large numbers of strangers becoming chargeable, but since the new Act required them to dispatch a stranger to his own place of settlement and not just to the next parish, they were hardly likely to embark on the costly process of removal unless there was a real chance of increased demands for relief. Though Adam Smith in particular criticised the Act of Settlement, it clearly did not prevent the social mobility which helped great cities to grow towards the end of the eighteenth century. Removals were still common, with their attendant miseries and cruelties; at the same time, as in earlier periods, punitive legislation aimed at vagrancy did not prevent people moving about.

Settlement was a question of universal interest to parishes yet did not produce a common practice, and the same was true of the institutions of relief which gradually merged into the workhouse. The tripartite division, poor-house for the impotent, workhouse for the able-bodied and houses of correction for the idle, never really operated in practice. Various experiments were tried, the most notable of which was that at Bristol where the parishes of the city combined in 1696 to provide their so-called 'pauper manufactory' or Corporation of the Poor. This attempted to make poor relief self-sufficient through the work done by the paupers, and while on the whole this did not completely succeed, the example of Bristol was copied by many other towns. Legislation, as ever, registered rather than initiated changing practice, and Sir Edward Knatchbull's Act of 1722 which encouraged workhouses confirmed the wider use of the workhouse both as a form of deterrent and as a source of profits.

Only the largest parishes could aspire to a 'pauper manufactory' in the Bristol fashion, and so amalgamations of parishes by local Acts became common. Thomas Gilbert's Act of 1782 made unions possible without special legislation, and by 1834 over 900 parishes had joined to form 67 unions under Gilbert's Act, most of them with paid relieving officers: the embryonic social worker was at hand. Gilbert's Act also encouraged outdoor relief as a method of sustaining paupers. The pension, dole or payment in kind was always the easiest and often the most appropriate form of relief to administer, and along with the 'roundsman system' (where local farmers employed the parish poor on a rota system) was one of the devices suggested by practical good sense. The 43rd of Elizabeth asked overseers to provide money for the impotent, work for the able-bodied and correction for the idle; two centuries of practice created in the Poor Law a tool of social policy of infinite variety and unlimited versatility. No contemporary then (and no historian since) was conversant with the whole nationally varying picture.

Variations in methods of poor relief were the result of the ingenuity of magistrates, overseers and vestries, and that ingenuity was increasingly taxed in the last quarter of the eighteenth century. Population growth, increased social mobility, industrialisation and economic fluctuations stretched to the limit a system which had been geared to a pre-industrial economy and had been finely tuned to social needs in the period 1600–1750. In the last five years of the eighteenth century, severe scarcity occasioned by bad harvests and the dislocation of war brought the Poor Law to an acute crisis. New remedies had to be found in exceptional circumstances, for not only were the unemployed to be sustained, but those in work were also in desperate need because of food shortages and increased prices. A solution was not forthcoming from Parliament. Samuel Whitbread's wage-regulation bill, which would have empowered magistrates to regulate wages according to the cost of living, was lost in 1796 after widespread criticism of what was in reality a confused though benevolent programme.

Parliament's failure to give a lead left the initiative where it had always been, in the localities, and from the 1780s local schemes had been intermittently introduced to subsidise labourers' income by 'allowances in aid of wages'. These wage subsidies became more common as the food crises worsened and so tended to become more systematised. The now famous meeting at the Pelican Inn in Speenhamland in 1795 was but part of a growing pattern of local initiatives to cope with acute economic dislocation and below subsistence-level wages. As an alternative to direct wage regulation, allowances were widely used as a temporary expedient to supplement low incomes. The so-called 'Speenhamland System' never existed in the form which the Poor Law reformer, Sir Frederick Eden, believed he was exposing, when in 1797 he gave the village of Speenhamland its false notoriety. We are on much safer ground in thinking in terms of a chronologic- ally and geographically varied allowance system, rather than of a uniform 'Speenhamland System'. Even where Speenhamland- type allowances were adopted they were often later abandoned as magistrates and overseers struggled to cope with changing economic conditions.

There was much confusion later over the different forms of relief that were used. Much abuse was to be heaped on outdoor relief *per se*, which was further encouraged by an Act of 1795 which released parishes from the workhouse test, but, as two centuries of practice indicated, outdoor relief was not a new feature of the 1790s. There were different sorts of supplementary benefits. First, these could be in money or in kind, and indeed there were widespread reports by 1800 of local subscriptions for distributing food which had replaced excess money payments. These wage subsidies were sometimes based on a bread scale (the Speenhamland index) but sometimes the two were separate. More common than either were the child and family allowances which were to be the object of Malthus's scorn. The essential element of them all was that they were devices used to help those in work, who in these times of crisis and scarcity were as much in need as the unemployed. Many historians now see the allowance system as a sensible and flexible response to economic and social dislocation. Many variants of the system helped to maintain a labour force where seasonal fluctuations were bound to produce troughs and peaks of demand for labour.[1]

In view of the harsh things that were later said about the consequences of the allowance system, it is worth recalling two points about these changes in the 1790s. First, whatever the economic consequences may have been (and that is very much an open question), the intent of the new modes of relief was human- itarian and benevolent. As always, those with wealth wished to ensure that those without it did not become disaffected and rebellious. At the same time there was genuine concern for those who, despite their labours, were below subsistence level. Here was an attempt to provide social welfare via a form of minimum wage and family allowances. The community was guaranteeing sustenance to all its members: Lloyd George was striving for this in 1911 and we are still searching for it today. Second, social policy is an expression of social philosophy, and a generation which resorted so quickly to allowances in aid of wages was clearly one which did not regard poverty or poor relief as degrading. Poor relief did not have the social stigma of debasement it was later to acquire. At that time it did not appear an act of mass demoralisation to offer relief via the Poor Law to labourers who were in need.

By and large English society accepted the increased cost of poor relief during the war years as one of the necessary consequences of a long-drawn-out military struggle with France. It was mainly after 1815 that the supposed evil consequences of the allowance system were pilloried severely. Indeed the developments of the 1790s stimulated a debate which had already been growing about the very nature of the Poor Law itself. That debate was to continue for forty years and reached its culmination in the great Poor Law Report of 1834 and its legislative sequel, the Poor Law Amendment Act.

II The road to 1834

Even during the war years it was recognised that there was a pressing need for a reform of the Poor Law, and as one observer remarked as early as 1807, 'The best, the wisest and most radical relief has ever been allowed to consist in a well-constructed plan to ameliorate the general condition of the labouring poor.'[2] Every magistrate, overseer, vestryman and relieving officer had his own panacea, and in an area of social policy where practice was so varied and contemporary familiarity with the system so fragmentary, it is difficult to give any coherence to the very diffuse debate on this pressing social problem. What the Webbs called a 'cloud of pamphlets' revealed the range of possible solutions. Sydney Smith surveyed them:

> A pamphlet on the Poor Laws generally contains some little piece of favourite nonsense by which we are told this enormous evil may be perfectly cured. The first gentleman recommends little gardens; the second cows: the third village shops; the fourth a spade; the fifth Dr Bell [the educationist], and so forth. Every man rushes to the press with his small morsel of imbecility.[3]

The shortcomings of the Poor Law induced a strong abolitionist case which wished to replace the Poor Law entirely. This opinion reached its high point with the report of a Select Committee in 1817. From about 1820 the abolitionist case was gradually eroded in the search for a compromise solution which would rid the Poor Law of its defects but would stop short of abolition. The Poor Law Amendment Act was the product of this search.

The high priest of abolitionism was the Revd T. R. Malthus, but the school of thought was by no means originated by him. During the eighteenth century there had been intermittent criticism of the Poor Law which was most vitriolic from the pen of the Revd Joseph Townsend. In 1786 Townsend had argued the central abolitionist tenet: 'These laws, so beautiful in theory, promote the evils they mean to remedy and aggravate the distress.' The normal stimulants to self-help (ambition and fear) were nullified by the Poor Law:

> What encouragement have the poor to be industrious and frugal when they know for certain that should they increase their store it will be devoured by the drones, or what cause have they to fear when they are assured, that if by their indolence and extravagance, by their drunkenness and vices, they should be reduced to want, they shall be abundantly supplied?[4]

Though the work of Townsend was quite widely known, it was not mainly to him that abolitionists looked for the text from which they should preach. Malthus provided the theoretical justification for what many came to believe in by instinct.

The influential *Essay on the Principle of Population* by Malthus was published in 1798 and went through five further editions by 1826. The oft-quoted precise ratio (that food production increases arithmetically while population increases geometrically) was less important as a mathematical formula than the simple (and to Malthus self-evident) proposition that, unless restrained by certain checks, population growth would outstrip the means of subsistence. In other words even the most optimistic growth in output of food could not keep pace with the potential natural population increase. Modern neo-Malthusians would argue that a country such as twentieth-century India illustrates the Malthusian case, since only by bringing population growth under control can there be any hope of solving the massive poverty problem.

Malthus was not arguing for birth control, though many subsequent thinkers drew this as the main conclusion, but for moral restraint and delayed marriages. Men should not marry until they could afford to support a family; only then could the increased population be adequately provided for. Even without any inducements mankind could overpopulate the country; hence the new Poor Law device of child allowances was deemed doubly misguided, for it seemed to offer a bonus on large families. The Poor Law was thus worsening what was already a pessimistic future.

The same conclusion was derived from the work of David Ricardo, who in his *Principles of Political Economy* (1817) produced the so-called 'iron law of wages'. He evolved the idea of a 'wages fund' in which only a certain proportion of the national wealth was available in the form of wages. Hence the more paid out in poor relief (and expenditure was rising substantially), the less remained for wages. It was a vicious circle in which more people were being drawn into pauperism all the time and wages were being forced down. There was much complexity in Malthusian and Ricardian economics, but people did not have to understand the theories fully to draw two simple conclusions: first, that as Malthus demonstrated, poor relief encouraged improvident marriages and offered inducements to unsupportable population growth; second, that according to Ricardo the more generous expedients of the war years actually worsened the position of all labour. The Poor Law was counterproductive and self-defeating and a positive cause of the problem it was trying to combat. The obvious conclusion was that it must be abolished.

But what should replace it? Potential reformers had plenty of suggestions to choose from. Increased government expenditure or reduced expenditure; repeal of the Corn Laws or increased protection; more workhouses or fewer workhouses; more enclosures or fewer: all these had their supporters. Some saw allotments as the answer; others, including Pitt, wanted every man to have his own cow. Friendly societies and contributory schemes seemed to offer much hope, and indeed there were roughly the same number of Englishmen in societies as were in receipt of poor relief. Savings banks too could provide for that rainy day when help would be required. All sorts of public works schemes were suggested (to return to the Elizabethan idea of setting the poor to work), but they were all damned in the eyes of the new classical economists in that they were always in unfair competition with free labour. Education was widely supported as the answer and was the central feature of Whitbread's Poor Law bill of 1807, which was another of his lost causes. All these had a common ancestry: they all stemmed from an increasing faith in self-help. The aim of all men ought to be to make themselves independent, whereas the tendency of the Poor Law was to make men dependent. After 1815 more and more people, inspired by the individualism of Adam Smith or perhaps by their own experience, were preaching the doctrine of self-help. When the mid-Victorians enshrined self-help as their great shibboleth they were not discovering a new notion but confirming a theory which had been imbibed with their mother's milk.

No one alternative commended itself to a large enough section of opinion, yet meanwhile, the post-war distress pushed up poor rates. In the crisis years 1817–9 expenditure on poor relief was nearly £8 million per annum, or 12 s. to 13 s. per head of population. A new edition of Malthus's *Essay* in 1817 seemed to be echoed by the 1821 census with its evidence of increased rural population. In 1817 also, the abolitionist case received its strongest support in the Report of the Select Committee on the Poor Laws. This report was written by Frankland Lewis, later to be first chairman of the Poor Law Commission, and it condemned the evils of the present system comprehensively. Yet the very distress of the post-war years which had brought the abolitionist case to such a pitch was the reason why the Poor Law could not be summarily abolished. Abolition may have been the logical conclusion to draw from the defects of the Poor Law, but abolition without replacement had no practical use in a society already torn by internal dissension and disorder.

Once the initial post-war crisis had been weathered, men searched for a solution which would reduce the burdens of poor relief while at the same time avoiding the demoralisation said to be the corollary of the allowance system. In the 1820s several local reformers, particularly in Nottinghamshire, saw great virtues in a deterrent Poor Law based upon indoor relief in the workhouse. One of the chief protagonists of this reformed system was George Nicholls, later an influential member of the Poor Law Commission and a historian of the Poor Law itself. He claimed a remarkable reduction in poor rates owing to the introduction of his new regime in Southwell and a similar one in Bingham, both in Nottinghamshire. His was a harsh approach, cutting back relief firmly and imposing the labour test without exception. At the heart of all was the deterrent workhouse: 'I wish to see the Poor House looked to with dread by our labouring class, and the reproach for being an inmate of it extend downwards from Father to Son...for without this, where is the needful stimulus to industry?'[5] These local reforms were to gain wider currency through their adoption by the Royal Commission of 1832, to which we now turn.

Expenditure on poor relief, which had fallen below £7 million in 1820 and below £6 million in 1822, began to rise again following the financial crisis of 1826. By 1831 the figure topped £7 million once more (just over 10s. per head), and again higher poor rates engendered a renewed debate on this perennial problem. It has often been said that had it not been for the increased demands of poor rates there would have been no new Poor Law. This is certainly true, but at the same time landowners would have dug deeper into their pockets had they believed that this was the price they had to pay for social stability. If it cost £7 million a year to preserve the King his crown, the peer his coronet and the squire his estate, then so be it. What doomed the old Poor Law was that despite paying £7 million a year there still occurred the frightening Swing Riots of 1830. The burning of hayricks and threats of spoliation in the south of England, coinciding apparently with the widespread use of the allowance system, convinced authority that reform must come. The Poor Law had not eradicated distress – indeed the rural populace had become disaffected and desperate. The new Whig Government of Earl Grey may have been intent on reform, but it would stand no nonsense as far as attacks upon property were concerned. Melbourne, the Home Secretary, treated the rioters as repressively as had the Tories at the time of Peterloo, and nine labourers were hanged and about 900 transported or imprisoned. The other side of the coin for a reforming Government was a full-scale inquiry into the operation of the Poor Laws, and in February 1832 a Royal Commission was appointed whose report was to be a classic document in the history of English social policy. That report was the work of Nassau Senior, one of the leading *laissez-faire* economists, and Edwin Chadwick, former secretary to Bentham, now launching out on his great administrative career.

The Poor Law Report of 1834 has been the subject of great controversy and debate among historians, but lest that debate becomes confused, it is as well to be clear from the outset that there are two quite distinct questions at issue. Whatever can be said in criticism of this report no one can deny its great influence, for the Poor Law Amendment Act was modelled upon it. Hence if we wish to understand the nature of social policy in this crucially important period we must understand the motivation and philosophy of the report itself, however wrongheaded that report might appear. What the Commissioners believed may not have been the truth, but the subsequent legislation was based on that belief: what people thought was happening was, for the purpose of social policy, more important than what was actually happening. All this is quite separate from the question of whether in fact the Commissioners were accurate in their assessment of the old Poor Law. It may eventually be demonstrated that the report was based on faulty data and doubtful evaluation, but this would not detract one iota from its importance in social policy. In other words the debate over the Poor Law Report is a matter of social and economic history, about whether the report is a reliable historical source on the early nineteenth-century Poor Law. Its reputation as a description of the old Poor Law may become tarnished, but its significance for the new Poor Law can never be diminished.

The Royal Commission employed Assistant Commissioners to go round the country and submit reports on the workings of the Poor Law in the provinces. The main accusation that has been made is that either these researchers were very selective in their coverage and fed back to London the sort of evidence which they knew would be favourably received, or that Chadwick and Senior were highly selective in extracting material from the local reports which conformed to their preconceptions. Both were convinced that the key problem was the allowance system and its effects upon the adult able-bodied rural labourer. The allowance system demoralised and pauperised the countryside and above all it depressed wages. Senior saw wage levels as a reflection of the free market economy, but the allowance system interfered with wage movements. Instead of wage levels being determined by the value of labour they were being decided by Poor Law authorities. What had been originally intended as a floor below which people could not fall had become a ceiling above which they could not rise.

Given this preconceived view of the evils of the old Poor Law the emphasis on the allowance system becomes understandable, and although Chadwick hailed the new Poor Law as 'the first great piece of legislation based upon scientific or economical principles', his report was in essence a piece of propaganda for a predetermined case. Despite the enormous weight of evidence collected by the Assistant Commissioners (much of it undigested by the Commission itself), much modern research tends to question the Report's assessment. According to one scholar (Blaug, 1963, 1964), many parishes had been persuaded to abandon allowances so that the system which dominated the Report was already in decline. Moreover, he argues, allowances were the result not the cause of low wages. Another researcher (Baugh, 1975) questions whether the allowance system was of any real significance at any time, for it was the changing shape of poverty which determined policy response. At times of agrarian depression, after the Napoleonic War but not before, bread scales and family allowances were more widely used, but they did not, even in the rural south-east, cause relief expenditure to soar as the Report claimed. The central tenet of the case that allowances depressed wages has been theoretically challenged in an analysis which distinguishes the 'income supplement' character of most allowances from the 'wage subsidy' nature of the less common work-sharing devices, such as the roundsman system (McCloskey, 1973). This work reinforces Blaug's argument that it was underemployment which demoralised rural workers and reduced wage rates. Even Malthus's infallible link between generous child allowances and increased population, so influential among members of the Royal Commission, has been turned on its head. A demographic historian (Huzel, 1980) has suggested that just as allowances may have been response to low wages and not the other way round, so too allowances may have been the response to and not the cause of population growth.[6]

All this will continue to be a subject of research and speculation, but the significance of the report will be immune from attack. Tawney called it 'wildly unhistorical' and Dr Blaug 'wildly unstatistical', yet its recommendations passed into a law whose influence pervades even our own times. Indeed one historian described the 1834 Act as having 'exerted a powerful influence on the intellectual, moral and social climate . . . which decisively affected the course of social history' and as the most important legislation since the original Poor Law was enacted. Another goes even further and asserts that the 1834 law was 'the single most important piece of social legislation ever enacted'.[7] Broadly, the Poor Law Report suggested three main planks for the new system: the principle of 'less eligibility', the dogma of the workhouse test and the bureau-cratic panacea of administrative centralisation and uniformity.

The new 'bastiles', as the workhouses became known, were the object of so much bitter criticism at the time that we are apt to think that the workhouse was the sole *raison d'être* of the new Poor Law. Yet we ignore the fact that the workhouse test was only the most appropriate expedient for implementing what *was* the central message of 1834, namely the principle of less eligibil-ity. If we wish to understand the philosophy of 1834 we must understand the notion of less eligibility. Chadwick and Senior viewed the allowance system with the jaundiced eye of those who in our day claim 'the Welfare State makes us soft'. Just as the Welfare State cushions people from disaster, so the allowance system removed the fear of hunger which kept men industrious. The Poor Law Report accumulated masses of evidence to demonstrate that not only did the allowance system demoralise people and depress wages, but that it offered an open invitation to idleness. As often happened, the public provision at subsistence level was superior to the private provision men could make for themselves by their own labour. Bentham had argued that men would always flee from pain and seek pleasure and so naturally, in the words of the report, men were 'under the strongest inducement to quit the less eligible class of labourers and enter the more eligible class of paupers'.

The inference is obvious. Most pauperism was wilful, the delib-erate choice of men who naturally pursued their own best interests. Instead of discouraging pauperism the Poor Law encouraged it by offering such generous benefits. To Chadwick's logical mind the solution was clear: simply reverse the syllogism. If men quit the class of labourer to join the more eligible class of pauper, then obviously they would quit the class of pauper and join the more eligible class of labourer were the relative conditions to be reversed. Instead of relief being of a standard above that of an industrious labourer, it must be *below*. Hence the Poor Law would be encouraging industry rather than idleness. It was devastatingly simple yet potentially a powerful inducement to self-help and, as Chadwick described it, 'a great engine of social improvement'. If men knew that the poor relief which was open to them would provide standards lower than that which their own labour could ensure, they would naturally prefer to work rather than become paupers. This was simply the perennial problem of incentive. In our own day, as then, many low wage-earners with large families would be better off on public relief than in work. The wage-stop was the device used in the 1960s to ensure that men did not quit the class of labourer and join the class of pauper. Less eligibility may not appear attractive but it is apparently necessary to combat human nature. (Document 2A.)

Chadwick made much of his own authorship of the principle of less eligibility. In truth it owed a great deal to Bentham's pleasure/pain idea and to his prison plan, the great Panopticon. In addition, Bentham in his own writings on pauperism in the 1790s had anticipated this notion:

> If the condition of persons *maintained* without property *by the labour of others* were rendered more eligible, than that of persons maintained by their *own* labour then...individuals destitute of property would be continually withdrawing themselves from the class of persons maintained by their own labour, to the class of persons maintained by the labour of others.[8]

Chadwick, as Bentham's secretary, had probably read this, but what was more important than the precise authority of less eligibility was its widespread acceptance in the 1830s. Though the terminology might be different, the idea behind less eligibility was completely in character with general opinion on the Poor Law in the early nineteenth century. Every clergyman, overseer and magistrate wished to restore the self-respect and initiative of paupers and all the varied suggestions for reform had, as we have seen, a common desire to stimulate self-help. The Poor Law Report was thus a synthesis of contemporary opinion.

With less eligibility as the principle we can now see the workhouse test as the means of putting that principle into practice.

The aged, infirm, orphan and widow needed residential care, so that there was no dispute about institutional relief for this category and the report had very little to say about such cases. Again, the able-bodied adult male was the problem and the Commissioners wished to provide him with institutional relief also. In Chadwick's view a great indiscretion had been committed in enlarging the function of the Poor Law to include the poor as well as the indigent. Here he was adopting Bentham's definition. Indigence was in effect destitution, but 'poverty is the state of everyone who in order to obtain *subsistence* is forced to have recourse to *labour*'. As the report makes clear, it was inappropriate and contrary to the original 43rd of Elizabeth to give relief to labourers in work. (Document 2B.) The allowance system had steered the Poor Law into dealing with poverty (i.e. low wages) rather than restricting itself to destitution, which was the true mark of the pauper. The 1834 report was concerned to deter pauperism, not to reduce poverty: the distinction between the two was absolutely crucial. The allowance system had of course also ignored the essential principle of 'setting the poor to work', so that again the 43rd of Elizabeth had been abused.

To enforce a workhouse test – that is, to abolish all outdoor relief and offer only institutional relief in a workhouse – would in Chadwick's opinion correct the three great faults of the allowance system. First, it would remove at once the 'poor' (i.e. the labourer whose wages were being subsidised) from the Poor Law and cater only for the indigent (the truly destitute), as was its proper function. Second, it would restore the principle of *work*, so that paupers would really provide some service in return for relief as the original legislation had intended. And third, in so far as it would provide a standard of living below that of the lowest independent labourer, the workhouse would remove the pernicious attraction the Poor Law had acquired by virtue of the allowance system. (Document 2A.)

Again this was not particularly original, and the report admitted that this was an attempt to generalise local reforms. It recommended 'That those modes of administering relief which have been tried wholly or partially, and have produced beneficial effects in some districts, be introduced, with modifications according to local circumstances, and carried into complete execution in all'.[9] The deterrent workhouse was a feature of the Nottinghamshire reforms already mentioned, and in 1828 J. R. McCulloch, an orthodox economist of the Senior school, had written:

> The real use of a workhouse is to be an asylum for the able-bodied poor...But it should be such an asylum as will not be resorted to except by those who have no other resource....The able-bodied tenant of a workhouse should be made to feel that his situation is decidedly less comfortable than that of the industrious labourer who supports himself.[10]

This was the remedy which would reduce poor rates. A harsh alternative to self-help and independence was to be offered to the prospective pauper which he would accept only when truly destitute. It was not intended to reduce poverty but to deter pauperism.

Some may find this so-called Benthamite programme difficult to reconcile with the apparently benevolent 'greatest happiness' principle. Happiness seemed to be the last thing the new Poor Law was intended to bring, yet of course we must not forget that the greatest happiness of the greatest number is satisfactory so long as we are part of the greatest number. Legislation in the interests of the majority sounds fine in the context of class legislation for the privileged few but very different when the minority are underprivileged. This report may not have been geared to the interests of the pauper, but it was geared to the interests of the majority (i.e. the happiness of the greatest number) by whom the pauper wished to be maintained. The remedies had in mind the wilful pauper who chose relief in preference to labour, but what of the enforced and unwilling pauper who found himself destitute through no fault of his own? The cold Benthamite answer was that he must suffer the injustice in the interests of the majority. 'The good of society' determined that he must accept such terms 'whatever they may be, which the common welfare requires'. To render justice in the small minority of cases where there was injustice would destroy the basis of the system. 'The bane of all pauper legislation has been the legislating for the extreme cases' – this was the harsh message of truth. (Document 2C.) The new Poor Law must be geared not only to the wishes of the majority (who were not paupers) but also to the needs of the majority of paupers for whom this reform was appropriate. The 43rd of

Elizabeth thought in terms of involuntary pauperism; 1834 acknowledged but dismissed it.

And yet beneath the harshness this was in a strange sort of way a benevolent programme, given the social philosophy of the day. It was widely believed that men were masters of their own fate, that the individual had within his grasp the power to find his own salvation. Men who had been encouraged to be idle by security could be stimulated to industry by fear. It seemed harsh to offer men a pit instead of a feather bed to fall back on should they slip, but perhaps the fear of the pit would prompt independence more than the security of the feather bed. Society was acting like the loving parent inflicting sharp, painful punishment on the miscreant child – being cruel to be kind. The child, like the pauper, resented the short-term discomfort but benefited from the long-term improvement in character. Fearing the workhouse, the prospective pauper would pick himself up by his bootlaces and find employment. The allowance system had offered the social cripple a pair of crutches and so permanently disabled him; the new Poor Law offered him nothing, and so he walked again. The Poor Law Commission was no more bent on sadistic exploitation of the working class than the parent punishing the child; both believed it had the best interests of the recipient at heart. The pauper, like the child, could become a useful independent citizen because of the chastening alternatives which faced him. (Document 2D.) The logic was impeccable so long as the basic premise was sound – that men were completely masters of their own fate. The industrial areas were to offer resounding proof that the original premise was not founded upon reality.

The administrative changes recommended by Chadwick were much more his own work. To his orderly Benthamite mind the 15,000 separate parishes administering the Poor Law were anathema. The report is full of anecdotal instances of parish incompetence which supported the case for administrative reform. Local discretion opened the way to corruption, intimidation and inconsistency, so Chadwick preferred a centralised, uniform system. The report recommended a central board to administer the Poor Law with powers to frame regulations and control local practices. Since 'well-regulated workhouses' would no doubt have to be fairly large institutions to cope with the various classifications of paupers, it was reasonable to suggest that parishes should join together to form unions of a viable size (this had, of course, already been progressing under Gilbert's Act). The day of parish sovereignty was over and there would apparently be no new Speenhamland. Poor relief was to become for the first time in its history uniform and centrally directed.

III The new Poor Law

The degree to which the report of the Royal Commission had reflected general opinions on Poor Law reform may be gauged by the speedy passage of the 1834 Poor Law Amendment Act. Though the Commission had taken two years to do its work, its final report was hurried in order to give the Whig Government a model for immediate action. This epoch-making measure passed both Houses of Parliament with comfortable majorities and received the royal assent in August 1834. There was all-party support for a measure which seemed to offer real hope of the much-sought-for reduction in poor rates. There was opposition in the press, notably from The Times, and in Parliament Radicals like Cobbett defended the right of the poor to relief. Most of those who were doubtful about the reform were worried about the centralisation involved and the enormous patronage that would be given by this creation of a bureaucracy to administer the Poor Law.

Though the measure passed quickly, it by no means gave Chadwick all he had wanted. He had always assumed that he personally would be in charge of the operation of the new system and so the report had only spelt out the overall structure, leaving some of the important practical details until later. In fact to his bitter disappointment he was only made secretary to the three-man Poor Law Commission and was made to feel very much the inferior partner in the enterprise. The Commission was independent of Parliament but did not have the power many people assumed.

Above all, the Commission could not compel local Poor Law Unions to build workhouses. The Cabinet had rejected this, for as Althorp, the Home Secretary, remarked, 'The landed interest were looking for immediate relief and relief to be purchased through expenditure would be rejected at once'. Many of the so-called 'collateral aids' which would have taken the edge off the harsh new Poor Law were left to private benevolence, and one scholar has gone so far as to say that the Act was 'a jejune and clumsy caricature of the Report'.[11]

Nevertheless the new Poor Law did initially achieve one of its main objectives; it reduced poor rates. In the ten years following 1834, poor rates nationally fell to between £4.2 million and £5 million per annum, and for the twenty years after that, expenditure fluctuated between £5 million and £6 million. Indeed the new Poor Law had a successful inauguration when it was applied to the southern counties between 1834 and 1836. Chadwick believed that the sharp fall in poor rates here was proof of the efficacy of less eligibility and the workhouse test. However, the good harvests of those years and the demand for labour for railway developments would in any case have reduced the pauper host. Chadwick, rarely a success at personal relationships, clashed frequently with the three Commissioners, and his advice that the boom years of the mid-1830s should be utilised to introduce the new Poor Law in the north was rejected. By the time the Assistant Commissioners moved north to form new unions, the economy had taken a sharp downturn, and the new Poor Law was to be accompanied by a major depression and mass unemployment.

There had been some popular opposition to the new system in the south, but this was nothing compared to the mass protest movement which developed in the industrial areas. The Poor Law Report had been so obsessed with the problem of the rural labourer that it had not fully inquired into the real nature of industrial poverty. A deterrent Poor Law might be justified if men were masters of their own fate, but was an unemployed factory operative truly blameworthy if his locality and industry were in a period of slump? The new Poor Law was geared to people who were work-shy, but the fluctuations of the new industrial economy made paupers of many who were, in later terminology, 'genuinely seeking work'. Residential relief was appropriate for the destitute, but could enough workhouse places be provided for the thousands who might temporarily be unemployed because of market forces? In short, the new Poor Law was constructed to meet the problem of rural destitution; the poverty of the industrial areas was that of temporary unemployment for which the workhouse test was an inappropriate remedy.

To men such as Richard Oastler the new Poor Law was consistent with the other examples of exploitation of the working class which his factory movement had exposed. The economic arm of the middle class, the factory owners, sapped the working class by factory labour, while the political arm, the Whig Party, also justifying itself by the tenets of heartless political economy, finally crushed the spirit of the people with these cruel 'bastiles', as the workhouses became known. Popular resentment spread rapidly among workers who knew that their employment was insecure. Temporary unemployment was a near-inevitable experience of all working-class lives, and the prospect of virtual imprisonment in a workhouse terrified men whose trades were liable to sudden fluctuations. Wild rumours spread about the inhuman practices which went on inside workhouses, which immediately took on the guise of prisons of terror. Already the new Poor Law was working. Relief had become a deterrent and only real destitution would induce a resort to the workhouse. Fear of the workhouse became part of popular folklore.

Spurred on by fear and anger, northern workers flocked to meetings protesting against the new Poor Law and the campaign completely swallowed the factory movement. There was much violent talk and in January 1838 the Methodist minister Stephens told a Newcastle audience:

> Sooner than wife and husband, father and son, should be sundered and dungeoned, and fed on 'skillee', sooner than wife and daughter should wear prison dress . . . Newcastle ought to be and should be one blaze of fire, with only one way to put it out, and that with the blood of all who supported this abominable measure . . . and let every man with a torch in one hand and a dagger in the other, put to death any and all who attempted to sever man and wife.[12]

The incitement to violence was also a feature of Oastler's oratory. According to him the Act was 'damnable . . . infernal anti-Christian, unsocial . . . the catechism of Hell . . . the Devil's own Book! It must be burnt *out* and out *burnt.*' It was during this campaign that Feargus O'Connor first became a popular hero, and at the great outdoor meetings he thrilled audiences with his bombastic Irish blarney.

Passions were so strong that riots did break out in 1837 and 1838 in Oldham, Rochdale, Todmorden, Huddersfield and

Bradford, some of which necessitated the calling-up of troops to restore order. The anti-Poor Law movement was, however, short-lived, partly because it was the midwife of Chartism. Working men were encouraged to seek political power in order to remedy all their grievances, and O'Connor led the anti-Poor Law crowds on to the Chartist road. There was another more important reason, namely the gradual realisation that local unions had a good deal more autonomy than had been anticipated and so could continue with local practice. It is sometimes assumed that opposition to the new Poor Law came solely from those who were prospective paupers, but the Assistant Commissioners knew that popular resentment would eventually die down, while the obstructionism of strong-willed guardians was much more permanent and difficult to handle.

Many magistrates and middle-class political leaders opposed the centralisation of the new system and resented the slur on their own administration implicit in the condemnation of the old Poor Law. Often the 'reforms' of 1834 had already been implemented by the collaboration of townships under Gilbert's Act and the employment of so-called select vestries and professional officials. As more research is being done on the Poor Law in the first half of the nineteenth century, it is becoming clear that there was a good deal more continuity between pre-1834 and post-1834 than the national story would suggest. While the Poor Law Amendment Act was a departure in the sense that it was legislating for the whole country and apparently removing local discretion, once more we are reminded of the factor mentioned earlier, that the real story of Poor Law practice is but dimly told by the progress of national legislation.

The central Poor Law Commission had very limited powers when faced with a union which failed to co-operate, rather like the struggle in the late 1960s between the Secretary of State for Education and stubborn local authorities such as Birmingham which refused to introduce comprehensive schools. New Poor Law Unions were quickly formed, but often the new guardians and relieving officers were the same men who had operated under the old system. Sometimes the new regimes refused point blank to implement the workhouse test, and in the case of Liverpool special Parliamentary dispensation was given to dissolve the new union and return to the former system of administration under a local Act. Popular opposition gradually subsided when it was realised that outdoor relief could not be dropped. Indeed the Poor Law Commission devised the 'labour test' (i.e. outdoor relief was given provided some work was done) in order to reconcile the continuation of outdoor relief with the principles of 1834. Indeed, throughout the whole of the mid-Victorian period, the overwhelming majority of paupers (something like five out of six) were relieved *outside* the workhouse. Those on indoor relief were always a small minority.

Proportion of paupers on indoor relief

Year	%
1840	14.30
1844	15.70
1849	12.26
1854	12.91
1859	14.00
1864	13.17
1869	15.49

Source: Annual Reports of the Poor Law Commission/Board (1840 and 1844: quarter ending March; 1849–1869: mean of 1 January and 1 July each year)

Perhaps the example of Leeds best illustrates the limits of the Poor Law Commission's authority. There the new system was not introduced until 1844, the main motive being to secure the building of a new workhouse. The old Leeds workhouse was a scandal, and according to the Benthamite Assistant Commissioner Charles Clements was 'altogether discreditable to a civilised country'. Physically it was squalid, and paupers of all kinds, young and old, infirm and able-bodied, male and female, were thrown together, the complete denial of the classification desired by Chadwick in his well-regulated workhouse. Respectable local opinion was aware of the need for a new workhouse, but the local ratepayers assembled in the vestry would not sanction the expenditure. The introduction of the new Poor Law was seen as a way of by-passing the vestry and using the Poor Law Commission's authority to get a new workhouse. In fact the election of guardians became a political battle and control went to Tories who were opposed to the new Poor Law. These new guardians were willing to build an industrial school but would not build a new workhouse. In vain did the Commission try to shame the Leeds guardians into action by urging the provision of a 'tolerably creditable' workhouse, 'where the aged and infirm can be accommodated with decent comfort, the sick properly attended to, the helpless idiot sufficiently protected and the unruly and shiftless able-bodied male pauper kept apart from the vicious and abandoned of the other sex.'[13] The guardians would not budge: there was certainly continuity here, and copulating in the privies which was the great public scandal of the old regime continued under the new. Only when local opinion and the local guardians wished it did the Poor Law Commission have the satisfaction of seeing Leeds build a new workhouse, and that was not for another fifteen years. In Leeds outdoor relief continued unabated and the cost of poor relief *went up* on the introduction of the new Poor Law.

It suited the Poor Law Commission's propaganda objectives to argue that the system was working under central direction and control, but research findings conclude that variety of practice was as characteristic of the New Poor Law as it had been of the old pre-1834 system. Most historians argue that this regional variation was the largely unintended consequence of the local resistance to centralisation. It has been suggested, however, that the very object of the New Poor Law was to strengthen local autonomy, largely through the coincidence of union boundaries with landed estates and the seating of magistrates on boards of guardians *ex officio* (Brundage, 1978). This is putting it far too strongly, for while ministers were concerned about the restoration of social authority, which the Swing Riots revealed to have been undermined, they were also concerned about reducing costs, improving efficiency and standardising administration. Indeed, although Lord John Russell could argue in 1837 that he had never intended to destroy local administration since the aim of 1834 'was to establish local self-government', he went on in the same speech to indicate that 'a kind of local government' had been established which had to operate 'under such general rules and general directions as the intelligence and experience of the Poor Law Commissioners prescribed'.[14]

The implementation of these 'general rules and general directions' was the responsibility of between ten and twenty assistant commissioners. When the Poor Law Commission was replaced in 1847 by the Poor Law Board under closer parliamentary control, these officials became Poor Law inspectors. As with the factory inspectorate, much depended on the personality of the individual inspector. The courteous and urbane Sir John Walsham secured much more local co-operation in the north-east, than did the bucolic Charles Mott in Lancashire and the West Riding, where the presence of the inspector immediately caused hackles to rise. With large districts to supervise, inspectors could visit unions only once or twice a year and so there was scope for much local discretion. A recent major study has confirmed on the basis of geographical analyses considerable regional variations in practice and variability in the imposition of Poor Law Commission rules. Issues such as the formation of union boundaries, the imposition of the labour tests, the building of new workhouses and the provision of specialist facilities gave considerable scope for differential local practice.[15]

We may perhaps understand the operation of the Poor Law bureaucracy if we think in terms of a 'macro' and a 'micro' level of administration. Most research suggests that on the macro scale of major policy issues (less eligibility, outdoor relief, the workhouse and labour tests, the building of workhouses, etc.) the central authority was forced to compromise and to draw up its regulations to accommodate local practice. By 1871, for instance, only one in six unions operated under the strict '1834 terms' of the 1844 Outdoor Relief Prohibitory Order; the rest worked under a much looser rein. A minority view has recently been powerfully argued (Williams, 1981) that the Poor Law Commission was successful in abolishing outdoor relief, a view which runs counter to a massive amount of localised research work. So the weight of opinion indicates a failure at the macro level of policy.

On the other hand, at the micro level of petty regulation the central authority was much more successful. It had important negative powers such as the refusal to approve appointments or to allow certain types of expenditure or to permit particular building schemes. It could insist on a standard form of collecting data, of recording minutes, of processing correspondence, of workhouse dietaries, of qualifications for appointments, of accounting procedures – and a whole host of minutiae down to the thickness of the porridge in the workhouse. Through these detailed regulations at the micro level the central authority imposed its will on the localities, so that in time the Poor Law had the appearance of a unified and uniform social service.

A similar macro–micro distinction may also assist in evaluating the popular distaste for the Poor Law which has already been mentioned. Through such novels as *Oliver Twist* and such Poor Law scandals as the Andover Case (where paupers were reduced to gnawing at rotting bones), an image was created of the workhouse as an instrument of cruelty and of the Poor Law authorities as bent on crushing the poor. On the macro level there is little evidence to support this view. Destitute indoor paupers were undoubtedly better housed, better fed, and better cared for than those 'merely poor' outside the workhouse, and Poor Law officials were usually trying to raise standards rather than depress them. Where scandals occurred they were often the result of unsupervised local abuse, rather than of central policy direction. As one regional study concludes, 'the Poor Law Commission was during the early 1840s the agency of restraint and enlightenment in the context of Durham's poor relief system'.[16] Thus at the macro level the Poor Law was not using cruelty as an instrument of policy.

But at the micro level of day-to-day life in the workhouse there was much psychological cruelty. There was cruelty towards those deterred from applying for much-needed relief and the cruelty of harsh regulations for those inside. Prison-like discipline, stigmatised uniform, the separation of families, routinised behaviour, a rigorous timetable – these were the forms of cruelty which depersonalised paupers within the workhouse regime. The most recent historian of the workhouse (Crowther, 1981) has explained this in terms of life inside a 'total institution'. The inhumanity of the workhouse revolved around the boredom, routine, petty regulation and official arrogance, with scope for personal abuse, which exist in any modern mental home, hospital or boarding school. These are intrinsic features of any large community inevitably under the duress of a small body of officials who have to keep the institution functioning. When scandals emerged (then as they do now) these merely reinforced from the macro level the popular image of heartless insensitivity well-established through the micro level of administration. By imposing on the Poor Law the principles of 1834, Parliament provided officials, both local and national, with the impossible task of marrying deterrence and humane relief within the same system. At different times, by different means and for different applicants the Poor Law could perform one or other of its tasks, but not both simultaneously. The contradictory objectives of the Poor Law were well recognised by the Liverpool philanthropist, William Rathbone, in 1867:

> It [the workhouse] does succeed in deterring those who can support themselves from applying for parish support; it does diminish pauperism, it has effectively checked the rapid progress of demoralisation and ruin under the old Poor-Law of Elizabeth. But as a system of public charity it fails altogether. It is beyond the omnipotence of Parliament to meet the conflicting claims of justice to the community, severity to the idle and vicious and mercy to those stricken down into penury by the visitation of God....There is grinding want among the honest poor; there is starvation, squalor, misery beyond description, children lack food and mothers work their eyes dim and their bodies thin to emaciation in the vain attempt to find the bare necessities of life but the Poor Law authorities have no record of these struggles.[17]

The Poor Law was saddled with the paradoxical aim of alienating its potential clientele and the stigma of pauperism induced a reluctance to seek official relief which became firmly rooted in popular culture. Yet for all its popular distaste and its capacity to divide and alienate the poor from the rest of society, the new Poor Law shared with its predecessor the ultimate confirmation that social obligations co-existed with social entitlement. Though the terms under which relief was granted may have been demeaning to the receiver, the fact that the relief was available exemplified the community responsibility of the giver. As a perceptive recent study explains:

> By applying for aid under the Poor Laws, people asserted their membership in a local community and, usually, present or past participation in a local labour market. They signified belonging, a sense of entitlement. Relief, both in the giving and in the receiving, solidified relationships of inter-dependence. Whatever the public rhetoric of 'pauperism' and the spirit in which relief was dispensed the poor laws transferred income from the propertied to the propertyless.[18]

3 Public health

I The nature of the problem

In many ways, despite periodic visitations of bubonic plague, there was no real public health problem in pre-industrial England. London and the centres of some of the provincial market or cathedral towns contained cramped houses, but the vast majority of the population were spread thinly over the rural areas. It was the Industrial Revolution, accompanied by a massive shift in population from rural to urban areas, which created a public health problem. As with so many other social questions, it was the very *concentration* of people which caused the difficulty. It was only in the so-called 'age of great cities' that society needed that essential combination of preventive medicine, civil engineering and community administrative and legal resources known by the generic term 'public health'.

The population of Great Britain doubled between 1801 and 1851, then doubled again in the next sixty years. Much of this growth was concentrated in the urban areas, some of them mere villages or hamlets before the impact of industrialisation. In 1801, London contained well over 800,000 people and there were only thirteen towns in England and Wales with a population of more than 25,000. By 1841, London had added a further million to its total and there were forty towns with more than 25,000, two of them with over a quarter of a million. It was not simply the *fact* of great cities but the *rate* of their growth which generated such serious social problems. The Table traces the growth of the largest cities outside London, and the figures give a clue to the dislocation and transformation which must have occurred. Clearly, decennial increases of over 40 per cent were not uncommon, with Manchester and Leeds as high as 47 per cent in the decade from 1821. Glasgow, deemed by many to be the worst city in the kingdom, doubled in twenty years and virtually quadrupled in forty. The pace of this phenomenal growth was such as to pose insuperable problems for urban communities, ill-equipped to face this challenge. Nor was this restricted to these first-rank cities, for some smaller towns grew at an even faster rate, so that Bradford's population, for instance, multiplied eightfold in the first half of the nineteenth century while that of Middlesbrough grew from only 154 in 1831 to 40,000 forty years later.

Population growth in British cities, 1801–61 (in thousands)

	1801	1811	1821	1831	1841	1851	1861
Birmingham	71	83	102	144	183	233	296
Glasgow	77	101	147	202	275	345	420
Leeds	53	63	84	123	152	172	207
Liverpool	82	104	138	202	286	376	444
Manchester	75	89	126	182	235	303	339
Salford	14	19	26	41	53	64	102
Sheffield	46	53	65	92	111	135	185

Such rapid growth posed enormous housing problems for urban communities, which first filled unused spaces such as cellars and attics and then embarked on providing private-enterprise cheap housing for the new industrial workers. In the absence of personal transport, houses and factories had to be in close proximity, and so began that process of residential zoning which characterised industrial cities, with workers living in the smoke and middle classes beyond it. The style of housing varied: sometimes the terraces of small cottages which had been a feature of industrial villages; sometimes the classic creation of the Industrial Revolution, the back-to-backs which dominated northern cities such as Leeds; sometimes the enclosed courtyard which was typical of Birmingham; and sometimes the great tenements which housed Glasgow's teeming population. Much is invariably made of this being 'jerry-built' housing, yet we really know too little about building standards before this period to make any safe judgements. We see every day, as our big cities now demolish the nineteenth-century slums, that these houses were in fact substantially built. Migrants from the countryside who came to an industrial city lived, perhaps for the first time, in a brick- or stone-built house with a tile or slate roof, and there is some evidence to suggest that during the Industrial Revolution rising rents were accompanied by slightly larger working-class houses.

The key problem was not in fact that of physical construction (though it is true that access to light and air was very limited in these styles of housing) but that of *amenity*. It was the lack of services to the house rather than the house itself which caused public health hazards. This was as true of the new houses on virgin building land in open spaces as it was of the cramped slums of the courts, yards, alleys and gardens which were infilled between streets. Essentially this residential development lacked the triple services of drainage, sewerage and water supply. Those very streets which were in most need of paving and cleansing were invariably least attended to and so refuse accumulated next to houses, accompanied by soil-heaps and cesspools which were the normal sanitary arrangements of the day. As one observer remarked, men would follow the call of nature where they could, so that 'soil and refuse water stand in every hole where a lodgement can be made there to remain until absorbed by wind or sun – a perpetual nuisance to the eye and a perpetual fever to the whole body'.[1]

Water was the priceless commodity which was in short supply, needed for drainage and sewerage and of course for drinking. Some cities like Birmingham had relatively good natural supplies, but in most cities the supply of wells and natural springs was augmented by the local river which was invariably an open sewer. One civil engineer described the Aire, which supplied many Leeds citizens with their drinking-water, as follows:

> It is charged with the contents of about 200 water closets and similar places, a great number of common drains, the drainings from dung-hills, the Infirmary (dead leeches, poultices for patients, etc.), slaughter houses, chemical soap, gas, dung, dyehouses and manufactories, spent blue and black dye, pig manure, old urine wash, with all sorts of decomposed animal and vegetable substances from an extent of drainage…amounting to about 30,000,000 gallons per annum of the mass of filth with which the river is loaded.[2]

Such minimal services as did exist in the form of private joint-stock waterworks companies were hopelessly inadequate to meet the needs of expanding cities.

Contemporary society tackles these problems now by environmental control and the provision of public services. Quite simply, there were no administrative organisations to take over these functions effectively to control building, to provide sewers, to pipe water to people's homes. Some of the older towns had corporations, but these were in no sense the equivalent of present-day local authorities. They were self-elected; many were corrupt and they lacked powers to exercise real local control. Often the newer cities, such as Manchester or Birmingham, did not have a corporation at all still being governed under parochial arrangements dating from their village days. In any case, in both sorts of towns such public health provisions as existed tended to centre on bodies deriving their powers from local Improvement Acts. These were invariably called Improvement Commissioners and it was they rather than other organs of local government which initiated the lighting, watching and cleansing of streets. Given the fact that those who paid the most improvement rates expected the best service, it is not surprising to find that it was the better-class streets and thoroughfares which were paved, lit, drained and scavenged at public expense rather than the insanitary areas with the greater needs.

As far as the central Government was concerned, only the sudden and tragic visitation of an epidemic could mobilise state action. There was a short-lived Board of Health established under the Privy Council in 1805–6 under the threat of yellow fever ('Gibraltar sickness'), which had assumed epidemic proportions in the Iberian peninsula at that time. Far more serious was the first visitation of the dreaded cholera in 1831–2, which returned again in 1848–9, 1854 and 1866–7. Cholera, being a water-borne disease, attacked all, notably the middle classes with their better water supplies, and struck fear into the hearts of the governors, local and national. This did produce some effective state concern for public health in the form of the Central Board of Health established by royal proclamation in June 1831 and eventually in no fewer than 1,200 local boards created by Orders in Council. There was even the so-called Cholera Act of 1832, which legalised the procedures and empowered local boards to finance their anti-cholera provisions out of poor rates.

However, since doctors could not agree on the causes of cholera or on the best treatment to be employed, it is doubtful if preventive measures such as lime washing achieved very much. Since the first epidemic coincided with the Reform Bill crisis, it added to the tension of those years and there were many anti-medical riots as ordinary people became fearful about the dissection of corpses infected with the disease. It is sometimes assumed that public health provision was simply a response to cholera epidemics. However, it is probably the case that many doctors working in the public health field on 'fevers' found cholera a distraction as much as a catalyst. The crucial feature of cholera was that it was an epidemic rather than an endemic disease, thus newsworthy and fearful, but overall not a great contributor to death rates. Hence while the appalling toll of the first cholera epidemic was some 22,000 deaths, generalised domestic fevers were killing over 50,000 annually in England and Wales.

Cholera, by virtue of its novelty and middle-class impact, created far more stir than the (statistically) much more deadly and common diseases which were the bane of the poor. Accepted by virtue of familiarity, these diseases swelled the death rate in early nineteenth-century cities. Notable amongst them were typhus and tuberculosis. Typhus, usually denoted simply as fever, was both widely endemic and more frequently epidemic in the nineteenth century. It was closely associated with cramped insanitary housing conditions and was the example *par excellence* of an environmentally caused disease. Hence it was almost exclusively a 'poor man's disease'; hence too, though doctors became increasingly aware of its nature, little was done in public terms to attempt to control it. This was even truer of tuberculosis or pulmonary consumption, which was so common as to be deemed a natural hazard of life about which nothing could be done. This disease clearly accounted for more deaths (perhaps one-third of all deaths) than any other in the first half of the nineteenth century. It persisted by virtue of a favourable environment, smoky atmosphere, squalid houses and deprived bodies. Only in the second half of the century did this disease begin to decrease in virulence, and then possibly because of the natural rise and fall of all epidemics. Scarlet fever, diarrhoea and measles were also common killer diseases; indeed only smallpox had been partially controlled by Jenner's discovery of a vaccine.

The pace of urban growth had, perhaps inevitably, been accompanied by insanitary housing conditions which had in turn increased the national death rate, which had been falling during the eighteenth century. Since actual death rates can only be verified after the beginnings of civil registration in 1837–8, we must be satisfied with the general consensus of an estimated rise during the first three decades of the century. Before 1831 the national death rate was probably something below 19 per 1,000, by 1838 it was 22.4 and by 1849, thanks to cholera again, it was over 25 per 1,000. There had been a fall in the mid-1840s, but these national figures always hid the basic discrepancy between urban and rural areas. The first Registrar-General estimated that in the 1830s the rate for rural areas was 18.2 per 1,000 while that for towns was 26.2. In the worst cities the rates could be over 30 per 1,000, and Glasgow in its cholera year of 1832 reached the stupendous 49 per 1,000. The Industrial Revolution had defined the problem: urban areas had higher death rates than elsewhere. Could state and society realise the significance of this and do something about it?

II Propaganda in the age of Chadwick

By the time that urban conditions were significantly increasing death rates, what was needed was some unequivocal and irrefutable demonstration of the connection between dirt and disease, environment and expectation of life. In fact, light had been shed on this problem over the previous half-century as doctors above all became increasingly aware of the health implications of urban life. Indeed, it may well be true that the medical profession did more to improve the nation's health by identifying the public health problem and generating interest in it than by any improved techniques in the treatment of patients. Doctors by their very profession were forcibly made aware of the mass killer diseases mentioned earlier, where other middle-class men noticed only the occasional cholera epidemic.

From the 1770s onwards doctors began to notice the impact of environment, and studies in London (1774), Manchester (1795) and Dublin (1806) identified medical problems in their social context. Perhaps more important were the more precise statistical surveys pioneered by John Haygarth of Chester, who in 1774 produced a survey of the town's population and the incidence of disease. Less than a decade later similar work was carried out by John Heysham at Carlisle, who stated categorically that disease 'is the offspring of filth, nastiness and confined air in rooms crowded with many inhabitants'.[3] A Leeds doctor, Charles Turner Thackrah, tackled the problem from another angle by examining in 1831 the impact of trade or occupation on illness and expectation of life. By the 1830s there was a steady flow of local surveys which unmistakably identified the health hazards of the environment. These included Robert Baker's survey and map of the impact of cholera in Leeds, Richard Millar's analysis of the spread of typhus, mainly in Glasgow, and above all James Kay's deservedly famous survey of Manchester, *The Moral and Physical Condition of the Working Classes* (1832).

Despite this growing accumulation of local evidence, a public health movement as such did not yet exist. There was merely a collection mainly of doctors working independently on their own local problems. The impact of these surveys was as yet diffuse, and someone or something was needed to concentrate the evidence so as to shatter public complacency and indifference. It was fortunate that just when, in the 1830s, the volume of literature was sufficient to make out a public health case, the great propagandist and administrator Edwin Chadwick should have been exposed to the evidence. The creation of the Poor Law Commission in 1834 (described in the previous chapter), together with the ancillary office of Registrar-General in 1837–8, combined to create an administrative momentum whose 'spin-off' effects vitally affected the public health question. From these two was generated the national statistical evidence which stimulated the interest and attention of reformers and eventually produced some legislative progress.

Chadwick had assumed in the Poor Law Report that his main problem was the able-bodied poor, and that reductions in the cost of poor relief would accompany the introduction of the principle of less eligibility. The first few years as secretary to the Poor Law Commission indicated to him that a large proportion of poor relief was concerned with widows and orphans, i.e. the dependants of breadwinners struck down by disease. Less eligibility had little relevence here, and Chadwick came to realise (as the

Commissioners did not) that disease was inextricably entangled with the Poor Law. He wrote in 1838:

> In general all epidemics and all infectious diseases are attended with charges, immediate and ultimate, on the Poor Rates. Labourers are suddenly thrown by infectious disease into a state of destitution, for which immediate relief must be given. In the case of death the widow and the children are thrown as paupers on the parish. The amount of burthens thus produced is frequently so great as to render it good economy on the part of the administrators of the Poor Laws to incur the *charges for preventing the evils where they are ascribable to physical causes* . . . [4] (My italics.)

In other words expenditure on poor relief could be reduced by taking preventive action with regard to environment, for, as he explained later in 1847, these causes of poverty 'upon due investigation are found to be preventible and generally with large pecuniary economy'.[5]

Out of this awareness of the economic cost of disease grew, in a very different image, Chadwick's famous sanitary report. Its immediate background lay in 1838 with the disallowing by Government auditors of sums expended by guardians in the East End of London on the removal of nuisances. The Whig Home Secretary, Lord John Russell, asked the opinion of the Poor Law Commission, which in turn inaugurated a sort of pilot study on the connection between environment and disease in the worst areas of London. Three doctors were employed for this survey, James Kay, James Arnott and Southwood Smith, and their work made possible the wider sanitary inquiry which Chadwick was to conduct. Their reports were not original in content but were the first to receive official sanction in that they appeared as appendices to the annual report of the Poor Law Commission. These 'fever reports' of 1838 gave Chadwick the ammunition he needed to substantiate the potential case for a full-scale Poor Law inquiry. In 1839 his chance came when the House of Lords ordered an inquiry into the sanitary condition of the labouring class. The Poor Law Commissioners, glad to be rid of their difficult and touchy secretary, in effect gave Chadwick leave of absence to undertake the survey, which was finally to appear in 1842.

As one of Chadwick's biographers put it, he believed that 'everybody had his story, his facts, his fragment of experience with lessons to instruct the acute and sympathetic investigator',[6] and in preparing this report Chadwick tried to collect as wide a range of voices as possible. The machinery of the Poor Law itself provided the bulk of his evidence via the questionnaires he sent to Poor Law Assistant Commissioners. Boards of Guardians and their relieving officers also contributed evidence, as did the Poor Law medical officers whose testimony was a central component of the whole report. The Registrar-General's returns were another mine of information which Chadwick quarried, and in Scotland, where there was no civil registry, personal contacts were utilised at Edinburgh University and elsewhere. Prison officers, model employers and a host of urban and rural doctors also added fuel for Chadwick's fires. The enormous range of contacts was finally supplemented by Chadwick's own personal visits to the main places mentioned in the report. Along the way Chadwick experienced considerable checks to his progress, notably by the Health of Towns Commission of 1840 whose report stimulated Lord Normanby (Home Secretary, 1839–41) to introduce a bill in 1841 and to forbid Chadwick completing his work. The 1841 election intervened and Chadwick received the green light from the new Tory Home Secretary, Sir James Graham, and so the report was finally published in July 1842.

Probably the greatest virtue of Chadwick's *Report on the Sanitary Condition of the Labouring Population of Great Britain* was its handling of statistical evidence which conclusively established the incontrovertible link between environment and disease. (Document 3A.) To find that the death rate in Cheetham was 1 in 45 while that in near-by Manchester was 1 in 26, or that the rate in the Leeds suburb of Chapeltown was 1 in 57 while that in the central area, Kirkgate, was twice as high at 1 in 28, was to indicate the environmental origin of disease. To demonstrate the sociological and geographical variations in life expectancy was to establish a close correlation between insanitary housing, deficient sewerage and water supply with the incidence of disease, high death rate and low expectation of life. This was the main and crucial element in the case the report was trying to establish. The economic cost of disease with which Chadwick began was by 1842 a relatively minor factor, though easily demonstrated by reference to the numbers of widows and orphans. Chadwick was much more interested in demonstrating the social evils *consequent* upon insanitary living conditions, and he turned current social theory on its head by arguing that the low moral standards (intemperance, prostitution, delinquency, etc.) were the result of the domestic physical environment, not the other way round.

Chadwick was convinced that the environmental controls necessary to *prevent* disease would require more powerful administrative organs than existed even within the reformed corporations. He wanted, in fact, a centralised and uniform administrative structure similar to that which he had suggested for the Poor Law, yet his final conclusions in the report were vague and rather unsatisfactory on this point. Far more definite was his solution to the civil engineering problem of sewage disposal. He strongly advocated the water-borne disposal of sewage via glazed round pipes, which is of course the modern method. (Document 3B.) Inevitably this would place even greater demands upon water supply, which became even more essential. Hence the search for more efficient modes of supplying urban areas with water both for consumption and drainage was a logical consequence of the evidence accumulated in the report. Indeed Chadwick assumed that the presentation of the case required few definite conclusions, since these would gradually evolve from the debate initiated by the report, and his only other major suggestion was the appointment of district medical officers.

Perhaps the greatest of the nineteenth-century Blue Books, the Chadwick Report, had an unprecedented sale for an official publication, possibly as high as 100,000. The Poor Law Commissioners had refused in the event to sign the report, which was thus circulated under Chadwick's sole name. Public complacency was certainly shattered and the early Victorian conscience was aroused, yet Chadwick knew that his report was only the beginning of what would be a long and arduous propaganda campaign. In 1843 he wrote a report on interment, arguing for the physical separation of burial grounds from urban areas, and in 1844–5 he unofficially directed the affairs of the Health of Towns Commission which the Peel Government set up, in effect to validate the evidence and conclusion of Chadwick's *personal* report.[7] More than this, the Commission delved more deeply into the technical and administrative details of possible legislation and so took the campaign on a stage further. It remained for the Health of Towns Association, begun in 1844 and organised mainly by Southwood Smith, to pursue the propaganda campaign for the implementation of legislation which was not to come until 1848.

While it is true that the main aim of Chadwick's report was to expose the public health problem rather than suggest any definite and extensive solutions, the contrast between 1834 and 1842 remains stark. Within six months of the Poor Law Report there was legislation mirrored in Chadwick's image; even six years did not produce the sort of public health legislation Chadwick wanted. Chadwick was apparently putting into words the common assumption of a widely influential social spectrum in 1834, whereas he was radical and original in 1842. The Chadwick of 1842 was clearly not the man of 1834. The reasons for the differing response and the delay in legislation were largely to do with the variegated issues raised by the public health question. Broadly these may be synthesised into four types of factor: technical, financial, ideological and political.

The *technical* questions involved those professions most centrally concerned in public health, namely medicine and civil engineering. Much has invariably been made of the lack of medical knowledge as a delaying factor, since Chadwick and most doctors of his day believed in the so-called miasmic theory, that is, that smells transmitted diseases. Yet although the bacteriological cause of disease was not established until the last quarter of the nineteenth century, the medical theories were not crucial since the right action could be taken for the wrong medical reasons. People did not have to know why the cesspool and the soil-heap caused disease; they had only to demonstrate the connection to produce the right conclusion, namely nuisance removal. Far more important were the civil engineering problems involved, first in water supply and second, as the water-closet came to be more widely used, in the disposal of liquid sewage. Laymen, who were often the prime movers in local attempts to solve these problems, were not competent to judge the merits of Chadwick's glazed pipe, or the difference between a one-foot and a two-foot fall, or the location of the siting of a reservoir, or the likely flow from a particular source, or the economic value of the sale of urban sewage. Yet often technical disagreements on questions such as these dogged well-meaning schemes and led to interminable disagreements such as that at Liverpool between the Pikists and anti-Pikists, so called because some wished to take water from Rivington Pike and some did not. The sheer physical size of the job of supplying large cities with water and disposing of sewage posed major engineering problems that could not be overcome easily or quickly.

Because of the size of the problem the costs were inevitably going to be great and there were serious *financial* aspects involved. Resources for social utilities are always scarce and sewerage was not a popular subject. Thus at Leicester a local Radical preferred to build 'magnificent Brummagean Town Halls': 'He did not care to meddle with the dirty work of Town Drainage. There was no glory to be gained in washing sewers with cold water, laurels were only to be won by the builders of Town Halls.'[8]

Even when there was local pressure for 'improvement', the enormous costs provoked doubts and produced periodic bouts of 'economist' activity where controlling or reducing expenditure was the main aim. As a Leeds councillor remarked, 'The people were more solicitous about draining rates from their pockets than draining the streets',[9] and calls for economy which often cut right across party lines could paralyse local municipal activity on the public health issue, as was the case in Leicester and Leeds in the mid-1840s and Birmingham in the mid-1850s. Demands for economy were the nervous psychological reactions of a public mind concerned for health in the midst of an epidemic but with a short collective memory when it had disappeared. Apart from doubts about soaring overall costs, there was the vexed question of who should pay. Wealthy people made their own private provision for water supply and sewerage and, as Chadwick complained, 'I am crying out Pestilence and for the relief of the masses but can get no one to hear of means which will affect the pockets of small owners...who set up the cry of self-government against any regulations which may lead to immediate expenditure for putting in better condition the houses for which they exact exorbitant rents'.[10]

The financial question inevitably thus involved basic *ideological* questions. Social utilities are now publicly financed, in effect by redistribution of wealth via taxation, but early Victorian England was sensitive to the inequity of this. If a town wished to finance its water supply and sewerage out of the rates, it raised the question 'Shall the town obtain money by a tax upon a few and appropriate it for the benefit of the many – and that tax interminable, without those few who find the money having any direct control over its expenditure or any possible means of having it repaid?'[11] Property owners, having expended money for their own sanitary needs, were to pay twice by being taxed to provide for the sanitary needs of their neighbours. An unknown hand inscribed the case of the propertied against the embryonic collectivism of a municipal water supply:

All they want is to expend other people's money and get popularity by letting what *they may call poor* have the water for nothing and also accommodating themselves and tenants at other people's expense . . . I have 10,000 pounds worth of property and have been at considerable expense in getting water. My neighbour has the same {but no water} and his property will be considerably benefited by having water brought to it and mine can't possibly be benefited at all – is [it] just that I should be made to contribute a yearly sum towards furnishing his estate with water and increasing the value of his property 15 or 20% [which] taxes me 1 1/4[?].[12]

The whole question of property rights and how far they could be invaded in the public interest was relevant here. Building regulations enforcing sewerage, for instance, involved infringements on individual liberty which many would not accept on ideological grounds. Men could be touched on the raw when interfering busybodies like Chadwick sought to establish regulations for social control, and so a mild by-law on the regular whitewashing of slaughterhouses produced the following sharp rebuke to the local council involved:

The legislature has not yet given them the authority to dictate to tradesmen in what way they shall carry out their business, as how often they shall whitewash their buildings and if they are once permitted to usurp such an authority . . . such is the spirit of busy officious intermeddling . . . that no man's place of business or even private house would be safe.[13]

Individual liberty was reinforced by self-interest, for those who were loudest in defence of property rights were often the owners of the property which needed sanitary improvement. Deference to an individualist ideology was sometimes therefore a rationalisation of economic self-interest and an excuse for inaction. One can sympathise with the working-class housing reformer James Hole and, a quarter of a century after Chadwick s report, his cynicism with democratic local self-government:

When contemplating an ugly ill-built town where every little free holder asserts his indefeasible rights as a Briton to do what he likes with his own; to inflict his own selfishness, ignorance and obstinacy upon his neighbours and on posterity for generations to come and where local self-government means merely misgovernment we are apt to wish for a little wholesome despotism to curb such vagaries.[14]

Forceful environmental control, which Hole wanted, meant enlarging the functions and authority of local government and dispensing with the erratic provisions of private enterprise via joint-stock companies. The choice between a joint-stock company deriving its income from those who used its services and a public authority financed by all through the rates and backed by legal statute was at heart an ideological matter but inevitably decided on largely *political* grounds.

Enormous powers were given to authorities as they enlarged their functions, and men were often suspicious of this extension of municipal patronage because of the individuals who could exercise this power. The local political situation often determined attitudes, so that at Leeds in the late 1830s, for instance, many Tories who had previously favoured a public scheme for water supply went over to a joint-stock company when it was realised that the Liberals were monopolising municipal affairs, and their spokesman commented: 'The Town Council and the Town Commissioners clutch the whole thing. They are in search of power – power, patronage – patronage.'[15] This reference to two bodies indicates that a political battle was being fought between rival administrative organisations within a local community. Water Commissioners, Commissioners of Sewers, Highway Surveyors, Poor Law Guardians, Select Vestries, Street Commissioners and Improvement Commissioners who were in various places and to a varying extent involved in public health matters would be dispensed with if powers were concentrated in one administrative health body. Politics is about the pursuit and exercise of power, and political considerations made many of these vested administrative interests (along with commercial vested interests like joint-stock water companies) resistant to change. It took Birmingham fourteen years to amalgamate the powers of the various Commissioners into the council, and in London there were some 300 bodies administering local Acts. As Chadwick found, there was always some administrative or commercial unit whose political power was sacrosanct, and he wrote to Ashley in 1844:

... frequently interested parties are seated at Boards of Guardians who are ready to stop anything which may lead to expenditure for the proper repair of the dwellings of the labouring classes.

Where measures of drainage are proposed and the works carried out by Commissioners of Sewers are found to be defective a cry is raised nothing must be done for fear of offending the Commissioners.

... When additional supplies of water are called for... one cry raised is 'Oh the interest of the companies is too powerful to be touched'.[16]

These political squabbles over who should exercise power within the local community were overshadowed by the wider debate about centralisation. Bodies might lock themselves in internecine battles locally, but they soon united against proposals to remove local control entirely and vest powers in a central administrative organisation. To Chadwick, local control meant either demarcation disputes between competing inefficient commissions or the deference to interested parties among electors and elected which produced inaction. Many urban communities feared the situation in which impersonal, impartial and powerful administrators (faceless bureaucrats, we would call them) could enforce action from London and incur expenditure over which there was no local control. They were correct in their interpretation, for Chadwick would have liked to take the public health question out of politics as the Poor Law had been taken out of politics by a centrally directed uniform administration. But the Poor Law Commission was not a precedent people wished to follow, for an irresponsible body (i.e. constitutionally responsible to nobody) was liable to get out of hand. In any case local communities knew their own problems best, and hence in the 1840s the largest cities obtained local Acts to cope with their own circumstances. It must be admitted, however, that the first of these, the Leeds Improvement Act of 1842, had originated partly in a desire to avoid the provisions of general Acts being discussed in 1841. In 1844 Manchester's Police Regulation Act was passed which enlarged the powers of the Corporation concerned with public health matters and involved much more than its title suggested. Leeds needed a further Act in 1848 to build its sewerage scheme, and no fewer than ten further Acts were obtained by Manchester by 1858. However, pride of place must go to the Liverpool Sanitary Act of 1846 which made the Corporation in effect a health authority and empowered it to appoint an engineer, an Inspector of Nuisances and above all a Medical Officer of Health (MOH). (Document 3C.) W. H. Duncan was the country's first ever MOH, and his work in tackling one of Britain's unhealthiest cities is justly famous. Before any national legislation had passed, these three cities had made important strides towards solving their water-supply problems. In 1837 Leeds had obtained a Waterworks Act which put the town's water supply half under public control (it was fully municipal by 1852), and ten years later Liverpool obtained an Act for the purchase of the town's private companies while Manchester obtained the Act for its great Longdendale scheme costing well over half a million pounds. These cities managed to keep the power where they wanted it, firmly in local hands.

These four areas of contention (technical, financial, ideological and political) were inextricably bound up with sanitary reform and help to explain delays in legislation and its eventual partial character. The last-mentioned fears about centralisation came strongly to the fore in 1847–8 when Lord Morpeth, a Minister in Russell's Whig Government, turned his attention to possible legislation. A public health bill in 1847 was lost owing to the opposition it aroused, but in that year, following another report on London's sewerage problems, there was established a Metropolitan Commission of Sewers, the embryo from which, in the course of time, the London County Council grew. Morpeth introduced his bill again in 1848 and was showered with petitions from local authorities against centralisation. The theme was always the same – we want sanitary reform but if the price to be paid is the loss of local self-government this would be too great a sacrifice. Though the weight of the opposition was mainly provincial, its arch-propagandist was Joshua Toulmin Smith, who wrote in the *Morning Chronicle* and who attacked centralisation in a famous work *Centralisation or Representation*. His antiquarian researches into the history of local government had imbued him with a righteous indignation against encroachments by the central administration. Chadwick and his supporters always had the evidence to fall back on. As a Nottingham propagandist had put it earlier, every doubter ought to make '100 inspections of privies, 50 examinations of drains, 20 enquiries with respect to backyards, 40 ditto with respect to light and prospect, 30 ditto with respect to air and ventilation . . . this dose to be taken every morning'.[17] The best case for centralisation lay in the urban conditions themselves.

The debate was not, however, about whether public action should be taken, but by whom. In the event Morpeth's Public Health Act, a great landmark in social reform, which was passed in 1848, was emasculated and generally ineffective in the short term. The main reason for this was its basic character as a permissive rather than an obligatory Act. Except where the death rate was higher than 23 per 1,000, the Act empowered, but did not compel, local Health Boards to pursue sanitary reforms. The General Board of Health set up in London under the Act with Chadwick as its salaried Commissioner was in essence an advisory, supervisory and co-ordinating body rather than an authoritative and powerful initiator of action. The cholera epidemic which greeted the establishment of the Board was a mixed blessing: its impact reinforced the need for legislative action and extended the scope of the Board, but its immediacy found the newly created Board unprepared for so demanding a task. A local Board of Health could be established if one-tenth of the ratepayers petitioned for it, but most of the larger cities preferred to operate under their own local Acts so they were not exposed to central inspection. The local commissions could still block progress, and at Birmingham one critic complained that 'the disinterestedness of the Commissioners is strong enough to divert the whole current of legislation into their own particular little sewer'.[18] Progress was slow in an area of administrative activity where the physical tasks of water supply and drainage precluded spectacular successes. By 1854 only 182 boards had been established under the Act, and of those only thirteen had established waterworks and sewerage schemes. In that year Chadwick was dismissed, as opposition to him personally and to centralisation generally grew, and though the Board continued until 1858 its effective demise may be dated from the departure of Chadwick.

Having conceived the 'sanitary idea' and laboured so hard for the cause of sanitary reform, Chadwick's achievements in legislative and practical terms seem minimal. This was, as we have seen, partly due to the immensity of the task, the weight of opposition and the combination of general factors raised by the sanitary issue. At the same time his own personality was a limiting factor, and a certain egoism, arrogance and impatience marred his effectiveness. The image was always of a one-man band, for all had to show

> unquestioning, blind, passive obedience to the ukase, decree, bull or proclamation of the autocrat, pope, grand lame of sanitary reform, Edwin Chadwick, lawyer and commissioner. . . . He was determined that the British world should be clean and live a century but on one condition only – that they consented to purchase real patent Chadwickian soap, the Chadwickian officially-gathered soft water and the true impermeable telescopic earthenware pipe and when they did die, were interred by his official undertakers in the Chadwickian necropolis.[19]

This mocking caricature must be set against other more sympathetic assessments of Chadwick's role. A letter to *The Times* in 1847 ascribed public health reform largely to Chadwick's zeal:

> There is one public man living and in full force known for . . . a power of acquiring and condensing and popularising the result of statistical inquiry . . . where can any moral filth be discovered, and my worthy friend Edwin Chadwick is not found stirring it, turning it over, analysing its pernicious power, proving the source whence it has arisen? – he is, indeed the great moral scavenger of the age.[20]

Part of the armoury of data which Chadwick was able to deploy derived from the work of office of the Registrar General, set up, with Chadwick's support, in 1837. The relentless and regular analysis of death rates in different districts provided the hard evidence to sustain intervention at the local level. Although the gradual improvement in health during the nineteenth century is usually ascribed to rising living standards, recent work suggests that sanitary reform was indeed a major contributory cause of health improvement.[21] This was the legacy which Chadwick bequeathed to Victorian England.

III Administrative growth in the age of Simon

It is sometimes assumed that the mid-Victorian period following the withdrawal of Chadwick was an anticlimax compared to the spectacular initial breakthrough made by him. In fact it was a period of achievement, the evidence for which lay below the surface of national political history. First, we must realise that regionally progress went on, especially in periods of general prosperity. Public health developments at the local level were not adequately represented by the pattern of national legislation. Municipal feeling was such that centralisation of the Chadwick variety was not possible, and more and more local improvement, waterworks and sewerage Acts were passed for the benefit of specific areas. Chadwick had resisted this trend, but John Simon, under whose aegis public health affairs developed in the mid-Victorian years, worked with it. Simon, a London doctor with a Huguenot background who pronounced his name Simone, had been appointed London's first Medical Officer of Health in 1848 and became Medical Officer to the General Board of Health in 1855. In 1858 the General Board of Health was wound up and its functions divided between the Local Government Act Office and, more important, the new Medical Department of the Privy Council, which appointed Simon as its first Medical Officer. This was the seed which sixty years later flowered into the Ministry of Health.

Simon sought to persuade where Chadwick bullied; Simon was willing to swim with the current where Chadwick opposed it and so was destroyed. With his inspectors, annual reports and personal industry, Simon was able to achieve slow administrative progress within the framework of permissive rather than obligatory legislation. It was important to endow local authorities with the powers to act if they chose to do so, though as always fears of central control made many areas prefer to operate under their own local Acts. There was much more on the statute book than contemporaries or historians realised, and the picture of no legislative progress between 1848 and 1875 is an erroneous one.

However, since so much of this legislation was little known at the time, its effect was clearly erratic and part of the problem was the confusion consequent upon overlapping legislation and jurisdiction. There were multifarious local bodies acting in the field of public health – Poor Law Guardians, town councils, local Boards of Health, Water and Sewer Commissioners, Highway Surveyors, Improvement Commissioners, Select Vestries and others – which produced a maze of administrative duplication and inefficiency. Equally, these bodies acted under a wide range of statutes which were also overlapping and confusing. There were four main areas of legislation in the public health field.[22] There were first of all straight Public Health Acts like that of

1848, or the Local Government Act of 1858 which gave local boards the powers to take preventive action and appoint officials. Secondly, there was the field of nuisance removal and a whole series of Acts of 1848, 1855, 1860 and 1863 which attempted to establish a national framework of nuisance authorities for the removal of nuisances. As time went on, so the definition of nuisances was enlarged and hence the functions and powers of nuisance authorities also. Thirdly, as the problem of water supply and sewage disposal spread into the countryside, a new group of 'sewer authorities' was created by the Sewage Utilisation Act of 1865. This not only spread public health legislation into rural areas but was the first public health Act to apply to the whole of Great Britain and Ireland. Finally, under the stress of epidemics, powers were granted for disease prevention in times of emergency under the Disease Prevention Acts of 1848 and 1855. These four areas of public health law – sanitary, nuisance, sewer and disease prevention – also competed with the whole range of local Acts which individual areas had procured.

Simon could offer little central direction and control, his powers being restricted to sanctioning loans for major improvement schemes. His inspectors could prompt local action, and where there was intransigence he might lash an indolent council in his annual report. Thus Leeds health administration 'in proportion to the importance of the town may perhaps be deemed the worst which has ever come to the knowledge of this department'.[23] Yet Leeds, described by Simon's biographer as 'the notoriously insanitary city', had gained a model Improvement Act in 1842 and had municipal sewerage and water supply by 1852, and here we have an illustration of the problem. Despite local and national legislation a citizen of Leeds could record in 1865:

> There was no power to compel the owners of property to sewer land before building human habitations on it . . . they had no power to prevent back to back houses . . . no power to compel the sewering and paving of the multitudinous new streets nor thoroughfares . . . there was no power to forbid cellar dwellings . . . to prevent the erection of *culs de sac* . . . no power whatever to compel the owners of old property to connect their dwelling houses with the drains.[24]

The lack of powers was the excuse for lack of action, yet the compulsory connection of a new house with the main sewer, for instance, had been a provision of the 1848 Public Health Act. Not all local authorities were committed to dilatory backsliding, and Tom Taylor at the Local Government Act Office found much pressure for progress coming from the local level. However, Parliamentary regulations could be frustrated by the whims of local pressures and so more compulsion was required.

After a decade in charge of national public health affairs Simon had come to the same conclusion: permissive powers must be replaced by obligatory powers. He wrote in his annual report of 1865:

> ... I venture to submit that the time has now arrived when it ought not any longer to be discretional in a place whether that place shall be kept filthy or not. Powers sufficient for the local protection of public health having been universally conferred, it next, I submit, ought to be an obligation on the local authorities that these powers be exercised in good faith and with reasonable vigour and intelligence. The language of the law besides making it a power should also name it a *duty* to proceed for the removal of nuisances to which attention is drawn.[25]

The immediate consequence of this report was the important Sanitation Act of 1866, which marked a significant turning-point in the history of public health. As *The Times* put it, 'it introduces a new sanitary era'. Essentially this Act did three things. First, it made available on a uniform and universal basis the sanitary powers previously restricted to local Boards of Health under the 1848 Act. Second it enlarged the definition of a nuisance to include a house for the first time and so enlarged the areas of jurisdiction and powers of nuisance-removal authorities. And third, it made it a *duty* for such authorities to perform their functions; in other words the powers were made compulsory. While enlarging the powers of local authorities over their citizens the Act, by *enforcing* action, extended the control of central over local government also.

Simon's initial enthusiasm was short-lived, for it soon became clear that the 1866 Act had been badly drafted and had added to rather than resolved the administrative chaos. However, the working of the Act initiated a debate into the whole question of public health legislation, which inaugurated a campaign for reform. This was led mainly by H. W. Rumsey, a Cheltenham doctor and well-known medical reformer, with Alexander Stewart, a London doctor, and his legal friend Edward Jenkins, who had written a joint paper for the Social Science Association in 1866. The initial demand was for a Royal Commission to inquire into the whole problem and the Royal Sanitary Commission was appointed in 1869, issuing its final report in 1871. Political partisanship inaugurated a debate on the relative merits of the Gladstonian Liberal legislation of 1871–2 and the Disraelian Conservative legislation of 1875. However, we should be nearer the truth if we saw the legislation of 1871–5 as the logical sequence to the Sanitary Commission's report. It was very much in the natural line of administrative departmental legislative development and was in many ways the product of joint Liberal–Conservative thinking.

The 1871 Local Government Board Act established the new Local Government Board in which were consolidated the functions of the Local Government Act Office, the Registrar-General's Office, the Medical Department of the Privy Council and the Poor Law Board. Thus was created a major Ministry which supervised most though not all of the activities of local government. The 1872 Public Health Act was the *local* counterpart of the 1871 legislation. By this Act the whole country was covered by Sanitary Authorities (town councils and local boards in urban areas, guardians in rural areas) whose sanitary duties were obligatory. The most notable provision was perhaps the compulsory appointment of a basic staff, particularly Medical Officers of Health. The example begun by Liverpool in 1847 was now made universal, and all Sanitary Authorities had to have an MOH. It had taken thirty years to implement one of Chadwick's main proposals of 1842.

The Liberals had not taken up one of the major recommendations of the Sanitary Commission, that powers under the dozens of Acts should be consolidated. This was left to the great Public Health Act of 1875, which was formerly seen as a central and original part of Disraeli's 'Tory democracy'. In fact Disraeli played little part in its passing, and it was a consolidation and codification of previous legislation rather than an extension of state activity. Yet to say this does not reduce its significance. It laid down in clear comprehensive terms the public health functions and duties of local authorities and was the essential basis of all public health activity until 1936. Also in 1875 Richard Cross, Disraeli's Home Secretary, introduced his Artisans' and Labourers'

Dwellings Act which enabled local authorities to replace deficient insanitary housing. This was an attempt to involve the state in the supply of housing which had been intermittently discussed over the previous quarter-century. In 1851 under the 'Shaftesbury Acts' local authorities were empowered to register, inspect and even provide common lodging houses. In 1866, an act permitted local councils and housing associations to borrow money at low rates of interest for the provision of working-class housing. In the same year a London MP, W. M. Torrens, tried to extend state involvement by an ambitious bill which would have permitted major slum clearance and municipal housing. His bill was naturally controversial and took two years to pass, and when finally enacted as the 1868 Artisans' and Labourers' Dwellings Act it was much emasculated. The Torrens Act allowed local councils to demand improvements of owners and to purchase and demolish insanitary properties. Where this act envisaged individual properties, the 1875 Cross Act permitted whole areas to be redeveloped, as in the great Corporation Street scheme in Birmingham, inspired by that city's most famou mayor, Joseph Chamberlain. Both acts were permissive and difficult to administer and had to be amended in 1879.

Key issues in the housing question remained the controversy over compensation and the power to build and supply houses at public expense. As ever, much of the pioneering work was under way through the initiative of local councils. As early as 1869 Liverpool had built an experimental block of council cottage houses and Leeds acquired the power to provide municipal housing under a local act in 1877. Some enterprising individuals had already explored the possibility of solving the urban public health problem by creating 'the ideal city' away from existing towns. In the 1850s Sir Titus Salt planned and laid out his famous model community at Saltaire near Bradford and by the 1890s Ebenezer Howard was developing his ideas for new planned 'garden cities'. The era of town planning was at hand. Parliament's response was the 1890 Housing of the Working Classes Act, which made more general, though still permissive, powers available to develop municipal housing.

By that time the so-called 'gas and water municipal socialism' had spread far and wide to transform the local authorities into really effective public health bodies. The pace varied and it was not until 1891, for instance, that Widnes established a municipal water supply, but the common theme was always there: central direction and compulsion with local authorities as the executive arm for national legislation. Gradually the 'civic gospel' spread as people realised the positive function local authorities could perform. As Robert Dale, the Birmingham Nonconformist minister, put it:

> Towards the end of the sixties a few Birmingham men made the discovery that perhaps a strong and able Town Council might do almost as much to improve the conditions of life in the town as Parliament itself...speakers...dwelt with glowing enthusiasm on what a great and prosperous town like Birmingham might do for its people. They spoke of sweeping away streets in which it was not possible to live a healthy and decent life; of making the town cleaner, sweeter, brighter; of providing gardens, parks and a museum; they insisted that great monopolies like the gas and water supply should be in the hands of the corporation; that good water should be supplied without stint at the lowest possible prices.[26]

Local initiative and central administrative growth created the patchwork, *ad hoc*, pragmatic, confusing structure from which a public health system finally emerged in 1875. Chadwick may have had a blueprint ready for implementation in the 1840s, but in the circumstances of the time the painstaking accumulation of powers and functions was the only solution possible.

4 Education and welfare

I Elementary education

That there was a social problem of education in the period following the Industrial Revolution was, as in the field of public health, the result of the distribution of wealth in English society. For those who could afford to pay the fees there was an educational provision leading to the universities, but for the mass of society there was a deficiency of educational opportunity. The rich could buy themselves out of the problems of squalor and ignorance, the poor could not and the state played little role in education. There were, indeed, only three ways of getting a state education: by being a cadet, a felon or a pauper, since the army, prison and workhouse did provide *some* schooling. For the rest there was the occasional attendance at charity or endowed schools supported by subscription, or dame schools, some of which were no more than childminding establishments.

Underlying the whole education debate, however, was the pyramidal structure of English society. The leisure of the few, the governing classes, depended on the labour and service of the many. Perhaps the poor should remain in ignorance lest they rebel against the way the social system worked. Just as the propertied classes opposed universal suffrage for fear that a mass electorate would not long tolerate the unequal distribution of property and wealth, so many feared that too much education might lead to disaffection. As an early eighteenth-century writer put it: 'If a horse knew as much as a man I should not like to be his rider.' The same idea was expressed more forcibly in an often-quoted Parliamentary speech against a bill of 1807 to instruct pauper children:

> The scheme would be found to be prejudicial to the morals and happiness of the labouring classes; it would teach them to despise their lot in life,

> instead of making them good servants in agriculture and other laborious employments to which their rank in society had destined them; instead of teaching them subordination it would render them factious and refractory as was evident in the manufacturing counties; it would enable them to read seditious pamphlets, vicious books and publications against Christianity; it would render them insolent to their superiors.[1]

In the same vein was the comment made later in the century, 'What caused the French Revolution? – books', and Bell, the educationalist, commented on the dangers of 'elevating by an indiscriminate education the minds of those doomed to the drudgery of daily labour above their condition and thereby rendering them discontented and unhappy in their lot'.[2]

Yet in some obvious ways the Industrial Revolution had turned this argument on its head, for the enormous growth in population and its concentration in the worst areas of industrial cities created a social milieu in which revolutionary disaffection was endemic. Some powerful antidote was needed to counteract the ideas of 'agitators' whose propaganda fed on the dismal ignorance of the labouring population. Much middle-class support for educational movements resulted from a desire to make sure that the 'right' attitudes and values were inculcated among the working classes, and such things as Mechanics' Institutes were patronised and directed by middle-class benefactors to this end. Education was thus seen as a means of social control and its role in this context was clearly appreciated by Leonard Horner in 1837:

> Independently of all higher considerations and to put the necessity of properly educating the children of the working classes on its lowest footing, it is loudly called for as a matter of police, to prevent a multitude of immoral and vicious beings, the offspring of ignorance, from growing up around us, to be a pest and nuisance to society; it is necessary, in order to render the great body of the working class governable by reason.[3]

Social deference, knowing one's place, was then a basic virtue to be imparted in any educational provision for the masses, and the Christian religion was a close ally here with its message of humility and acceptance of one's lot in life – the inequity of this world being counterbalanced by the equality of the next. Even more important, the purpose of all education was to teach morality, and morality was based on Christianity: hence some form of religious instruction was central to any basic elementary education. Most of those concerned to promote the education of the working classes were anxious to continue the essentially voluntary character of English education. It should be provided by the charitable benevolence of those whose station enabled them to help the less fortunate.

These three characteristics – social deference, Christian morality and voluntarism – were the key features of the educational provisions made by charitable societies in the early nineteenth century. Since religion was central, the Sunday school movement played a major role in the teaching of reading, often using the Bible as the sole text. Furthermore, since dogma varied within Christianity it followed that religious education would be fragmented denominationally. The basic religious confrontation of nineteenth-century society was between Church and Dissent, and this was reflected within the education movement: the Anglicans had their National Society, founded in 1811, which took over the work of the famous SPCK (Society for Promoting Christian Knowledge), which dates from 1698, while the Nonconformists organised their schools through the British and Foreign School Society, which evolved from the Royal Lancasterian Society of 1808.

The natural religious hostility between these two societies was exacerbated by the fact that they were the patrons of the two great educational innovators of the age, Bell and Lancaster, who were bitter personal rivals. Andrew Bell evolved his techniques while in India and introduced them into a number of parochial schools on his return, while the Quaker Joseph Lancaster had run his own school in Borough Road, London, and had evolved similar methods. Each had arrived at his conclusions independently, but there was a fierce controversy over who had originated the scheme. Essentially this was educational innovation in response to scarce resources: Bell's sandtrays and Lancaster's roof slates, for instance, were used for writing owing to the high cost of paper. The basis of both schemes was the monitorial system, an expedient used to cope with the chronic shortage of teachers. Older and able pupils taught children set exercises in small groups under the overall supervision of a teacher. The voluntary societies by their funds and teaching methods tried to remedy the deficiencies of the two essential educational resources – buildings and teachers.

It was wholly typical of the way social policy developed in the second quarter of the nineteenth century that Parliament's concern for education should originate not from some overall general conviction about the role of state education but as a pragmatic response to these deficiencies. In trying to aid the process of providing more schools and teachers, the state became irreversibly committed to intervention in the educational field. From the beginning of the century some had argued that the state must adopt the role of educator, and in 1807 Samuel Whitbread's bill for pauper education was lost. In 1818, Henry Brougham chaired a Parliamentary Committee of Inquiry into the state of education for the poor, but despite its finding that only 7 per cent of the population were attending day schools, his own bill for parochial schools was defeated in 1820. The Whig Chancellor, Viscount Althorp, provided £20,000 in 1833 to be spent on education and from this small beginning state intervention was bound to grow, since once Parliament had granted money it would eventually want to supervise its expenditure. Since there was no official department to spend this money it was granted to the education societies on the basis of funds they themselves could raise. The state was thus helping to finance voluntarism not in proportion to demonstrable educational need but according to a scale of subscriptions.

The 1833 grant concerned school building and inevitably there was pressure for involvement in teacher training, not least in response to growing working-class demands for education. Many in authority were indifferent or hostile, notable among them Lord Melbourne, the Whig Prime Minister in the later 1830s. He told Queen Victoria in a now famous conversation: 'I do not know why there is all this fuss about Education. None of the Paget family can read or write and they do very well.' Despite this, it was his ministry which alarmed the Anglican establishment by proposing in 1839 to set up a Committee of the Privy Council which would among other things run non-denominational training colleges (normal schools) and appoint Government inspectors. Tory Party tactics at the time were geared to a 'church in danger' assault upon the Whigs, and these proposals seemed to represent a levelling-up of Dissent to equal the position of the Established Church. The whole Tory-Anglican machine was set in motion to oppose any system of state education that was not based on the Church of England, and so this proposal was dropped. However, the Committee of the Council was established in 1839 and provided departmental bureaucratic responsibility for education. In addition it was to have inspectors who were to prove crucial in the campaign to improve standards.

The Anglicans had won in 1839, but they themselves were frustrated in 1843 by an equivalent agitation from the Dissenters against Graham's factory bill, which proposed a general system of factory education under the supervision of the Church. Even Methodists and Roman Catholics joined Dissenters in a massive campaign against the educational clauses of the bill, which Graham was forced to withdraw. Dissenters travelled the short distance from anti-*Church* education to anti-*State* education by emphasising the achievements of voluntarism (exaggerated by the inclusion of all Sunday schools in statistics).

The privileged position of the Anglican Church posed a religious problem which could not be overcome, hence the poetic refrain:

> All must tell the State
> She has no right to educate.

As Graham himself had commented in 1841: 'Religion, the Keystone of education, is in this country the bar to its progress.' The rivalry between Church and Dissent precluded the growth of a state system as each side withdrew into its defensive denominational position. The year 1843, a lost opportunity in the history of English education, illustrated the futility of trying to merge the sects, and in Ashley's words:

> 'Combined Education' must never again be attempted – it is an impossibility, and worthless if possible – the plan is hopeless, the attempt full of hazard. So I will never vote for combined education – let us have our own schools, our Catechism, our Liturgy, our Articles, our Homilies, our faith, our own teaching of God's word.[4]

However, even within the limits of this separatist denominational friction there were forces working for the extension of state control. The Committee of the Council's most important decision was to appoint Dr James Kay, later Sir James Kay-Shuttleworth, as its first Secretary. His early work as a doctor in the slums of Manchester, his experience as a Poor Law official and his ideas on teacher training (which led to his college at Battersea becoming the model for the rest of the century) combined to make him an ideal choice. His inspectors were men of high quality who had vision and imagination to concern themselves with much more than the physical amenities of a school building. Under Kay-Shuttleworth's guidance, they acted as disciples in the great educational cause, spreading ideas, encouragement, advice and dispensing criticism. Education inspectors found allies within the factory inspectorate which supervised the half-time factory schools required by child employees. The most famous, Horner (already discussed) saw in education the means of promoting social cohesion, 'by bringing the children of the employers and the employed into the same school to humanise both and create a right feeling between them'.[5] The work of the inspectors provided evidence and propaganda for the further extension of state intervention.

At a different level, opinion in the 1840s was moving in the same direction. Some learnt from the crises of 1839 and 1843 that neither Church nor Dissent could reign supreme; a working compromise would have to be found which would provide secular education. A leading figure here was W. F. Hook, Vicar of Leeds, whose years among the Dissenters of the West Riding led him away from an exclusive Anglican position. By 1846 he was suggesting a state system of education which did not involve domination by the Church:

> The Church has no more claim for exclusive pecuniary aid from the State or for any pecuniary aid at all, than is possessed by any other of those many corporations with which our country abounds. To call upon Parliament to vote any money for the exclusive support of the Church of England is to call upon Parliament to do what is unjust. The taxes are collected from persons of all religions and cannot be fairly expended for the exclusive maintenance of one.[6]

It was in this more propitious atmosphere that Kay-Shuttleworth revived the idea (dropped in 1839) of state supervision of teacher training.

This represented a move away from the so-called 'monitorial humbug' of Bell and Lancaster towards an eventual state-run adult training scheme. For the moment Kay-Shuttleworth, in the Minutes of the Committee of the Council for 1846, evolved the pupil-teacher training scheme, which involved a five-year apprenticeship from the age of thirteen. (Document 4A.) During the five years the pupil-teacher would receive instruction from a master and do some teaching himself for which he was paid. After five years' apprenticeship he could go on a Queen's scholarship to a training college for final qualification.

The scheme involved more generous payments to schools and required in 1847 a vote of £100,000 by Parliament. The Anglicans supported the scheme, as did Wesleyans and Roman Catholics, who saw the opportunity to qualify for grants. Many Unitarians had by now become convinced that voluntarism would not work, since a couple of hours in a Bible class did not represent an adequate education for the rising generation. Though less numerous than in 1843, the Dissenters who opposed the scheme, led by the Congregationalist Edward Baines, editor of the *Leeds Mercury*, were more virulent in their attacks on what was in 1847 a Whig-Liberal Government. They wanted voluntary education based on their own religions, and for them state education could only mean Godless indoctrination by subservient state-employed teachers who, of necessity, would do their masters' bidding. Though the scheme was passed by Parliament easily, the Dissenters continued the fight in the 1847 election, convinced that education must have total freedom. 'It is the air we breathe, if we do not have it we intellectually die. In fact we are waging our present electoral warfare ... [against] a rebellious conspiracy for the dethronement of Religion from her seat at the right hand of God.'[7]

Many Nonconformists thus retreated into an extreme sectarian voluntarism and by 1851 over 350 Dissenting schools had been opened which were independent of state aid. Conversely, however, many had by now accepted the view that the state must acknowledge responsibility for education. As one Anglican periodical put it:

Popular education must be an affair of the State – of the State not merely making grants to the different societies and demanding the right of inspection over schools which receive such grants; but as establishing some system administered by an efficient and responsible board for providing masters to work on some well-matured plans, with books under a proper supervision and paid at least in part by the State or by compulsory and local assessments. The schoolmaster must become a public functionary, duly qualified for his office and under due control.[8]

It was a measure of Kay-Shuttleworth's achievement that by the time of his resignation in 1849, despite the absence of general education legislation, state intervention had become firmly established virtually by a process of administrative growth.

Gradually the work of the Education Department (as it became in 1856) grew despite the humourless, unsympathetic direction of R. R. W. Lingen, Kay-Shuttleworth's successor. He curtailed the freedom of the inspectors and generally imposed greater rigidity on educational administration. This was partly the result of the growing burden of running the scheme. The Parliamentary grant increased from £100,000 in 1847 to over £500,000 ten years later. In the decade from 1849 the number of pupil-teachers increased more than fourfold to over 15,000, and by 1859 over 15,000 individuals were in the receipt of some teaching fees. Though Parliament had approved the annual grant, there had never really been any impartial review of this enormous growth in function and expenditure since 1833. Such a review was to be undertaken by a Royal Commission under the Duke of Newcastle, which sat from 1858 and reported in 1861. The report of the Newcastle Commission was a mixture of congratulations and criticism. The essential structure of state aid for voluntary religion-based schools was felt to be sound, given the estimated attendance which was just under 13 per cent of the population, nearly double that found in 1818. On the other hand, it was still short of the 1 in 6 figure which most aimed at, and very few children attended regularly (38 per cent attended for less than one year) or beyond the age of eleven. While some advanced (then thought unnecessary) work was taught, they found the education of younger children neglected. The level of elementary education to be aimed at, the ability to read a newspaper, write a letter or add up a bill (Document 4B) was not attained by a majority of ten- or eleven-year-old school leavers. Their recommendations for 'the extension of sound and cheap elementary instruction' in an age searching for economies in Government expenditure involved the reduction of the multifarious grants to two, a central grant based on attendance and a local grant financed from rates based on the achievements of pupils.

Robert Lowe, the Vice-President of the Education Department since 1859, and his friend Lingen, the Secretary, both feared the uncontrolled growth of education and were determined to implement the essentials of the Newcastle recommendations. Though the proposal for local boards and rates was dropped because of the old religious feuding, the system of 'payment by results' was implemented in the new regulations for Government grants embodied in the so-called Revised Code of 1862. The state would pay schools (in addition to building grants) 4s. per child based on regular attendance and a further 8s. if the pupil passed examinations arranged in six standards in reading, writing and arithmetic – the three Rs. It was the adoption of market forces in education, for as Lowe said, 'Hitherto we have been living under a system of bounties and protection – now we propose to have a little free trade'. Teachers would redouble their efforts knowing that their salaries were geared to the attainments of their pupils. The new vogue in examinations would be extended to elementary education and give pupils something to work for. Lowe posed his famous contrast between economy and efficiency: 'I cannot promise the House that this system will be an economical one and I cannot promise that it will be an efficient one but I can promise that it shall be either one or the other. If it is not cheap it shall be efficient, if it is not efficient it shall be cheap.'[9]

Educationists, then and since, have roundly criticised the Revised Code because of its cramping effects on the curriculum, henceforward to be narrowly utilitarian with emphasis upon the three Rs. It is doubtful, however, whether 'liberal' education in the classroom had progressed very far by the early 1860s and there may, therefore, have been more continuity in school practice than is sometimes allowed. While normally viewed as an anti-education ploy, the Revised Code has been defended by a few historians as a not unreasonable attempt to secure mass literacy and numeracy. In the short term it did achieve its purpose of reducing expenditure, for the grant which had been over £800,000 in 1861 fell to £636,000 in 1865, despite a sizeable increase in attendances.

Ironically it was only eight years after the Revised Code that Gladstone's Liberal ministry introduced the 1870 Education Act which established in principle the right of every child to some form of schooling. It is by no means clear why this Act should have been passed at that time, and several reasons have been suggested. The most obvious was the connection between the second Reform Act of 1867 with its enfranchisement of the urban working class and the need to educate the new electorate. As Lowe put it, 'I believe it will be absolutely necessary to compel our future masters to learn their letters', or as it became in the more popular version, 'We must educate our masters'. A factor sometimes rather ignored is that there was a healthy economic climate and a feeling that there was money available to finance education. Also important was the growing propaganda for a universal state system, and in 1869 the National Education League was born. W. E. Forster, Vice-President of Education in Gladstone's first ministry, did pilot surveys of four great cities and found less than 10 per cent of their population in schools. It was clear that there were gross deficiencies in school places which voluntarism was not going to fill. Even many of the extreme Dissenters were coming round to the view that voluntarism had been given a fair trial and had failed. The Congregationalist Education Union, which had originated in the 1840s to oppose state education, was wound up in 1867 and the symbolic acceptance of defeat was registered when the great voluntarist Edward Baines wrote: 'I confess to a strong distrust of government action, a passionate love for voluntary action and self-reliance but now as a practical man I am compelled to abandon the purely voluntary system.'[10]

Forster's 1870 Act did not provide universal free or compulsory education, but it did allow for the glaring deficiencies in English education to be removed. Its significance may be gauged by comparing the system before and after 1870; the period before 1870 was one characterised by state *subsidy* of voluntary education, the period after by state *supplementation* of voluntary education. School Boards were to be established where there was clear educational need, and these could provide non-denominational elementary schools financed out of the rates in addition to Government grants. These board schools did not replace voluntary schools, which continued with increased grants. The two schemes existed side by side, in theory complementary, in practice in competition. A way round the religious problem was found by the provision that 'no religious catechism or religious formulary which is distinctive of any particular denomination shall be taught', and there was a 'conscience clause' by which all schools, whether board or voluntary, which received a Government grant had to permit the withdrawal of children from religious instruction on parental demand. The 1870 Act was a compromise which tried to make use of and not destroy existing educational resources. Much research remains to be done on the national and local effects of the Act, but it is clear that it did not solve the problem overnight, and one scholar has estimated that 'although the overall educational and social objectives remained limited, it took thirty years to make a national system of elementary schools fully a reality'.[11]

The religious squabbling continued in the election for School Boards and in the attempts, particularly by the Anglicans in county areas, to forestall the imposition of the School Boards. Clearly the initial advantage lay with existing voluntary schools, and even by 1880 only one-sixth of children were in board schools, but the potential for future growth lay with the School Boards with their support from rates and grants, and by 1900 54 per cent of the elementary school population were in board schools. Many of the large boroughs had imposed by-laws making education compulsory, which in turn increased revenue, since grants were still related to attendance, and it was partly as a means of helping the rural voluntary schools that Disraeli's ministry turned its attention to compulsion. Lord Sandon, the Vice-President, told the Cabinet in 1875 that for these schools 'the question of general compulsion has become under the Education Act of 1870 a matter of life and death', and he also thought that to allow democratic School Boards to take over would damage Conservative control in the countryside.[12] Thus with partly political and partly educational motives Sandon's Education Act of 1876 set up School Attendance Committees and placed the responsibility for ensuring attendance firmly upon parents.

The various loop-holes were removed by the incoming Liberal ministry, which by Mundella's Education Act of 1880 made attendance compulsory for children aged between five and ten. This inevitably sharpened the debate about fees, which averaged about 3d. per week per child, and many School Boards waived the fee for needy children. The 1891 Fee Grant Act virtually established free elementary education, and by 1895 only about one-sixth of the 5 million needy elementary school-children were paying fees. The availability of free education through School Boards made it easier to integrate pauper children into the general education system. An Act of 1873 had made school attendance a condition of outdoor relief for children, an option which had been open to guardians since Denison's Act of 1855 had empowered guardians to pay school fees. By the end of the century the vast majority of unions sent children to their local board school and so the distinctive badge of pauperism was gradually removed.

In fact, that had always been the aim of the ambitious pauper education scheme which had been devised in the 1830s by Kay-Shuttleworth (then as Dr James Phillips Kay, a Poor Law inspector) and his colleague E. C. Tufnell, for over thirty years an inspector of Poor Law Schools. Kay and Tufnell believed that hereditary pauperism could be eradicated through the removal of children from the contamination of adult pauperism and the separate education of orphans in district schools. They had no time for the argument that the pauper child might be in a superior position to that of the child of the labourer by virtue of attendance availability and industrial training. Less eligibility had no relevance to the child whose pauperism was blameless and where educational provision so clearly conduced to the good of society. (Document 4C.) Tufnell never lost faith in the district school, where groups of unions could collaborate to provide schooling away from the union workhouse. In his final report in 1874 he extolled their virtues by recounting the story of a pauper boy 'showing his ascent from the condition of street arab to competence and respectability...typical of the life of innumerable children who have been raised from the lowest grade of misery and heathendom to a state of complete and honest independence by the aid of a district school'.[13] Despite Tufnell's enthusiasm not many industrial schools were built, yet pauper education benefited under the 1846 scheme whereby teachers could be trained and their salaries paid from central funds. The five inspectors of Poor Law Schools, attached to the Board of Education until 1863 and to the Poor Law Board thereafter, like their counterparts elsewhere were agents for improved standards and opponents of parsimony.

By the time the presence of pauper children in board schools became commonplace, the pernicious effects of payment by results were being removed. This system had been severely criticised by the Cross Commission which reported in 1888, and the 1890 Code abolished grants for examinable attainments in the three Rs. A new horizon opened up and, in the words of George Kekewich, the Secretary of the Department, the aim was now 'to substitute for the bald teaching of facts and the cramming which was then necessary in order that children might pass the examination and earn the grant, the development of interest and intelligence and the acquirement of real substantial knowledge'. 'Where are the 3 Rs now?' asked the educational journal, the *Schoolmaster.*

'No; the age of the 3 Rs is dead, buried and pulverised into invisible dust.'[14] By a process of accumulation the nineteenth century had made provision for primary education; the problem of secondary schools and beyond was left to the twentieth.

II Medical services

There are some similarities between the educational and medical services available to the poor in the early nineteenth century. Again, the rich could afford to pay doctors' bills and buy medicines, while for the poor there were quacks and patent elixirs or the charitable hospitals – the medical equivalent of the charity schools. The voluntary hospitals, many of which date from the eighteenth century, provided medical attention for those above pauperism who would have gained most from a state medical service. Broadly they were of two types: general hospitals, started by benevolent laymen, and specialist hospitals, usually launched by doctors in effect for research. Both employed the letter or ticket system whereby subscribers could introduce patients of their acquaintance. In addition, from the end of the eighteenth century many cities built public dispensaries modelled on the General Dispensary opened in the City of London in 1770. These became, in a sense, the out-patients' departments of the voluntary hospitals. As always, voluntarism based on charitable effort responded to deficiencies exposed by genuine need, but the voluntary hospitals were inevitably patchy in their coverage of the country. London had the best voluntary hospitals and Liverpool was the best endowed of the provincial cities. In many places the Poor Law authorities subscribed to these hospitals and used them for the treatment of paupers, a procedure finally legalised by a Poor Law Act of 1851.

As in the field of education, only the armed forces, the felons and the paupers received state medical treatment and it was out of the Poor Law that a rudimentary health service evolved. The voluntary hospitals had emerged to supply a pressing need, and when it was found that voluntarism could not cope with the problems of a vastly increased population, the Poor Law, especially after 1847 when the Poor Law Commission became the Poor Law Board, was forced into the unexpected provision of medical services for the masses. In 1834 this seemed highly unlikely, since it was envisaged that medical relief would play its part in the crucial distinction between poverty and pauperism. In the confusion of the early nineteenth century medical attention was not restricted to paupers, and it was hoped that after 1834 the Poor Law medical officers would concern themselves solely with paupers. However, less eligibility was always the keystone of the new Poor Law, hence the medical treatment of paupers had to be inferior to that which an independent workman could provide for himself. The dangers of a too-efficient pauper medical service were already apparent by 1841:

> If the pauper is always promptly attended by a skilful and well-qualified medical practitioner ... if the patient be furnished with all the cordials and stimulants which may promote his recovery: it cannot be denied that his condition in these respects is better than that of the needy and industrious ratepayer who has neither the money nor the influence to secure equally prompt and careful attendance nor any means to provide himself or his family with the more expensive kind of nutriment which his medical superintendent may recommend. This superiority of the condition of the pauper over that of the independent labourer as regards medical aid will ... encourage a resort to the poor rates for medical relief.[15]

In order to avoid this general resort to the Poor Law, medical and sick clubs, provident and friendly society schemes were encouraged to promote medical self-help among the working classes. The line between poverty and pauperism was a thin one and illness could soon cause a person to traverse it: indeed 72 per cent of all pauperism in the mid-nineteenth century was the result of sickness.

The whole panoply of medical voluntarism, including the hospitals, was geared to protecting patients from the stigma of Poor Law treatment, yet the Poor Law medical service grew in response to the inadequacy of voluntary efforts. The key figure in this development at the local level was the Poor Law medical officer, who gradually became a sort of general practitioner for the poor at large. This process was greatly stimulated by developments in vaccination in the mid-nineteenth century. Public treatment developed along separate paths, and to this day we receive our medical treatment via a completely different set of authorities (the NHS) from that which regulates sanitary conditions (the MOHs of the local authorities). Vaccination procedures to some extent combined the two.

Jenner had discovered vaccination in 1798, and in 1808 a National Vaccine Establishment had been set up supported by Government funds. The neglect of vaccination prompted Parliament to legislate in 1840 for free vaccination on demand. The Poor Law was the only national administrative network and the Poor Law medical officer the only widely available vaccinator, and so the operation of the Vaccination Act *for all* became his responsibility. In 1841 Parliament confirmed that vaccination by a Poor Law medical officer did not pauperise the recipient: a medical service was being provided by the Poor Law for everyone. In 1853 vaccination was made compulsory for infants, a unique interference with personal liberty. We do well to remember the significance of vaccination, which 'constitutes the first continuous health activity promoted by the state . . . an extraordinarily early development of state interference: a free, compulsory and nationwide health service in miniature'.[16]

The Poor Law medical officer's function as public vaccinator accentuated his non-pauper medical role, which was already growing in two ways. Medical officers could treat outdoor paupers on order from the relieving officer, and the numbers so treated grew enormously in mid-century. It was generally accepted that accidents and childbirth should normally be dealt with by Poor Law medical officers, and for domiciliary sickness a much less stringent definition of pauper was utilised than the destitution envisaged in 1834. Inability to pay doctors' fees came to be the criterion, and in 1852 a Poor Law Board order authorised medical relief in such cases, where the head of the family was still employed and thus not necessarily totally destitute. This increased contact between the medical officer and the general public was accompanied by a second development, the increased use of the sick wards of workhouses. By a mutually complementary process, Poor Law medical officers insisted on treating more patients in the sick ward where recovery would be speedier, and Poor Law Guardians applied the labour test increasingly so as to treat the able-bodied out of the workhouse. Hence workhouses took on the characteristics of public hospitals as they came to cater more for the sick than the able-bodied. Those who could be were treated at home, more serious cases being taken into the sick ward of the workhouse, and this growing specialisation was further aided by the Lunacy Acts of the period. By the Acts of 1842 and 1845 Lunacy Commissioners were appointed to inspect the asylum which every county was empowered to erect. The 1845 Lunacy Commission was given powers not only to inspect but also to license asylums and to discharge patients judged to be unreasonably detained in the asylum. As the leading historian of mental health comments, 'the Commissioners' power to inspect and remedy abuses was a notable step forward in human rights'.[17] The Lunacy Act of 1862 empowered the Commissioners to transfer lunatics from the workhouse to an asylum or vice versa in the case of harmless imbeciles. The increased load of indoor and outdoor medical relief led many unions to appoint separate doctors for each district: medical officers for outdoor work and workhouse medical officers for the sick wards. From the 1850s many unions opened public dispensaries for the issue of medicines and it became increasingly common for these to come into general and not just pauper use. From 1866 the term 'state hospital' was widely used to describe workhouse infirmaries. There remained appalling problems, inadequate facilities and the shortage of trained personnel, so that the mass of the population still suffered serious ill health.

The scale to which workhouses had become a public hospital system may be gauged from the estimate that of 65,000 hospital beds available in England and Wales in 1861, 50,000 or over 81 per cent were provided by workhouse sick wards, the rest by the voluntary hospitals.[18] Many welcomed the transformation of the workhouse (or part of it) into a hospital, and Florence Nightingale wrote: 'The sick can never be properly treated in the same establishment as the able-bodied pauper... there is absolutely no more real connection between an infirmary and a workhouse than between an infirmary and a railway establishment.'[19] There was pressure in the 1860s for this public hospital provision to be extended, not least by the Poor Law medical officers themselves. The whole medical profession was strengthened by the establishment in 1858 of the General Medical Council and the Medical Register, and the profession was an important propagandist for a better medical service. In the 1860s, the public was shocked by two pauper deaths due to lack of treatment in London workhouses and two separate surveys were made, one for the Poor Law

Board and one by the medical journal, *The Lancet*. This led to a reform of Poor Law medical services in London by the Metropolitan Poor Act of 1867, which many regard as the starting-point for an efficient state medical service. This Act combined London unions into 'Asylum Districts' under the Metropolitan Asylums Board, which enabled a whole range of specialist, general, fever and isolation hospitals to be built as well as an ambulance service to be established in the capital. By 1871, when the Poor Law Board was absorbed into the Local Government Board, a different attitude permeated the Poor Law from that which had reigned thirty years earlier. By then it was generally admitted that the harsh deterrent features of 1834 were inappropriate for the treatment of the sick. Gathorne-Hardy, the President of the Poor Law Board, made this point specifically in introducing the Metropolitan Poor Bill:

> There is one thing which we must peremptorily insist on – namely, the treatment of the sick in workhouses being conducted on an entirely different system, because the evils complained of have mainly arisen from the workhouse management, which must to a great degree be of a deterrent character, having been applied to the sick, *who are not proper objects for such a system*.[20] (My italics)

George Goschen, Hardy's successor at the Poor Law Board, supported the idea of 'free medicine to the poorer classes' and clearly envisaged some general medical service. This largesse was not always welcome to the guardians and their hard-pressed ratepayers. In Bradford in 1869 a protest was recorded against poor law patients in the infirmary being 'better off than they were in many respectable families and much better off than workpeople with 20s, 30s or 40s per week and living in £10 houses'. When called upon to justify his 'generous' treatment, the workhouse medical officer asserted, somewhat anachronistically, 'the life of a sick pauper is as valuable as that of a prince and when sick we ought to treat them both alike'.[21]

Similar conclusions about the level of medical provisions for paupers came from Dr Edward Smith, the first medical inspector for the Poor Law Board, who concluded in 1866 after his inquiry on London infirmaries: 'No one can walk through these great institutions without appreciating the fact that the inmates are better fed, better clad, better housed and better cared for than they were before their admission and better than the great mass of the working classes who earn their own living.'[22] This conclusion was supported by an independent observer who commented on the value of Poor Law medical services to the working class:

> A poor rate is an insurance of the labourer's life and health. It maintains him in old age, assists him in sickness and protects him when labouring under mental disease, and supplies him with the services of a highly skilled person in the shape of a medical officer.... At the existing rate of agricultural wages a farm labourer and to some extent the artisan could hardly supply these services for himself.[23]

The fears expressed in 1841 (see p. 98 above) proved well founded: less eligibility had been banished from the infirmary and people had turned to the Poor Law for a medical service. This process continued in the last quarter of the nineteenth century, accentuated by the Local Government Board's attack upon indiscriminate outdoor relief. Following the example of London, many places in the 1870s and 1880s built public infirmaries and dispensaries separate from the workhouse. It was clear that these new hospital facilities were used by those above pauperism, and so 'paupers' became 'patients'. There was still local discretion, regional variation and the stigma of applying to the Poor Law, but the provision of hospital beds via the Poor Law did increase (it reached 83,000 by 1891) and the building of specialist hospitals separate from the workhouse reduced the reluctance to apply, though in Birmingham patients still had to enter by a workhouse door to remind them where they were. Already by 1891 over 16 per cent of Poor Law hospital beds were in infirmaries rather than workhouse sick wards. The drive against outdoor relief pushed more people into the Poor Law infirmaries and so reinforced their character as public state hospitals. Many felt that as a matter of preventive medicine it was sound sense to allow all to use hospitals, since infectious diseases did not restrict their attack to paupers. A Royal Commission in 1881 recommended such general accessibility to hospitals, and by 1891 London citizens had been given the universal right to hospital treatment for infectious diseases. Earlier in 1885 an anomaly had been removed when it was confirmed by Parliament that resort to Poor Law medical services did not deprive a man of his franchise, which had been one of the punitive aspects of less eligibility. The Medical Relief

(Disqualifications Removal) Act decreed that Poor Law medical treatment did not pauperise. This was, as one historian points out, 'a seemingly miniscule measure but one that nevertheless breached the hallowed constitutional principle that voting rights should never be exercised by those without independent means of support'.[24]

Thus through the medical officers and the workhouse infirmaries the Poor Law had become an embryo state medical authority providing, in effect, general practitioners and state hospitals for the poor. This had been unexpected, contrary to the ethos of the new Poor Law and the pragmatic response to practical need. Such were the devious ways in which social policy developed in the nineteenth century.

III Law and order

That same concentration of population which produced other social problems posed enormous difficulties in the maintenance of law and order. During the troubles of the early nineteenth century, such as Peterloo, it had been the army which had in the last resort maintained order, and the same was true of the Chartist period. Yet it was in this period that the modern police system originated. Many Benthamite thinkers, such as Chadwick, devised schemes to 'solve' the problem of crime which so worried early industrial society. Basically, Chadwick's proposals involved a variation of the less eligibility principle combined with a preventive police force. Theoretically, crime would diminish if the condition of the criminal were made less eligible than the condition of law-abiding citizens and if there were so many policemen obviously visible to deter the potential lawbreaker.

The establishment of the Metropolitan Police Force in 1829 was an important step on the road towards a civilian unarmed law-enforcement body in contrast to an armed militia, which was another possibility. On occasion the Metropolitan Police were sent to other places which did not have a force, such as Birmingham in 1839, much to the chagrin of the local inhabitants. When municipal corporations were reformed in 1835 the new councils were instructed to form efficient constabularies under the local Watch Committees, and the counties were empowered to do likewise under the Police Act of 1839. Given the concern felt about attacks upon property (most nineteenth-century crime was concerned with gain), it was surprising how lethargic many places were about organising a police force. By the mid-1850s half the counties and more than a dozen boroughs had not established a force. Two contemporary fears prompted more effective action. First, the ending of the Crimean War led to concerns that discharged soldiers would inject into the country a potent source of disaffection. This fear, combined, secondly, with worries about the potentially dangerous impact of ex-prisoners released under the 1853 Penal Servitude Act, which ended transportation as a punishment. Such fears led to a political climate which made police reform possible. The erratic coverage of police forces was remedied by the 1856 County and Borough Police Act which made it compulsory for counties and boroughs to establish police forces and which imposed inspection and Exchequer grants to enforce the new policy. Home Office supervision by the three Inspectors of Constabulary did not restrict local initiative, but it did, through the 25 per cent grants available, ensure that all forces were efficient by conforming to certain minimum standards. It was a typical mid-Victorian compromise between local action and central supervision and compulsion. The pattern of regional forces persists to the present day, and England has not thus far adopted the suggested national police force which was recommended in the Constabulary Report of 1839.

Despite the national coverage of efficient police forces, the preventive principle did not markedly reduce the statistics of crime, and the main emphasis came to be on detection. This raised questions about the appropriate form of punishment. Peel, in the 1820s, had begun the process of reducing the number of offences punishable by death, which, by mid-century, had been reduced to murder, treason, piracy and arson in royal dockyards, and the last public execution took place in 1868. Transportation, much reduced from 1841, finally ended in 1867 and two years later imprisonment for debt virtually ceased. Those who were incarcerated in prisons found them better organised, more efficient, but more chastising than before. In 1842 Pentonville was opened and the 1840s saw the building of over fifty prisons on the solitary-cell Pentonville system developed there. Separate confinement had come to be regarded as the best of all disciplines. A Prison

Act had been passed in 1824 but without adequate administrative machinery. In 1835 the deficiency was remedied again by central inspection to supervise local control. Such inspection did not necessarily prevent local abuses continuing, and there were scandals revealed in the treatment of prisoners at Newgate, Leicester and Birmingham. However, inspection of prisons did strengthen Home Office supervision which was reinforced by further legislation in 1853 and 1865. It had long been realised that for full control over prisons the Home Office would eventually have to take power out of local hands, and as early as 1850 a Whig Home Secretary had commented: 'If...we were to take on ourselves the whole charge...we must at the same time supersede local management...The whole of the appointment of the prison officers would also be taken into the hands of the government.'[25] This finally happened in 1877 when the prisons were placed fully under national control by Disraeli's Government. Joshua Jebb, the Inspector-General of Prisons and a firm believer in punishment by long hours on the hand crank, a manual version of the treadmill, was concerned that juvenile offenders were imprisoned, transported or even on occasion hanged along with adult criminals. He reported in 1847:

> The whole system hitherto pursued with respect to youth appears to be open to the most serious objections both as regards the practice of sentencing mere children to transportation or committing them to the penal discipline of the prison. The bulk of the convicts below the age of thirteen and fourteen are the objects of pity rather than justice.[26]

He took a personal hand in the running of Parkhurst, which from 1838 to 1864 was admitting solely juvenile offenders and which was in his words 'the only establishment which had been formed for receiving young criminals from prison and making any endeavour to combine the punishment due to crime with a reformatory and industrial training'.[27] Despite this the methods and concept of Parkhurst as a *prison* for young offenders came under severe criticism from reformers, notably Mary Carpenter, author of *Reformatory School* in 1851, whose concern was for the so-called 'children of the perishing and dangerous classes and for juvenile offenders'. Already voluntarism had produced a few such reformatory schools, the best of which was run by the Philanthropic Society, a group dating back to 1788. Sydney Turner, from 1857 first Inspector of Reformatories, had become chaplain at the society's school in 1841 and in 1848 had transferred the reformatory to Redhill to implement the rural family methods developed in France. In 1851 reformers held a conference in Birmingham to attempt to push the Government towards reformatory rather than deterrent punishment, and this led to the establishment of many voluntary reformatories like Mary Carpenter's Red Lodge in Bristol.

The mid-Victorian solution to this problem was once more a fusion of voluntary effort and state supervision. The Youthful Offenders Act of 1854 was a turning-point in the history of the treatment of English juvenile delinquency, and Matthew Davenport Hill, a legal reformer, called it 'the Magna Charta of the neglected child'.[28] It enabled voluntary bodies to set up reformatory schools to which the courts could send convicted youths under sixteen years of age for a period of two to five years (after a brief taste of 'real' prison). The central Government paid a maintenance grant to the schools which were under state inspection, first by the Inspectors of Prisons and from 1857 by a separate Inspector of Reformatories.

By 1861 there were forty-seven certified reformatories, and contemporaries saw the whole system as a confirmation of the virtues of an alliance of voluntarism and state subsidy and supervision. Mary Carpenter had always seen these reformatories as part of a tripartite attack upon the problem of the outcast child. Basic education for destitute children was to be provided by so-called 'ragged schools', near-delinquent vagrant children ('street Arabs') were to go to industrial schools and the reformatories were to deal with convicted juveniles. The whole vision did not quite materialise, however. The Ragged School Union was formed in 1844 under the presidency of Lord Ashley, and by 1861 it ran more than 170 schools, staffed by over 400 paid teachers and with an average daily attendance of about 25,000 children. The movement was in effect made redundant by the 1870 Education Act, but it continued its missionary work for underprivileged children. While the ragged schools remained completely voluntary and without state subsidy, the industrial schools in 1857 were given the same status as the reformatories. Magistrates could commit vagrant children to certified industrial schools, though there were far fewer of these than reformatories and they received a smaller proportion of their income from the state. A parallel development were the industrial schools run by local guardians for children, often orphans, who came under the aegis of the Poor Law. From 1848 large district boarding schools were being built for pauper children, and so provision for destitute and delinquent children shaded into the general education and welfare schemes of Victorian England.

5 Laissez-faire and state intervention in the mid-nineteenth century

I Social ideas to c. 1870

The case studies in social policy described in previous chapters were at once a part of and a response to the social philosophy which emerged in the first half of the nineteenth century. Inevitably such an explosive social change as the Industrial Revolution was accompanied by new ideas in economic and social affairs. Men sought to understand what had happened and to find a rationale for the new society created by economic change. Industrial capitalism came to be justified by the so-called 'political economy' of a group of thinkers known collectively as the 'classical economists'. The demonstration of the general principles of economic theory which explained the role of capital and free competition (the essential elements of the new society) crystallised into a *laissez-faire* synthesis. The nature of behaviour in human society was closely related to the economic role performed, and so ideas about the structure and function of society emerged as a social equivalent or adjunct of economic theory.

Just as the economic changes themselves were a challenge to the old pre-industrial society, so too the economic theory that accompanied the Industrial Revolution challenged the doctrines of a prior age. From the sixteenth to the eighteenth century, Governments operated on an accumulated body of experience and doctrine known as 'mercantilism'. In its social aspects it was, in a sense, the inheritor of feudalism, with the state acknowledging a social responsibility for the welfare of its citizens; much paternalistic Tudor social legislation, for instance, was of this character. In its economic aspect mercantilism was a collection of economic policies based on the assumption that the state could regulate the character and direction of the nation's economic activity. Typical mercantilist devices included a tariff policy geared to the accumulation of gold through a favourable balance of trade, rigorous protection of home industries by national and local regulations and the safeguarding of colonial trade via restrictive controls on shipping.

The mercantilist approach was comprehensively undermined by Adam Smith, the originator of the school of political economy. Smith's *Wealth of Nations* was first published in 1776 and had gone through eight editions within twenty years. For Smith the whole panoply of mercantilist regulation was a conspiracy in the interests of a few producers at the expense of the majority of consumers. As he said, 'Consumption is the sole end and purpose of all production' and the consumer would be best served by market forces operating *freely* under competition. All regulations were restraints upon trade and restricted economic development. The full potential of economic growth would be achieved by leaving all to pursue their own self-interest, and since society was itself only the sum of the individuals in it, then the general welfare would be served by the collective pursuit of individual welfare. In fact, by pursuing his own self-interest a man is 'led by an invisible hand to promote an end which was no part of his intention', i.e. the common weal:

> Every individual is continually exerting himself to find out the most advantageous employment for whatever capital he can command. It is his own advantage indeed and not that of society which he had in view. But the study of his own advantage naturally or rather necessarily leads him to prefer that employment which is of most advantage to the society.[1]

Essentially, Smith was asking for the liberation of the economy from mercantilist regulation either in the form of restrictionist tariffs or of the almost anti-social monopolies which had been created. In so far as he wanted *free* trade and economic forces to work in a *free* market this was designated a liberal school of economics. In its widest context it allowed the individual to fulfil his true potential unrestricted by the trammels of unnecessary restrictions and regulations which were infringements on his liberty. Above all, Smith's concept of society presupposed it to be a collection of *individuals*: just as a sand-castle was the particular configuration of so many individual particles of sand, so social structure was the particular relationship between individuals. Self-interest was for society what gravity was for the solar system, the basic universal force continually at work to keep the whole system in operation. Smith envisaged the individual entrepreneur freely investing his capital, bringing together the factors of production, making the decisions, taking the risks and finally, after selling in competition with others in the open market-place, taking his profits. The notion of individuals freely pursuing their own self-interest in competition with others was the common social ethic deriving from Smith which underlay early industrial society. It was in the liberal tradition dating from Locke that the individual should be free from coercive power. However, at the outset it is important to realise that Smith did envisage a positive role for the state in providing public services which no individual alone could maintain. (Document 5A.)

The principles of classical economics were further refined by other writers building on Smith's work. As we have seen in the chapter on the Poor Law, Malthus was concerned that the pressure of population growth could outstrip the means of maintaining it, and the demand for food with its consequent pressure on resources was one strand in David Ricardo's *Principles of Political Economy* (1817). Ricardo has been called the high priest of the capitalist middle class, for he demonstrated the crucial central role of capital in a society – 'that fund by whose extent the extent of productive industry of the country must always be regulated'. At the same time his rigorous division of income into rent, wages and profits led him to the conclusion that since the first two were increasing (because of population growth), profits must be reduced in the long term. Above all, he identified the non-productive landlord whose property increased in value and whose rents soared without performing any extra work or service. In the emerging struggle between the middle and the landed classes Ricardian economics provided the well-authenticated image of the parasitic privileged landlord. Ricardo strengthened the case for freeing the commercial classes from the shackled protected market in which agriculture held a self-perpetuating supremacy. Both Smith and Ricardo wanted the natural liberty of a free market system. In searching for an understanding of the self-adjusting price mechanism so crucial to Smith, Ricardo concluded that in fact labour was the source of all value (a notion welcome to the early socialists), though it needed the application of active capital to make it productive. Nassau Senior established the wage-fund theory (mentioned earlier in discussing the Poor Law) with its ultimate vision of ever-increasing wages completely swallowing profits, and the wage-fund concept was firmly held down to 1869, when it was repudiated by John Stuart Mill. Senior also introduced the 'stick and carrot' stimulus of fear of poverty and ambition for the so-called decencies and luxuries, which would encourage incentive and reduce population growth.

The economic theories of political economy were closely allied to the philosophy of government which emerged alongside, through the work of Bentham. Jeremy Bentham applied one of the most powerful minds of modern times to the problems of society using principles of clear logical thought untrammelled by previous history. Accepting the broad basis of a free market economy of the classical school, Bentham realised that the state might sometimes have to ensure that a real community of interest was catered for. This was in effect an elaboration of Smith's third duty of government into a clear ethic of political philosophy. Bentham and his followers wished to apply the test of utility to all institutions: were they efficient, economical and above all conducive to 'the greatest happiness of the greatest number'? Because of this, Benthamites were called 'utilitarians' (or alternatively the 'philosophical radicals') and many of the reforms of the nineteenth century sprang from some direct or indirect Benthamite source. Though Benthamism envisaged collectivist state action, it was to be geared to the needs of individualism. Utilitarianism wished to release the potential of individual interests working *naturally* in harmony together, but recognised that a minimum of efficient, economical state intervention was necessary to produce artificially the same harmony.

Bentham's disciples, notably James Mill, spread the gospel of utilitarianism, and it was Mill's son John Stuart Mill who struggled in the mid-nineteenth century with the divergent concepts which clashed in the alliance between political economy and utilitarianism. The question really was how far *laissez-faire* should go. No one seriously believed in total *laissez-faire*, for that would produce complete anarchy, and all civilisation and law involve some restraining of individual liberty in the interests of the common good. Mill's view, expressed in his highly regarded *Principles of Political Economy* of 1848, was that *laissez-faire* was the ideal from which the Government should depart only in the exceptional case where an overwhelming need existed for state action. He acknowledged that there were obvious areas where the state rightly intervened, but wished all to beware of over-government by a repressive dictatorial state. Every inroad into *laissez-faire*, however necessary, was a step *away* from the ideal: 'Letting alone should be the general practice, every departure from it unless required by some great good is certain evil.' (Document 5B.) Mill feared than an overprotective state would weaken individual responsibility and an opponent of state vaccination echoed Mill's view:

> It is only by the voluntary and judicious exercise of their own powers that the people can progress; it is clear so far as the state does for them . . . the duties which are within their own sphere and competence, to that extent it limits and retards their development . . . if even vaccination were the greatest blessing in existence it would not be the duty of the state to enforce it.[2]

Such abstruse theorists as Ricardo and Bentham were known at first hand by only a small minority, but there were always popularisers of these ideas, which percolated, sometimes in an attentuated form, through all levels of society. It has often been the case in the history of ideas that concepts discussed esoterically by experts become in a simplified form the intellectual loose change of a popular culture. Thus the Ptolemaic system of cosmology was an extremely complicated structure full of mathematical variations, but Dante could see in the *Divine Comedy* the simple earth-centred model with the heavenly spheres above, the same image which is common in Shakespeare. So too by the mid-nineteenth century, a synthesis of political economy and utilitarianism had emerged in that body of attitudes often called 'Victorianism', so well popularised by Samuel Smiles.

By the time of the Great Exhibition in 1851 England had survived the social tension of the second quarter of the nineteenth century and had entered the calm prosperity of the 'age of equipose'. With the whole fabric of society more secure and the obvious progress made through industrialism evident all around, men could foresee a solution to the problem of want through the beneficial effects of prosperity for all: 'In this age of improvements scientific, social and legislative...it seems by no means impossible...that the whole of the working classes should be raised above the dread of poverty – that all should be comfortable, all educated, all well fed, well clothed, well lodged.'[3] In such circumstances the virtues which had sustained the capitalist middle class and produced these benefits were elevated into a moral code for all, almost a religion. The social philosophy of Victorianism crystallised into four great tenets: work, thrift, respectability and above all self-help. The gospel of work was central to the practical efficient approach of the entrepreneur and to the growth of the urban industrial society. As Dickens wrote in *Hard Times*, 'You saw nothing in Coketown but what was severely workful', and Carlyle laid down the dictum: 'Properly speaking all work is religion'. Work was the most 'useful' thing a utilitarian could imagine, and could be practised by all no matter what their talents or their station. The corollary was the other side of the coin: if work was a virtue, idleness thereby was an evil. The attack upon the idle, unproductive aristocrat on the one hand and the idle Speenhamland able-bodied pauper on the other was an expression of this faith in work as a virtue.

The capitalist had worked hard, but he had also inevitably been forced to forgo present enjoyments by applying his capital usefully rather than frittering it away in conspicuous consumption. Thrift was the brother of work in this dour Puritanical outlook, which produced the capital and the human energy to spark industrialisation. As Senior put it, 'Wages and profits are the creation of man. They are the recompense for the sacrifice made, in the one case of ease, in the other of immediate enjoyment.'[4] The whole process of capital investment was made possible by the willingness of individuals to save rather than consume. Here was Smith's invisible hand at work, for an individual saving for a rainy day turned out to benefit the whole society.

Working and saving were elements in what was essentially a sober, respectable attitude to life, and it was in the mid-nineteenth century that manners and good conduct became important. As many have pointed out, the respectability of the Victorians was a hypocritical façade where real feelings were hidden and surface behaviour highly regarded. Nevertheless it did produce a growing sensitivity to suffering, a concern for others, an assault on the public vices (drunkenness and prostitution), the sober English Sunday and a moral code in which a decent family life could function unblemished by improprieties. Deriving in part from the earlier work of the Evangelicals of the 'Clapham Sect', middle-class morality imposed a public respectability to which even the royal family conformed.

Above all, this middle-class Victorian social philosophy was underpinned by self-help, the supreme virtue. The stupendous achievement of producing the so-called 'progress of the nation' had been the result of Smith's ideal individuals pursuing their self-interest. The open, competitive society with its enormous opportunities enabled all to rise by their own talents, unaided by Government agency. Samuel Smiles was able to survey the men who had achieved great things by their own efforts and generalise their experience into a universal principle. There could be no doubt that heaven really did help those who helped themselves. (Document 5C.) Man, master of his own fate, working to achieve his full potential, was an image derived from the real world: all things were possible given the initiative and industry. Self-help was the middle-class justification for the *status quo* which in the last resort was not static. Men could climb the social ladder. It required only a small logical extension to enlarge the proposition that universal opportunity existed into a social theory in which men found their due place in society in proportion to their talents. Herbert Spencer in the third quarter of the nineteenth century evolved a social Darwinism in which the fittest reached the top and conversely those really inferior were at the bottom. This was the context in which a deterrent Poor Law had a logical place.

Though the self-help ideology was essentially of middle-class origin and application, its impact was society-wide. Its influence floated upwards into the ranks of the landed aristocracy which became permeated with notions of service, respectability and, at least in public, a stricter religious observance and moral code. Such diverse areas as the reform of the public schools and universities, the decline of duelling and patronage, the opening-up of the civil service to competition, reform of the army and the formal regulation of sporting activities indicated a growing acceptance of the middle-class values implicit in Victorianism. This spread of bourgeois attitudes was paralleled by important political changes. In 1832 the electoral system had been reformed by the first

Reform Bill which established a middle-class franchise; in 1835 the local oligarchies were opened up by municipal reform; and in 1846 Peel repealed the Corn Laws in deference, apparently, to the needs of middle-class interests. To Cobden it appeared that 1846 had made 1832 a reality: 1832 had signalled and 1846 had established middle-class government. As another observer pointed out:

> By the Reform Bill the predominance of the middle classes in the most active and important branch of our senate . . . was solemnly and irrevocably affirmed. And it is by the middle classes that our recent important improvement has been commenced, by them has it been sustained and by them has it been carried on to its final though over-reluctant answer. . . . [Free trade] proves the actual existence of that which it was foretold the Reform Bill would eventually found, the Monarchy of the Middle Classes.[5]

Where some saw this middle-class monarchy, others saw a strategic withdrawal by the governing classes to preserve the essence of aristocratic power. While Professor Perkin talks of the victory of the so-called entrepreneurial ideal, Professor Burn deemed it 'extravagant to think of England in this period as being governed by and in the interest of the middle class'.[6] For present purposes it is not essential to resolve this disagreement; it is sufficient to state that there was a fusion in politics and society of aristocratic and middle-class interests, an alliance of property and capital to form a new dominant ruling class.

This merger was perhaps predictable, since it brought together the two main forms of wealth in English society. What was far more surprising was the adoption of the ideas of the propertied by the property-less, for the self-help philosophy spread down as well as up. *A priori*, one would have assumed that the class antagonisms flowing from an unequal distribution of wealth between masters and men would not have produced a shared social philosophy. Working-class poverty appeared to many to be encouraged by a system which deprived labour of the full produce of its toil and in which labour was crushed between property and capital. As John Francis Bray, an early socialist, put it: 'The present arrangements of society enable masses of capital to grind between them masses of labour and thereby necessarily doom the majority to toil and deprivation for the benefit of the minority.'[7] In such circumstances anti-capitalist theories spread along with industrialisation.

Thomas Paine's *Rights of Man* (1791) was an enormous influence on nineteenth-century radicalism and advocated the natural rights of which the masses had been deprived by individual owner-ship of land. Thomas Spence envisaged a democracy of farmers renting land under public control, while Charles Hall, also believing in land nationalisation, analysed the inequalities of wealth and their effects on social contracts. This challenged Smith's concept of equal individuals pursuing their own self-interest; as Hall observed, unequal distribution of wealth precluded equality of opportunity. However, the near-anarchist William Godwin, writing at the end of the eighteenth century, believed that man's reason was limitless and that he could master the circumstances of his environment.

Socialistic ideas were further stimulated by Ricardo's assump-tion that labour was the source of all value, though it proved difficult to integrate this into a satisfactory anti-capitalist social theory. William Thompson criticised competition in his attempt to adapt Benthamism in the working man's interest, while John Gray analysed the likely consequences of differences between demand and production. These two, Thompson and Gray, wished to set up voluntary communistic cells based on co-operative production, while Thomas Hodgskin and John Francis Bray emphasised more the organisation of labour, Hodgskin favouring combinations of workers against capital and Bray believing in a form of workers' control of industry. None of these theorists could boast the practical achievements of Robert Owen, whose book *A New View of Society* (1813) emphasised how social environment affected men's personality and character. His mill at New Lanark pioneered humane industrial practices and the Owenite co-operative communities were an attempt to create an alternative society within capitalism.

Many of these theories, some anti-industrial, some communistic, were present within the Chartist leadership, but once this movement had spent its strength there was a sort of hiatus, in a sense waiting for Marx. Between the failure of Owenism and the rise of Marxist socialism, working-class social philosophy was affected by middle-class values as working men became increasingly concerned to get a better deal from capitalism rather than overthrow it. This consensus is usually described as the *embourgeoisement* of the working class, the imposition of middle-class ideas upon working-class culture.

Yet it may be that the mid-Victorian period witnessed the resurgence of older artisan values, re-emerging after the chaos of industrialisation. Whereas Sunday schools may have been instruments of social control as they brought working-class children under the tutelage of middle-class teachers, they may equally have been a haven for independent working-class activity. The adoption of supposed bourgeois values was often not the result of manipulation by social superiors but the logical outcome of workers' own experience in the workplace and the community. The stabilisation of social relations within the emergent factory culture allowed a new industrial paternalism and an endemic working-class consciousness to co-exist. That *bourgeois* and artisan ideology should converge may have been the result of a common intellectual origin in the Enlightenment. Hence in attempting to isolate the 'rough' by colonising the 'respectable', the middle-class social strategist was not automatically undermining the independence of the working class, for the assumption of 'respectability' did not necessarily compromise artisan values.

Whether the conflict or the consensus model is more appropriate, there was much in mid-Victorian working-class behaviour which impressed the middle class. Trade unionism had turned away from the revolutionary tendencies implicit in the attempts during the 1830s to organise the whole of labour, and the 'new model unions' of the 1850s were based upon highly-paid, highly-skilled trades like engineering. These shunned militancy, seeking to establish unions as respectable institutions of Victorian life, and they ran self-financing insurance schemes for their members. The seriousness, diligence and industry of such unions earned for trade unionism a growing social acceptance. Members of these unions were often concerned with adult education, which developed rapidly in the middle decades of the century. Developments such as the Mechanics' Institutes, the Society for the Diffusion of Useful Knowledge and the Working Men's Union encouraged working men to educate themselves in adult life. Self-education was a prime example of self-help and considerably reduced middle-class fears about the disaffection of working men in two ways. First (as was mentioned in the section on education), many of these adult education ventures were sponsored by middle-class patronage and were channels of communication for middle-class ideas, spreading the authentic self-help gospel. Second, the very fact of adult education confirmed a working-class belief in self-help and self-improvement. Education was seen by many as the lever by which working men could gain their political and social rights and fulfil their potential. The Chartist leader William Lovett aimed to develop 'the mental and moral energies of our population, to the great end of their political freedom and social happiness...to develop all the powers and energies God has given them to the end that they may enjoy their own existence and extend the greatest amount of happiness to all mankind'.[8]

The growth of friendly societies was viewed as further evidence of the basic soundness of the English working class. The friendly societies were the prime example of working-class self-help in what was an ameliorative rather than revolutionary social philosophy. With fewer than a million members in 1815, they totalled 4 million members by the 1870s and in size outstripped all other working-class activities of the mid-Victorian years. Some of these mutual insurance schemes involved little more than burial funds to avoid a pauper's grave, others were far more ambitious with medical, accident and unemployment benefits, or widows' and old-age pensions. They represented the collective efforts of men to finance their own protection from the vagaries of an industrialised system and combined the classic virtues of thrift and self-help. Though in periods of social tension in the first half of the nineteenth century they were regarded as potentially subversive, by the mid-century they had an official Registrar, J. Tidd Pratt, who ensured that they were soundly managed and socially acceptable. They were convincing evidence that the same values and attitudes which inspired masters were shared by their men, at least the more affluent of them. They went a long way towards convincing people that working men had listened to the advice Smiles had given in the 1840s: 'Every working man should strive to elevate himself in his social position and become independent. With this view, every working man in times of prosperity and good wages should strive to *save* something and accumulate a fund in case of bad times.'[9]

Ironically, the co-operative movement also, in the long term, confirmed a working-class faith in self-help. Begun as an alternative to capitalism, it became, especially in its retailing activities, a means of mutual profit sharing to short-circuit the normal trading pattern. Consumers were helping themselves to buy in the cheapest market and by their own efforts were seeking to mitigate the deleterious effects of the competitive system. By the mid-nineteenth century less was heard of the founding of co-operative communities and more of efficient trading practices which would best serve the financial interests of members. As one supporter explained: 'Modern Co-operation means a union of working men for the improvement of the social circumstances of the class to which they belong... it is the working man's lever by which he may rise in the world.'[10] Once more working-class activity shared the values of middle-class philosophy.

Trade unionism, adult education, friendly societies and the co-operatives were four facets of working-class life which suggested a shared value system between the two classes. There were other examples, such as the savings banks patronised by the humble, the building clubs, the Sunday school teaching, the volunteer and teetotal movements. For the most part these activities were participated in by the better-paid skilled artisan, the so-called 'aristocracy of labour', and the virtues proclaimed were such that could appeal only to those well above the poverty-line. What use was thrift to the man without the means to meet his current needs? Yet even in the great distress caused by the Lancashire cotton famine the response of working men displayed in Gladstone's words 'self-command, self-control, respect for order, patience under suffering, confidence in the law, regard for superiors'.[11]

The widespread acceptance of the virtues of self-help through these activities confirmed the existence of a large number of working men who had means well above subsistence level. As Smiles so perceptively saw, the more affluent the working man the less revolutionary he became; the more he got out of capitalism the less likely he would be to overturn it and replace it with a doubtful alternative:

> The accumulation of property has the effect which it always has upon thrifty men: it makes them steady, sober and diligent. It weans them from revolutionary notions and makes them conservative. When workmen by their industry and frugality have secured their own independence they will cease to regard the sight of others' well being as a wrong inflicted upon themselves and it will no longer be possible to make political capital out of their imaginary woes.[12]

Hence the fear of working-class spoliation gave way in the mid-Victorian period to a respect for the diligence, industry and soundness of the English working class. There were still many who foresaw that society must be radically altered by a social revolution of the masses, but others came to the view that the working class was safe and could be trusted with the vote. The millions of members of friendly societies, the hundreds of thousands of co-operators, Sunday school teachers and trade unionists, the thousands of investors in savings banks and building societies – these men could not be dangerous. Disraeli, who displayed, even in passing the 1867 Reform Bill, an ambivalent attitude towards a massive working-class enfranchisement, could none the less put a brave face on it when a million urban workers gained the vote and say 'I have no fear of England'. Working-class acceptance of the middle-class social philosophy ensured the enfranchisement of the working class, which in the long term represented a major political threat to the *laissez-faire* ideology. Yet already state intervention had turned social theory on its head.

II   Social theory and state intervention

The simplified Smilesian view of the ideal society composed of industrious, thrifty individuals pursuing their own self-interest in competition with others in a situation of equal opportunity gave to the state a purely negative role: 'The function of government is negative and restrictive rather than positive and active.' Part of this popular synthesis involved the assumption that 'the best government is that which legislates least' and took up Mill's proposition already quoted that 'letting alone should be the general practice'. The widespread feeling that 'we cannot go on legislating for ever' gladdened Smiles's heart, and the great jurist A. V. Dicey, looking back from the end of the century, could characterise the period from 1825 to 1870 as one dominated by Benthamism or individualism (the later years of the century being a period of collectivism). Though Benthamism was not the precise equivalent of *laissez-faire*, it seemed to Dicey that the two came to be merged and that the four decades from about 1830 were marked by a minimum of state activity in deference to Benthamite individualism.

The limits on state activity so dear to Smiles and identified in practice by Dicey are difficult to reconcile with the state intervention only partially recorded here in earlier chapters. While Smiles could claim that the negative role of the state was 'every day becoming more clearly understood', *The Times* could record that 'session after session we are amplifying the province of the legislature and asserting its moral prerogatives'.[13] To begin to list the activities the state had adopted by 1870 indicates the paradox: the state maintained paupers, limited the employment of women and children, regulated emigration via the Passenger Acts, controlled pollution via the Alkali Acts, financed and supervised schools, reformatories, prisons and police forces, enforced nuisance-removal, vaccination and the civil registry of births, marriages and deaths. The list could be considerably extended, and to it would have to be added the multifarious services provided by a typical town council, for the long arm of the state had extended to such humble areas as public wash-houses, libraries and parks. That arch-opponent of state activity Herbert Spencer had already by mid-century written two books (*The Proper Sphere of Government*, 1843, and *Social Statics*, 1851) bitterly criticising the over-legislation and over-government England was suffering. As Dr Parris points out: 'Spencer prescribes *laissez-faire* but describes government growth'.[14] Another historian has identified sixteen central adminis-trative departments created in the second quarter of the nineteenth century. The very age of individualism and *laissez-faire* apparently saw the birth of the centralised administrative state. This conundrum has given rise to a major historical debate, which one historian at least deems unnecessary, for he considers the juxtaposition of *laissez-faire* and state intervention 'a false antithesis' (Perkin, 1977). His advocacy of individualism and collectivism as part of the same continuum still leaves a paradox to be explained.

There are a variety of ways in which we can resolve this paradox and they fall broadly into five categories. They are by no means exclusive and there is a considerable degree of overlap, yet they each have a distinctive feature and each casts on this problem a shaft of light peculiar to itself. The first is the simplest and most obvious and – who knows? – perhaps the one nearest the truth, which is that the paradox results from the old human failing of saying one thing and doing another – the difference between theory and practice. While men held genuinely to a belief that *laissez-faire* was at heart the best answer, they had to accept that the prob-lems posed by urban industrial society of necessity enlarged the practical activities of the state. This could happen to confirmed classical economists and expert administrators who could not consistently argue the case for *laissez-faire* given the course of state intervention and who, like Mill, tried to rationalise the discrepancy. But even more common was the discrepancy between the esoteric reality and the popular simplified myth, that wide gulf already noticed between the complex expert ideology and the sometimes garbled version suitable for popular consumption. Although the patterns of law came increasingly to affect everyone, it was still possible to turn a blind eye, to withdraw into that large area of apparent freedom and assume that individualism really did exist and was a virtue to be extolled.

As Professor Burn pointed out, it was perfectly feasible for a wealthy, independent, middle-class man to forget the all-embracing role of the state which underpinned his liberty. Burn painted for us the picture of a Mr Brown ensconced in his fine house and park:

> He appears to enjoy liberty in the highest possible degree, to be as nearly isolated from coercive forces or authority as a civilised man living in a civilised community can be. But, in fact, the liberty which he so happily enjoys is dependent to a large extent on the existence of coercive power, his own or that of the state.... Mr Brown, on balance, enjoys a notable amount of liberty ... is the beneficiary of coercion, but of coercion which in his day and for him has come to be so quietly and decorously applied that he, and Mill, and Dicey could almost ignore its existence.[15]

If it was possible with one's domestic environment to imagine a near-total liberty, it was equally possible to seem unaware of the encroachment of the state in public everyday life. Individualism could be proclaimed within an unconsciously collectivist milieu such as Sidney Webb described in the story of the practical man who became a collectivist despite himself:

> The individualist town councillor will walk along the municipal pavement, lit by municipal gas and cleansed by municipal brooms with municipal water, and seeing by the municipal clock in the municipal market that he is too early to meet his children coming from the municipal school, hard by the county lunatic asylum and municipal hospital, will use the national telegraph system to tell them not to walk through the municipal park, but to come by the municipal tramway to meet him in the municipal reading-room by the municipal art gallery, museum and library where he intends to consult some of the national publications in order to prepare

his next speech in the municipal town hall in favour of the nationalisation of canals and the increase of Government control over the railway system. 'Socialism, Sir,' he will say, 'don't waste the time of a practical man by your fantastic absurdities. Self-help, Sir, individual self-help, that's what made our city what it is.'[16]

This long and well-known quotation dates from a later period (1889), but sums up perfectly the way men could preach ideas which current practice was rendering obsolete before their very eyes. Indeed in another sense there may be a connection, for the undermining of dearly held values may have produced the need to proclaim the gospel of self-help all the more loudly.

The second explanation sees a discrepancy not so much between theory and practice as between theory and practice in one field and another. Halévy identified an inconsistency between the utilitarian approach to law and politics, which presupposed intervention to produce a harmony of interests, and the desire for the free play of market forces in economic affairs.[17] We can synthesise this into the proposition that while many *social* problems required state intervention, *laissez-faire* was to be the rule for the *economy*. Hence the discrepancy arises between the means to be used in social and economic affairs. Many historians have taken up Halévy's distinction, arguing for the separation of social and economic aspects of Government policy, and this was the sort of position Macaulay had arrived at by mid-century. As we have seen in the discussion on the Leeds election of 1832 and the factory question, Macaulay at that time believed in the sort of negative state function later supported by Smiles. However, in 1846 he argued for a negative role (free trade) in commercial affairs, but a more positive interventionist approach to 'transactions which are not purely commercial'. Here he would allow a 'meddling government': 'It is not desirable the state should interfere with the contracts of persons of ripe age and sound mind touching matters purely commercial.... The principle of non-interference is one that cannot be applied without real restrictions where the public health or morality is concerned.'[18]

Certainly, it is true that the classical school wanted economic affairs to be free from interference so that market forces could freely operate (to the benefit of the consumer), and here free trade had obvious attractions. Yet there are difficulties about the distinction between society and economy. To start with, the line between the two was blurred. Were not the Poor Law, public health and the factory question as much involved with economic as with social affairs? Certainly, the Poor Law and factory reform were closely bound up with the labour market. Furthermore, even in overtly economic matters the state was taking a greater initiative. The Passenger Acts regulating emigrant shipping interfered with freedom of contract, the Alkali Acts told the chemical industry how to run its business, railway legislation imposed some forms of price control, legislation for gasworks limited dividends, and above all the various company legislation of the mid-nineteenth century introduced legally backed rules into commercial affairs. Thus while there is some truth in the feeling that there was a greater reluctance to interfere in economic affairs, the distinction is not altogether satisfactory.

The third way of looking at the problem would be to attempt to see Benthamite utilitarianism as more a synthesis of *laissez-faire* and collectivist intervention rather than an exclusive brand of self-help. Some would go even further and argue that Dicey's identification of Benthamism with individualism was a complete reversal of the true position, and Brebner has written: 'In using Bentham as the archetype of British individualism he was conveying the exact opposite of the truth. Jeremy Bentham was the archetype of British collectivism.'[19] This view is perhaps compounded with the same error as Dicey's in seeing collectivism and individualism as mutually exclusive alternatives, for in practice there were elements of both in any utilitarian approach. The question was what the proportions ought to be in any given case; it was all a matter of balance.

Given the assumption (strongly supported by Dr Parris) that Benthamite utilitarianism could be a mixture of collectivism and individualism, we may go further along this line of argument and, using Professor Perkin's terminology, say that there was a synthesis of the entrepreneurial and professional ideals. The former corresponded broadly to the self-help philosophy already described, the latter involved the professionalisation of government, the accumulation of expertise, the solution of problems by the application of reason and the creation of an administrative state. It was in the field of social policy that the tension between the two concepts stretched to breaking-point. The origin of this lay in the nature of the social philosophy itself, with its conflict between the *natural* harmony of interests (Smith's view) and the need in certain circumstances to create, by intervention, an *artificial* harmony (Bentham's view). Hence in this case the paradox of the creation of an administrative state in the period described by Dicey as one of Benthamite individualism may be resolved, assuming a process whereby the inherent contradictions of utilitarian philosophy were worked out by an application of the components (individualism and collectivism) in proportions which varied according to circumstance. The crucial point here is that intervention or *laissez-faire* could be equally Benthamite depending on the context. Here there is no conflict between theory and practice but simply a varying of emphasis within the same theory.

These three explanations are in some way concerned with Benthamite theory and its implications, but in the fourth, the so-called MacDonagh model, Benthamism has no central role. Professor MacDonagh's study of the Government's growing involvement with emigration and shipping in the first half of the nineteenth century produced a five-stage model of Government growth.[20] The first stage involved the revelation of some 'intolerable' evil (such as children in mines or emigrants exploited at sea) which, it was assumed, could be legislated out of existence by a prohibitory Act. The second stage involved the realisation of the ineffectiveness of the initial legislation and its replacement with new legislation involving the use of inspectors for enforcement. Third, the momentum created by a body of professionals familiar with the problems (as most MPs were not) led to a growing centralisation and superintendence by some central agency. Fourth, the growth of professional expertise among the administrators brought an awareness that the problems could not be swept away by some magnificent all-embracing gesture but would require continuous slow regulation and re-regulation. Finally, the bureaucratic machine pursued research and brought in scientific aids to produce adequate preventive measures which passed almost unnoticed into law. A self-generating mechanism gave to the administrators discretionary executive powers typical of modern bureaucracy.

MacDonagh's thesis centred on two main principles, the pressure of intolerable facts and an inherent administrative momentum, and these two also figured strongly in Professor Roberts's picture, which saw the administrative development of the 1830s and

1840s as the true origin of the British Welfare State.[21] In neither of these pictures was Benthamism more than incidental to the process, and this initiated a debate among the academics which to some extent became a semantic discussion over what was meant by the term 'Benthamite'. Are we talking of people who had read Bentham, or his followers, or who were influenced directly or indirectly by him or them, or who had even heard of Bentham? Furthermore, as we have already seen, there is a considerable area of disagreement about what Benthamism stood for. The other point in the debate concerns the significance of the five-stage model, which has been attacked especially by Dr Parris, who substitutes another of his own, which is essentially based on the concept of Benthamism as a mixture of *laissez-faire* and intervention (the third explanation discussed above).[22] In particular, it has been argued that MacDonagh's model breaks down when examining other areas of social policy either because men had not in fact learnt from experience or because, without giving themselves time, men plumped for inspection anyway (as, it may be added, it was an obvious utilitarian device). While it is clear that the model derives from the Passenger Acts and does not therefore fit all situations, there is nevertheless much of value in the basic concepts involved. Even Dr Parris admits the importance of executive officers playing a leading role in the process of further legislation and in the extension of their own powers, and many other historians have accepted some version of the administrative momentum idea.

Indeed the fifth of our explanations takes the MacDonagh–Roberts approach a stage further by arguing that the evolving administrative state had little to do with concepts of collectivism and individualism (terms which contemporaries did not widely use) but with the conflict between two views of the role of government, a traditional and a so-called incrementalist view. It has been recently suggested by Dr Lubenow[23] that, assuming the existence of intolerable evils, either created or exacerbated by industrialisation, then the response of the state was conditioned by these two models of government. In his view what we are looking at was not a sort of Victorian Welfare State but a modification of existing administrative practice on the basis of a compromise between local and central government. Opposition to these changes derived not from individualism but from historical and legal assumptions about the English Constitution, and support for them was not Benthamite in origin but stemmed from the revelation of intolerable evils.

By studying opinion, mainly in Parliament, on four issues – the Poor Law, public health, railways and the factory question – Dr Lubenow concludes that men saw the problems very differently from the way in which historians analyse them. There was here a conflict not between theory and practice nor between collectivism and individualism but between these two models of government. The traditional model put great faith in the historic rights and customs enshrined in the past practice of English government, with prime emphasis on local self-government. It assumed, therefore, an attack via a growing centralisation upon the traditional freedom of English institutions. The incrementalist model faced up to the new problems not with any clear-cut, predetermined programme of action (Benthamite or otherwise), but hesitantly and empirically. As knowledge increased so the approach changed: it was admittedly a continual choice between options of only marginal value. This mode of analysis as before is strong on certain areas but weak on others. It was in the field of public health that this picture has most relevance; in the Poor Law it has less and in the railways and factory question the facts are fitted forcibly in an unconvincing way. However, this approach does highlight the importance of localism in the growth of an administrative state and the enormous variety of opinion on this problem.

It was by a very complex process that social policy gave birth to the Victorian administrative state and, as we have seen, the collective views of historians are nearly as complicated. In order to attempt to pull some of these ideas together it is worth highlighting four characteristics of the developments in social policy in the mid-nineteenth century. First, any explanation which does not emphasise the practical, pragmatic, unplanned, *ad hoc* response of the state is in a major respect deficient. It cannot be overemphasised that social policies and their administration were geared to meet real and pressing problems, not to breathe life into some abstract theory or to satisfy some metaphysical whim. It was the pressure of facts, and unpalatable ones at that, which produced unexpected and (by most) undesired administrative growth. The whole spirit of the age was geared to the accumulation of facts, for society had an insatiable appetite for knowledge of itself, with the mushrooming of statistical societies and surveys both by Government and private agency. It was the practical man's approach to life to deal in facts; to quote Dickens's *Hard Times* again: 'Now, what I want is, Facts. Teach these boys and girls nothing but Facts. Facts alone are wanted in life. Plant nothing else and root out everything else. You can only form the minds of reasoning animals upon Facts.... Stick to Facts, Sir.'[24]

It was in facing up to very real human practical problems that men devised the administrative expedients necessary to cope with the deficiencies of an ever more complex competitive society. Children working long hours, able-bodied males unemployed, women dying in childbirth, foetid cesspools and sewers, desperately dangerous mines, ships or railways, adulterated food, the scourge of smallpox, these and many more were the practical facts of life with which early Victorian society had come to terms. Just as the varied allowance system of the Poor Law had evolved to meet the practical problem of low wages, so the continuance of outdoor relief and the growth of Poor Law medical services were a response to the real world which faced the guardians. The social problems consequent upon industrialisation were the origin of that administrative state which few anticipated or at heart wished for.

The second important characteristic of the attempted solution to these problems of social administration was the essential relationship between central and local government. Especially, though not exclusively, in the field of public health, the problem was not whether the state should act, but by what agency. Centralisation was in many respects an evil to be feared more than the insanitary conditions which required immediate action, and a Liberal editor asked whether the people should 'quietly stand by while the municipal institutions – the boast, the characteristic of England and the bulwark of her liberties – are offered up a holocaust on the altar of that newest of idols – centralisation?'[25] It was in defence of municipal authority that most anti-centralisation feeling was expressed, yet there were important implications for the whole field of local government, rural as well as urban. Charles Wood warned of the likely consequences of centralisation:

This tendency is most dangerous. We have hitherto been for the most part locally governed. Responsibility had been very much distributed; ... This is . . . the black cloud on the horizon, that we are gradually approaching the state of Continental countries where the government is responsible for everything, for whatever goes wrong the government is blamed. That which twenty years ago might have changed a parish vestry may change a ministry and the nation be involved in difficulty from some petty local grievance. I am against doing anything to forward this tendency. If country gentlemen are not to have some power and responsibility, they will not act.[26]

If centralisation superseded the power of the local amateurs who sat on the bench, acted as councillors, aldermen, guardians, surveyors and commissioners, then real local government would disappear. Hence the characteristic development in social policy was for the state to grant first permissive and then obligatory powers to local agencies for the enforcement of regulations. Sometimes, as the later years of the Local Government Act Office showed, initiative came from the local level, but as in police and public health questions, central supervision, inspiration and inspection with local executive action was the normal rule until the latter part of the nineteenth century. As the evidence from the Poor Law shows, even when centralisation was apparently intended there was a great deal of local initiative which could in fact run against specific legislative direction. This balance between central and local was highly regarded by many contemporaries, for as Mill wrote: 'The principal business of the central authority should be to give instruction, of the local authority to apply it. Power may be localised, but knowledge, to be most useful, must be centralised.'[27]

If there was an alliance between central and local government where it was generally agreed there ought to be intervention, there was also, third, an alliance of voluntary and state action where greater doubt existed. Because these problems were so new, because there were in fact no clear guidelines as to action, men held very ambivalent views on the same issue and were often inconsistent between what we might deem similar issues. The analysis of division lists in the House of Commons shows that men did not vote the same way on all social policy questions. Social policy cut right across normal party lines and a whole range of personal and political factors could affect men's views. As we saw in the chapter on public health, paternalistic Tories switched from a public to a private scheme for water supply when it was realised that all the power and patronage would go to the local Liberals. Provincial Nonconformists might oppose centralisation as a blow against a London-based Anglican establishment; university-educated clergymen might support inspection because they hoped to land some of the posts.

We tend to see state intervention as a step forward, but to some it was a means of shrugging off individual responsibilities:

> Men who find their duties to the public interfere somewhat inconveniently with their selfish purposes club together and ask government to relieve them of obligations they would fain get rid of. All they want is to be left at liberty to acquire wealth or to employ it without being burdened with the heavy responsibilities which its possession involves.[28]

On this argument individuals were wrongly shifting their responsibilities on to the community, yet others could say that the reverse process was equally reprehensible. Thus in the case of dispensaries maintained by philanthropic individuals, Lord Clarendon wrote: 'It is the duty of the whole of the parish adequately to provide for the life and recovery of the poor in the case of sickness. . . . If the dispensaries are so constituted as to shift this burden from the whole parish and imposing it only on those who are charitably disposed . . . they are insomuch objectionable.'[29]

The only answer was to combine voluntary and state action, and many felt that this compromise was the only way progress could have been made. A society of doctors in favour of a free health service was forced to admit in 1840: 'The public mind is not yet prepared for the national provision of medical relief, or of its necessary consequence – the "establishment" of a profession in connexion with the state', and the voluntary/state compromise in education was described by the *Quarterly Review* in 1861 as 'the only scheme that could have been introduced into our free, tolerant, dissentient and jealous country'. So the elementary schools, dispensaries, hospitals and reformatories of Victorian England were examples of state-aided, state-supervised private philanthropy. One might add that much state action resulted from some private initiative by individuals agitating in the cause of social policy.

Once the state had stepped in, there can be no doubt that there was a vital element of self-generating administrative momentum. This is the fourth important characteristic, and we do not necessarily have to go all the way with MacDonagh's rejection of Benthamite influence or with Roberts's identification of the origins of the Welfare State to recognise the significance of administrative growth *per se*. As we have seen, the definition of Benthamism was elastic and Senior did state that 'The only rational foundation of government...is expediency – the general benefit of the community. It is the duty of a government to do whatever is conducive to the welfare of the governed.' Critics of the growth of state activity were right to scorn a definition like that under which all things were possible.

At the same time neither Benthamism nor individualism (if they were opposites) could provide universal solutions neatly packaged and ready for use. In this essentially pragmatic approach, the evidence had first to be accumulated; inquiry had to precede action. Even men who had no notion of Benthamism were unconsciously following a Benthamite methodology by a process of inference which elicited a course of action from an impartial review of the evidence. This method of advancing meant that at the point of departure people rarely knew their destination, which was itself constantly shifting. We need only compare the work of Chadwick and Simon in public health to see that both an avowed Benthamite and a non-Benthamite could be led to support state action far beyond the initial intention; Chadwick by becoming fully aware of the problem, Simon by discovering in practice that state regulation would not work properly without compulsion.

Once men came face to face with the complexity of the problems, the vested interests and social and political ideologies involved, they soon lost their faith in heroic sudden charges upon a clearly defined and exposed enemy. Implicit in this trial-and-error, learn-from-experience approach was an element of the blind leading the blind, as one keen interventionist admitted in the *Edinburgh Review* in 1846:

> They do not disguise from themselves the uncertainty and risk which attend all political and social reformations. They are aware of the blindness even of the most keensighted when the future is concerned. They admit that society advances by groping its way in the dark, like miners exploring a vein. But they can discover no other mode of social progress, and they believe that experience, the only light, points steadily in this direction.[30]

If interventionists were like miners groping in the dark, what we can say is that the Benthamites had lamps in their helmets, they had some idea where they were going. The forms used in this process of administrative growth were Benthamite: the use of Commissions to investigate, action based upon inquiry, professional experts to enforce the legislation and advise upon further developments.

Moreover, in the mid-Victorian period there emerged a powerful and influential forum, the Social Science Association, which brought together the expert opinion from which social legislation could evolve. John Stuart Mill saw the body as an association for social improvement and as 'a means of gaining adhesions to important practical suggestions fitted for immediate adoption'. Another prominent member, Edwin Chadwick, identified the Association's key role in bringing together 'persons who give their attention to special subjects as sanitarians, educationalists, law reformers and political economists'.[31]

The crucial point was that whether the bureaucracy was set up consciously as a Benthamite device or was even composed of officials imbued with Benthamism was less important than the fact that men who were professionally involved in these problems were of necessity agents of spontaneous growth. To start with, many of the inspectors were appointed because of their prior expertise in the area concerned. Men like Horner and Kay-Shuttleworth were prepared to use their positions as propagandists and were not, at least at first, restricted by the constraints upon a modern civil servant. Nor was the impact of this spontaneous growth restricted to one department. The establishment of the Poor Law Commission led, through the work of Chadwick, to the illumination of the public health problem, and the office of the Registrar-General generated mountains of social statistics on a wide range of subjects. Inspectors could exercise enormous personal powers, for instance where grants were involved, and school, prison and police inspectors had wide discretionary authority. Whether acknowledged by Parliament or not, delegated legislation was involved here, so that the Committee of the Privy Council for Education, for example, itself appointed by Order in Council and not specific Parliamentary authority, was able to make new rules simply by issuing minutes which were laid on the table of the House of Commons. Above all, the inspectors, by their very familiarity with the problems themselves and the response of interested parties to the regulations, were uniquely equipped to provide the basis for future, more effective legislation. The bureaucracy was the means by which the Government learnt by the very act of governing: Horner's work on the 1847 Factory Act or Simon's draft of the 1866 Sanitary Act were only two examples of many where administrative feedback generated a new and deeper level of state involvement. Once professionals were appointed there existed the nucleus of an establishment with the power of self-generative growth. This is exactly what Lowe feared with regard to education:

> The great danger is that the grant for Education may become a grant to maintain the so-called vested interest of those engaged in education. . . . If Parliament does not set a limit to this evil, such a state of things will arise that the conduct of the Educational system will pass out of the hands of the Privy Council and the House of Commons into the hands of the persons working that educational system, and then no demand they choose to make on the public purse would any Ministry dare to refuse.[32]

It was not sheer selfish bloody-mindedness that caused a bureaucracy to grow and attract greater powers, but a growing realisation of how much needed to be done to create that real state of equal opportunity in which meaningful natural liberty could flourish. Contracts between individuals could not be freely negotiated by equals where the dice were loaded all one way, as between a factory owner and a child employee. Wherever the self-interest of one person was incompatible with the self-interest of another, wherever (as the contemporary play on words had it) the rights of property became the wrongs of the poor, then there was a case for intervention to create the very conditions in which mutual self-help and competition could freely operate. *Laissez-faire* was not so much a coherent philosophy as a widely held, deeply felt aspiration that ought, in the best of all possible worlds, to be the ideal. The onus of proof, so to speak, was on the prosecution, those who challenged the ideal and claimed it to be inappropriate. Where a case was made out – and invariably Parliament did not move until some private or official body did substantiate a case – then with a doleful glance *back* at the promised land of *laissez-faire*, the state was prepared to embark on a journey which eventually led to a centralised administrative state. Gradually various groups were officially exempted from the full rigours of self-help – paupers, child labourers, women workers, lunatics and so on.

But for the rest, and even for some of these in need, Victorians hoped that private philanthropy would render the necessary temporary palliatives. In a sense the efficacy of private charity was the main Victorian bulwark against a totally collectivist approach. Once charity was found to be ultimately inadequate to meet the pressures placed upon it, then the floodgates opened and the collectivist tide flowed in.

6

The growing awareness of poverty

I Victorian philanthropy and the Charity Organisation Society

It was clear even to the most assiduous upholder of the individualist ethic that not everybody was able to practise the virtues of self-help or to benefit by them all the time. John Stuart Mill's gradual conversion from a strict Benthamite individualism to a near-socialism was evidence of an intellectual's acceptance of the limitations in practice of a theoretically justifiable credo. It was all too easy to assume, like one of Dickens's self-made masters, that everyone could make £60,000 out of 6d.; that, in the words of Matthew Arnold, 'You have only to get on the back of your horse Freedom . . . and to ride away as hard as you can, to be sure of coming to the right destination.' As a perceptive cultural historian has remarked, 'Although Victorian didactic literature constantly insists on the necessity of self-help, one of the dominant themes of a major tradition within Victorian fiction is *the powerlessness of the individual*.'[1] Writers such as Mill and Thomas Carlyle exposed the paradox that, though a more egalitarian and democratic society might be emerging, the individual was becoming increasingly absorbed in the mass, losing identity and purpose. The Victorian response to the powerlessness (or, as it was often conceived, moral weakness) of the individual was an over-liberal dose of charity. The phenomenal variety and range of Victorian philanthropy was at once confirmation of the limitless benevolence of a generation and implicit condemnation of the notion of self-help for all.

It was small wonder that self-congratulation was so common a theme in contemporary surveys of Victorian philanthropy. So many different good causes were catered for – stray dogs, stray children, fallen women and drunken men; there was apparently no subject which could not arouse the philanthropic urge of the Victorian public. This produced an impressive growth in charities in the nineteenth century. One survey of London estimated that in 1861 there were no fewer than 640 charitable institutions, of which nearly half had been founded in the first half of the nineteenth century and 144 in the decade from 1850. London charities had an annual income of £2.5 million, and though this underestimates the full amount by not including private individual charity, it still exceeded the amount spent by Poor Law authorities in the capital. Public assistance through the Poor Law was thus accommodating only part of the public's need for help.

To list some of the areas of charitable activity indicates the scope of Victorian philanthropy. To start with, practically every denomination had its own 'benevolent' society to cater for its own poor. Anglicans, Non-conformists and Roman Catholics all maintained their own charitable funds and in 1859 the significantly named Jewish Board of Guardians was set up, a sort of sectarian Poor Law within the Poor Law. These religious denominations were often the source of temporary charities in times of economic distress, either national or local. An interesting development in the nineteenth century was the growth of visiting societies, an attempt to bridge the gap between the so-called 'Two Nations' by personal contact. Many of these were denominationally based and the most famous, the Metropolitan Visiting and Relief Association launched in 1843, was an Anglican charity led by Bishop Blomfield. These visiting societies made a positive effort to go out and see needy people in their own homes, while other charities were seeking to provide a sort of refuge for the needy. Charity schools, hospitals, dispensaries, asylums, orphanages, reformatories and penitential homes for prostitutes were examples of this sort and they were multiplied throughout the country.

Many housing charities such as the Peabody Trust sought to provide cheap homes for the working classes, but these tended to accommodate those in work and it was only Octavia Hill's housing experiments which really reached the destitute. There is an interesting parallel between her and Mary Carpenter, since both were aiming at those at the very bottom of society. Both saw the deficiencies of existing charities for the people they wished to help: schools and some charitably maintained houses were available for the poor, but these did not cope with the 'perishing classes', hence Mary Carpenter's ragged schools and Octavia Hill's housing settlements. From the nineteenth century date many of the charities for distressed gentlefolk, those formerly independent but now fallen on hard times, and the best known in this category was the National Benevolent Institution which granted pensions to needy gentlemen or members of professions. Many very famous charities date from this period, the RSPCA, the YMCA, Dr Barnardo's, the Salvation Army and the RNLI, the latter of which is to this day a vigorous defender of voluntary as opposed to state action. To this list could be added all sorts of street, missionary and Bible societies, while the temperance, anti-slavery and Sabbatarian organisations were at once charities and political pressure groups. One might well inquire what motivated such a torrent of charity raining down upon the poor. It would appear that charity was the response to four types of motivation: a fear of social revolution, a humanitarian concern for suffering, a satisfaction of some psychological or social need and a desire to improve the moral tone of the recipients.

Underlying much Victorian willingness to support charitable enterprises was a genuine and persistent fear of social revolution. Symbolic gestures in defence of property in times of tension, such as the enrolling of middle-class special constables in the Chartist crisis of 1848, were less common than the steady and consistent middle-class patronage of charities which would lift the masses from the depths of despair. The most frequent image used was that the *bonds* of society would snap under the strain of abject misery and deprivation. In order to prevent an assault upon the whole basis of society and the division of wealth within it, men were prepared, almost as an insurance against social revolution, to siphon off some of their wealth for use by those in need. Perhaps most were confident that the misery of the poor was temporary and that these charities were, in effect, a tiding-over process, yet even in the relatively prosperous mid-Victorian period the charities persisted, for the tension was never far below the surface. As Gladstone reminded a critic of his policies, 'Please to recollect that we have got to govern millions of hard hands; that it must be done by force, fraud or goodwill; that the latter has been tried and is answering'.[2] The goodwill could be fostered either by benevolent legislation to which Gladstone referred or by philanthropic benevolence which would show that both Parliament and the social groups which dominated it were genuinely concerned with those outside the pale.

Of course there is no reason to doubt that many Victorians were genuinely concerned for suffering and that this motivated their philanthropy. Again, deriving from the Evangelicals of the previous generation, there was a society-wide increase in sensitivity to the suffering of others. Charity was a Christian virtue and many in the nineteenth century were moved to try and save souls in the belief that, as Andrew Reed, with a lifelong concern for orphans and lunatics, put it, 'the Divine image is stamped upon all'. In the course of the Victorian period the emphasis shifted from man serving God to man serving his fellow-man. Especially in the latter part of the nineteenth century much religious activity came to be socially oriented, religion became imbued with an essentially social conscience. The Christian Socialists F. D. Maurice and Charles Kingsley were examples here. What had occurred was, in Beatrice Webb's phrase, 'the transference of the emotion of self-sacrificing from God to man...the impulse of self-subordinating service was transferred consciously and overtly, from God to man'.[3] The desire from a religious motive to help desperate and deprived individuals such as orphans, climbing boys, tramps, drunks, prostitutes and lunatics was an important stimulus to Victorian philanthropy.

At the same time, charity often helped the donor as much as the recipient. A humanitarian religious concern for the consequences of poverty could be closely allied with self-conscious guilt-complexes about the possession of wealth. Conscience money well describes the contribution of many for whom the sight of beggars in the street evoked a sense of personal pain. This was not restricted to individuals, for there was what Beatrice Webb called 'the class consciousness of sin' which permeated the middle class as a whole. Charity often satisfied some emotional deficiency perhaps caused by a bereavement or a childless marriage, and it has been argued that Gladstone's charitable work was a means of overcoming internal tension. For many a leisured (and perhaps bored) wife or spinster, charity had its recreational and creative aspects. It could be a very satisfying personal experience and, as one titled lady recalled after a touching deathbed reunion with an old man she had been visiting, 'These little incidents make "slumming" a real pleasure. One can give so much happiness with so little trouble.'[4]

Psychological or emotional motives merged into social motives. There was a good deal of *noblesse oblige* about much Victorian philanthropy, a social duty which had to be done and seen to be done. Charitable activity was imbued with social snobbery and a royal patron could considerably enhance any society's prospects. The published subscription list was a very fruitful stimulus to increased contributions, as people could reflect smugly on their own offerings and scorn the parsimony of their neighbours. A degree of social mobility and ambition was bound up with charitable work, as men mixed with their social superiors on the endless committees and at the many social functions. Charity, in short, assumed the guise of a fashionable social imperative beautifully caricatured by a Liverpool satirist:

> The most fashionable amusement of the present age is philanthropy.... We have the religious philanthropists, the social and moral philanthropists, the scientific philanthropists. Everyone who stands in need of the smallest assistance or advice from his neighbour, and a great many who do not, must become the pet or prey of some one or all of those benevolent classes... because [philanthropy]... elevates you, don't you see – makes you a patron and a condescending magnate and all that.... Take up Social Science as nineteen twentieths of Liverpool folk do, as something which makes a shopkeeper hail-fellow with a lord and flatters an alderman into believing himself a philosopher.[5]

The whole concept of charity presupposed a class of superior wealth with the means to dispense bounties, and in the Victorian period it equally presupposed a class of superior attitudes and values. Charity was a means of social control, an avenue for the inculcation of sound middle-class values, and the widespread practice of visiting was in effect a cultural assault upon the working-class way of life. Few saw poverty and its consequences as a function of the economic and social system. The majority assumed, as in the spirit of 1834, that poverty stemmed from some personal failing. Hence charity was a way of initiating a moral reformation, of breeding in the individual the self-help mentality which would free him from the thraldom of poverty. This aim was quite explicit in Victorian philanthropy. The constitution of the Metropolitan Visiting and Relief Association stated the aims of the society, which included the 'removal of the moral causes which create or aggravate want; to encourage prudence, industry and cleanliness'. Octavia Hill told the Royal Commission on the Housing of the Working Classes that rather than improving old houses she was 'improving tenants in old houses', and while admitting that her rule was a despotic one she added: 'It is exercised with a view of bringing out the powers of the people and treating them as responsible for themselves within certain limits.' The idea of philanthropy as an essentially educative tool was best expressed by the casework pioneer C. S. Loch: 'Charity is a social regenerator. ...We have to use charity to create the power of self-help.'[6] This attempt to employ charity as a way of spreading the self-help philosophy and of combating revolutionary ideas (the first of the four motives discussed above) provided a built-in method of validating the efficacy of philanthropic activities. Thus the complacency of one group of Vitorian philanthropists was shattered when, in the middle of a subscription to provide relief from the distress of 1839–40, an unemployed workman proclaimed that the hungry were entitled to take bread where they could find it. It appeared that something had gone terribly wrong, since charity was supposed to produce deferential and grateful men imbued with a desire to profit by industry and initiative, not by spoliation. Increasingly in the mid-Victorian period, doubts were expressed about how effective the multifarious charities really were. In particular these doubts crystallised into two main accusations, that the charities had a built-in inefficiency and that charity was, like the old Poor Law, counterproductive, helping to promote that very poverty it sought to alleviate.

The inefficiency of much Victorian philanthropy was in many ways an inevitable consequence of the stupendous growth in the number of charities themselves. There was a great deal of duplication of effort and much wasteful competition between rival groups in the same cause. The multiplicity of charities produced small vested interests which made active co-operation difficult. There was sometimes conflict between London and the provinces in national organisations, and the same Church versus Dissent antagonism which characterised Victorian politics plagued Victorian philanthropy. This could cause dissension in well-meaning attempts at interdenominational combined efforts; for instance, in Leeds in 1840 a benevolent fund had to be divided *pro rata* and disbursed separately to Anglican and Nonconformist applicants. There was little inquiry or research into the real needs of recipients and nobody in the breathless activity of collecting and spending funds had time to work out an order of priorities. Given the haphazard development of charities, it is hardly surprising that some good causes were over-patronised and others completely ignored. The very structure of Victorian philanthropy meant that not all the money collected actually reached the poor. Apart from the increasing number of charity frauds, the splendid dinners and balls, the impressive buildings for headquarters, the ostentatious propaganda and advertisements all resulted in an increase of 'necessary' expenses and a reduction of the funds to be disbursed.

Some rationalisation might have reduced inefficiency, but the way in which charity contributed to the very problems it sought to remove was far more serious. The lack of co-operation between the charities meant that multiple applications for relief were quite common, which encouraged indiscriminate dispensing of funds. The availability of such money did little to encourage thrift or self-help among those aided and, as a professor of political economy put it, 'One chief cause of poverty is that too much is done for those who make no proper effort to help themselves and thus improvidence in its various forms is encouraged',[7] while the *Westminster Review* pontificated: 'It is as dangerous to practise charity as to practise physic without a diploma.' The historian J. R. Green looked with dismay on the growth of benevolent funds in the East End of London: 'A hundred different agencies for the relief of distress are at work over the same ground, without concert or co-operation or the slightest information as to each other's exertions. The result is an unparalleled growth of imposition, mendicancy and sheer shameless pauperism.'[8] From a Manchester writer came similar views:

> The number and extent of our charitable institutions and the large amount of indiscriminate relief are a growing evil. If habits of self-respect and an honest pride of independence are the safeguard of the working classes and a barrier against inroads of pauperism it will follow that any public institutions which lead them directly or indirectly to depend upon the bounty of others in times of poverty or sickness and which tend to encourage idleness and improvidence are not public charities but public evils.[9]

The whole concept of charity was one that tended to degrade rather than uplift the recipient and, as Lovett once remarked, 'Charity, by diminishing the energies of self-dependence, creates a spirit of hypocrisy and servility.'[10] It therefore required a careful, thoughtful approach to compensate for these characteristics, and Victorian philanthropy was most unscientific in its methods. This was in itself one of the evils complained of, for, as Loch explained when comparing charities with lighthouses, they had not been 'placed with care precisely on those points of the dangerous coastline of pauperism, where their lights will save from shipwreck the greatest number of distressed passers by'.[11]

It was this sort of deficiency which the Charity Organisation Society (COS), begun in 1869, was hoping to remedy. Broadly, it aimed to put the charities of London on a more sensible footing by defining proper areas of competence, to devise and execute scientific methods of social casework and to educate and reform the recipients of charity so that they might become once more independent, self-respecting individuals. It is important to make a distinction between the social casework of the COS and the social philosophy which underlay it. In method the COS was a pioneering body which was of great significance in the development of professional social casework in the nineteenth century. The social philosophy of the COS was rigorously traditional and the COS became one of the staunchest defenders of the self-help individualist ethic long after it had been challenged on all sides. The essential duality of the COS was then that it was professionally pioneering but ideologically reactionary.

To the early leaders, however, there was no paradoxical duality. Charles Bosanquet, Edward Denison, Octavia Hill and above all C. S. Loch (secretary from 1875 down to 1913) all believed that the casework methods devised should be geared to the moral improvement of the poor; that was the real purpose of charity. Neither this moral reformation (which would suppress mendicity) nor the organisation of London's charities (which would reduce the unsystematic philanthropic chaos) could take place unless there was adequate inquiry into the background of applicants for relief. All charities had to be on their guard against fraudulent applicants, but the very thought of applying for help, the act of supplication, was itself so degrading a prospect for the dispensers of charity that it was generally assumed that the humbling experience of asking for succour was adequate proof of the *bona fide* nature of the applicant. This, for the COS, was the reason for indiscriminate charity, which would cease only when every applicant was vetted. A proper systematic investigation by personal contact was the seed from which all else would grow; it was the very foundations on which the COS was built.

The basic method of personal inquiry and follow-up was by no means original. The visiting system had originated in Hamburg in the eighteenth century, and from Germany had also come the Elberfeld system which also involved visiting and reporting. In Britain the pioneer had been Thomas Chalmers, a Glasgow Free Churchman, whose parish organisation of 1819 used investigators. Chalmers's work was a definite inspiration to the COS, while Bishop Blomfield's visiting society (mentioned earlier) also developed a reporting system. Despite all these precursors it was the COS which developed casework fully as a professional activity by its insistence on rigorous inquiry into the nature of the problems facing applicants and their families. Theirs was a stern approach, being one of the few charities that would actually turn people away if they had been put in the 'undeserving' category. Completely lost souls – the alcoholic, the chronic idler or the totally depraved (perhaps in modern casework those most needy) – were rejected as being hopeless cases immune to the medicine which the COS could administer. They had no interest in a man whose 'condition is due to improvidence or thriftlessness and there is no hope of being able to make him independent in the future';[12] their ideal client was the person in whom the seed of self-help and independence could be nurtured. Cash payments were appropriate as a temporary measure so long as they were followed by positive signs of moral improvement. Hence a typical COS benefit was for a widow to be given a mangle so that she could take in washing, for, as Loch had said, 'We must use charity to create the power of self-help'. The COS approach was in line with a late twentieth-century anti-famine slogan: 'Don't give him a fish – teach him how to fish.'

The belief in self-help as the supreme virtue, coupled with the notion that most poverty was the result of personal failing, was central to the COS outlook. Massive philanthropic state help was not only unnecessary but, as Samuel Smiles would have said, was 'positively enfeebling'. The normal contingencies of a normal working-class life – illness, unemployment, old age – were predictable and hence could be anticipated. Provision ought to be made for such normal interruptions of earnings by a man himself, and where the distress was too great then the COS was ready to step in. (Document 6A.) In the wider contemporary debate about poverty Loch and his colleagues firmly supported two propositions: first, that poverty was avoidable through personal initiative and was not a consequence of the social and economic system; and second, that the extent of poverty was well within the capability of voluntary philanthropic effort which precluded the need for any large-scale state intervention. At the very time when the COS was building up its strength, those propositions came under severe attack. The COS approach was well summarised by the organisation's most recent historian, Jane Lewis:

> The objects of COS were to improve the condition of the poor by co-operating with the poor law, to repress mendicity, to investigate and effectively assist the deserving and to promote good habits. Above all the aim of COS was to restore the deserving to 'self-maintenance', so that they became capable of engaging in market exchange and participating fully in civil society.[13]

She has also explained that the COS was not a monolithic organisation and that some its leaders, such as Helen Bosanquet, did support a form of 'social collectivism'.

II Poverty revealed

In the midst of the growing concern over poverty in the 1880s the *Illustrated London News* remarked that 'Recent *revelations* as to the misery of the abject poor have profoundly touched the heart of the nation'.[14] The crucial word is that italicised here – revelations – for there was a very real sense of society forcibly being made aware of unknown conditions within it. In the ferment of ideas which wellnigh overwhelmed the *laissez-faire*, individualist ethic in the last quarter of the nineteenth century there was no more crucial element than this growing awareness of poverty, caused by the attention focused upon it. At first sight this is difficult to understand, for there had been a good deal of prior propaganda on this subject. As we have seen, Chadwick was instrumental in arousing a similar public indignation four decades earlier, and in the first half of the nineteenth century there had been a host of novelists – Dickens, Disraeli, Kingsley, Mrs Gaskell and others – who had exposed the poverty-stricken conditions of the new society. Above all, if factual reporting was required to stimulate this interest then this had already been provided by Henry Mayhew in the mid-Victorian years. Mayhew, a London journalist, had written a series of articles in the *Morning Chronicle* following investigations made by him, and a selection of these was published in 1851 under the title *London Labour and the London Poor* and reissued a decade later. Mayhew described the people in his book as 'a large body of persons of whom the public had less knowledge than of the most distant tribes of the earth', and one review of the book commented that it 'is full of facts entirely new; throws light where utter darkness has hitherto existed'. Despite this, the same sort of remarks accompanied the revelations of the 1880s. Somehow, partly by a process of 'podsnappery' ('I don't want to know about it') and partly by virtue of the seemingly infinite capacity of the economy to create wealth, the real facts of continuing poverty were obscured from a large part of the Victorian generation.

In the last twenty years of the century this changed, most decisively because from the late 1870s and particularly in the mid-1880s England's faith in unlimited economic progress was shattered by the so-called 'Great Depression'. Increased competition from the USA and Germany and a failure to innovate in strategically placed new industries such as chemicals and electrical engineering were the main factors which produced a depression of profits, prices and interest rates which undermined the confidence of both landed and commercial classes. Within the depression, usually dated from 1873 to 1896, there were also periods of very high unemployment which exacerbated the problem of chronic low wages and underemployment. The governing classes were concerned enough to appoint a Royal Commission in 1885 to inquire into the trade depression. There was clearly no reduction in national income and real wages rose, yet this was an economic climate in which the paradox of abject poverty in the midst of growing national wealth found a more inquiring and attentive audience. More people were forced to admit that a generation of self-help had not produced a better deal for all, for, in the words of a very famous book by the American Henry George, there had been progress *and* poverty.

The English publication of Henry George's *Progress and Poverty* in 1881 opened a period characterised by books and surveys which focused public attention on the problems of poverty and squalor, particularly in London. One of the most influential was a short pamphlet by a Congregationalist minister, Andrew Mearns, *The Bitter Cry of Outcast London* (1883), which in evocative and emotional language put the case of those forced to exist in the slums of London. It was a great blow in favour of the environmentalist case, pioneered by Chadwick, that the moral degradation of the poor was a *consequence* of their housing conditions and not the other way round; that, as Macaulay once remarked, if people are forced to live in hog-sties they eventually behave like hogs. Mearns was aided in his work by others, notably by another Congregationalist minister, William Preston (who claimed the authorship of the pamphlet), and his impact was heightened by the fact that W. T. Stead took up the cause of housing reform and sensationalised it in his *Pall Mall Gazette.* In the short term, the campaign produced a Royal Commission on Housing and, in the longer term, it further stimulated a religious and humanitarian concern for poverty. Similar work was done by the playwright and journalist G. R. Sims, whose articles on London's poor had appeared in the *Pictorial World* shortly before Mearns's pamphlet without creating the same impact. Later these were published as a book under the title *How the Poor Live and Horrible London* (1889), and Sims posed the contrast between the Imperial mission ('civilising the Zulu and the Egyptian fellah') and the destitution conveniently ignored at home. It was a paradox Oastler had first highlighted in 1830.

The same sort of image was evoked by William Booth, founder of the Salvation Army, whose *In Darkest England and the Way Out* (1890) claimed to be a sort of traveller's guide into the unknown parts of England (an obvious parody on contemporary guides to 'darkest Africa'). Like Mayhew forty years before, he wanted to expose to civilised Englishmen the conditions that existed in the midst of the wealthiest, most civilised, most Christian country in the world. Again, the environmentalist case was put in describing people such as 'The bastard of the harlot, born in a brothel, suckled on gin, and familiar from earliest infancy with all the bestialities of debauch, violated before she is twelve, and driven into the streets by her mother a year or two later, what chance is there for such a girl in this world – I say nothing about the next?'[15] Perhaps even more important was Booth's concept of the famous Cab Horse Charter with its two points: 'When he is down he is helped up and while he lives he has food, shelter and work.' As Booth commented, even this humble standard was beyond the reach of millions of human beings.

Booth's long-term answer was a sort of agricultural retraining programme and emigration; in the short term, he worked within the Salvation Army to make contact with the destitute to save bodies and eventually souls. This desire to go out and mix with the poor also characterised the university settlement movement which sprang up in the East End in the 1880s as an attempt to bridge the gap between rich and poor, so acutely mirrored by the juxtaposition of the East End and West End of London. Arnold Toynbee, a supporter of many reforming movements and the originator of the term 'industrial revolution', confessed to a working-class audience just before his death in 1883: 'We have neglected you; instead of justice we have offered you hard and unreal advice;...we have sinned against you grievously...but if you will forgive us...we will serve you, we will devote our lives to your service.'[16] It was, therefore, appropriate that the first settlement established in 1884 by Canon Samuel Barnett, himself a profound influence on late Victorian philanthropy and social work, should be given the title Toynbee Hall. The settlement movement spread and by the end of the century there were some thirty houses established in urban slums. They gave to a generation of young humanitarians invaluable personal contact with poverty and exposed to many the practical fallacies of the individualist ideology, now theoretically challenged by the philosopher T. H. Green.

The philosophy of idealism which Green promoted encouraged a more positive approach to state intervention rather than relying on the free market individualism. However, these were not seen as necessarily opposing forces. As Jose Harris explains, 'idealism strongly emphasised both the fundamental unity of state and society and the participation of private citizens in the larger social whole'. Hence, she argues, the growth of the state and the growth of the market responses to social and economic problems were inter-related. As the view gained hold that society was like a social organism subject to environmental and structural forces beyond the control of the individual, so matters previously considered private were now viewed as legitimate part of the 'public sphere'. This trend was reinforced when concerns over eugenics and demographic decline surfaced in the so-called 'national efficiency' movement. What later came to be called 'New Liberalism' had an authoritarian aspect, justifying intervention for the greater good of society. As one historian puts it, 'New Liberalism contained the potential for the tyranny of the minority'.[17]

Though in the 1880s there was this increased realisation that environment, social and physical, played so decisive a part in men's fortunes that they clearly could not control their destiny, yet at the same time nobody had any clear notion of how extensive this poverty was. The traditionalists of the COS had always acknowledged that men might need help via charity, but were convinced that the amount of poverty was limited and could be dealt with by private agency. The accumulated statistical evidence did not yet exist to disprove this contention, and it was in this ignorance that Charles Booth began his work. Booth, originally a Liverpool merchant, was concerned about the sensational reporting of individual cases of hardship and wished to know how typical these cases really were. As he later said:

> The lives of the poor lay hidden from view behind a curtain on which were painted terrible pictures: starving children, suffering women, overworked men; horrors of drunkenness and vice, monsters and demons of inhumanity; giants of disease and despair. Did these pictures truly represent what lay behind, or did they bear to the facts a relation similar to that which the pictures outside a booth at some country fair bear to the performance or show within?[18]

To search out the reality of poverty, to distinguish between the emotional superstructure and the statistical basis, was Booth's aim. He wished to put some meaningful quantified sense into the much-bandied term 'starving millions'.

Two pilot studies on Tower Hamlets in 1886 and East London and Hackney in 1887 showed that about one-third of the population lived at or below the 'poverty line', a concept invented by Booth himself. These surveys led on to the massive seventeen-volume *The Life and Labour of the People in London* which appeared in stages between 1889 and 1903. Essentially this was a tripartite work – a poverty series on budgets and causes of poverty, an industry series which dealt with comparative earnings in a trade inquiry, and a final and later seven-volume religious influence series which analysed the moral condition of the poor. Booth virtually had to invent his own social classifications and had to pioneer methods of social investigation; these achievements alone ensured him an important place in the history of social science. For contemporaries he provided the real statistics of poverty which were essential if sensible solutions were to be found, for, as he once pointed out, 'In intensity of feeling and not in statistics lies the power to move the world. But by statistics must this power be guided if it would move the world right.' Booth highlighted the problems of casual earnings and old age, but more importantly provided essential ammunition in the battle between voluntary and state aid. Booth's conclusion that some 30 per cent of London's population was living in poverty confirmed that the problem was far beyond the scope of private charitable benevolence. (Document 6B.) The notion of a submerged tenth which could be nursed through temporary difficulties by philanthropic individuals was replaced by one of a submerged third requiring massive state intervention.

There was perhaps some haziness in Booth's work on the concept of the poverty-line where this involved wasteful expenditure, and the COS was unwilling to believe that the 30 per cent figure was national, given London's exceptional circumstances. In both these respects Booth's work was built on by Seebohm Rowntree's survey of York, *Poverty: A Study of Town Life* (1901). Rowntree, a member of the cocoa and chocolate family, was inspired by Booth's survey and wished to see how far a small historic town would compare with the metropolis. His finding of 28 per cent in poverty was near enough to Booth's figure to suggest that approaching a third of the urban population of the whole country was living in poverty. Rowntree distinguished between primary poverty (where earnings were below subsistence) and secondary poverty (where earnings were above subsistence but expenditure was wasteful). (Document 6C.)

That Booth and Rowntree are discussed in harness, rather like other literary duets such as Marx and Engels, should not obscure important differences between them. Booth still considered some aspects of poverty primarily from a moralistic standpoint and his support for punitive treatment for the feckless by withdrawal into labour colonies was reminiscent of the embryonic concentration camps envisaged in Bentham's National Charity Company. Booth, then, stood at the end of an essentially Victorian tradition while Rowntree, an important influence upon twentieth-century social policy, was perhaps at the beginning of a more progressive line of thought. As well as identifying the existence of secondary poverty, Rowntree also exposed a cycle of poverty in a labourer's life, comprising 'five alternating periods of want and comparative plenty'. At three stages of working-class life poverty was highly likely to occur – in childhood, in the early years of marriage and child rearing, and in old age. It followed that women were likely to be in poverty throughout the whole of their child-bearing years. In order to illustrate this cycle, Rowntree devised a graph which showed the standard of living weaving above and below the poverty line and he used other innovative visual aids (such as pie-diagrams and histograms) to get his message across. In this way and because Rowntree's book was a single and more man-ageable volume than Booth's massive compendium, the York survey probably had a greater impact than the earlier one on London.

Together, these surveys provided the compelling statistical jus-tification for a more collectivist policy. Such a policy would have to take account of the growing acceptance that much poverty was the consequence of complex economic and social factors beyond the control of the individual. The nature of that policy would depend, as ever, upon the political arena.

III   Poverty and late Victorian politics

This growing public awareness of poverty was accompanied by important political developments which would, in the long term, ensure that the relief of poverty became a crucial political question. Parliamentary democracy had been brought appreciably nearer by the enfranchisement of urban workers in 1867 and of rural workers in 1884, and by the redistribution of seats in 1885, by which date most constituencies were single-member seats with electorates of roughly similar size. At last population was gaining the political influence previously reserved for property – numbers were beginning to count. The new situation was not lost on politicians, who realised that they needed to placate voters, not merely keep the unfranchised hordes out. Even Lord Salisbury, the Conservative Prime Minister denounced by Chamberlain as the leader of those 'who toil not neither do they spin', took up the cause of housing reform in the 1880s. Certainly he had a genuine interest in homes for the working class, but he also knew that housing was an issue dear to the hearts of the new electorate.

The new electorate was also assailed with specifically working-class propaganda, for the 1880s witnessed a revival of British socialism, now for the most part on a Marxist basis. Partly spawned by the depression of the 1880s, a variety of socialist groups were formed. Henry Hyndman, a wealthy intellectual, founded the Social Democratic Federation, an avowedly Marxist association whose most important recruit was the poet and artist William Morris. Morris was disturbed to find the extent of working-class hostility towards socialism, and he also found the irascibility and argumentativeness of his socialist colleagues unnerving. So in 1884 he and Marx's daughter, Eleanor, seceded to form the Socialist League, which was itself split by dissensions within a short period. Also in 1884 was founded the Fabian Society, which aimed to convert intellectuals by argument and propaganda to the socialist cause. It did not anticipate or support a sudden revolutionary explosion, preferring a gradualist approach within the existing governmental system. Fabians such as Sidney and Beatrice Webb and George Bernard Shaw believed that state socialism would come by degrees as government policy evolved to face practical difficulties. One of Hyndman's fundamental beliefs was that 'workers can never hope to gain anything unless they stand together for the interests of their class',[19] and there were important developments in both the economic and the political sphere which suggested that this was happening in the last years of the century. In 1868 the Trades Union Congress (TUC) had been formed and by the 1890s it had over a million members. Following the famous London dockers' strike of 1889, trade unionism spread to a large number of unskilled workers via the so-called 'new unionism'. There was a very real sense of labour organising itself into a separate interest in society which was soon reflected within the political system. The first two working-class MPs in 1874 had been Liberals sponsored by their unions; by the 1890s many were thinking of a separate working-class party, and the Independent Labour Party (ILP) was launched in Bradford in 1893 led by Keir Hardie. 1900 marks the birth of the Labour Party itself when the ILP, the Social Democratic Federation, the Fabians and the trade unions came together to form the Labour Representation Committee. This later took the title of the Labour Party, and within a quarter of a century it had produced a Labour Prime Minister and had replaced the Liberals as the alternative party to the Conservatives.

For the moment socialism and the organisation of labour represented a threat to the other two parties in view of the more democratic franchise that existed. Though socialists were an infinitesimal minority of the electorate they had an influence far beyond their numerical strength. On the one hand they provided a series of collectivist programmes from which the other parties could borrow policies (this was especially true of the Fabians), and on the other they provided the spectre of an ultimately socialist society which might eventuate if discontent with the existing order became excessive. Hence socialists became a sort of bogey-man to haunt the politicians and stimulate their social concern. British politics adopted an essentially Bismarckian stance by trying to use social policy as a means of undermining and heading off socialism itself. As A. J. Balfour, later a Conservative Prime Minister, put it just before the election campaign of 1895:

> Social legislation, as I conceive it, is not merely to be distinguished from Socialist legislation but it is its most direct opposite and its most effective antidote. Socialism will never get possession of the great body of public opinion ... among the working class or any other class if those who wield the collective forces of the community show themselves desirous to ameliorate every legitimate grievance and to put Society upon a proper and more solid basis.[20]

Hence both parties sponsored a mass of detailed legislation in the 1870s and 1880s which dealt, as we have already seen, with social problems. Public health, housing, education and working conditions all became issues of political importance following the widening of the franchise.

Yet though the extension of state intervention was impressive, it had appeared at one time that it would become even more important. Though Disraeli and Lord Randolph Churchill might try to make social reform an exclusively Conservative property, the politician who excited the public most on this question was the radical Liberal Joseph Chamberlain. Mayor of Birmingham from 1873 to 1875 when he pioneered a new civic gospel of town government, he had entered Parliament in 1876. He led the very powerful National Liberal Federation which championed the urban Liberal constituency organisations against the old Whig families which were still important in the Liberal Party. From 1880 to 1885 he was President of the Board of Trade in Gladstone's second ministry, and it was in these years that he really put himself at the head of the social reform movement. His famous criticism of Lord Salisbury has already been mentioned, and in that speech in 1883 he went on to point out that aristocratic fortunes had 'originated by grants made in times gone by for the services which courtiers had rendered kings and have since grown and increased, while they have slept, by levying an increased share on all that other men have done by toil and labour to add to the general wealth and prosperity of the country'.[21]

The generation that had been advised by Henry George that a simple land tax on the unearned increment in land values was the panacea was stunned by the attack from a Minister of the Crown on the inequalities of wealth consequent upon landownership. In 1885, Chamberlain went even further in a speech at Birmingham which attracted international attention when, while attacking property owners for depriving the rest of the nation of their historic rights, he posed the famous question: 'What ransom will property pay for the security which it enjoys? What substitute will it find for the natural rights which have ceased to be recognised?' During the election campaign of 1885, Chamberlain electrified audiences with his enthusiastic speeches for his so-called 'unauthorised programme' which would deal with the great evil of 'the excessive inequality in the distribution of riches'.

Here, indeed, appeared the possibility of a leading Minister conducting an assault upon capitalist society in the interests of the masses, and this was apparently confirmed by the so-called Chamberlain Circular of 1886. Following alarming riots by unemployed workers in London on 8 February 1886, in which there were indiscriminate attacks upon property, Chamberlain, as President of the Local Government Board in Gladstone's short-lived third ministry, issued a circular in March which authorised municipal schemes of public works to relieve unemployment. At last, under the excuse of an unusual depression, the state was prepared to allow that there were categories of people in need (i.e. the normally industrious) for whom the deterrent and degrading Poor Law was inappropriate. Chamberlain's Circular implicitly acknowledged that unemployment was not the result of personal failing, that such poverty ought to be relieved by the state and explicitly that in such cases the stigma of pauperism must not be attached to these unfortunates. Some relief *outside* the Poor Law was called for. (Document 6D.) It was a significant disruption of the unity of the Poor Law and, through the subsequent reissuing of the circular, it eventually produced the Unemployed Workmen's Act of 1905. Though the twenty years' experience of public works schemes did not convince people that this was the real answer, nevertheless the Chamberlain Circular had established the principle that unemployment was in the last resort the responsibility of the whole society and was inappropriately dealt with via the Poor Law. As Harris explains, 'that some applicants for poor relief were now admitted to be victims of uncontrollable social forces was an unexploded time bomb ticking away inside the structure of the New Poor Law'.[22]

So auspicious a departure in social policy was not, however, capitalised on by Chamberlain, who, like Lloyd George after him, found that the politics of a wider world enticed him away from the cause of social reform. In 1886 Chamberlain, opposed to Gladstone's policy of Home Rule for Ireland, broke with the Liberals and formed his own Liberal Unionist group. Gradually Chamberlain drifted towards the Conservatives, who were also calling themselves Unionist, i.e. in favour of preserving the union between England and Ireland. In the twenty years from his challenge to Gladstone the issues which aroused Chamberlain were those of Ireland, the Empire, tariff reform and Imperial preference He entered Salisbury's Unionist Cabinet in 1895 as Secretary for the Colonies, and though the Government had promised to implement a social policy based on Chamberlain's programme of 1885 in fact Chamberlain did not really press the Cabinet hard, and the only important measure passed was the 1897 Workmen's Compensation Act which made employers fully liable for accidents to their employees while at work. Chamberlain's known support for old-age pensions, already introduced into Germany in 1889 and New Zealand in 1898, did not produce legislative action by the Salisbury ministry.

Though more might have been achieved had the political history been different, nevertheless the last quarter of the century witnessed so much progress in social policy that Sir William Harcourt, the Liberal Chancellor who in the 1894 budget introduced death duties, as a means of reducing great landed wealth, could make the famous remark 'We are all socialists now'. Of course, then as now, socialism was a debased word whose meaning varied according to individual usage. Strictly speaking, socialism means the collective ownership of the means of production, distribution and exchange; that, as Robert Blatchford put it in his widely-read socialist book *Merrie England* (1894), 'the land and other instruments of production shall be the common property of the people, and shall be used and governed by the people for the people'. There were very few, least of all among those who reached Cabinet office, who subscribed to that notion. If socialism meant the abolition of private property and an equal distribution of wealth, then few supported it, but as the Liberal John Morley said in 1889:

> If Socialism means a wise use of the forces of all for the good of each; if it means the legal protection of the weak against the strong; if it means the performance by public bodies of duties which individuals could not perform either so well or not at all for themselves, why, then, the principles of Socialism are admitted all over the field of our social activity.[23]

In other words, socialism for Morley and many like him meant, in effect, collectivism, the use of the collective force of the society to mitigate the worst effects of a capitalist system, to intervene within but not to overturn a capitalist society.

At the same time there was enough in late Victorian politics to alarm the individualists who believed that England really was on the road to socialism. The enormous growth in municipal activity was itself an apparent precursor of things to come. Sidney Webb's famous comments about what councils had already done under the very noses of the practical men of the self-help school was quoted in the previous chapter, and the 1890s were a heyday for so-called 'gas and water municipal socialism', with London leading the way. Nobody had yet coined the phrase 'welfare state' but already in the early years of the century a Liverpool historian could identify, in his local council's wide role, a municipal 'cradle to grave' provision:

> It offers to see that the child is brought safely into the world. It provides him in infancy with suitable food. It gives him playgrounds to amuse himself in and baths to swim in. It takes him to school...it trains him for his future trade. It sees that the citizen's house is properly built and sometimes even builds it for him. It brings into his rooms an unfailing supply of pure water from the remote hills. It guards his food and tries to secure that it is not dangerously adulterated. It sweeps the streets for him and disposes of the refuse of his house. It carries him swiftly to and from his work. It gives him books to read, pictures to look at, music to listen to and lectures to stimulate his thought. If he is sick it nurses him; if he is penniless it houses him; and when he dies, if none other will, it buries him.[24]

Some were appalled to find so respectable an upholder of Liberal free trade principles as Gladstone advocating anti-landlord, anti-property measures in Ireland, or so aristocratic a figure as Salisbury supporting the public provision in the Acts of 1885 and 1890 of homes for working men. In principle this could only lead inexorably towards a socialist destination, for, as Lord Wemyss asked in the House of Lords, 'If they built houses would they furnish them? Would they put fire in the grate or food in the cupboard? And if not, on this principle, why not?'[25] Wemyss was the chairman of the Liberty and Property Defence League begun in 1882 which opposed the extension of state intervention and whose slogan was 'self-help versus state help'. The League campaigned vigorously and kept a watchful eye on all bills going through Parliament. Its great prophet was the veteran individualist Herbert Spencer whom it called 'our modern Aristotle' and who wrote the most forceful late-Victorian attack upon state intervention in a series of four articles published in 1884 in the *Contemporary Review* and printed as a book, *The Man versus the State*. Spencer and his supporters were alarmed to find that both political parties were advocating increased state coercion. In 1902 *The Times* carried a series of articles critical of municipal trading and this began a flood of books and pamphlets hostile to 'municipal socialism'.

Such agitation could not prevent the various inroads into the self-help philosophy already mentioned, yet many felt that little had so far been done by the state to attack the basic problem of the inequality of wealth in society. This paradox of a changing philosophy of welfare co-existing with the stubborn persistence of harsh realities was well exemplified in the late-Victorian Poor Law. On the one hand, the Poor Law developed increasingly specialised agencies for particular categories of pauper, for whom the workhouse became an approximation of a welfare institution. Children, the sick, the elderly and lunatics may indeed have received more sympathetic treatment as the end of the century approached. On the other hand, for the generality of paupers needing outdoor relief, particularly those suffering from inadequate or irregular wages, the Poor Law remained in the icy grip of the philosophy of 1834. Indeed there is much to support Michael Rose's argument that the classic Victorian deterrent Poor Law was the creation of the 1870s rather than of the 1830s.[26] As we saw, the principles of 1834 were considerably vitiated by compromises in practice which left many of the objectives of the New Poor Law unachieved. Rose argues that a series of crises in the 1860s (the Lancashire cotton famine, workhouse infirmary scandals, financial collapse) led to a major reappraisal of Poor Law policy. This coincided with the emergence of the Charity Organisation Society and its more rigorous restatement of the individualist philosophy which underlay the original 1834 proposals.

From 1869 it is possible to detect a conscious purge on outdoor relief which was reinforced in the early years of the Local Government Board whose ethos was dominated by the Poor Law Division. In 1869 the Poor Law Board issued to London Unions the so-called Goschen Minute, which urged co-operation with voluntary bodies and a closer control on outdoor relief. The COS willingly participated and, for example, in Marylebone Octavia Hill organised a voluntary committee which screened applicants before they ever reached the relieving officers. Under strong COS influence the practical rule emerged that the 'deserving' should receive charitable help, while the 'undeserving' should be consigned to the Poor Law. This moralistic classification reinforced and justified the harsher treatment of those judged undeserving. The stricter enforcement of the workhouse test and the revival of the 1834 ideology was well-illustrated in a conference of London Poor Law guardians whose resolutions were much praised by the Local Government Board. (Document 6E.)

Within five years the trend was clear in the statistics of poor relief.

Poor relief and expenditure, 1868–74

	1868–9	1873–4
Poor Law expenditure per head of population	7s. 0.3/4d	6s. 6d.
Poor Rate in £	1s. 5.9d.	1s. 4.4d.
Paupers as proportion of population	4.7%	3.5%
Adult able-bodied as proportion of paupers	16.77%	13.53%
Proportion of paupers on indoor relief	13.86%	15.48%
Proportion of adult male paupers on indoor relief	21.80%	28.64%

The rate of expenditure was down, the poor rates were lower and the overall rate of pauperism had declined, despite a worsening of the economic situation. A higher proportion of paupers, especially of adult males, was relieved in the workhouse, while a lower proportion was adult able-bodied. So vagrants, casual or itinerant workers, single women, deserted wives, alcoholics and a whole range of unemployable 'inadequates' found themselves subjected to the harsh regime belatedly imposed in conformity with less eligibility and the workhouse test. The ambivalence of the poverty problem was sharply exposed in the statistical discrepancy between the investigators and the officials. When Edward VII ascended the throne, it was asserted that pauperism in his kingdom was between 2 and 3 per cent, whereas poverty was between 25 and 30 per cent. The old dichotomy between poverty and pauperism, so crucial to the Bentham–Chadwick analysis, was now irrelevant. As Alfred Marshall told the Royal Commission on the Aged Poor, 'While the problem of 1834 was the problem of pauperism, the problem of 1893 is the problem of poverty'. It was to explore how far this assertion was well-founded and, if well-founded, how the Poor Law should respond that in 1905 Balfour appointed a Royal Commission on the Poor Law, some seventy years after the first. By the time the Commission reported, British social policy had already entered a new age.

7 Liberal social policy, 1905–14

I The young and the old

When Balfour resigned as Conservative Prime Minister in December 1905 it was partly on the expectation that a weak and disunited Liberal Party would fragment in office and therefore lose the next election. In fact, the sensible Scottish Liberal leader Sir Henry Campbell-Bannerman was able, by firm leadership, to outgun the potential dissidents of the 'aristocratic' wing of his party (Asquith, Grey and Haldane), and in the event all three served in his very powerful Cabinet which, on its radical wing, included the promising figure of Lloyd George at the Board of Trade and the former trade union leader John Burns at the Local Government Board. Though Burns himself no longer had the 'fire in his belly' which had motivated the dockers' leader of 1889, his appointment was of enormous significance since he was the first working man to achieve Cabinet rank. He personally achieved little in his eight years in this post, but his very presence next to 'marquises and belted knights' symbolised a new democratic age and concern for the masses.

Campbell-Bannerman judiciously decided on an immediate election which, in January 1906, resulted in the biggest land-slide since 1832. The Conservatives dropped from 402 to 157 (Balfour himself was defeated at Manchester) while the Liberals totalled 401, including 24 so-called Lib.-Labs., and could count on the support of a further 29 Labour members and the 82 Irish Nationalists. It was a stupendous Liberal victory which produced a House of Commons with a Government majority of

356.* It seemed to many that after nearly twenty years of Conservative rule the democratic changes of the 1880s had at last borne fruit.

Historians and contemporaries have been equally perplexed to explain the reasons for this surprising election result. Social reform, though vaguely mentioned by some Liberals, was not a key electoral issue although it was to become a major preoccupation of the Liberal Government. 'Chinese slavery', the importing of indented Chinese labour, in South Africa was much more widely discussed, to the discomfort of the outgoing Unionist ministry. Chamberlain, who had resigned from Balfour's Government in 1903 to lead his tariff reform campaign, saw Imperial preference as a means of cementing colonial links, protecting British industry and providing the revenue to finance social reform. It was a bold programme but it failed to capture the imagination of the working class and tended to produce discord in the Conservative camp while uniting Liberals behind their traditional shibboleth of free trade. The Nonconformist conscience, also a traditional element in the Liberal make-up, had been outraged, almost anachronistically in this a-religious early century, by Balfour's Education Act of 1902. The Act had legalised secondary and technical education (which was being provided unconstitutionally by many School Boards) by abolishing the School Boards and vesting control in the local authorities, which were also to finance and control all the former voluntary religious schools. It was an attempt to provide uniform local administration, but since so many of the voluntary schools were Anglican it inevitably produced the cry of 'Church on the rates' and again strengthened Liberal support.

For those perceptive enough to realise it, the most significant element in the new Parliament was the group of 53 Labour members, 29 of whom were sponsored by the Labour Representation Committee (LRC) which, after the election, began calling itself the Labour Party. This success was partly due to a secret compact by which about 30 previously Conservative seats were left uncontested by the Liberals, a free anti-Conservative field for

---

* As often, the electoral system distorted the true voting strength of the defeated party, and though the Conservatives obtained only 23 per cent of the seats, they had actually received over 43 per cent of the votes. They thus had a substantial popular base from which to rebuild.

Labour activity. Some trade unionists still saw themselves as allies of the Liberals (the Lib.-Labs.), for it was still quite natural to see Liberal and Labour as both parties of the Nonconformist Left, allies rather than competitors. The key issue which had increased both LRC and TUC membership in the years before the election had been the Taff Vale case by which unions were held to be responsible for a company's loss of income due to a strike. This, in effect, removed the strike weapon from a union's armoury and produced much anti-Conservative feeling.

This Labour strength, as yet numerically insignificant in the context of Liberal euphoria, was in fact the symbol of the distress of the masses which, if not placated, would in the long term destroy the Liberals. Labour was growing because working men felt they needed special, sectional representation within the political system. The 1906 election provided the Liberals with the chance to show that there was a party of concern and conscience which could legislate in the interest of the poor and that there was no need for a party designated to this one sole interest in society. *The Times* was among those observers who rightly judged the significance of the infant Labour Party:

> The emergence of a strong Labour element in the House of Commons has been generally recognised as the most significant outcome of the present election. It lifts the occasion out of the ordinary groove of domestic politics and will have a far wider influence than any mere turnover of party voters.... Though the Labour party has used the Liberals in this election to help them to what they want...they show no gratitude to the Liberal party.... The reason is that the system of commercial organisation that now galls them is the work of the Liberals and is founded upon the ideas now outworn which gave Liberalism its period of supremacy.[1]

Labour members in short were a visible challenge to the unlimited competition of traditional Liberalism.

Indeed it was a Labour back-bencher who introduced a bill which in December 1906 finally became law as the Education (Provision of Meals) Act, which empowered local authorities to feed necessitous schoolchildren. Public interest in meals for needy children dates back to voluntary efforts in the 1860s, but the real stimulus was the Boer War with its deficient recruits and the consequent moves for national efficiency. In that bizarre way which again and again seemed to link imperialism and social reform (sometimes as allies, sometimes as competitors), it seemed to some that Britain would only be able to sustain its Empire in the future if she ensured that the new generation of children, tomorrow's Imperial Army, was properly nourished. Public concern was aroused by the apparent evidence of what was called 'national deterioration', and a Royal Commission on Physical Training in Scotland recommended in 1903 that education authorities should, in conjunction with voluntary agencies, provide school meals. Far more authoritative was the Report of the Interdepartmental Committee on Physical Deterioration of 1904, which strongly urged that both medical inspection and feeding should be undertaken within the state educational system.

The cause of meals for poor children was taken up by the renegade Tory John Gorst, but the Balfour ministry would not allow any measure that would involve increased local or national taxation and so left this significant element of social policy for the Liberals. The Unionists would go no farther than to issue a Poor Law circular to encourage guardians to take up this duty. The Liberal measure of 1906 empowered local authorities to provide meals for needy schoolchildren, if necessary by a halfpenny rate. It was a small measure and produced only limited progress, for it was not until 1914 that Exchequer grants of half the cost were made available. Yet it had once more extended the scope of the state by removing from the parent the responsibility of feeding the child and at the same time exacting no punitive *quid pro quo*. In the last resort, it proved impossible to make parents pay, so that in effect this began a system of publicly financed free school meals. Parents were not deprived of their rights of citizenship as was the pauper, and so the principles of the old individualism were once more eroded. In 1885 it had been admitted that a resort to the Poor Law medical service did not pauperise; in 1886 Chamberlain's circular had advised that a resort to public works by involuntary unemployed did not pauperise; and now in 1906 it was admitted that resort to a free school meal did not pauperise. Thus the state was little by little acknowledging responsibility for the sick, the unemployed and the hungry. As always, from little things great developments grow.

The other main plank of the Physical Deterioration Report of 1904 had been school medical inspection, and this was implemented by the Liberals in 1907, again stimulated somewhat by back-bench activity. A back-bench amendment inserted a medical provision into the abortive 1906 Education Bill which was lost in the Lords, and in the following year another back-bench measure was withdrawn when the ministry brought in its own Education (Administrative Provisions) Bill. R. L. Morant, the active and influential Permanent Secretary of the Education Board, was anxious that the case for school medical treatment (which the Liberals were unwilling to accept) should be established by the revelations that would inevitably follow the introduction of school medical inspection. He drew up the 1907 bill and in effect smuggled medical inspection through by surrounding it with other, much less significant administrative proposals. It was yet another example of that administrative momentum described earlier. A medical department was thus established within the Board of Education which would supervise the provision of a new school medical service. The school clinics, the brainchild of the reformer Margaret McMillan, began to be introduced and, from 1912, grants were made available for treatment as well. Another step had been taken towards a general medical service.

In order to ensure that children did receive proper medical attention, neglect of a child's health by a parent was made a legal offence by the Children Act of 1908. This long and cumbersome Act, which was successfully steered through Parliament by the young Herbert Samuel, then Under-Secretary at the Home Office, was so all-embracing that it has been termed the 'children's charter'. Like so many well-known major pieces of legislation (such as the Public Health Act of 1875) its importance lies partly in consolidating and codifying a number of earlier disparate Acts. Children's legal rights were clearly established and their welfare in the event of parental negligence became the responsibility of the community at large. The Act also embodied a more enlightened attitude to juvenile delinquents, who from 1907 could be sent to the new 'borstals'. Child offenders were now to be kept in remand homes while awaiting trials which were to take place in specially designated Juvenile Courts. The general concern for the protection of young infants, which had been growing since the 1890s and which had culminated in the Children Act of 1908, also spilled over into the fields of maternity, and it was in the Edwardian period that maternity and child welfare clinics began to be established by voluntary bodies. Sir Arthur Newsholme, the Chief Medical Officer at the Local Government Board and himself a researcher into child health, supported these clinics, which from 1914 began to receive Government grants.

These significant developments in official concern for the welfare of children were by no means as important as the major measure concerned with the welfare of the old, namely the belated introduction of old-age pensions in 1908. Once more the Liberals needed to be prodded into action by back-bench and extra-Parliamentary activity, but the implementation of the Liberal promise to provide pensions (coinciding with the death of Campbell-Bannerman and the elevation of Asquith to Prime Minister) did inaugurate a period of positive legislative action in the field of social reform by the ministry itself. From 1909, the Liberal Government began leading the march forward where they had earlier been pushed from behind.

The issue of old-age pensions, though a remarkable breakthrough in English social policy, was not the subject of controversy by the time they were introduced, because of the long and popular campaign on their behalf. As early as 1878, Canon William Blackley proposed a scheme of compulsory contributions into an annuity fund early in life which would finance sick pay and pension later on. This proposal was effectively squashed by the powerful opposition of the friendly societies, which opposed any competition with their own schemes and which became perhaps the most important brake on the progress towards pensions. However, in the later 1880s, Charles Booth's revelations of how much poverty was due to old age seemed to clinch the case for pensions, and he himself became a prominent supporter of them. Indeed success seemed assured when, in 1891, Joseph Chamberlain took up this subject. As always, social policy was ultimately decided in the political arena and it was vital to have a prominent politician to support pensions. There was, however, one fundamental difference between Booth and Chamberlain: the former wanted a non-contributory scheme, the latter a contributory one.

If Chamberlain's political prominence, particularly as a Unionist Cabinet Minister from 1895, seemed to indicate that his scheme was more likely to prevail, its contributory basis, sound enough actuarially and indeed ideologically, earned it the implacable opposition (as had Blackley's) of the friendly societies. They would tolerate no state competition for that same pool of working-class earnings which financed the contributions of their several million members. They were not yet fully aware that the fall in death rate was throwing increasing burdens on them and that in effect the friendly societies were providing pensions by a liberal interpretation of sick pay in old age. Only slowly did they realise that a non-contributory pension financed out of taxation (Booth's idea) would be of great benefit to them, and so they opposed Chamberlain's scheme because it was contributory and Booth's even though it was not. Chamberlain certainly recognised that without the support of the friendly societies any proposal would be abortive:

> They are in touch with the thriftily-minded section of the working class. Their criticism of any scheme would be very damaging: their opposition might be fatal. They have very great Parliamentary influence and I should myself think twice before attempting to proceed in the face of hostility from so important and dangerous a quarter.[2]

Booth's scheme for its part was deemed prohibitively costly and no government in the 1890s was prepared to find the money, perhaps as much as £16 million, to pay for pensions without contributions. The pension question, despite the evidence and public support, arrived at an impasse: Chamberlain's contributory scheme was not practical because of friendly-society opposition, while Booth's non-contributory scheme was not practical because of its cost.

In an attempt to resolve this difficulty, several reports were presented in the 1890s. The Gladstone ministry appointed the Royal Commission on the Aged Poor in 1893 which included both Booth and Chamberlain, but its Majority and Minority Reports were inconclusive and led only to Poor Law circulars instructing guardians to relax some of the deterrent aspects of relief for the aged and encouraging them to use domiciliary outdoor relief in preference to the workhouse. Salisbury's ministry appointed a Treasury Committee in 1896 which reported two years later in favour of contributory pensions, but in 1899 public interest, stimulated by the introduction of pensions in New Zealand, led to the appointment of a Commons Select Committee which included Lloyd George and which recommended in favour of non-contributory pensions, the first official support for pensions financed from taxation.

Though the massive expenditure on the Boer War removed the possibility of such pensions in the near future, and their former supporter, Chamberlain, was now seeking ways of shelving what had become an embarrassing demand, there was a tide of opinion moving inexorably towards some form of old-age pension. In 1899 Booth had helped to launch a national movement in favour of pensions, whose activities were directed by F. H. Stead, a Congregationalist minister-cum-journalist, and the able trade unionist Frederick Rogers, the first chairman of the Labour Representation Committee. The Fabians, the TUC, the co-operative movement and the Labour Party all supported universal pensions financed out of taxation, and by the time the Liberals were in office even two former implacable opponents were coming round. The Charity Organisation Society, which had always opposed state pensions in principle, was now prepared to accept a voluntary contributory scheme, while conversely the friendly societies were reluctantly acknowledging the advantages to them of a non-contributory scheme. Asquith, as Chancellor, was therefore faced with a mass of opinion in favour of pensions, and when meeting a large deputation of supporters of pensions in November 1906 he and Campbell-Bannerman promised that they would be introduced and on a non-contributory basis.

Despite this promise, many back-benchers in the Commons found Asquith dilatory in implementing it. For his part there was the problem of how to finance pensions, the cost of which would be determined by such tedious but important administrative details as age, coverage, exemptions, etc. There is much to support the view that the Liberals were finally forced into action by a series of poor by-election results in which Liberals were defeated by Labour; allies were becoming competitors for lack of concrete reforms. Opinion in Parliament was clearly in favour of pensions financed from taxation, as was demonstrated by the overwhelming support given to an abortive private member's bill introduced in 1906 by W. H. Lever, the great soap magnate. The ministry had been frustrated in some of its major legislation by the opposition of the House of Lords. Its two years in office had produced disappointing results and the threat to Liberal pre-eminence of a growing Labour Party was becoming manifest. Political expediency therefore chimed with social concern to make 1908 an appropriate moment to introduce pensions. There was always a strong element of political motivation in Liberal social policy and Lloyd George admitted as much to his brother: 'It is time we did something that appealed straight to the people – it will, I think, help to stop this electoral rot and that is most necessary.'[3]

By the time Asquith introduced his pension proposals into Parliament in the 1908 budget he was already Prime Minister and the bill was actually taken through the Commons by Lloyd George, his successor as Chancellor. Both men emphasised that old-age pensions, which were to be non-contributory, would reduce the number of aged paupers and so relieve the Poor Law whose future was itself under examination by an important Royal Commission. Though many had talked of pensions at the age of sixty-five, the financial demands were such that Asquith's proposals provided 5s. per week at the age of seventy. As an economy it was recommended that a married couple should get only 7s. 6d., but this reduction was deleted by back-bench opposition during the bill's passage. A sliding income scale was also introduced so that a smaller pension was paid to those with incomes between 8s. and 12s. per week. Though some in the Lords still opposed pensions as 'thinly disguised outdoor relief' and others still favoured a contributory pension as ideologically more respectable, the 1908 Old Age Pensions Bill found widespread support and came into operation on 1 January 1909.

Though 5s. was a paltry amount, its impact was swift by virtue of it being non-contributory, so that those over seventy could immediately draw pensions instead of having to wait for an entitlement through contributions, which would have been the case in a contributory scheme. Pensions were paid through the Post Office and were quite separate from the Poor Law and immune from its moral stigma. Largely because of this, far more applied for pensions than had been anticipated, revealing in Lloyd George's famous phrase 'a mass of poverty and destitution which is too proud to wear the badge of pauperism'. This refusal to use the Poor Law services available and the consequent need to construct a system of social services separate from the Poor Law rather than upon its foundations is of great significance in the history of English social policy. Looking back, it may seem obvious that the old 1834 Poor Law would have to be replaced, but it is quite remarkable that a country should provide a universal, all-embracing service for the relief of destitution which could, as we have seen, deal with a wide variety of conditions (sickness, old age, unemployment, etc.) and yet find that when it wished to extend these services it did not increase but rather reduced the scope of its pre-existing universal Poor Law. The deterrent stigma of moral shame which was deliberately implanted in 1834 did its work too well, so that popular reluctance to apply, and therefore the need for an alternative, condemned the Poor Law in the long term to ossification rather than providing the possibilities of self-sustained growth and adaptability to meet new conditions. Much of the social policy on the twentieth-century road to a Welfare State has been concerned with removing categories of need from the remit of the Poor Law and providing socially more acceptable alternatives. To the grateful recipient, pensions could never be a form of outdoor relief; it was a new birthright of an Englishman, a part of his citizenship, not a deprivation of it. State pensions paid as of right* and financed out of taxation set the Liberals firmly on a course which was to involve basic departures in social policy. In particular old-age pensions provided Lloyd George with the immediate budgetary task of finding the money to pay for them, and they introduced him to the problem of extending state pensions to other needy groups for whom the Poor Law was equally inappropriate. In the same month of August 1908 in which the Pensions Bill received the royal assent, Lloyd George made his famous trip to Germany, not as a diplomatic messenger but as a curious observer of the German insurance scheme. Here lay the origins of national insurance in Great Britain.

II   Lloyd George and the origins of the Welfare State

David Lloyd George, born in 1863, had been brought up by his uncle in Wales in very humble circumstances. Personal history had made him familiar with the poverty he did so much to alleviate while a Liberal Minister. More than any other leading politician in the Edwardian period, he had sprung from the people and, rising by virtue of his own talents, he became the first real outsider

---

*Initially pensions were paid only to those whose conduct marked them as the 'deserving poor' but by 1911 Lloyd George had considerably relaxed the regulations, which until 1919 excluded criminals, drunkards and malingerers.

to achieve the highest office. Without wealth or family connection he had made a political career for himself by his anti-imperialist, anti-landlord campaigns. It was Lloyd George who personified the so-called 'New Liberalism' of the left wing of Asquith's Cabinet, a ministry which also included strong supporters of traditional Gladstonian Liberalism. Asquith's assumption of the Premiership in the spring of 1908 produced not only Lloyd George's promotion to Chancellor but also the entry into the Cabinet as President of the Board of Trade (Lloyd George's post since 1906) of the youthfully exuberant Winston Churchill, who at this time was imbued with the cause of social reform. Churchill had captured the idea of collectivism and translated it into a party doctrine. He had spoken positively on the social reform agenda as early as 1906:

> I should like to see the state embark on various novel and adventurous experiments. . . . I look forward to the universal establishment of minimum standards of life and labour. . . . I do not think liberalism . . . can cut itself off from this fertile field of social effort.[4]

It was Lloyd George and Churchill in partnership who carried Asquith's Government forward into a progressive and active social policy. Indeed by 1910 Churchill was convinced that they were crucial to any ministry, and he told Lloyd George: 'If we stood together we ought to be strong enough either to impart a progressive character to policy or by withdrawal to terminate an administration which had failed in its purpose.' Lloyd George had recognised the nascent threat to Liberalism posed by Labour from 1906, but was confident that a new party would oust the Liberals only if they failed 'to cope seriously with the social condition of the people, to remove the national degradation of slums and widespread poverty in a land glittering with wealth'.[5]

The recurring theme of indescribable and hideous poverty co-existing with abundant and incalculable wealth, characteristic of so many of Lloyd George's speeches since he first became an MP in 1890, was to impart to his first and most crucial budget that special flavour of social justice which made his financial proposals so controversial. Faced with an impending deficit of £16 million (an amount whose significance is now reduced by a generation made familiar with taxation involving hundreds of millions) caused by present and future social service and naval expenditure, Lloyd George chose to raise the extra revenue in a manner which earned his 1909 budget the title of 'the People's Budget' and made it the most famous in modern English history.

Lloyd George proposed to increase the duty on beer, spirits, tobacco and petrol and to levy an excise duty on the use of cars. These were unexceptionable and were not as significant as the changes proposed in income tax which would make it more progressive. By developing Asquith's earlier budgetary innovation of a distinction between earned and unearned income, Lloyd George was able to produce a sliding scale which, depending on size and nature of income, varied the rate of income tax between 9d. and 1s. 2d. in the pound. Those on middling and lower incomes (below £500) were now allowed to earn a tax-free £10 per child every year, a small bounty but one that acknowledged the extra burdens imposed by a family, while those with higher incomes (over £3,000) were now to be faced with a supertax of an extra 6d. in the pound. These proposals were controversial but they did build on earlier tendencies and only extended the principle of a progressive and equitable income tax. It was significant that the income-tax proposals passed through the Commons without much opposition. The most controversial and original proposals were a series of land value duties, clearly aimed at Lloyd George's long-term *bêtes noires*, the landowners. There was to be a 20 per cent capital gains tax on the unearned increment of land values as revealed on sale, a capital levy on unused land and mining royalties, and a tax payable when leases expired and the land reverted to the landlord.

These land duties were an attempt to deal with the long-standing grievance of untaxed landed wealth, which as Ricardo had predicted had soared as the general prosperity had grown. This was closely, though not solely, associated with urbanisation, for landowners had found their holdings inflating in value as land was required for urban housing development. Yet to neither the national nor the local budget did the landowner contribute, while the value of his land was enhanced through the efforts of others. Churchill put the position very clearly:

the landlord who happened to own a plot of land on the outskirts or at the centre of one of our great cities...sits still and does nothing.

Roads are made, streets are made, railway services are improved, electric lights turn night into day, electric trains glide swiftly to and fro, water is brought from reservoirs a hundred miles off in the mountains – and all the while the landlord sits still. Every one of those improvements is effected by the labour and at the cost of other people. Many of the most important are effected at the cost of the municipality and of the ratepayers. To not one of those improvements does the land monopolist as a land monopolist contribute. He renders no service to the community, he contributes nothing to the general welfare . . . the land monopolist has only to sit still and watch complacently his property multiplying in value.[6]

The Liberal answer in 1909 was the dual thrust of the People's Budget and the Housing and Town Planning Act introduced by John Burns. By the latter measure local authorities were empowered to control suburban development and so could plan the utilisation of suburban land. But neither measure was more than a start in dealing with the unearned augmentation of land values. Local authorities were not allowed to speculate in land and could acquire only those sites where specific plans were in hand. The land duties for all their political controversy turned out to be fraught with technical and legal difficulties, which meant that they cost far more to administer than they ever yielded. Ironically, the less tendentious taxation changes proved to be brilliantly successful as tax-raising measures and were to bring Lloyd George considerable surpluses in revenue.

The financial details are important, but the general principles underlying them are more so. This budget was frankly and overtly redistributing wealth through taxation. It was seeking to raise revenue by taxing the wealthy few for the benefit of the penurious many. It embodied precisely that principle which so offended the early Victorian opponents of a publicly owned water supply financed out of the rates (quoted above, p. 73). Though appearing to raise class war, in fact in attempting to tax the real wealth of the country the People's Budget symbolised another sort of war, described at the end of Lloyd George's budget speech:

This is a War Budget. It is for raising money to wage inplacable warfare against poverty and squalidness. I cannot help hoping and believing that before this generation has passed away we shall have advanced a great step towards that good time when poverty and wretchedness and human degradation which always follow in its camp will be as remote to the people of this country as the wolves which once infested its forests.[7]

Here was the essence of the novel approach: financial policy geared to the social needs of the people; the budget as a tool of social policy.

As always, Lloyd George's policies had a political as well as social motive and this budget raised (as perhaps was intended) a constitutional crisis with the House of Lords. Stung by the vituperative public attacks on the landed aristocracy by Lloyd George and Churchill (both of whom received a royal rebuke), the House of Lords threatened to throw out the budget. The Chancellor warned that '500 men chosen accidentally from among the unemployed' (his definition of the House of Lords) could not frustrate the wishes of a democratically elected government. (Document 7A.) Ill-advisedly the Lords did reject the budget and so provoked a major constitutional battle between Lords and Commons which ended only with the Parliament Act of 1911. Two elections were held in 1910, in effect one on the budget and one on the powers of the Lords, and the People's Budget was eventually passed in that year. In 1911 the Lords, under the threat of a creation of Liberal peers, agreed to the conversion of their absolute veto into a power to delay non-monetary legislation for a maximum of two years. Money bills would pass automatically. Thus, by spoiling for a fight over the social and political implications of a revolutionary budget, the House of Lords, 'Mr Balfour's Poodle', had its teeth drawn.

If the budget produced a revolutionary constitutional settlement, the ultimate social purpose of Lloyd George's increased revenues, social insurance, was no less revolutionary. The crisis with the Lords delayed the introduction of a major piece of social legislation which had been under consideration since 1908. The People's Budget had cut the Gordian knot of shortage of funds, which for instance had so long delayed even the widely supported innovation of pensions. Now the money was available and the question was how it could best be used. There were plenty of ideas around, for the Reports of the Royal Commission on the Poor Law had appeared just before the budget. The Commission of 1905–9, unlike that of 1832–4, was composed of experts in the field of social administration and included several guardians or officials of the Local Government Board, people (including C. S. Loch, Helen Bosanquet and the venerated Octavia Hill) who were attached to the Charity Organisation Society, four religious leaders, two Labour leaders, two economists and two social investigators, Charles Booth (who retired from the Commission in 1908 because of ill health) and Beatrice Webb. However, the Commission resembled that of 1834 in the desire of many members to produce a report which would substantiate preconceived doctrines. While Beatrice Webb furiously denounced the Local Government Board's stratagem of leading the Commission by the nose to 'recommend reversion to the "principles of 1834" as regards policy, to stem the tide of philanthropic impulse that was sweeping away the old embankment of deterrent tests to the receipt of relief',[8] she herself hoped to lead or rather bully the Commission into the Fabian socialism she and her husband, Sidney Webb, personified.

When evidence was heard it was clear that the top echelons of the Local Government Board were still preaching the doctrines of less eligibility. J. S. Davy, head of the Poor Law Division, was convinced that, as in pre-1834 days, relief was indiscriminate and over-generous and that Poor Law administration again lacked uniformity. He was alarmed by the growth of services (e.g. under the Education (Provision of Meals) Act or the Unemployed Workmen's Act) outside the Poor Law. Davy firmly believed that, in order to make the condition of the pauper less eligible than that of his independent neighbour, it was vital that he should suffer first 'the loss of personal reputation (what is understood by the stigma of pauperism); second, the loss of personal freedom which is secured by detention in a workhouse; and third, the loss of political freedom by suffering disfranchisement'.[9] Davy's often-quoted evidence indicates how strong a hold the individualist ethic still had, and when asked whether a deterrent Poor Law was fair for someone unemployed through a trade depression, Davy's reply was that the man 'must stand by his accidents: he must suffer for the general good of the body politic'. That sounded very much like the sentiments in the 1834 report – 'it is a hardship to which the good of society requires the applicant to submit... he must accept assistance on the terms, whatever they may be, which the common welfare requires'.

That very diversification which made the Poor Law so universal and adaptable and which convinced Davy that it could embrace all the newer services was itself inimical to less eligibility. More and more was done for paupers which independent labourers could never afford to do for themselves; for instance, in the field of medical relief the provision itself was a contradiction of less eligibility, since in the words of one of the Poor Law medical inspectors 'it is not possible to make the condition of the sick pauper less eligible than that of the independent wage-earner; the patient must be treated with a view to cure, and that means, in practice, extra comforts, good nursing and skilled medical and surgical treatment'.[10] This had been the precise fear of the early Victorian supporters of the stringent new Poor Law (see above, p. 98). Indeed all the medical evidence pointed inexorably towards the conclusion that sickness was a major cause of poverty and hence less eligibility and a deterrent Poor Law were inappropriate.

Even the Majority Report of the Royal Commission, signed by the chairman, Lord George Hamilton, and fourteen members, did not seek to defend the principles of 1834 which Davy and the Local Government Board preached. However, they did accept that a remodelled Poor Law could be an all-embracing social institution. Davy, though perhaps ideologically reactionary, was right in believing that the structure existed on which to build such a reformed Poor Law and, as was mentioned above in discussing pensions, it seemed more logical to extend existing services rather than contract them by creating new ones. Hence the Majority Report wished to reverse the recent trends in removing categories of social need from the Poor Law. Acknowledging that the term 'Poor Law' and the office of guardian had acquired a bad odour, they recommended the use of the term 'public assistance' with control vested in public assistance authorities and committees to be run by local authorities. It was a copy of the administrative changes in the 1902 Education Act whereby local authority Education Committees had replaced the School Boards. The Majority Report envisaged all social services coming under the remit of the Public Assistance Committees, which were to make effective use of voluntary charities and social casework agencies (clearly the influence of the COS here). Indeed in some respects the voluntary agencies were to act as a sieve through which only the really destitute would need to pass. Though the

Majority Report was not simply a statement of self-help individualism, notions such as this confirmed deeply entrenched prejudices in favour of poverty still conceived of as a personal failing. Despite their ideas for change, the majority of the Royal Commission could still agree with the proposition that 'The causes of distress are not only economic and industrial; in their origin and character they are largely moral'.[11] They could not resist the remark that the destitution and misery of the poor resulted 'possibly from their own failure and faults'.

Though Beatrice Webb was a lifelong believer in the moral improvement of the individual, her Minority Report (which Sidney Webb drafted), supported by George Lansbury, a future Labour Minister, Francis Chandler, a trade unionist, and the Revd Russell Wakefield, later Bishop of Birmingham, stressed the problem of poverty as a social condition resulting from the organisation of the economy. Where the Majority Report wished to make 'a swollen Poor Law' into an all-purpose relief organisation, the minority wanted to destroy the Poor Law completely. There was agreement that local authorities should take over the functions of the Poor Law, but the Minority Report advocated administrative specialisation by which separate departments (such as education, health, pensions, etc.) would deal with separate problems. Where this was criticised on the grounds of creating four or five Poor Laws, the Webb proposal was to have a co-ordinating registrar of public assistance who would dovetail the work of individual departments and assess by a means test what, if anything, ought to be charged. The Minority Report advocated a quite distinct, nationally organised service for the able-bodied. A powerful Ministry of Labour was envisaged which would organise the labour market through the use of labour exchanges and retraining programmes and, in times of cyclical depression, embark on great schemes of public works. Here ten-year programmes at the rate of £4 million per year were suggested, to be implemented not regularly but in times of depression so as to encourage economic growth. It was a version of the full-employment policy advocated during the Second World War. Indeed the whole Minority Report outlook anticipated much of the modern Welfare State, and though in the short term its influence on policy (though not on ideas) was negligible, in the longer term much of the Webbs' vision has materialised.

Never can so important a Royal Commission have produced so little in the way of immediate action, for not even the more moderate suggestions of the Majority Report were enacted. Thus to take an example, though both groups recommended the abolition of the guardians this did not occur until 1929. The powerful vested interest of the Local Government Board itself was resistant to change, and its President, John Burns, was able to persuade the Cabinet that circulars amending Poor Law practice would be sufficient to meet the criticisms that were common to both reports. Burns was supported by Lloyd George who was equally reluctant to be stampeded into Fabian socialism and who was working on his own insurance scheme. On insurance, the Majority Report was equivocal and the Minority Report positively hostile.

It is clear that Lloyd George was drawn towards insurance by his desire to extend state pensions to deserving cases other than the elderly. While floating the idea of a coalition to solve the constitutional crises he explained that he favoured

> provisions against the accidents of life which bring so much undeserved poverty to hundreds of thousands of homes, accidents which are quite inevitable such as the death of the breadwinner or his premature breakdown in health. I have always thought that the poverty which was brought upon families owing to these causes presents a much more urgent demand upon the practical sympathy of the community than even Old Age Pensions. With old age the suffering is confined to the individual alone; but in these other cases it extends to the whole family of the victim of circumstances.[12]

Though often accused of insincerity, Lloyd George did have a genuine and abiding concern for poverty and hoped to be able to give financial security to the sick, the unemployed, the widow and the orphan as well as to the aged. The cost of pensions (£8 million in the first year instead of the expected £6.5 million) convinced him that benefits could never be extended if they were to be financed by taxation alone, since the costs would be prohibitive. Insurance, by drawing on the funds of workers and their employers, could provide the necessary revenues.

More than this, insurance had many positive advantages over benefits financed out of taxation. People were happier about benefits which they had actually paid for by contributions – they earned a contractual right to benefit. As W. J. Braithwaite (the civil servant who worked closely with Lloyd George and drafted the 1911 Act) put it, 'Working people ought to pay something! It gave them a feeling of self-respect, and what cost nothing was not valued.'[13] Churchill was convinced that the great virtue of insurance was its emphasis on the rights earned by the insured worker. A strict application of insurance principles was essential, he said: 'The qualification for insurance must be actuarial. You qualify, we pay. If you do not qualify it is no good coming to us. That is the only safe and simple plan upon which the administration of such a fund can be conducted.'[14] Indeed Churchill fully accepted the corollary that a man who had earned his right to benefit was entitled to it even if he was personally responsible for his destitution, and the insurance fund would have to 'stand the racket'. Similarly Lloyd George, refusing to debar an insured man from medical benefit even where he was sick through his own negligence, commented that 'most illnesses are due to abuse of some prudent rule of Nature', and he instructed Braithwaite to insert a clause in the 1911 bill 'that medical treatment shall be given without regard to cause or nature of disease'.[15] Two great protagonists, Lloyd George and Churchill, saw no place in insurance for the concept of the undeserving poor, since it was irrelevant to the issue, which was universal entitlement earned by contributions.

Insurance, which was thus financially practicable and socially acceptable, also had a positive political appeal to Lloyd George, for we should never forget that he was a politician first and foremost. The political expediency of insurance was of three sorts. First, there could be no question that this would be an important stimulus to social progress and, as Asquith told the King, taken with pensions the insurance scheme represented 'the largest and most beneficial increase in social reform yet achieved in any country'. It had always been Lloyd George's intention to make a great stir, to do something really big that would attract public attention. A revealing though brief entry in Braithwaite's diary records that Lloyd George was 'bound on getting a scheme which will not be a "wet squib"'.[16] The sheer excitement of being involved with a major piece of social legislation had its own built-in political kudos and the Conservative Austen Chamberlain grudgingly commented in 1911: 'Confound Ll. George. He has strengthened the Government again. His sickness scheme *is* a good one and he is on the right lines this time.'[17]

The expectation (by no means fulfilled) of political advantage was a general factor. Far more specific was, second, that insurance would be a means of solving the political choice offered by the two reports of the Poor Law Commission. Lloyd George found neither report particularly attractive and indeed was well advanced in his plans before he read the reports carefully, yet he was fully aware that insurance would cut the ground from under the conservative remodelling of the majority and the Fabian socialism of the Webbs. As John Burns said to him enthusiastically, 'You know this is a bigger thing than either the Majority or Minority Report and renders them both unnecessary'.[18] The Chancellor had in fact, in Burns's famous phrase, found a means of 'dishing the Webbs'. Insurance was in this sense a brilliant political compromise between rival Poor Law reformers. Third, in the longer term social insurance was deliberately used as a means of making socialism less likely. The National Insurance Act is sometimes hailed as a major step on the road to a socialist Britain, but just the opposite was intended. Lloyd George and Churchill were using that strategy propounded by Balfour at the 1895 election (quoted earlier, p. 152) which would use social policy to head off socialism. Liberal collectivism was not to be a half-way house to socialism but its opposite, for as Churchill pointed out in his election campaign at Dundee in 1908: 'Socialism wants to pull down wealth, Liberalism seeks to raise up poverty....Socialism assails the maximum pre-eminence of the individual – Liberalism seeks to build up the minimum standard of the masses. Socialism attacks capital, Liberalism attacks monopoly.'[19]

Insurance, by helping to provide that 'national minimum' of which the Webbs were always speaking, would make changes in the organisation of the whole society less likely. Indeed insurance was the capitalist's answer to the problem of want, and by reducing it insurance covered up what the socialist saw as the root cause of poverty. Keir Hardie saw this side of Lloyd George's policy clearly, and bitterly explained to a constituency meeting of miners in Merthyr Tydfil that when miners asked for a decent minimum wage the answer was 'No say the Liberals, but we will give you an Insurance Bill. We shall not uproot the cause of poverty but we will give you a porous plaster to cover the disease that poverty causes.'[20] It was not just in the details but also in the underlying aims that the British insurance scheme was modelled on that of Bismarck. As early as December 1908 Churchill was advising the Prime Minister bluntly to 'thrust a big slice of Bismarckianism over the whole underside of our industrial system',[21] and more explicitly a radical Liberal close to Lloyd George urged the 'English Progressive' to take 'a leaf from the book of Bismarck who dealt the heaviest blow against German socialism not by his laws of oppression...but by that great system of state insurance which now safeguards the German workman at almost every point of his industrial career'.[22]

It now appears that most Edwardian protagonists who quoted the German precedent misunderstood the diversity of the German system. What was attractive about the German insurance scheme was its capacity to provide benefits for workers without having recourse to increased direct taxation or duties. So the links between Bismarck and Asquith and Lloyd George were fiscal rather than political. Moreover, as indicated above, Bismarck used 'laws of oppression' to contain socialism, whereas Lloyd George bought Labour support for national insurance by promises of trade union reform.[23]

The above discussion on the insurance principle makes clear that Churchill was as much involved in the early work on insurance as Lloyd George. However, he recognised that his work on unemployment insurance (discussed in the next section) would have to wait until Lloyd George's 'invalidity scheme' had been completed, and he urged, as was to happen, that the unemployment scheme, Part II of the 1911 Act, should be introduced alongside health insurance. The health scheme was in any case the more complex and controversial of the two, not simply because it was ideologically progressive but more because of the vested interests involved. Indeed the Webbs warned that any attempt at compulsory insurance would be foredoomed because of this:

> Any attempt to *enforce* on people of this country – whether for supplementary pensions, provision for sickness or invalidity, or anything else – a system of direct, personal, weekly contribution must, in our judgment, in face of so powerful a phalanx as the combined Friendly Societies, Trade Unions and Industrial Insurance Companies, fighting in defence of their own business, prove politically disastrous.[24]

Had the Minister responsible for the legislation been any other than Lloyd George this prophecy would doubtless have been fulfilled, for it needed all the Chancellor's consummate political skill to get a scheme through. Never has the phrase 'politics is the art of the possible' been more clearly demonstrated.

Not only did Lloyd George have to fight a major public political battle, but, as is now clear from Professor Gilbert's research into the making of the 1911 Act,[25] he was also engaged in a delicate balancing act behind the scenes between the vested interests concerned. What finally emerged in 1911 as Part I of the National Insurance Act was very different from the embryo implanted in Lloyd George's mind in 1908. The end result was moulded into shape by the tripartite pressures of the competing and conflicting aims of the friendly societies, the medical profession and the so-called industrial insurance interests. As we have already seen, the friendly societies were extremely touchy about any state competition in their fields of action. They already operated sick clubs and medical benefits, but Lloyd George won them over in 1908 by promising that any new scheme would be operated by them. The medical profession felt justifiably exploited by the friendly societies' medical contracts and wished to free itself from friendly-society domination, but not by selling itself into state medicine. Finally, there were the commercial industrial insurance companies, the most famous and largest of which was the Prudential, whose thousands of collectors visited millions of homes every week to collect coppers for the life policies which gave minimal death benefits, used to avoid a pauper's funeral. The extent of the business was stupendous and the companies were fearful, on the one hand, that the widows' and orphans' benefits proposed by Lloyd George would compete with their own death benefits and, on the other, that their rivals, the friendly societies, were to get exclusive control of the new scheme and so promote their own business. The commercial insurance interests were brilliantly protected by their spokesman Howard Kingsley Wood, who was at the end of his life Chancellor in Churchill's War Cabinet, and Lloyd George ruefully complained in 1910 that insurance had been easy in Germany, but in Britain

> one would have to encounter the bitter hostility of powerful organisations like the Prudential, the Liver, the Royal Victoria, the Pearl and similar

institutions with an army numbering scores if not hundreds of thousands of agents and collectors who make a living out of collecting a few pence a week from millions of households...they visit every house, they are indefatigable, they are often very intelligent and a Government which attempted to take over their work without first of all securing the co-operation of the other party would inevitably fail in its undertaking.[26]

Given that his 1910 proposals failed to produce a coalition, Lloyd George was left to negotiate the best scheme he could and come to terms with the companies. Balancing the wishes of the three major vested interests produced a mixture of victories and defeats for Lloyd George. Thus, as examples, Lloyd George was able to use the medical profession to pressurise the friendly societies into giving up medical benefit entirely to the local Insurance Commissions, which had been his long-term aim; on the other hand he had to pay a dear price for the support of the commercial companies by discarding, early in 1911, his cherished widows' and orphans' benefits. As he had forecast in 1910, the scheme would have to be 'confined to Invalidity and the most urgent and pitiable case of all must be left out'.[27] Such were the messy compromises that lobby politics imposed upon the Chancellor. Generally the friendly societies were sacrificed to the more powerful commercial interests and the medical profession used its power after the passage of the Act to secure its own financial position. Besides these delicate negotiations there were also extraordinarily complex actuarial problems about the workings of any scheme, notable among which was the question of whether there should be an accumulated fund out of which benefits were drawn, or the 'dividing out' system where current contributions finance benefits.

When the details were complete the Chancellor introduced a bill into the Commons in May 1911 of which Part I was the health insurance scheme. It proposed that weekly contributions should be made for all wage-earners at the rates of 4d. from the employee, 3d. from the employer and 2d. from the state (Ll.G.'s famous 9d. for 4d.), which would be paid into an accumulating fund to finance benefits. The scheme was to be administered by 'approved societies' which employees would join at their choice, but was to be legally compulsory and supervised by the state. In other words the state was compelling its citizens to provide insurance for themselves rather than providing simple state medicine and sickness benefits. In return for these contributions an insured worker received sick pay of 10s. per week from the approved society and free medical treatment from a doctor selected from a panel organised by local Insurance Commissions. Doctors were paid a capitation fee depending on the number of 'panel patients' they had. There were also to be certain extras such as maternity benefit of 30s. and sanatoria allowances for tuberculosis. Apart from the lack of general hospital provision and the continued fragmentation of health services (public health, Poor Law, voluntary and insurance), the major deficiency of the scheme was its failure to include dependants of insured workers for medical treatment. This was really because the plans of Lloyd George were concerned originally with financial security and the sickness benefit was to be part of the extended pension scheme. Medical treatment was added to get the worker back in harness again. His financial destitution was not dependent on the health of his family, though the family's destitution might result from his sickness. The position was well put by Government actuaries in 1910:

> Married women living with their husbands need not be included since where the unit is the family, it is the husband's and not the wife's health which it is important to insure. So long as the husband is in good health and able to work adequate provision will be made for the needs of the family, irrespective of the wife's health, whereas when the husband's health fails there is no one to earn wages.[28]

As Hennock explains, this limitation to the breadwinner demonstrates 'how little legislation was designed to improve the physical condition of the nation'. National insurance addressed sickness mainly as a cause of interruption of earnings.[29]

With all its shortcomings (and Lloyd George designated it as only a beginning) the health insurance scheme was a tremendously important extension of state aid. Lloyd George, having settled details with the vested interests, then had to face a major political storm in getting the controversial measure through Parliament. The Unionists, bitter about their defeat over the Parliament Act, turned their wrath on the insurance scheme and in the later stages were negatively obstructionist. The press stirred up public opposition, especially among mistresses and their servants, against the 'monstrous scheme of stamp licking'. It appeared for a time that the general breakdown of respect for the law (this was the age of the syndicalists, the suffragettes and in 1912 of the

Ulster Volunteers) would extend to the insurance scheme, which might be stillborn because of public refusal to comply with the regulations. Lloyd George rose to the occasion and defended his scheme as an urgently needed measure of social reform. He was, he said, driving 'an ambulance wagon', and the image stuck. (Document 7B.)

Much of course remained to be done, and had it not been for the First World War reform would no doubt have come sooner, yet it was a major non-socialist injection of social welfare into the British system. The Unionists' specious opposition on the grounds of confiscation of working-class earnings was in fact well based, though they were unaware of it. The Fabians, particularly the Webbs, saw through it and had warned Lloyd George beforehand: 'It's criminal to take poor people's money and use it to insure them, if you take it you should give it to the Public Health Authority to prevent their being ill again.'[30] Flat-rate insurance contributions are in fact regressive direct taxes which, unlike income tax, are not adjusted according to means, and so they remained for over half a century. As the Minority Report put it, they are in effect a poll tax and England had not had one of those since 1381! Despite this, insurance became entrenched in the British way of life and laid the foundation of the Welfare State.

Lloyd George thought that the overwhelming benefit which the poor would derive was well worth any short-term unpopularity. He reviewed the position in December 1911 in a speech based on the following notes. If the Act was lost it would be:

> Back to old position where millions with no provisions for sickness. Universal testimony greatest benefit derived by very class who generally fail to keep in insurance.... Five millions back again to the wretched days of no doctor in a case of sickness – furniture sold up – outdoor relief for themselves and their families... Act undoubtedly for a time an electoral disadvantage. Inevitable objections to paying, some from principle, some from poverty, some because they wish to have the money for much less useful purposes.... May for some time lose small employers' votes – some workmen who do not realise advantages of insurance. We will go through with it rather than consign those miserable millions back to beggary. In any event Act an enormous improvement.[31]

Time would familiarise the English people with the advantages of insurance, and in time Lloyd George envisaged in his typical imprecise but perceptive way the replacement of insurance by a general welfare scheme. Another famous note has been described as a key document in the history of the Welfare State:

> Insurance necessarily temporary expedient. At no distant date hope state will acknowledge full responsibility in the matter of making provision for sickness, breakdown and unemployment. It really does so now through Poor Law, but conditions under which this system has hitherto worked have been so harsh and humiliating that working-class pride revolts against accepting so degrading and doubtful a boon. Gradually the obligation of the State to find labour or sustenance will be realised and honourably interpreted. Insurance will then be unnecessary.[32]

Lloyd George saw the crucial point that a system of services would have to be created separate from the Poor Law. Insurance was, for the time being, the most that could be achieved. It was socially acceptable and soundly based financially. Yet the wider social welfare which Lloyd George glimpsed in the future would, he hoped, be something better. The vagaries of fate determined that it would not be he who extended these, the origins of the British Welfare State.

III Liberal social policy and the problem of work

The significance of the National Insurance Act of 1911 was enhanced by the inclusion in Part II of a selective unemployment insurance scheme on which Churchill and his advisers had been working since 1908. However, the attempt *as an experiment* to deal with unemployment by insurance should not be seen in isolation, for the Liberals pursued a broad policy concerned with various aspects of work. As we saw in an earlier chapter, the statutory limitations on hours of work had applied to children and women first in the textile industries and from the 1860s and 1870s in other industries as well. However, legislative interference in conditions of work and contract was ambivalent in terms of social ideology, at once an erosion of *laissez-faire* for those groups protected and a confirmation of it for those outside. The adult male still remained in terms of his work the free agent first officially recognised in 1833, and it was not until the early twentieth century that there was legislative protection for him. In 1908 the Home Secretary, Herbert Gladstone, introduced a bill to give the miners an eight-hour day for which they had been campaigning for forty years. This was partly a reflection of the large number of mining MPs, including Keir Hardie, in Parliament and partly in deference to the growth of the Labour Party itself. Churchill inspired everyone by his speech on this measure when he forecast that 'The general march of industrial democracy is not towards inadequate hours of work but towards sufficient hours of leisure', and, while Home Secretary, he introduced the Shops Act of 1911 which established half-day closing once a week, a boon to shop workers. More significant was Churchill's Trade Boards Act of 1909, which established boards to negotiate minimum wages in the so-called 'sweated trades', such as tailoring. Later on a minimum wage was established in mining, and this was a sizeable infringement of the sacrosanct feedom of contract between masters and men. Once more the state was protecting those who were unfairly exploited by capital, this time in pursuit of the Webbs' national minimum, to which Churchill had been converted.

It had been through the Webbs that Churchill met the young economist William Beveridge, a man who was to have so great an influence on twentieth-century social policy. Indeed never have the ideas of an adviser been so quickly put into practice, for not only were Churchill's letters and speeches in 1908 and 1909 full of Beveridge's notions, but the plans also bore immediate fruit in the rapid establishment of labour exchanges. Beveridge's crucial analysis of unemployment had revealed distinctions between various causes and notably had identified the problem of underemployment. A man who was casually employed reflected the characteristics of another who was unemployed and yet he was not totally without work. His real problem was finding other work quickly once his casual employment had ceased, and this was where Beveridge's labour exchanges would produce, in the phrase used in his book *Unemployment: A Problem of Industry* (1909), 'the organised fluidity of labour'. (Document 7C.)

In July 1908 Beveridge entered the civil service as a member of Churchill's team at the Board of Trade. Though labour exchanges were loudly called for in the Minority Report of the Poor Law Commission, his influence and Churchill's prior interest had already ensured their creation before that report appeared. In line with other developments in social policy, Beveridge was convinced that labour exchanges, to be successful, must have absolutely no connection with the Poor Law or any other destitution-relieving authority. He had advised that:

> Labour Exchanges will always be most seriously hampered in their work so long as they have any apparent association with the direct relief of distress. As instruments of industrial organisation they need industrial management. The central supervising authority should be the Board of Trade. The local management should be in the hands of a body or bodies representative of local employers and employed working either directly under the Board of Trade (the expense being made a national burden) or also under the principal local authorities, L.C.C., Town or County Council (not on any account Distress Committees or their like) if the expense remained still in part a local burden.... Labour Exchanges need to be recognised, industrialised, nationalised.[33]

In the event there was no link with the Poor Law and in 1909 the Labour Exchanges Act was passed by a Parliament whose main attention at the time was devoted to the much more sensational People's Budget. When the new service began in 1910, with Beveridge its first director, it took over the exchanges already operated by local authorities under the 1905 Unemployed Workmen's Act. Though not controversial, the introduction of state-run, nationally financed labour exchanges (whose use was to be voluntary) was a notable innovation in a free market economy. In one sense it enabled the market economy to function more smoothly by establishing a general point of contact between an employer and a potential employee. Previously the factory gate, aided by rumour, had been the only channel of notification of vacancies. Yet in another sense it was a service geared to the interests of the man looking for work. To men out of work labour exchanges were a boon. From the first, it was intended that labour exchanges should be only one half of a policy to deal with unemployment, the other half being insurance. Indeed at one time Churchill envisaged these two as part of one great bill. This idea was rejected in favour of a separate measure on labour exchanges, with unemployment insurance as part of Lloyd George's health scheme. Beveridge was convinced that labour exchanges were closely allied to insurance. The former reduced the intervals between jobs while the latter shared the risks of longer periods without work between all the workers in an industry. (Document 7D.) This was the 'magic of averages', as Churchill called it, which averaged the good times with the bad which the trade cycle appeared inevitably to bring.

Churchill relied on Beveridge and Llewellyn Smith, Permanent Secretary at the Board of Trade, to work out the details of an unemployment insurance scheme. It is interesting to note that while health insurance was the more contentious of the two, both as regards the vested interests and the public political battle, it was unemployment insurance which was more original. Health insurance had been introduced in Germany but unemployment insurance was, in the title of an article Churchill wrote in 1908, 'the untrodden field'. The few continental experiments had consisted mainly in subsidising trade union schemes, and some British unions did have unemployment funds. It was agreed at an early stage to restrict the British scheme to a certain number of trades and to make it contributory, with state support. There was much departmental discussion on the question of relating benefits to contributions and even of relating contributions to earnings, but the main debating-point was whether benefits should be withdrawn from men who were to blame for their own unemployment. As we have seen, both Churchill and Lloyd George believed that insurance entitlement made any moral connotations irrelevant. Churchill explained to Llewellyn Smith, who wished to debar men dismissed for misconduct:

I do not like mixing up moralities and mathematics. Some admixture of personal considerations is no doubt inevitable in the working of any such scheme but safety lies in the discovery of clear, ruthless, mathematical rules to which the self-interest of individuals prompts them to conform and failure to conform to which automatically relieves the fund.[34]

The rules had to be mathematical (i.e. actuarial) and not moral (i.e. distinctions between deserving and undeserving). Churchill believed that any insurance scheme would have to comprise all the factors in the risk, which might include alcoholism and bloody-mindedness as well as technological redundancy or a trade depression. In his view nothing at all would be gained by deviation into the moral aspects of individual responsibility, and his defence of this universalism has been described by Professor Gilbert as 'a classic statement of the principles of social insurance and of the essentially unconditional nature of the British welfare tradition'.[35] (Document 7E.) Churchill was in fact overruled and men dismissed for misconduct were deprived of benefit, but even Llewellyn Smith's view was based on the actuarial point (that the risk could not be calculated) rather than the moral one (that such men were undeserving poor).

Churchill did not in the event introduce the measure into Parliament in 1911 as by then he had moved to the Home Office. The scheme was well advanced before he left the Board of Trade and he therefore deserves much of the credit for it. Beveridge had insisted in 1909 that 'the principle of proportioning benefits to contributions must clearly be embodied in the Bill',[36] and Part II of the National Insurance Act of 1911 established a ratio of one week's benefit for every five contributions paid. The scheme was compulsory in a clearly defined range of industries susceptible to fluctuations (building, construction, shipbuilding, mechanical engineering, ironfounding, vehicle construction and sawmilling) in which employees and employers paid 2½d. each and the state subsidy was a third of the total, approximately 1⅔d. Benefits were to be 7s. per week up to a maximum of fifteen weeks, with opportunities for subsidies for trade unions which ran their own schemes and paid higher benefits. In all, some 2¼ million men were to be covered against unemployment, the major hazard in a working man's life. Apparently devoid of Parliamentary interest, Part II of the Act passed entirely without the bitterness associated with Part I. As the experiment accumulated evidence, it was hoped that the scheme would be extended to other trades. Again the war intervened and there was no general extension until 1920, in very different circumstances. Pressure of numbers was to change its character, but in the beginning it had been, as Beveridge later put it, 'a measure not of relief but of industrial organisation'.

The National Insurance Act covering health and unemployment was the kingpin of the social policy of a Liberal Government which had also introduced labour exchanges, old-age pensions, school meals, school medical inspection, trade boards and a redistributional budgetary programme. The question naturally arises as to why this government at this period should have embarked upon such an ambitious social policy. Three issues seem to have had an important bearing upon government motives. First, there were the assumed political advantages to be derived from an active social policy dealing with questions close to the interests of ordinary voters. Now that these voters were being wooed by Labour, many Liberals saw an attack upon inequality as a means of killing off the Labour challenge, and even beyond that as an antidote to socialism. That state welfare was not necessarily popular among working-class voters does not invalidate the idea that Liberals expected social reform to be an electoral asset.

The second important aspect was the ideology of New Liberalism. In many respects, the social policy of the government represented a working out of tensions in the Liberal party, the contradictions between traditional Gladstonian Liberalism, based on equal opportunities and low government expenditure, and New Liberalism, based on progressive finance and greater state intervention. The Liberal rejection of Lloyd George's radical 1914 budget proposals, to tax more effectively true land values and to reform municipal finance, may have represented the limit of mainstream Liberal tolerance for New Liberal social policy. Many Liberals were alarmed at the rate of middle-class desertions as revealed in the 1910 elections. To counter this, it could be argued that New Liberalism provided a strategy to contain Labour and to prevent that political polarisation between Conservative and Labour which would squeeze the Liberals. Some regional research does suggest that New Liberalism was indeed a vote winner and could promise the prospect of working-class replacements for middle-class defectors.

Yet New Liberal theorists had never seen their ideas solely as bait for the working class, but rather as a policy geared to national social needs. This relates to the third issue in Liberal motivation, the question of national efficiency. British imperial pride had received a jolt when it proved so difficult to subjugate the Boers and this was compounded by the revelation that so many volunteers had been rejected on health grounds. We have seen how this led to concern over 'physical deterioration' and an atmosphere of international Darwinism plus an arms race in Europe gave a novel importance to social questions. Moreover, the 'survival of the fittest' took on added domestic significance when theories about eugenics began to identify differential fertility rates with the 'inferior' (i.e. poorer) classes breeding indiscriminately. To this concept may be added the realisation by some businessmen that competition in the international market-place could make welfare provision an asset. This convergence of complex and sometimes inconsistent ideas into a national efficiency mentality created an informed public opinion which viewed welfare legislation as conducive to British imperial and economic interests. No longer was it a matter of humanitarian philanthropy, social policy was now good patriotic business. It should not be forgotten that, though opposing Liberal financial and legislative strategies, the Conservatives had their own positive social policy proposals, not least tariff reform which also married social and imperial issues.

These three factors – electoral advantage, New Liberal ideology and national efficiency – combined with humanitarian concern, bureaucratic initiative, social investigation and popular demand to produce a comprehensive programme, which, some Liberals today assert, represented the 'creation of the Welfare State'. In answer to this claim, one scholar complains that 'to talk of this "laying the foundations of the Welfare State" is to sacrifice historical perspective and analysis to facile metaphor and terminological anachronism'.[37] How may this conflict be resolved? It is certainly true that in such things as education, employment, housing and health, Edwardian Liberalism was deficient as compared with the standards applied in the mid-twentieth-century Welfare State. On the other hand, the two key ministers involved in these policies, Lloyd George and Churchill, were aware of the revolutionary changes they were embarking upon, not least in the conception of the positive role of the state. Churchill told Asquith in 1908: 'I believe that there is an impressive social policy to be unfolded wh. would pass ponderously through both Houses and leave an abiding mark on national history,' and again: 'There is a tremendous policy in Social Organisation. The need is urgent and the moment ripe.'[38] Furthermore, both men had more or less explicit ideas on how these minimal beginnings could be built on. Lloyd George's note on the development of a welfare service has already been quoted, and Churchill's more precise plan was as follows:

1. Labour Exchanges and Unemployment Insurance;
2. National Infirmity Insurance, etc.;
3. Special Expansive State Industries–Afforestation–Roads;
4. Modernised Poor Law, i.e. classification;

5.   Railway Amalgamation with State Control and guarantee;
6.   Education compulsory till 17.[39]

As early as 1908 Churchill, the man who reputedly refused to be locked up in a soup kitchen with Mrs Sidney Webb, was anticipating future welfare policies on a broad and comprehensive basis.

It was already possible to discern in Liberal social reform new forms of social and economic organisation which made the Liberal government's policies a clear watershed in the history of social policy. A comparison with the German system showed the clear lines of innovation:

The creation of new state welfare institutions increased the role of central over local government, enlarged the sphere of government intervention in social and economic life and strengthened the trend towards an expanding and increasingly professional state bureaucracy.[40]

As Lloyd George had significantly pointed out, many of these newer developments were actually being provided for by the Poor Law, so that Liberal social policy was not just involved with extending state aid but of providing it on different, socially more acceptable terms. A person who was sick, hungry, unemployed or old could in fact turn to the Poor Law for help, and almost all the categories of social need for which the Liberals were now catering were already being dealt with by Poor Law Guardians. The crucial development was the withdrawal from Poor Law authority of various social conditions and consequently the protection of the beneficiaries from the social or political disability of being categorised a pauper. The origins of this tendency lay in the mid-1880s with the Medical Relief Act of 1885 and Chamberlain's Circular of 1886, where the sick and the involuntarily unemployed were given limited exemption from the rigours of the Poor Law. This tendency became almost a general rule in the hands of the Liberals. School meals were provided outside the Poor Law; school medical inspection and treatment was available outside the Poor Law; a non-contributory pension could be drawn by those over the age of seventy outside the Poor Law; labour exchanges notified the unemployed of vacancies outside the Poor Law; many millions of workers were compulsorily insured against sickness and given free medical treatment outside the Poor Law; and a smaller number were insured against unemployment again outside the Poor Law. In each case it had been a deliberate act of policy to separate these newer provisions from the all-embracing but socially unacceptable scope of the Poor Law, and the Local Government Board was clearly right in anticipating that the ultimate result of such a policy was that the Poor Law would not so much be killed as die away through neglect. When all its functions were appropriated by other social institutions the Poor Law would fall apart. Whatever historical perspective is used, one cannot escape the conclusion that Liberal social policy before the First World War was at once at variance with the past and an anticipation of radical changes in the future. The work of continuing these developments was not performed by Liberal hands, for the greatest of all Liberal Governments turned out to be the last.

8 Politics and policy, 1914–39

I War and post-war

The First World War had a profound influence upon British society, for quite simply it swept away a whole world and created a new one. Things would never be quite the same and the Edwardian epoch became a vision of the distant past as though a great chasm separated 1918 from 1914. This war was in fact the greatest watershed of modern British history. However, the effects of total war in the twentieth century have been as much concerned with accelerating as with diverting the course of social policy. In very significant ways the stress of fighting the First World War accentuated developments which were already discernible in the pre-war years. The crucial developments in the much-expanded role of the state paralleled themes of the Edwardian age in two important respects. First, the greatest single stimulus to the enlargement of the function of the state was national defence. As we shall see, the quest for national security in the war effort caused the state to traverse fields very remote from military strategy. This was, in effect, a massive extension of the whole national efficiency movement of the early years of the century. Then, prospective fears for national efficiency motivated much pre-war social policy; now, the practical needs of self-defence dictated a greater amount of state intervention, what the *Manchester Guardian* called 'War Socialism'. The break between Asquith and Lloyd George in December 1916 may be viewed in many ways – personal, political or military – but perhaps the most significant underlying development was the growth of a strong collectivist urge which Asquith reluctantly accepted but which Lloyd George welcomed and carried forward.

The pressure of war, the need to mobilise the full resources of the country, led the British Government to adopt powers and enact policies undreamt of when the war began. A sort of inexorable logic forced the state forward, every step necessary as an effective enforcement of the previous one. Everything really stemmed from the Defence of the Realm Act, passed in 1914, which, with its subsequent amendments, granted large powers to the Government. It was vital to get men, materials and supplies about the country and so the railways were put under a form of quasi-nationalisation. Some shipping was requisitioned and this was vastly extended towards the end of the war. As the war was fought, various crises arose which prompted increased Government intervention, one example being the shortage of munitions. First, compulsory priority was given to government orders, and, later, state control of the munitions industry was extended by the opening of state factories. National defence had brought the state into open competition with private enterprise.

However, the state relied mainly on manufacturers and so there were huge profits to be made in war industries in a situation of full protection. Hence the question of price control became important. Coal, rents and food prices were controlled and in the later stages of the war agriculture was stimulated by state direction. By 1917 there were food subsidies and by 1918 rationing of essentials such as meat, sugar and butter. War meant deprivation, imposing a need for an order of priorities, and in facing up to this the Government was provided with the opportunities for novel modes of action. As one observer commented in 1916 in a pamphlet of newspaper articles: 'It is not one of the least compensations for this war that it has necessitated experiments on an otherwise impossible scale in the handling and rationing of the people's food and drink and upon the conversion of private into quasi-public businesses.'[1]

By no means the least significant 'experiment' was the fact that, when faced with a major crisis, the national budget could bear unimagined burdens. In 1915 the war was costing 3 million a day; by 1917 this was £7 million. Public expenditure increased sixfold during the war and the National Debt rose from £650 million to nearly £7,500 million. The political will generated by the need to raise such enormous sums of money could equally be used to meet the peace-time needs of society. Indeed Lloyd George, very much aware of the potential problems of peace-time, set up a Ministry of Reconstruction in 1917 headed by Dr Christopher Addison. The War Cabinet had asserted that reconstruction was 'not so much a question of rebuilding society as it was before the war, but of moulding a better world out of the social and economic conditions which have come into being during the war'. This theme of the state of flux caused by the war and its consequent opportunities for the literal reconstruction of society was close to Lloyd George's heart, and he told Labour leaders in 1917:

> The present war... presents an opportunity for reconstruction of industrial and economic conditions of this country such as has never been presented in the life of, probably, the world. The whole state of society is more or less molten and you can stamp upon that molten mass almost anything so long as you do it with firmness and determination.... The country will be prepared for bigger things immediately after the war... will be in a more enthusiastic mood, in a more exalted mood for the time being – in a greater mood for doing big things; and unless the opportunity is seized immediately after the war I believe it will pass away.[2]

Lest the opportunity be missed, the Ministry of Reconstruction with its various committees operated as a sort of 'think-tank' and converted ideas into practical proposals for legislation. Apart from schemes of demobilisation (which were to run into great difficulties when the time came), the main items on the agenda for reconstruction were health, housing, education and unemployment insurance, and these four issues were to figure prominently in the post-war settlement.

To an even greater extent than the Boer War, the First World War exposed through its deficient recruits the low physical condition of the British people. One survey revealed that only one in three conscripts was fit enough to join the forces. This situation strengthened the hand of health reformers. In such circles the central aim had always been the creation of a Ministry for health which would unify the various health services operating under so many different agencies (education authorities, Poor Law, public health authorities, Insurance Commissions and voluntary). Addison was a strong supporter of this and had written a Cabinet report on such a proposal even before his Reconstruction appointment. As early as March 1917 Lord Rhondda, one of the businessmen

Lloyd George brought into politics, had submitted to the Cabinet as head of the Local Government Board a memorandum on the creation of a Ministry of Health as a *war-time measure*. Public opinion, he argued, was already clamouring for improvement in health services because of deficiencies in infant and maternity care and in the treatment of war-disabled:

> These and other crying evils can only be remedied by the immediate establishment of one Central Ministry of Health in place of the two or three separate and competing Government Departments, which at present separately supervise various elements in the national health problem.... [This] would be popular and would raise no party controversies. It would be essentially a war emergency measure for making possible the immediate development of the maternity and infant welfare and other services ... which have become doubly needed by reason of the war havoc and doubly urgent if they are to be started before the difficulties of demobilisation render such an initial step both too late and impossible.[3]

The dangers Rhondda so perceptively anticipated were not heeded and the promise he elicited from the Prime Minister on his departure from the Local Government Board was not to be redeemed until 1919, when demobilisation was already well advanced.

The reason for delay lay in the old problem with which Lloyd George was bitterly familiar, the vested interests of the 'approved societies', both friendly societies and industrial insurance companies. The picture was further complicated by the vested interest of the Poor Law Division of the Local Government Board, which feared that the creation of a new Ministry might be a cloak over the belated implementation of the Minority Report's proposal of 1909 to break up the Poor Law. The approved societies were, as ever, fearful of their own position, this time anxious about the proposals that the local authorities, perhaps as the thin end of the wedge, were to take over maternity benefits and infant welfare. They were also anxious that insurance should not be detrimentally linked with the Poor Law and so favoured a Ministry which included the Poor Law medical services but left the rest fragmented elsewhere. These pressures frustrated Addison and not only delayed the introduction of a measure until 1918 but also forced him to withdraw his bill for further discussions. It was not, therefore, until 1919 that the Ministry of Health was created.

Addison was made its first Minister, with Sir Robert Morant, a lifelong supporter of the idea of a Health Ministry, as its first Permanent Secretary. In effect the new Ministry was a merging of the old Local Government Board with the Insurance Commissions and it meant that the Poor Law remained intact within the Ministry of Health. Though under immediate attack, the Poor Law was not to be remodelled until 1929.

One of Addison's first tasks in the new Ministry concerned housing, the deficiencies of which had also been exposed by the war. The inevitable cessation of house-building in war-time had produced an estimated shortage of 600,000 houses which Lloyd George was committed to remedying by his euphoric promise to provide 'homes fit for heroes'. Ever since 1875 local authorities had been empowered to replace substandard housing, and since 1890 to build council houses. The particular problem facing post-war Britain was that the massive inflation caused by the war in effect priced those most needy out of the housing market, and furthermore rent control, introduced in 1915, meant that working-class house-building was just not a profitable possibility. There was an unavoidable financial gap between a reasonable rent based on actual building costs and a rent which those in need could afford. The deficiency would have to be supplied from public funds. Once more state intervention lay in the logic of the practical housing situation.

Political fears gave a particular urgency to this logic. Throughout the early post-war years the Cabinet received regular reports from Basil Thomson, Home Office Director of Intelligence, on the threat of revolution. These alarmist reports created an atmosphere of panic among some ministers, fearful of the spread of 'Bolshevism'. The natural reaction for a government was to think in terms of repression, as had happened after the Napoleonic Wars. A cabinet official perceptively identified for the Prime Minister an alternative strategy: 'Bolshevik propaganda in this country is only dangerous in so far as it can lodge itself in the soil of genuine grievances. . . . A definite reiteration by yourself of the government's determination to push forward with an advanced social programme is the best antidote'.[4] This, indeed, was what Lloyd George advocated, for he saw an ambitious social policy as a means of creating social unity. He warned his colleagues that unthinking reaction had led to the

Bolshevik revolution in Russia and that honouring election promises in the social field would be the best security for the fabric of state and society.

In this strategy, housing occupied a particularly critical position, since both the supply of housing and its design promised valuable potential results. A vigorous housing programme offered tangible gains to the working class from the existing political structure. Moreover, the 'garden city' design with high-quality, low-density, 'parlour' houses could genuinely be advertised as a reward to returning heroes. Housing policy thus became part of the insurance against revolution where the undoubted public cost could be written off as a necessary premium on social stability. As Lloyd George reminded the Cabinet in 1919, 'Even if it cost a hundred million pounds, what was that compared to the stability of the state?'[5]

Housing had been under discussion in the later stages of the war, but effective planning was undermined by the delays in creating the Ministry of Health. It was not therefore until July 1919 that Addison's Act (the Housing and Town Planning Act) became law. This embodied two main developments. First, it invested local authorities with the duty of remedying housing deficiencies in their areas, and second, it provided Treasury subsidies first to the local councils and later to private builders for so doing. The short-lived Addison housing programme firmly committed the state to housing as a social policy based upon local initiative and central supervision, compulsion and subsidy. Addison, who displayed a Chadwickian personality which in social policy never allowed achievement to match ambition, was faced with an intolerably difficult task. On the one hand there was a crying need for new housing, which was a central plank in Lloyd George's social reform policies, while on the other shortages of materials and skilled men, higher land prices and interest rates grossly inflated the cost of implementing the housing programme. Addison assumed that housing had a higher priority than retrenchment, and his tendency to push the programme forward almost regardless of cost earned him the enmity of the Bank of England and the Treasury and led the Chancellor, Austen Chamberlain, to regard him as financially irresponsible. In a welter of recrimination Addison became a scapegoat for Lloyd George's failed social programme and was dismissed from the Government in 1921 with his housing policy terminated. Though it was costly (he was paying £800 for houses which cost £300 a year later), a final total of 213,000 were built under Addison's scheme. Indeed in 1922 an overall total of 110,000 houses were completed, and this was the largest number built with state subsidy in any inter-war year.

Once the post-war boom dissipated itself, financial pressures forced the Ministry into a deflationary policy with cuts in Government expenditure. The 1922 'Geddes axe' curtailed the housing programme and was equally severe on education, which was another social deficiency revealed during the war. The minimal state provisions for education under the 1902 Education Act were eroded by the industrial pressures of war production which led so many juveniles to quit school prematurely for factory work (though higher wages did produce more secondary school pupils). In education as elsewhere, the war provoked deprivation but also opportunity and new resolve. The Board of Education reported in 1918 that the war 'has certainly brought a clearer and wider recognition of the value of education, and, while showing the defects and shortcomings of our system, has produced the resolution to improve it'.[6]

H. A. L. Fisher, a university vice-chancellor, had been brought into the Government in 1916 and he proposed far-reaching changes in the educational system. He introduced a major Education Bill into Parliament in August 1917 which aroused so much opposition from local authorities and industry that it had to be withdrawn. Even his watered-down proposals which were finally passed in 1918 involved major extensions of state education. In particular, Fisher's Education Act of 1918 established a principle which was subsequently to be implemented over the years, that 'children and young persons shall not be debarred from receiving the benefits of any form of education by which they are capable of profiting through inability to pay fees'. This was a precursor of the idea in the 1944 Act that all children should have the education best suited to their needs and talents. A start was made in 1918 by the abolition of all fees in elementary schools, and local authorities were instructed to submit proposals for complete schemes covering all types of education in their areas. The school leaving age was raised to fourteen, continuation classes for those over fourteen were encouraged and the practice of half-time schooling was ended. Government grants to local authorities and teachers' salaries were both increased. It was a brave measure carried forward by the tide of reconstruction and it envisaged a total educational provision from nursery to university. Educational vision was overtaken by financial stringency and some of Fisher's proposals, notably the continuation classes, were victims of the 'Geddes axe'.

The most obvious sign that the post-war boom was over was the sharp increase in unemployment, which was to dominate the inter-war years as a whole. From the end of 1920 to the summer of 1940 unemployment was never below one million and at times was over three. This put an enormous burden on the unemployment insurance scheme, first begun experimentally in 1911. Retrospectively it appeared a mistake not to have extended the scheme during war-time, for in those days of full employment a big surplus would have been accumulated. Even so, with only the addition of munitions workers, the fund had a surplus of £21 million by the end of the war and this was thought sufficient to finance any new demands. The problems attendant upon a general extension of the scheme in times of distress had been well anticipated by a sub-committee of the Ministry of Reconstruction which had reported in February 1918:

> So far as hardship due to unemployment is not met by insurance the Government of the day will inevitably be driven to fall back on 'measures for the relief of distress', in other words a system of doles. It will be impossible in the middle of a great crisis to improvise any satisfactory machinery for administration and large sums will inevitably be spent in the least effective... and most demoralising way.... Unless a scheme of general insurance is devised and launched at the earliest possible date it may be impossible to avoid the disastrous chaos of unorganised and improvised methods of relieving distress.[7]

Once more planning proved no substitute for action, which in the event was 'unorganised and improvised'.

The first of the *ad hoc* responses to the practical problems of unemployment was Addison's 'out-of-work donation', at first intended for demobilised soldiers and then extended to civilian workers. This established certain precedents which were of far-reaching significance. First, it was both non-contributory and at subsistence level, which firmly established the principle that the state had a commitment to relieve and maintain the unemployed. Second, it involved dependent allowances which made their inclusion in 1921 in the unemployment scheme inevitable. Since the benefits payable were superior to those available in either of the insurance schemes (health or unemployment) or through the Poor Law, there is much truth in the notion that this out-of-work donation effectively sabotaged any future programme. Indeed it was sheer fear of the social and political consequences which might attend the abrupt ending of these schemes which caused both their extension (the civilian one until November 1919 and the military until March 1920) and the introduction of a universal insurance measure.

Thus, instead of a planned approach, the Lloyd George Coalition was, at the end of 1919, stampeded into a new scheme. The Unemployment Insurance Act of 1920 was a logical extension of the 1911 scheme to virtually all workers earning up to £250 but was unfortunate in its timing. Just at the moment when insurance was being extended to the labour force at large, unemployment was rising steeply to undermine the *insurance* aspects of the scheme. The anticipated level and duration of unemployment quickly converted the insurance fund's surplus into a massive deficit. In addition to the legitimate demands of insured workers there were many who had either exhausted their benefit or who had never earned the right to benefit. Hence began in 1921 (even before the 1920 Act was fully operational) that almost annual juggling with the levels of contributions and benefits and the grafting-on to the insurance scheme of a series of devices which sought to preserve the fiction of insurance but in reality were a system of thinly disguised outdoor relief. With the so-called extended or uncovenanted benefit began the dole. This was the age of the depression.

By 1921, the four characteristics which were to dog the treatment of unemployment relief for the decade and a half from the armistice were already present. First, it was a totally *ad hoc*, unplanned response to events, a process of devising expedients as the need arose. Not until the mid-1930s was any conscious pattern imposed. Second, it involved the system of doles (as anticipated in the report of 1918 quoted above) which effectively undermined the insurance principle. As Beveridge explained some years later, there occurred the replacement of 'the principle of insurance by the practice of largesse':

The insurance scheme of 1911 giving in exchange for contributions a strictly limited allowance to tide men over passing depression under

> a contract which though compulsory was to be something like a fair bargain for each man and each industry has been replaced by a general system of outdoor relief to the able-bodied administered by labour exchanges and financed mainly by a tax on employment.[8]

Third, the reason for this transplanting of destitution relief from the Poor Law to the insurance fund lay in the inability of Poor Law authorities to cope with so great a task as the relief of mass unemployment and the refusal of the unemployed to be left to the Poor Law. Throughout, the dole was protection for the unemployed against the Poor Law and vice versa. Fourth, underlying all, was the fear of social revolution which was a recurring theme in the history of social policy. In the early post-war years there was large-scale industrial unrest, widespread disaffection and fears of 'Bolshevism'. To leave the unemployed unaided would be to court social disturbance. The many-sided dole was thus an expedient for the defence of capitalism. It produced a demoralised, not a revolutionary, nation.

II   The central problem of unemployment

No government of the inter-war years could escape the dilemma imposed so acutely by unemployment: to throw the unemployed on to private charity would be socially and politically impossible, yet to help the unemployed might bankrupt the nation. Lloyd George's Coalition, falling apart in 1921–2, could only flounder in the necessary expedients already described, and no other ministry of the 1920s provided any decisive alternatives. Uncovenanted benefit, sustained as an insurance myth by the notion that the unemployed man could draw benefits to which future contributions would entitle him, was disliked by those involved in insurance and was regarded as a temporary though necessary expedient. As labour exchange officials were reminded:

> Uncovenanted benefit is confined to persons who are normally employed in insurable employment and who may be expected by the payment of contributions in respect of such employment in future to assist in extinguishing the deficit. *It is obviously important that the Unemployment Fund should be restored to solvency at the earliest possible moment and that a return should be made to the strict principle of contributory insurance.*'[9] (My italics.)

This belief underlay all the expedients, but only a revival in trade could rescue the insurance principle from its debasement. In fact only slowly was there an awareness that the insurance scheme was trying to cope with two quite distinct economic conditions, cyclical and structural unemployment. For those normally in work, the insurance scheme offered the 'magic of averages' tiding over bad times by thrift in the good. But for long-term unemployment due to irreversible depression in specific industries unemployment insurance benefit was destitution relief. For a long time governments assumed that the main aim was to find means of making the *insurance scheme* viable. It was an impossible task.

Nor were any more progressive notions forthcoming from the first Labour Government of 1924, under Ramsay MacDonald, for the Prime Minister's cautious approach and the need for Liberal support precluded radical action. Labour continued the 'insurance juggle' by raising benefit to 18s. (it had been reduced from 20s. to 15s. as an emergency measure in 1921) and by emphasising the need to protect the unemployed from the moral disgrace attached to the Poor Law. Extended or uncovenated benefit was relieved from its previous time limit which had left a gap between periods of benefit. Labour decreed that the unemployed should have limitless access to the unemployment insurance scheme. The Liberals, unhappy about this further diminution of the actuarial principles enshrined in 1911, forced Labour to accept a time limit of two years on these changes. This meant a further review and, in 1925, the incoming Baldwin ministry appointed the Blanesburgh Committee to inquire into the insurance scheme.

The Blanesburgh Committee has been widely criticised, though it did face up honestly to the myth of uncovenanted benefit. Its report recommended in 1927 that the actuarially unsound uncovenanted benefit should be replaced by a new standard benefit, effectively unlimited in duration, secured by a minimum of thirty contributions in two years. Thus was rejected the essential requirement of the 1911 scheme that length of benefit be proportional to amount of contributions. It implemented the notion that so long as a man had contributed something by way of an insurance premium he was entitled to draw benefits according to his need. It also reinforced the tendency by which the maintenance of the unemployed became increasingly the financial responsibility of those in work. For those who, because of exceptional unemployment, could not satisfy even the new minimal requirements there was to be a special temporary provision to be known as transitional benefit, drawn as of right but totally unrelated to any insurance contribution. Transitional benefit was yet another device to protect the unemployed from the Poor Law, for the Blanesburgh Report commented: 'The dislike of most insured persons to resort to poor relief is natural and laudable. We would encourage it...an Unemployment Insurance Scheme should provide for the great bulk of genuine unemployment in a manner honourable to those whom it benefits.'[10] The Blanesburgh Committee was trying to accommodate the interests of left and right by facing both ways simultaneously. It held out to the employers' lobby the prospect of a supposedly actuarially sound scheme on the basis of 6 per cent unemployment (an unrealistic figure): it offered to the trade union lobby as of right transitional payments for those who could not meet the '30 in 2' contribution requirements.

In implementing these new benefits (standard and traditional) under the 1927 Unemployment Insurance Act, the Baldwin government adopted the policy of allowing a more generous treatment of the unemployed, while limiting the effects by tightening up the administration of the scheme. This was exactly the justification used by Labour in getting its improved terms through Parliament in 1924. Both parties found it expedient, for financial and political reasons, to make a great issue of the prevention of abuse, and the device they used was the 'genuinely seeking work test'. Under the original insurance legislation it had been assumed that the proportioning of benefits to contributions (1 in 5 in 1911, 1 in 6 in 1920) would automatically prevent abuse. The malingerer, it was said, could only cheat himself since unnecessary claims would reduce entitlement to benefit when it was really needed. Once that principle was eroded then some alternative was required and the same Act in March 1921 which introduced uncovenanted benefit also introduced the seeking work test. Claimants had to prove that they were really trying to obtain employment otherwise they could be deprived of benefit.

At first this aroused little controversy and the provisions were considerably strengthened by Labour in 1924 so as to allay fears that increased benefits would exploit the taxpayer. The effects were immediate as rejected claims jumped from 10 to 17 per cent within three years. Baldwin's government still further intensified the attack upon supposed abuse and in some categories and in some areas those disallowed amounted to 1 in 3. During the life of the test from March 1921 to March 1930 nearly three million claims were disallowed (Deacon, 1976). It was no wonder that by the time of the 1929 election the abolition of the test was a major Labour demand, despite Labour's own extension of it. Yet the test had been part of a package aimed at protecting insured workers from the stigma of the Poor Law. It became increasingly clear during the 1920s that a reform of the Poor Law itself was a necessary part of any comprehensive treatment of unemployment. Neville Chamberlain began this task with his major Local Government Act of 1929.

Since the war there had been friction between the central Government and some guardians over what was deemed to be excessively generous relief. The most famous case was at Poplar in the early 1920s, and in 1926 Chamberlain had taken new powers to supersede errant guardians, powers which he implemented after the General Strike, in West Ham, Chester-le-Street and Bedwellty. Now in 1929 he went even further. After nearly a century of existence the guardians were swept away and their powers over the Poor Law were vested in the local authorities, who were instructed to form Public Assistance Committees (PACs) for the relief of destitution. The authorities were encouraged to allocate to their appropriate committees the Poor Law functions that were not concerned with the relief of the able-bodied (such as child care or chronic illness), and so by local initiative it was possible to begin to implement some of the proposals of the 1909 Minority Report, which had been echoed by the Maclean Report on administration in 1918. To the unemployed the new PACs were merely the old guardians writ large, and shortly to be armed with even greater inquisitorial powers. By the time local government reform came into operation the 1929 election had brought into office Ramsay MacDonald's second Labour Government, which had to face the onset of the worst world-wide depression ever experienced. By the end of the 1920s two separate approaches to the problem of unemployment were crystallising. They represented the difference between social and economic policy, or between maintenance and work, the alternatives traditionally demanded by the Labour movement. With unemployment a persistent feature of the whole decade and sticking at the apparently irreducible million, or 10 per cent of the insured labour force, there were many who, gripped by helplessness, came increasingly to feel that unemployment, like some plague from heaven, would simply have to be endured. Hence the task of *social* policy was to decide on what terms and at what level and by whom the unemployed should be maintained. Others were struggling towards the notion that unemployment could actually be cured by creating work for the unemployed. Hence the task of *economic* policy was so to organise capitalism that the nation could once more make full use of its most valuable asset, its manpower. As Beveridge concluded in 1930, repeating words he had first used in 1909, 'the problem of unemployment... is insoluble by any mere expenditure of public money. It represents not a want to be satisfied but a disease to be eradicated.'[11]

There were a variety of policy options of this second sort open to MacDonald's ministry. To start with, Labour was in a minority, relying on Liberal support, and the Liberals' 1929 election manifesto had been Lloyd George's *We Can Conquer Unemployment*. When Lloyd George fell from power in 1922 it was widely assumed that he must some day return to office. In the mid-1920s the Liberal Party pieced together a tenuous unity and various working parties produced in 1928 the so-called 'Liberal Yellow Paper' which also set out schemes to cope with unemployment. The Liberal solution involved a £250 million scheme of public works (road building, housing, electricity, telephones, etc.) financed by loans. These ideas show the influence of J. M. Keynes, the economist, who already saw in them the possibilities of the multiplier effect he was to formulate fully in his general theory of employment of 1936:

> The fact that many workpeople who are now unemployed would be receiving wages instead of unemployment pay would mean an increase in effective purchasing power which would give a general stimulus to trade. Moreover the greater trade activity would make for further trade activity: for the forces of prosperity like those of trade depression, work with cumulative effect.[12]

Keynes disliked deflationary policies which by wage reduction would force people out of depressed industries, and preferred to attract men to newer jobs by using the Sinking Fund to promote public investment.

If MacDonald disliked turning to the Liberals, then there were the ideas of Sir Oswald Mosley and Ernest Bevin within his own ranks. Mosley, a junior Minister in the Labour Government, was frustrated at the lack of drastic action on the unemployment question, and the Mosley Memorandum of 1930 was a mixture of ideas: loan-financed public works, early and increased retirement pensions, reorganisation of banking, import control and state credit for industrial development. Part Keynesian liberalism, part Hobsonian socialism and part Italian fascism, the Mosley Memorandum was a remarkable document, acceptance of which by the Labour Government would surely have made Mosley a future Labour leader. Bevin led the TUC towards a managed currency policy which involved devaluation and the dropping of the gold standard, a revenue tariff, the financing of state planning by a graduated levy on all citizens, and the weakening of the control of the rentier class. Even within Conservative ranks men such as L. S. Amery, Oliver Stanley, Robert Boothby and Harold Macmillan were advocating expansionist economic policies and a decline of *laissez-faire*. Those who believed in positive economic policies were in fact scattered through all three parties, though masters of none.

Indeed, as one historian has recently argued, the most significant division in the politics of the depression years was not the traditional one between the political parties but the argument over unemployment policy between the economic radicals and the economic conservatives.[13] The economic radicals discussed above differed in the fiscal details, but running through all of them was the realisation that public expenditure and taxation had the power to determine the level of investment and employment. The economic conservatives were those, such as MacDonald and his Chancellor Philip Snowden, who followed orthodox financial theories, the credo of the City and the Bank, the Treasury view, which comprised a desire for retrenchment and a balanced budget and dislike of great public borrowing. As one staunch deflationist put it in 1931, 'The best contribution which the State can make to assist industry and promote employment is strict economy in public expenditure and lightening the burden of debt by prudent financial administration'.[14] The economic conservatives, holding almost to a wage-fund theory as applied to capital, believed that public expenditure must inevitably divert the limited supply of capital from its normal channels. MacDonald had assured fearful capitalists in 1924 that he would not 'diminish industrial capital in order to provide relief':

> I want to make it perfectly clear that the Government have no intention of drawing off from the normal channels of trade large sums for extemporised measures which can only be palliatives . . . the necessity of expenditure for subsidised schemes in direct relief of unemployment will be judged in relation to the great necessity for maintaining undisturbed the ordinary financial facilities and the reserves of trade and industry.[15]

Above all, financial security lay for a nation, as for an individual, in a balanced budget. Criticisms of MacDonald for not employing spending to counter unemployment are to a degree anachronistic, for a coherent Keynesian theory was not available until 1936. There was no one obvious alternative, rather a plethora of possibilities, sometimes conflicting, each supported by its own experts. It was about 1930 that the quip was born 'Where five economists are gathered together there will be six conflicting opinions and two of them will be held by Keynes'. However, Keynes had already demonstrated the weakness of the official view by his confrontation with Bank and Treasury officials at the hearings of the Macmillan Committee, set up to look into the relationship of finance and industry. If Labour Ministers understood the developing Keynesian theories (which is doubtful), they rejected them in favour of orthodox 'respectable' financial opinion. Keynes eventually went to America and inspired the New Deal; Lloyd George continued in the political wilderness; Mosley left the Labour Party in disgust and later led the British fascists; and the economic radicals like Harold Macmillan remained Conservative oddities. As time passed the options narrowed and the social policy of less stringent relief for the unemployed led MacDonald into the impasse of 1931, to defend gold or resign. The background to the 1931 crisis must now be discussed.

Beveridge was convinced that the ending of distinctions between covenanted and uncovenanted benefit had been the last stab in the back for the insurance scheme: 'It was the Conservative Government of 1927 which on the bad advice of the rather stupid Blanesburgh Committee made the insurance benefit unlimited in time and formally divorced the claim to benefit from payment of contributions.'[16] If this was so, the evil was compounded by Labour in 1930 when it made the transitional benefit a charge upon the Treasury rather than the insurance fund and removed the last control officials had by reversing the 'genuinely seeking work' clause so that the onus was put on officials to prove that the applicant was not genuinely seeking work. The unemployed were now deemed innocent until proved guilty. Making benefit easier to obtain at a time when unemployment was rising above 2 million was bound to produce a budgetary deficiency at some point, and that time was not long delayed. Within two months of the changed regulations the numbers receiving transitional benefit jumped from 140,000 to 300,000, and this form of benefit cost the Treasury £19 million in its first year. Snowden, perhaps anticipating back-bench Labour opposition to the unpalatable measures he deemed necessary, agreed to the appointment in February 1931 of a committee under Sir George May to advise on how to balance the budget. The Report of the May Committee on 15 July 1931 began a chain reaction which was to destroy the Labour Government.

It is not necessary here to recount the details of the 1931 crisis, which have been fully analysed many times before. The most significant factor for the history of social policy was that the crisis represented a victory for the economic conservatism which characterised the May Committee Report. So insistent was it that debt redemption via the Sinking Fund was sacrosanct and that the budget must be balanced mainly by cuts in expenditure that in the event it exacerbated the currency crisis (which had originated in central Europe) and left the Cabinet no room for manoeuvre. Bank officials told MacDonald on 11 August:

> (1) that we were on the edge of the precipice and, unless the situation changed radically we should be over it directly; (2) that the cause of the trouble was not financial but political and lay in the complete want of confidence in H.M.G. existing among foreigners; (3) that the remedy was in the hands of the Govt. alone.[17]

It was a 'bankers' ramp', not in the sense that financial opinion deliberately sought to throw out a Labour Government, but in that the bankers (i.e. economic conservatives) decided the terms of reference within which the crisis was to be solved. The gold standard had to be preserved; this could only be done by a restoration of confidence, which in turn depended on balancing the budget. Nobody in the Labour Cabinet suggested any alternative way of looking at the problem, any alternative concept to the traditional Treasury view; it was simply a question of finding an agreed package that would balance a budget deficit of £170 million. Arthur Henderson came to support Bevin's radical schemes only after the break-up of the ministry; while it existed he offered no constructive alternative.

The crucial question came to be the unemployed. Once more the Poor Law was precluded as a remedy and Arthur Greenwood recorded that 'It was agreed that it was unpracticable to place even the partial maintenance of unemployed workers not in receipt of statutory benefit on the Poor Law'.[18] As the crisis neared its climax financial opinion decreed that a 10 per cent cut in the dole was a *sine qua non* of the restoration of confidence. No other juggle of figures would do. A *Daily Telegraph* editorial observed:

> There is only one thing that will impress the people who know in this country and abroad and that is the sight of an axe honestly laid at the upas-tree of colossal expenditure . . . . New taxes are no substitute for a lessened burden . . . . Unemployment benefit is the crux . . . as it has been the culminating cause of the present emergency.[19]

The fate of the whole ministry, indeed of the nation, depended on whether an unemployed man should live on 17s. a week or 15s. 3d. Social policy, which so many in the previous century had deemed outside the realm of government, was now central to a government's existence. Had not Charles Wood forecast in 1850 'That which twenty years ago might have changed a parish vestry may change a ministry'? All those policy options open in 1929 had narrowed to one by August 1931 – cut the dole or resign.

One should perhaps say – to give perspective – cut the dole or resign and let others cut the dole; for a Conservative–Liberal coalition, which was a likely consequence of MacDonald's resignation, would certainly have gone ahead with the package of cuts necessary for the restoration of confidence. Hence the choice for Labour Ministers was not whether the dole should be cut (for that was inevitable) but by whom. MacDonald, supported by eleven of his team, felt that, since it was unanimously agreed that cuts were 'necessary', then a Labour Government ought to face up to doing its national duty. Henderson was in the minority of nine which could not, in terms of their social conscience, be a party to laying even heavier burdens on those least able to bear them. As Hugh Dalton put it, 'This is not the kind of thing that *we* can do. Better keep the party together in opposition than break it up in office', and Walter Citrine commented that the minority had 'acted as Labour ministers would be expected to act by the Labour movement'. Forced to resign by the Cabinet split, MacDonald found himself Prime Minister of an all-party National Government, necessitated in the King's mind by a crisis of war proportions. What probably began as a political act of national self-sacrifice became for MacDonald a means of remaining Prime Minister for a further four years. Though without the Welshman's talent, MacDonald became a second Lloyd George, a prisoner in a Conservative coalition. Confidence, of course, was not permanently restored and within a month Britain went off the gold standard despite the cuts in expenditure. A bitter election sent Labour crashing to only 49 seats (though still with 6.6 million votes) and gave the National Government its 'doctor's mandate' to treat the sick patient, i.e. the nation. Retrenchment, protection and patience were the policies employed by Mac-Donald's National Government and the nation sat it out, waiting for prosperity to return.

The impact of the political crisis on the unemployed was immediate. Insurance benefits were cut by 10 per cent (from the 17s. established in 1928 to 15s. 3d.), standard benefit was limited to twenty-six weeks and transitional benefit, now called transitional payment, was to be administered by the PACs of the local authorities which were empowered to enforce a stringent means test. The means test, like the workhouse before it, was destined to leave an indelible mark on popular culture, a powerful image long after its official demise. The means test of the early 1930s was a family means test which involved a household assessment of need, taking into account the income of all its members, be it the few shillings pension of the aged parent or the coppers earned on the son's paper round. Its inquisitorial tone produced resentment and frustration among applicants and heightened family tension, already aggravated by the loss of patriarchal dignity and discipline consequent upon unemployment itself. Receipt of transitional payment through the PACs in effect put the unemployed right back on to the Poor Law (though not in name) which, locally administered, exhibited wide regional variations in scales and conditions of benefit. Injustice only added to the demoralisation.

In order to appreciate the popular resentment of the means test it is necessary to highlight what a radical change of policy it represented. The various expedients of the 1920s which so compromised the insurance principle had one thing in common – they protected the insured worker from means-tested poor relief. Beveridge, at this time, though not later, wedded to an inflexible actuarial definition of insurance, has already been quoted roundly criticising these devices. What he quite failed to understand was that claimants themselves preferred uncovenanted, extended or transitional benefits, whether actuarial or not, because these were paid as of right as *insurance* benefits, and therefore were free from the stigma of poor relief. Indeed it was official policy throughout the 1920s, no matter which party was in power, to keep the insurance classes off the Poor Law. It was almost a translation of the values of Victorian philanthropy into the world of insurance. In both, the undeserving got the Poor Law, but whereas the deserving were formerly protected by charity they were now protected by extended insurance benefit. The dictates of humanity, practicality and expediency all combined to spare those normally in work from the stigma of the means test.

So the 1931 household means test exposed large numbers to the means test who had never before been deemed appropriate for this form of discretion. In the first seven weeks of operation the household means test disallowed or reduced benefit in some 53 per cent of claims. At the end of 1931 some 400,000 people, entitled to benefit before November, felt the immediate icy blast of retrenchment. The indignity of supplication was sharpened by the novelty of the humiliation. These changes symbolised a more profound form of modernisation, as Vincent explains:

> The terms of exclusion of the poor from society were redefined to meet the conventions of the modern state. In place of disenfranchisement and the workhouse, there was the means test and the inspecting officer policing the management of the family economy. In theory the bureaucratisation of welfare promoted access and justice, in practice it engendered alienation and fear.[20]

The remarkable fact was that the indignities and humiliation of unemployment were remote from the experience of the majority of the nation. Unemployment, albeit a national problem, was not equally distributed throughout the country. The unemployment rate varied from the 67 per cent of Jarrow to 3 per cent in High Wycombe, a consequence of the concentration of the worst structural and cyclical unemployment in the nineteenth-century staple industries, coal, textiles, shipbuilding and heavy engineering. Even these variations hide the true picture, for long-term unemployment (the cruellest of all) was still more heavily concentrated in the decaying areas, as the Pilgrim Trust survey *Men without Work* shows. (Document 8A.) It is perhaps not without significance that London, the seat of power, was in the most prosperous area (that south-east of Birmingham) where consumer and service industries were expanding, while the 'distressed areas', Wales, Scotland, Lancashire and the north-east, were remote from the capital. Even at its height of over 3 million, unemployment still left over three-quarters of the labour force in work, and those fortunate enough to stay in work experienced substantial increases in real wages. This majority of the nation, in asking the unemployed to bear the full brunt of the depression, displayed a lingering feeling that somehow the men out of work deserved to be less eligibly placed than the rest. It still lay in the logic of the Benthamite greatest happiness principle that the unemployed should suffer, for the greatest happiness of the majority (i.e. the national interest) decreed that the dole should be cut and the means test imposed. Again one is drawn back to the phrase of 1834: 'Requesting to be rescued from that danger out of the property of others, he must accept assistance on the terms, whatever they may be, which the common welfare requires'. And so mllions in the 1930s found they were refused either work or adequate maintenance, for in Wal Hannington's words 'There were men anxious to work and produce not only their own maintenance but wealth in addition, yet denied both the right to work or a decent existence during enforced idleness'.[21]

Damned for ever in the eyes of the unemployed, the National Government did embark on a programme of reorganisation which by the later 1930s had rationalised the *ad hoc*, pragmatic, much-amended insurance system. At the end of 1930 the Labour Government had set up the Holman Gregory Royal Commission to inquire into unemployment insurance. Its final report in December 1932 confirmed the view Chancellor Neville Chamberlain already held, that the whole unemployment question must be taken out of politics and removed from inconsistent local control. The Royal Commission recommended that the insurance scheme proper be completely separated from the problem of long-term unemployment and destitution relief which, it said, should be dealt with by an Unemployment Assistance Committee. The Treasury was already pressing for greater central control over the disbursement of transitional payments which were costing more than insurance benefits. From these origins grew the Unemployment Assistance Board, established by the Unemployment Act of 1934 which has been described as 'a notable piece of social legislation, by which the Conservatives consolidated the welfare state'.[22]

The 1934 Unemployment Act had two distinct parts, Part I on unemployment insurance and Part II on unemployment assistance. Part I further extended the coverage of compulsory insurance so that with a separate agricultural scheme there were 14.5 million workers covered by 1937. Contributions were established on the equal thirds principle (employee, employer, state) and the 1931 cuts in benefit were rescinded. The insurance scheme was to be run by an independent statutory committee which retained no responsibility for insured workers once they had exhausted their twenty-six weeks' benefit. It attempted to make unemployment insurance a self-supporting scheme for those normally in work.

Part II of the 1934 Act dealt with those who had no entitlement to insurance benefits and who were to be the responsibility of the newly established Unemployment Assistance Board (UAB). This body was to disburse Treasury funds for 'unemployment assistance' and was to be shielded in day-to-day administration from political pressures. The UAB was to provide a new form of destitution relief for all the able-bodied on a *national* basis, and on two appointed days was to assume responsibility first for about 800,000 maintained on transitional payments by the Public Assistance Committees and later for a further 200,000 in receipt of poor relief from the PACs. It was empowered to produce its own regulations, scales and means test and from this developed its initial crisis, for when the UAB began its work in January 1935 it was discovered that its scales of benefit were lower than those operated by many of the PACs. A popular Poor Law was indeed a novelty and a major political row broke out in which the National Government, despite its 400 majority, was forced to give ground. Oliver Harvey, Minister of Labour, hurriedly ordered the so-called standstill by which applicants were temporarily given the right to claim either the PAC or the UAB scale, whichever was more favourable. It was not, therefore, until April 1937 that the able-bodied maintained by the Poor Law were absorbed into the new scheme. By then new scales had been agreed and declining unemployment helped to smooth the transition. The UAB provided at the end of the 1930s benefits according to need based on personal circumstances and family responsibilities for all those who satisfied the technical requirements of being normally in insurable occupations. Labour had finally got maintenance, if not yet work.

The 1934 Act had a profound effect upon the Poor Law, which lost almost all its able-bodied adult males and became a generalised relief agency meeting a variety of residual conditions. The old 1834 Poor Law had virtually disappeared. In 1929 the guardians had been disbanded and the 1930 Poor Law had abolished the workhouse test and the term 'pauper'. Without the able-bodied unemployed to support, the PACs could fragment the remainder of their functions and still remain an all-embracing, last-resort, general assistance service. Indoor relief still remained as a form of specialised institutional care for children, the old or the sick. Only 13 per cent of those in receipt of poor relief on 1 January 1936 were in institutions, the largest single group being the sick, while the remaining 87 per cent were receiving domiciliary relief in cash, kind or service. The sick, aged, widows, deserted wives, and unemployed still not in the UAB charge were among those relieved at home. The change in the Poor Law was indeed dramatic, as one survey reported in 1937:

> As the other public social services have grown up and have relieved the Poor Law authorities of some part of their burden, the Poor Law itself has mellowed and become more expansive. Instead of the grim Poor Law of the nineteenth century with its rigorous insistence on the principle of 'less eligibility' and the workhouse test we have a liberal and constructive service supplementing the other social services, filling in gaps and dealing with human need in the round in a way which no specialist service could ever be expected to do.[23]

Unemployment had indeed been the central issue of the inter-war years. Its malignant canker had poisoned millions of homes; it had blighted whole industrial regions; it had disinherited a generation; and it had laid low an elected government. The state's response to unemployment was the other side of the coin; unemployment had eventually produced the UAB which once and for all destroyed less eligibility (in some cases UAB scales were higher than local wage rates); it had mellowed the Poor Law; it had even forced the cautious National Government into a measure of direct action by the 1934 Special Areas Act which tried to stimulate investment in the distressed regions. Above all, unemployment had demonstrated the ultimate weakness of *laissez-faire* capitalism, and Keynes wrote that the failure to provide full employment was 'the outstanding fault of the system in which we live.... It is certain that the world will not much longer tolerate the unemployment which, apart from brief intervals of excitement, is associated ... with present-day capitalistic individualism.'[24]

When the rearmament programme of the later 1930s reduced unemployment and war production in 1940 caused it to all but disappear, the British Government unconsciously proved Keynes right.

III   Other areas of social policy

It was an ironic reversal of their pre-war positions that transposed unemployment and health insurance during the inter-war years:

> The unemployment insurance scheme found its way on to the Statute Book quietly and unobtrusively but its subsequent history has been eventful and stormy. The health insurance scheme on the other hand was forced upon the country amid a great uproar of opposition but it has since had a comparatively smooth and prosperous course.[25]

Health insurance and treatment as a panel patient became the norm for the 18 million insured workers who by 1937 were in the approved society scheme first launched in 1911. There were no major structural changes in the health insurance scheme in the inter-war years such as the half-dozen overhauls the unemployment scheme received.

The most important changes were the reduction of the state's contribution in 1926 from two-ninths to one-seventh as a Government economy measure and the cuts made in benefit to married women in 1932, as a means of retaining the solvency of the health scheme. Broadly the inter-war years witnessed a working-out of both the strengths and the weaknesses of the 1911 scheme.

As time went on, two general criticisms were increasingly voiced; one concerned the impact of unemployment and the other revolved around the powerful role and functions of the approved societies. The danger of *ad hoc* action to meet a crisis is always that it creates anomalies that are hard to justify. Once it was admitted in the early post-war years that unemployment benefits should be at subsistence level and include family allowances, the sickness benefits under the health insurance scheme were invidiously exposed. Raised to 15s. per week at the end of the war, they remained at this level throughout the inter-war years, still without dependent allowances. Since unemployment might well promote illness it was common, for instance, for a man to cease to draw a higher benefit with dependent allowances and because of sickness draw a lower one without them. The inequity was only exaggerated by the inevitable extra medical or nursing purchases required in the family. The feeling of injustice did not prevent a large-scale resort to the insurance scheme, particularly by insured married women, as a means of supplementing family income in times of depression. Doctors, who were paid a capitation fee of 9s. for each patient, were generally unwilling to refuse sick notes, particularly when unemployment was so high.

In theory it was always in the hands of the government to provide a remedy by integrating these schemes; yet in practice the powerful position of the approved societies, especially the industrial insurance companies, militated against reform. There was no question that the approved societies did, on the whole, run the scheme well, within the terms of reference as they saw them. However, there were inefficiencies and inequities about their administration of health insurance. To start with, the approved societies varied enormously in size from a hundred to a million or more members who might be scattered all over the country. Extraordinary duplication of administrative effort was involved. For instance, in a factory in the south-west, 337 employees were members of thirty-seven different societies, sixteen of which had only one member at the firm; and in 1926 it was stated that ninety-eight societies had one member each in Glasgow. The range involved may be seen from the fact that though 65 per cent of the societies insured 2 per cent of the population, 76 per cent of the population were insured by 2.5 per cent of the societies. All the societies had to pay the statutory benefits and beyond this had the power to provide discretionary extras. Apart from being costly to administer, these extra benefits varied from one company to another. Hospital and consultant services were not provided under the Act, but some societies did provide these while others could not afford to. The main extras were concerned with dental and ophthalmic services which were fairly general, while others such as convalescent or nursing allowances were not.

The need to generalise and extend the extra benefits, essential if the scheme was really to be universal, was recognised at an early stage. The question was always how to finance this at a time when governments of all parties were bent on retrenchment. A possible way out was suggested in 1926 by the Majority Report of the Royal Commission on National Health Insurance which recommended a pooling of the surplus funds of all the societies. This would have solved the financial problem of the weaker ones; but the larger, richer and more powerful societies naturally resisted this proposal. They deeply resented, moreover, the scathing attack on approved societies as a whole in the Minority Report of 1926, which wished to sweep them away altogether. As was manifest from the first discussions in 1908–11, the insurance world was a powerful political lobby. When Baldwin's Cabinet discussed the 1926 recommendations, Neville Chamberlain advised his colleagues that 'the political power and influence of the Approved Societies make it desirable in present circumstances to meet their views';[26] and so no action was taken. Though many societies allowed their members virtually no say in affairs and used the insurance scheme to promote their own private burial policies, the approved societies were to survive until after the Second World War. By 1939 it was becoming apparent that further development was not really possible within the insurance scheme, simply because priorities were wrong. As a Fabian Society tract put it in 1943:

The sick are considered not as citizens but as insured persons. The drive for them to recover comes not from the State, which has a vital need – economic, social, political, for *national health*, but from the

Approved Societies, which want to cut the cost of sickness. The whole system is based on an arbitrary distinction between the insured and the non-insured; for the latter, unless they are destitute we provide no general medical service and no maintenance during sickness.... The scheme which was remarkably progressive thirty years ago has not moved forward with the times and now is obsolete. Health insurance has served its turn.[27]

Perhaps the most significant omission in the health scheme (apart from the exclusion of dependants from medical treatment) was the lack of hospital provision. A public hospital service developed in only a piecemeal way despite the creation of the Ministry of Health which was supposed to integrate all the public medical services. By the 1929 Local Government Act the local authorities were empowered to take over Poor Law infirmaries as municipal hospitals, and Neville Chamberlain hoped that this would be the beginning of a new national hospital service. However, outside London the authorities were dilatory in taking up the opportunities offered by the 1929 Act. Between 1921 and 1938 public provision of hospital beds increased by only 4,000 to about 176,000, while the voluntary hospitals provided a further 87,000. In 1936 only thirty-nine county boroughs and ten county councils were providing a general municipal hospital service. However, many more did provide specialist hospital services such as maternity, child welfare, isolation, tuberculosis and venereal disease hospitals or clinics. By the time the war began Poor Law infirmaries and dispensaries still provided just under half of the public hospital provision. The fears expressed in 1929 that hospitals were about to be nationalised were thus proved groundless.

The multifarious functions of the Ministry of Health encouraged progressive thinkers to envisage a real *health* service widely pitched which would promote the well-being of the nation through public health, housing, town planning and industrial organisation as well as the curing of sickness. Even today it is argued that the NHS is a sickness service (i.e. curative) rather than a health service (i.e. preventive), and as early as 1937 the pressure group PEP (Political and Economic Planning) was advising:

While everyone knows that cholera, bubonic plague, malaria, scurvy and other scourges have been eliminated by the engineer or through raising the standard of living rather than by medical treatment, we are

all too apt to think of health in terms of curing and treating disease, and
to ignore or underrate the extent to which habits of life, the layout of
our towns and buildings, labour management, transport, food manufacturing and distribution and so forth can and must be brought into the
campaign for fitness.[28]

Major consolidating measures, the 1936 Public Health Act and
the 1937 Factories Act, were introduced and something of a start
was made on this ambitious programme in the field of housing
which was a major responsibility of the Health Ministry. Addison's
rather extravagant programme has already been mentioned, and
this was succeeded by two important schemes which between them
resulted in nearly a million houses being built. Neville Chamberlain's
Housing Act of 1923 was primarily aimed at private building and
offered a subsidy of £6 per house per year for twenty years. He
hoped it would allow moderately affluent workers to purchase
cheaply priced houses and so by a natural momentum move up
into better housing. In the following year John Wheatley, the
most successful Minister in MacDonald's first administration, put
the emphasis firmly on rent-aided property in the public sector.
The 1924 Housing Act offered a subsidy of £9 per house per
year for forty years for houses built to rent only at controlled
rents subsidised from the rates. Though Chamberlain himself
reduced both subsidies somewhat as a retrenchment measure in
1927, these Acts were successful in stimulating house-building.
Altogether Chamberlain's Act produced 438,000 houses while
Wheatley's topped 520,000. Together with the private houses
boom of the 1930s they helped to solve the physical shortage of
houses. War would of course renew the problem of a deficiency
in the stock of houses, yet between the wars 4 million houses had
been built: 1.1 million by local authorities, 400,000 by private
builders with public subsidies and a further 2.5 million by private
builders alone. The housing problem had been solved, or so it
seemed.

The very fact of remedying the deficiency in housing, perhaps
even by the later 1930s providing a surplus, only served to highlight the narrowness of the concept which saw the problem simply
as equating housing units with numbers of families. Rising living
standards and an increasing awareness of the pernicious impact of
bad housing, which Chadwick had first exposed nearly a century
earlier, gradually transformed the housing problem from the

need to supply a physical deficiency (which was dealt with by 1939) into a task of replacement of substandard housing or slum clearance (a problem clearly not solved by 1939). Since the nuisance-removal legislation of the nineteenth century (especially the 1875 Artisans' Dwellings Act), the local authorities had been empowered to demolish insanitary slum houses. These seeds did not flower until Arthur Greenwood included in the 1930 Housing Act subsidies for slum clearance based on the number of families rehoused and local authorities were instructed to draw up five-year plans for slum clearance. The National Government concentrated efforts on rehousing rather than new building and in 1933 suspended the previous subsidies while producing a programme of slum clearance which involved the replacement of over a quarter of a million houses and the rehousing of over a million people. Rehousing had been joined to traditional nuisance removal in public housing policy. By the 1935 Housing Act overcrowding was made a penal offence for local authorities which permitted future infringements of minimum standards now established by law.

Under the Act a census of overcrowding was taken in 1936 which even on a narrow definition of overcrowding found that some 4 per cent of working-class houses were overcrowded. Predictably there were wide regional variations; for instance, while over 20 per cent of families were overcrowded in Sunderland, in Bournemouth the figure was 0.3 per cent. Less predictably, the survey showed that size of family was as important a cause of overcrowding as size of income, which provided further evidence in favour of family allowances. The census could also be used in a Chadwickian way to correlate overcrowding (i.e. bad housing) and infant mortality (i.e. poor health). Thus taking the two towns already quoted, Sunderland had an infant mortality rate of 92 per 1,000 while Bournemouth's was only 40, at a time when the national average was 57. Even more extreme was the range between Jarrow, with 17.5 per cent of its families overcrowded and infant mortality at 114 per 1,000, and Oxford with only 1 per cent overcrowding and infant mortality at 31. While the stock of houses increased, the problem of *bad* housing continued, and not even the limited 1933 programme of rehousing was completed by 1939. As Mayhew and Mearns before and 'Shelter' later, the Second World War, by exposing 'how the other half lives', generated a renewed public indignation about bad housing conditions, a problem not likely to be solved completely during this century. Certainly the cheap money, plentiful labour and adequate materials of the 1930s made this a missed opportunity.

In housing, as in the other problems discussed, the name of Neville Chamberlain has been prominent. As Minister of Health in the 1920s and Chancellor in the 1930s he was closely concerned with local government reorganisation, the reform of the Poor Law, health insurance, hospitals and the establishment of the UAB. Indeed Professor Gilbert has argued that Chamberlain was 'the central figure in British social politics... the most successful social reformer in the 17 years between 1923 and 1939...: after 1922 no one else is really of any significance'.[29] His concern was more to do with efficient social administration than with social justice, and his most important achievement, contributory pensions in 1925, showed his skill in detailed complex legislation. Pensions under the 1908 non-contributory scheme were inevitably costly and because of inflation were raised to 10s. in 1919. Furthermore the age structure of the population meant that the numbers entitled to draw pensions at the age of seventy would grow. Before the First World War the Labour movement had been demanding pensions financed out of new taxation at the age of sixty; and a widows' and orphans' scheme (i.e. financial help on the death of the breadwinner) had been one of Lloyd George's reluctantly discarded aims in 1911. In establishing contributory pensions for the aged and for widows and orphans, Chamberlain found himself opposed politically by a Labour Party committed to non-contributory benefits and by an insurance world ever fearful of its own death benefit insurance business.

Neither of the opposition groups deflected Chamberlain from his course, and the 1925 Widows', Orphans' and Old Age Contributory Pensions Act reached the statute book safely. The scheme, which was to be financed by equal contributions of employer and employee with an elastic state subsidy to meet expenditure, was integrated into the existing health insurance system. It provided an insured worker as of right and without means test an old-age pension from sixty-five to seventy, with benefits for his widow and children on his death. At the age of seventy an insured worker would transfer to the existing non-contributory pensions, though without the statutory limitations of means, nationality and residence attached to them. The benefits were established as 10s. for an old-age pension (£1 for a married couple), 10s. for a widow, with 5s. for a first child and 3s. for subsequent children, and 7s. 6d. for orphans. Apart from the widows and orphans there were thus from 1925 three types of old-age pensioners: first, those over seventy drawing non-contributory pensions under the 1908 scheme with test of means, nationality and residence; second, those between sixty-five and seventy drawing contributory pensions under the 1925 scheme; and finally, those over seventy drawing pensions under the 1908 scheme but by right of contributions under the 1925 Act who were exempt from the limitations of means, nationality and residence. The 1925 scheme was extended in 1929 to widows first over sixty and later over fifty-five, and in 1937 to previously uninsured 'black-coated' workers. Chamberlain was thus the architect of a pension programme which survived intact until after the Second World War.

Partly because the 1925 scheme was highly complex and partly because Chamberlain's forte was mastery of a detailed technical brief, the new pensions programme has sometimes been viewed as a mere administrative development growing out of the 1908 scheme. In fact, Chamberlain's Act was of much broader social and political significance, in three important aspects.

First, the Act (along with other developments in health and unemployment) firmly embedded the contributory insurance principle within the British welfare system. The contractual entitlement, the pooling of risk and the anathema to overt social taxation made the insurance principle attractive, even to Labour in the longer term. The 1924 Labour government had missed the opportunity to extend the non-contributory scheme and to deliver the traditional socialist demand for 'work or maintenance'. The 1925 Act and its principles became incorporated in the Beveridge scheme and the Welfare State itself.

Second, this Act was the central plank in a coherent strategy, delivered in different ways by Baldwin as Prime Minister, by Churchill as Chancellor and by Chamberlain as Health Minister, to promote 'New Conservatism'. The new mass electorate could be wooed away from Labour by what Macnicol has called 'a new kind of populist capitalism' and he concludes that Chamberlain 'boldly seized the opportunity to make pensions the flagship of

New Conservatism'. As a fellow Tory wrote congratulating Chamberlain, 'not only is it a great personal triumph for you but it is also a historic event in the development of Conservative policy'.[30]

Beyond the party rivalry, thirdly, lay a broader social and political purpose, the containment of a radical socialist threat. Both politicians and civil servants consciously used social policy to defeat socialism and pushed through social reform for fear of something worse. As Chamberlain explained, 'the added security given to the worker is going to make him more contented and less restless' and Churchill believed that contributory pensions 'must lead to the stability of the general structure'.[31] Macnicol concludes:

> Pension funding became the litmus test of whether the British state could absorb, contain and render harmless the radical challenge from organised labour that had grown steadily since the 1880's.... Indeed, the period 1918–25 was probably the most important in the evolution of British welfare policy, witnessing a concerted and ultimately successful civil service strategy of containment.[32]

Education, equally regarded by many as central to social policy, was to a great extent a minor concern of governments in the interwar years, suffering particularly from the desire for retrenchment in public expenditure. There was in fact no major Education Act between Fisher's in 1918 and the great Butler Act in 1944. There were two important reports which helped to formulate the structure on which the later educational system was based. The Hadow Report of 1926 firmly established the notion of a division at eleven between what had previously been called elementary schools and the higher, central or senior schools. New terminology came into use with the primary and secondary education levels. Those higher schools established under the 1902 Act were now to become grammar schools and the others, including the senior departments of the old elementary all-age schools, were to become modern schools. The crucial turning-point at eleven-plus was thus established and 'Secondary Education for All' became a Labour slogan. The Spens Report of 1938 added a third category at the secondary level with the notion of a technical school, in addition to the grammar and modern schools. This was an attempt, again confirmed in the 1944 Act, to provide different sorts of education for different sorts of pupil. The idea, never really fulfilled, was that all three types of school would be equal in merit but catering for different needs. Educational needs were also apparent in the important Children and Young Persons Act of 1933 which built on the great 1908 Act and emphasised still more that for children in need or juvenile delinquents priority must be given to rehabilitation.

The real experience for so many of the two decades between the wars as wasted years of misery and deprivation should not cloud the genuine achievements that were registered. A revisionist school of history is seeking to amend the popular image of the 1930s as a 'decade of depression', for these were the years when consumer goods such as radios, vacuum cleaners, electric irons and even cars were first brought within the reach of the mass market. Lower prices and better housing were part of the reality of social conditions as well as grinding want and slums. Technically advanced car factories as well as silent shipyards featured on the industrial landscape. Rowntree, doing a second survey of York, found enormous progress yet still eradicable poverty. Living standards had improved by 30 per cent, he estimated, owing to smaller families, increase in real wages and the growth of social services. Yet he had taken only a bare subsistence level as his base line and he recognised that people would not be satisfied with mere subsistence as general living standards rose. (Document 8B.) Rowntree was right to highlight the role of the social services, for the Englishman of 1939 was very much better protected than his father forty years before. Pensions, health insurance, unemployment insurance, long-term unemployment relief, housing subsidies, a more humane Poor Law, an embryonic municipal hospital service, all these and more were available to a large proportion of citizens.

The pattern of government expenditure reflects this growth in the social services which some now describe as a 'social service state'. Social expenditure represented 2.4 per cent of GDP in 1918. It had grown to 11.9 per cent by 1938. To counterbalance this impression of social improvement, some historians, (for example Webster), challenge the rise in average living standards, since this hides regional variations. Official figures offer underestimated ill health, malnutrition and local blackspots of infant mortality, while many social surveys simply ignored the most deprived areas. There also appears to have been official reluctance to acknowledge the mutually re-inforcing connection between ill health and unemployment.[33] Some historians also point out that the changes in both unemployment and health administration reduced democratic control and accountability and increased centralisation.[34]

Even where there was legislative progress, policy had, however, evolved pragmatically, was unco-ordinated and still far from universal. As the PEP commented in 1937, 'The greatest single gap in the coverage of public social services is the failure to extend the insurance medical services to the dependants of the existing insured persons and others of the same income group'. Despite real progress, an overall, general, planned social policy was still not present, and to quote PEP again: 'We attach great importance to the emergence of a mature philosophy and a broad strategy of the social services which can take the place of piecemeal political and administrative improvisation.'[35]

Such ideas were becoming more widespread and by 1939, in the word of one social historian, 'a new consensus was beginning to emerge which accepted the necessity of greater state intervention, planning and the provision of full employment as a majority priority'.[36] The war showed just how much still needed to be done and generated the political will to do it.

9

War and welfare
in the 1940s

I The Second World War

If the essential theme of the 1930s had been selectivity, that of
the 1940s was universalism. That specious universalism which in
1931 had required the unemployed to share in the national sacrifice
by a 10 per cent cut in income did not hide the fact that society
and social policy were riddled with arbitrary distinctions and selective
treatment. Just as unemployment was uneven in its impact, making
it an experience depressingly familiar to specific regions and
industries, so too the evolving services were uneven in coverage.
Accidents of classification vitally affected the nature and scope
of the services available. Insured workers were covered for
unemployment, sickness, medical, old age, widows' and orphans'
benefits, non-insured workers were not; insured workers had free
access to a doctor, their families did not; a sick man received less
financial aid during his incapacity for work than one who was
unemployed; the unemployed were selectively treated, for twenty-six
weeks by the insurance scheme, then by the UAB, but a minority
of 40,000 able-bodied men who were technically not normally in
insurable occupations were left with the Poor Law; non-contributory
pensioners over seventy were subjected to a means test, contributory
pensioners were not. Common social conditions did not produce
common social security benefits as classification and technical
qualifications had usurped need as the determining factor. The
war was to have decisive influence in producing a common
experience and universal treatment for it. George V had reiterated
the need to re-create the political will to solve gigantic problems
which had characterised the years 1914–18 and had advised
Lloyd George in 1921 and Ramsay MacDonald in 1931 to tackle

unemployment as though it were a crisis of war proportions. The Second World War did, in fact, generate the political and social determination to overcome enormous difficulties, and in its wake the spirit and practice of universalism affected the course of social policy.

Much of what might be termed the spin-off effects on social policy resulted from the nature of the Second World War as a total war. When Churchill replaced Chamberlain the total war replaced the phoney war, all-out effort replaced partial effort, victory at all costs even involving social reconstruction replaced avoidance of defeat and social conservatism. In his famous phrase Churchill promised only 'blood, toil, tears and sweat', and almost by way of a *quid pro quo* the nation accepted limitless sacrifices in the war effort in return for an implied promise of a more enlightened, more open post-war society. The nearer to a total war, the greater tends to be the degree of social equality involved and so the Second World War tended to reduce social distinctions. This flowed from the character of the war as perhaps the first 'people's war', wholly dependent on the efforts and support of the whole population, not just the military prowess of a professional army. Since so many were in a very real sense participants (though not in the armed forces), the wider definition of the war effort produced a growing concern for the health and welfare of an ever-widening circle of people. The distinction between military personnel and civilians was inappropriate in such a war as this; hence the welfare of the whole society was part of the total war effort.

In such a war and to a much greater extent than in 1914 the state was forced to adopt new and powerful policies. Food shortages necessitated rationing, fears of inflation produced food subsidies, bombing led to evacuation, the needs of production brought about the almost communistic direction of labour. Total war posed in an acute form the problem of the utilisation of the full resources of the society (resources so obviously under-utilised in the unemployment of the 1930s), and so the war provided the opportunity to use the painfully learned Keynesian lessons of economic control. The cramping limitations of orthodox finance were discarded as Keynes (now with a roving commission in the British Treasury) saw increased production under state stimulus and planning demonstrate the validity of his theories. What was possible in war-time could be practised in peace as well.

These tendencies were accentuated by the universalism inherent in the problems facing English society during the Second World War. Bombs, unlike unemployment, knew no social distinctions, and so rich and poor were affected alike in the need for shelter and protection. Food rationing produced common shortages and even the royal family ate spam. An excess profit tax ensured that there would be no profiteering as in the First World War, and production was much more geared to communal national goals under state control. Though much debased by subsequent political attempts at revivification, the so-called Dunkirk spirit did bring the nation together in a common united purpose, a remarkable achievement in 1940 considering the divisive policies pursued in the 1930s. That war affected everyone while unemployment had blighted only some was a key factor in the transformation from the divided society of 1931 into the united people of 1940.

The contrast was not lost on contemporaries, and the sober, serious-minded determination to pull together and win the war was accompanied by a process of self-examination in which the constraints and deficiencies of pre-war Britain was exposed. If Britain was fighting for total victory it was surely not simply to re-create the lost opportunities of the past. Self-criticism in 1940 could only mean hopes for a brighter future of greater opportunity, and so conservative a voice as *The Times* led the way in crystallising opinion on the post-war world. (Document 9A.) The universalism, the nature of a people's war, the introspection and hopes for the future all made it likely that plans for reconstruction would be a much more important part of this war than previously. It was of great significance that from a very early stage thoughts were turning towards post-war reconstruction. There was general agreement that the major post-war aim of 1919, to return as quickly as possible to the pre-war situation, would certainly not be the priority once the Second World War was over, indeed just the reverse. In social and economic affairs the tragedy of unemployment and the possibilities created by Keynesian policies produced an overwhelming desire to build a better future. Perhaps this was where the majority of the British people and Churchill were out of step: he looked no further than winning the war; they looked beyond it. The most famous of the fruits of reconstruction, the 1942 Beveridge Report, appeared at an early stage, when defeat was certainly unlikely but victory still remote. As Beveridge explained, public interest in reconstruction 'represents simply a refusal to take victory in war as an end in itself; it must be read as a determination to understand and to approve the end beyond victory for which sacrifices are being required'.[1] In short, a people's war had to produce a people's peace.

The Beveridge Report certainly embodied the aspirations of the war years, but perhaps the war-time problem which most epitomised the impact of the war upon social policy was evacuation. Evacuation comprised the two factors which were the crucial characteristics of the social policy of the war years. First, it was pre-eminent among those situations which required a much greater involvement of the state in social affairs. Second, the very fact of evacuation acted as a mirror to society and revealed the blemishes that still remained, so generating an even greater degree of universalism. The extension of state security and the consequent stimulus to social concern on a universal rather than a selective basis characterised the war years as a whole and the problem of evacuation in particular. Evacuation was part of the process by which British society came to know itself, as the unkempt, ill-clothed, undernourished and often incontinent children of bombed cities acted as messengers carrying the evidence of the deprivation of urban working-class life into rural homes. Evacuation, which aroused the nation's social conscience in the very first year of war, became 'the most important subject in the social history of the war because it revealed to the whole people the black spots in its social life'.[2]

Evacuation and rationing were twin pillars on which was built what Paul Addison has called 'a consensus of social democracy'. The political unity of wartime, symbolised by the party truce and Labour's entry into Churchill's Coalition, generated an acceptance of progressive welfare objectives across a broad spectrum of opinion. The radicalising effects of total war were reinforced as Labour ministers insisted that domestic social problems were as important as military strategy. A kind of benevolent conspiracy emerged which recognised that the working class had to be offered a new deal if the war was to be won. In 1940, Addison argues, 'the political influence of the ration book' shifted opinion decisively to the left and a progressive consensus was established which survived for the whole decade and made possible radical social and economic policies on the basis of broad consent. The consensus was, admittedly, based on a suspension of conflict over important political and economical questions which, in the interests of war-time unity, thereby led to the temporary disappearance of certain tendentious elements in public opinion. The flowering of egalitarianism perhaps generated unrealistic hopes of social improvement and the spirit of 'fair shares' might well be dissipated once the stimulus of war was removed.[3]

The war years which thus transformed social attitudes and social expectations also witnessed important developments in social policy itself, especially in the crisis years of 1940–1, further evidence that this war was not to be fought on battlefields alone. The general tendency of much war-time social policy was to accelerate the move away from selective Poor Law services, a process which we have already noticed from the late nineteenth century onwards. Developments in the provision of school meals and milk were a good example here. We saw earlier that school meals were first provided out of public funds before the First World War, and studies in nutrition had emphasised their importance during the inter-war years. As often in the history of social policy, the popular mind refused to recognise the subtleties of social administration and still regarded school meals and milk for needy children as in some vague way an adjunct of Poor Law charity. The war years transformed this. In July 1940 increased Treasury grants produced an improvement in supply which in a year doubled the number of meals taken and increased school milk by 50 per cent. In September 1941 the requirements of an overall food policy for the nation brought school meals and milk into greater prominence as a universal measure. Rich and poor children suffered from the same war-time shortages and, as a Cabinet memorandum put it, 'There is a danger of deficiencies occurring in the quality and quantity of children's diets ... there is no question of capacity to pay: we may find the children of well-to-do parents and the children of the poor suffering alike from an inability to get the food they need.'[4] The Cabinet in the midst of war authorised increased expenditure on school meals and milk which produced a dramatic change in the coverage and nature of these provisions. Roughly one-third of all children ate at school in 1945 where one in thirty had done so in 1940, and those taking milk increased from about half to about three-quarters. Some 14 per cent of children taking meals received them free and about 10 per cent of those taking milk, and the scheme had been extended to fee-paying and private schools. A charity for the needy had been transformed into a normal school provision for all.

Similarly, the national milk scheme for mothers and infants was put on a stable footing during the early stages of the war. Direct state stimulus to the consumption of milk had begun in the 1930s and had been strengthened in 1939, though without producing much public response. In 1940 began the scheme which for three decades became the normal practice of family life, one pint of milk at about half price for every child under five, and for expectant or nursing mothers. Without means tests or social discrimination and organised nationally through the Ministry of Health with a government subsidy, the national milk scheme became immediately popular so that in 1944 only 5 per cent of those entitled were not participating. A less successful take-up rate was recorded by the scheme to provide fruit juices, vitamins and cod-liver oil for infants. The general food policy ensured that priority groups such as mothers and young children were not just entitled to essentials like milk but actually received supplies as well. War once more provided the opportunity to rectify deficiencies discovered in pre-war days, and the war-time food policy so ably directed by Lord Woolton owed much in inspiration to the nutritionist Sir John Boyd Orr, whose famous dietary survey of 1936 had concluded that 'a diet completely adequate for health according to modern standards is reached only at an income level above that of fifty per cent of the population'.[5] Since workers needed to be healthy to be able to withstand the production demands of the war effort they had to be adequately fed, and so again 'warfare necessitated welfare'. The extra state nurseries enabling young mothers to work and the better provisions for the disabled facilitating employment in useful occupations also lay in the warfare/welfare logic.

The universalist demands of a total people's war likewise diversified the activities of the UAB, which perforce dropped its association with unemployment and became simply the Assistance Board. It was now required to deal with a much wider variety of people and social need. To start with, inflation in the first year of war created enormous problems for pensioners, and in 1940 the Old Age and Widows' Pension Act empowered the Assistance Board to pay supplementary pensions based on proven needs.

As in 1908 when pensions were first introduced, the numbers in receipt of Poor Law relief was no guide to the true poverty which existed, and approximately three-quarters of a million people drew supplementary pensions in addition to the quarter of a million already on poor relief. This development by itself altered the whole character of the Assistance Board which, established to deal primarily with the long-term unemployment, was by 1941 dealing with ten pensioners to every one man unemployed. It was in the long-term continuity of social policy that this supplementation required by pensioners should be provided not by the Public Assistance Committees of the local authorities (the stigma of the Poor Law once more) but by a national agency untainted with poor relief. The desire to protect pensioners from the Poor Law applied equally to the variety of other people in war-time poverty, the victims of the blitz, those in need of hardship allowances, evacuees, dependants of internees, foreign refugees and the infinite number of people who for so many reasons were in distress because of the war. All were now dealt with by an Assistance Board whose image and character was much softened by the new form of means test imposed by the Determination of Needs Act of 1941, which owed much to Ernest Bevin, the trade union leader who was the powerful Minister of Labour in Churchill's War Cabinet. The 1931 means test had provoked a popular outcry and had been modifed somewhat in practice during the 1930s. It still left only half of claimants with their full benefit intact and even at the end of the decade the UAB was disallowing 10 per cent of claims and reducing a further third. Bevin had been a bitter critic of the household means test and was determined to abolish it. The dislocation of war-time with the consequent increased personal mobility made the old test virtually impossible to administer. So instead of the rigorous and distasteful personal enquiry, the new test assumed certain contributions from non-dependent members of the family. Immediately about a quarter of a million people benefited from the new regulations and the Assistance Board gained further popular esteem through its 1944 increased scales of supplementary allowances. Increased benefits, a more sensitive means test and an enhanced welfare role thus transformed the UAB of the 1930s into the NAB (National Assistance Board) of 1948; from a specialised unemployment relief institution to an all-purpose welfare agency.

The role of the Assistance Board in war-time thus anticipated post-war developments, and in some ways the same is true of the hospital service which also had to be radically reorganised to meet war-time needs. Chamberlain's Local Government Act of 1929 had not stimulated as much hospital municipalisation as had been hoped, and it was Chamberlain's ministry which in 1939 on the outbreak of war organised the emergency medical service which included over two-thirds of all British hospitals. It is important to realise that the emergency medical service divided an already divided hospital system. In 1939 there were the public hospitals provided by the local authorities or Public Assistance Committees and there were the far more prestigious voluntary hospitals which included the famous teaching hospitals. After 1939 both public and voluntary hospitals were to deal with two quite distinct categories of patients, those who were included in the emergency service (primarily service personnel to start with), who received free treatment financed and organised on a national basis, and those who were not. Pushed on by that same pragmatic logic in dealing with practical problems which characterised so much of the history of social policy, the war-time government was forced to extend the emergency service little by little to patients other than service personnel, munitions workers, evacuees, people with fractures, firemen and so many others that by 1944 there were twenty-six main categories of patients eligible for the emergency medical service. Large numbers of people received the benefits of an embryonic national hospital service. Since enough beds were not available to meet the whole need for hospital treatment, war-time priorities dictated that those most easily identifiable as participants in the war would get most favoured treatment, and the chronic sick and the old tended to suffer because of this. Though the emergency medical service exposed once and for all the deficiencies and inequities of the voluntary system, it thereby promoted the case for a national state hospital service. The remarkable achievements of the emergency medical service (albeit a temporary war-time expedient) in providing new operating theatres, bandages and dressings, extra beds and specialised treatment were evidence of what might be achieved by a universal hospital system.

Such a system was implicit in the Beveridge Report, which at once both expressed and augmented the essential universalist spirit of wartime. Many others besides Beveridge had assumed that the general tendencies of the later 1930s, accentuated by the war, would lead to the removal of poverty; for instance, Seebohm Rowntree wrote to a friend in 1942:

> I think it is probable that after the war a scheme of family allowances will be introduced and national minimum wages will be fixed and I think it is almost certain that the scale of benefits under the various social insurance schemes will be raised to levels which will provide the families concerned with the essentials of physical efficiency. I think therefore that there is no need to be seriously concerned about the continuation of extreme poverty.[6]

Beveridge put these aspirations into concrete form in a report which immediately caught the public imagination. Arthur Greenwood, the Minister without Portfolio in charge of reconstruction, had appointed Beveridge in 1941 chairman of an inter-departmental committee of civil servants to inquire into the whole field of social insurance. When it became clear that the proposals of the committee were likely to be controversial, it was decided that Beveridge would sign the report himself and that the members of his committee as civil servants would be regarded as his advisers. He had in any case already taken full charge by laying out the clear objectives of the committee. In December 1941 he had outlined for the committee his so-called 'heads of a scheme', and in a memorandum circulated in January 1942 he stated categorically that their aim must be 'the total abolition of that part of poverty which is due to interruption or loss of earning power'.[7] Though the committee held forty-four meetings and received in all 194 papers, the decisive ideas were contained in these two memoranda. (Document 9B.) As Beveridge later explained, once the objectives were laid out it only became a matter of finding the means of attaining them.

The Beveridge Report was published in December 1942 and was an immediate bestseller, with total sales of some 635,000. It was the culmination of a lifetime's influence upon social administration which had begun with Beveridge's advocacy of labour exchanges and insurance in 1909. Beveridge now, in 1942, used three guiding principles. First, it was time for revolutionary changes not hide-bound by past experience. Second, social insurance was only a part of a comprehensive social policy which involved attacking the five giants of Want, Disease, Ignorance, Squalor and Idleness. The concept of the five giants had been born in June 1942[8] and the insurance scheme would only tackle Want. Finally, social security was to be established by combining the functions of state and individual in such a way that personal initiative would not be stifled. Guided by these three principles, the Beveridge plan was based on three assumptions which themselves were perhaps more revolutionary than the rest of the report. Beveridge in effect was saying that any sensible Government would first of all grant family allowances, create a comprehensive health service and maintain full employment. These three prior assumptions were essential to the success of the plan.

Given these, the Beveridge plan for social insurance envisaged in return for a single weekly contribution a cradle-to-grave provision of sickness, medical, unemployment, widows', orphans', old-age, maternity, industrial injury and funeral benefits. It was universal in coverage of both risks and persons and would provide subsistence benefits for all. It was a well-organised scheme of *planned* social insurance based on the six components: flat-rate subsistence benefits, flat-rate contributions, unification of administrative responsibility, adequacy of benefits, comprehensiveness and classification. (Document 9C.) The Beveridge Report did indeed seem to be the gateway to a promised land of universal social security without means test, uniformly administered by a Ministry of Social Security.

In attempting to gauge the significance of the Beveridge Report it is worth making three general points. First, the plan of social insurance was not as revolutionary as Beveridge later maintained or as public enthusiasm assumed. Its attractive symmetry and simplicity perhaps obscured the fact that the Beveridge plan was no more than a rationalisation of the existing insurance scheme, whose gaps in coverage had been frequently exposed. It was generalising previously selective benefits, and as a scheme of social security (i.e. income maintenance in times of loss or interruption of earnings) it was a practical expression of the desire to provide a national minimum for all, a concept which originated half a century before. Certainly its single contribution for all risks and the funeral benefit was novel, and a radical departure was the inclusion of industrial injury benefits on the insurance scheme, thus taking the problem of industrial accidents out of the tortuous field of legal process. However, we miss the truly revolutionary flavour of the Beveridge Report if we restrict our attention to the insurance scheme, which was admittedly nine-tenths of the report. What was really revolutionary was the whole concept of a society so organised that it could fight what Beveridge imaginatively called the five giants. He was only dealing with want, but he was aware that his proposals had to be placed in the context of a social policy which would tackle the other four evils as well. A country whose history had been so much concerned with freedom, the freedom *to* speak, *to* write, *to* vote, was now being given a new lesson in liberty, that true freedom lay in freedom *from* want, *from* disease, *from* ignorance, *from* squalor and *from* idleness. Here, in the totality of the vision, was the revolutionary element of the Beveridge Report.

Second, a prime example of the non-revolutionary character of the social insurance plan was that it was designed as an insurance scheme. It was time for a revolution, but it was to be a British revolution which meant enshrining the best of the past in the plans for the future. As Beveridge explained, 'The scheme proposed here is in some ways a revolution but in more important ways it is a natural development from the past. It is a British Revolution.'[9] It thus rejected a socialist solution which would simply have maintained all out of taxation on the principle of from each according to his means, to each according to his needs. Beveridge was quite clear on this for it was of crucial importance. Explaining his proposals on radio the day the report appeared he said: 'The Plan for Britain is based on the contributory principle of giving not free allowances to all from the State, but giving benefits as of right in virtue of contributions made by the insured persons themselves', and in the press three months later he reiterated that freedom from want meant 'not a claim to be relieved by the State on proof of necessity and lack of other resources, but having, as of right, one's own income to keep one above the necessity for applying for relief'.[10] Since social acceptability is an important element in any social policy, Beveridge rightly judged from the history of popular resentment of the Poor Law that the British people preferred contributory benefits earned as of right to discriminatory doles. As Sir William Jowitt, the war-time Minister, explained it in 1944, social insurance 'is well known to our people ... it has been a central feature of every government scheme since 1911 and our people are therefore well versed in the idea of a system whereby they get benefit as of right'.[11] Culturally conditioned by capitalism to respect contract, British society resented means-tested relief which penalised thrift and impaired personal dignity, while respecting benefits of contractual entitlement. History and social psychology dictated that insurance, in Beveridge's phrase, 'is what the people of Britain desire'.

The Beveridge Report was significant, thirdly, because it tuned so well with the popular spirit of universalism which was so characteristic of the war years. Social acceptability because of entitlement was only strengthened by that universalism which treated everyone exactly the same. All were to be in the insurance scheme and, whether prince or pauper, would pay the same and receive the same. Flat-rate universal contributions in return for flat-rate adequate subsistence benefits, this was the magic formula which would render justice to all. So popular was it that people were prepared to pay the price of a regressive poll tax for it and invest insurance contributions with a degree of popularity. That a form of taxation with this element of inequity should be popular is a comment on the premium people place upon universal contractual entitlement. Beveridge was of course aware that flat-rate contributions which bore heavily upon low wages would limit what could be actuarially financed in the level of benefits, but the scheme was to provide no more than subsistence benefits for all, i.e. the national minimum, with the exception of industrial injury benefits which were to be earnings-related. Subsistence benefits provided both financial security and the opportunity for private thrift to supplement a minimum standard, thus neatly combining individual and community responsibility for personal and social welfare.

Perhaps here rather than in the field of unemployment Beveridge was thinking of pre-war conditions rather than likely post-war developments. His scheme would work with unemployment at up to 3.5 per cent, and he had assumed that the government would maintain full employment, which he later defined as an irreducible minimum of 3 per cent unemployment, so he did not plan his insurance scheme with the depression in mind. He did, however, assume that a universal provision of *subsistence* benefits was primarily needed, and this was thinking in terms of what Rowntree always called 'the maintenance of physical efficiency'. Affluent post-war Britain did not think of simply avoiding starvation but of maintaining in times of loss or interruption of earnings something approaching the accustomed standards of individuals and their families. Poverty becomes a relative thing once the whole society is secure against starvation, and benefits related to need have to be adjusted according to income. Universal flat-rate subsistence benefits were in fact an aspiration of the past; the future would move more and more towards earnings-related benefits.

The reception of the Beveridge Report was euphoric and this enthusiasm was largely based on the universalism which would reflect a new social cohesion. As the *Daily Mirror* headlines put it, 'Beveridge tells how to BANISH WANT. Cradle to Grave Plan. All pay – all benefit...from duke to dustman.'[12] It is significant how in the next decades the perspective on Beveridge changed quite remarkably. Social policy specialists and social historians now line up to condemn the Beveridge Report. Digby calls it, 'an ambiguous and eclectic document that was less bedrock than shifting sand', while Lowe describes, 'an ineffective and conservative document'. Abel-Smith, an influential poverty expert in the 1950s and 1960s, regrets that the report was 'flawed and failed to live up to its promises', echoing the most recent study which concludes that Beveridge was 'an unsound foundation' on which to build a Welfare State.[13]

Such criticisms are quite separate from the initial concerns over costs which were to persist over the next half century and become the staple flaw for right wing politicians and thinkers. One northern Tory MP's diary entry the day the report was published characterised a worry that was to prove long-lasting:

> It seems to me to make a big promise on an insufficient basis – a vast increase of expenditure on social services based in the supposition that our trade and industry will be as great after the war as it was before the war and that unemployment figures will not exceed a million...it seems to me sheer folly to promise higher benefits unless you are sure you can guarantee them.[14]

Half a century later Correlli Barnett had elevated such concerns into a whole interpretation of a period when 'New Jerusalem constituted a piece of romantic fantasising...the dreamers of new Jerusalem disregarded the real life problem of funding its construction out of what was now a bankrupt and backward industrial economy.'[15]

The social scientists who now criticise Beveridge do not base their critique upon such worries over welfare largesse. Indeed, they do not at all subscribe to the view that a proper Welfare State is unaffordable. Rather they are drawn to some of the incongruities and implied contradictions in the Beveridge scheme. We may see the great strength of Beveridge's emphasis upon insurance entitlements, which removed any behavioural conditions, thus fulfilling Churchill's Edwardian aim to take the 'moralities' out and put the 'mathematics' in. Yet an insurance record of contributions required regular employment and therefore was to exclude large numbers of women, the disabled and those casually employed. Though the philosophy was universalist, welfare benefits were not an adjunct of citizenship but a consequence of insurance based entitlement.

The social attractiveness of flat-rate benefits in return for flat-rate contributions proved difficult to reconcile with the equally attractive promise of adequate living standards. Though not for the want of trying, Beveridge never quite conquered the challenge of the poverty line, largely because of the problem of variable rents. Beveridge rejected separate rent allowances for fear it would complicate a symmetrical and essentially simple system. Hence it proved impossible to define a poverty line that was equally applicable in different regions where rents varied considerably. A quarter of a century later housing benefits, as a supplement to other welfare benefits, was a belated attempt to addresss this difficulty.

In any case, it would prove impossible to provide adequate benefits that were genuinely actuarially based, because of the regressive nature of insurance contributions and their impact on low wage earners. It may, therefore, have been naïve (or perhaps self-deluding) to assume that the selective, Poor Law-type, national assistance safety net would gradually become unnecessary. Paradoxically, while Britain came to be identified as the archetypal Beveridge-inspired Welfare State, the universal protection against poverty was in time largely to be guaranteed by tax-based, means tested benefits, rather than by the classic Beveridge model of insurance based and earned entitlement.

More speculatively, Beveridge has been criticised for sorting the problems of the past rather than anticipating future needs. Of course, few are blessed with a capacity to predict the future. Many of Beveridge's assumptions about social and family structure came to be undermined, such as the nuclear family or the non-working dependent wife. One parent families, divorce, cohabitation, homelessness, homosexuality, disability and mental illness, all characteristic of late twentieth-century Britain, society came to be intractable problems for the Beveridge Structure to accommodate.

For the moment, Britain in 1942 viewed the Beveridge Report as a sort of Utopia and it helped to swell the euphoria engendered a few weeks earlier by the victory at El Alamein. The massive publicity given to the report ensured widespread public awareness of its proposals, at least in general terms, and popular hopes of some immediate action were aroused. Indeed by the very publication of the report the government had, in the words of one observer, 'delivered a hostage to political fortune. Its credit, external and internal, has become bound up with the putting through of a great scheme of social security.'[16] Despite great public enthusiasm the reaction of Churchill's ministry was, to say the least, equivocal. The Army Bureau of Current Affairs (ABCA) issued a summary of the report written by Beveridge himself – and then withdrew it two days later on orders from the War Office. The withdrawal of the ABCA summary implanted in the serviceman's mind the notion that Churchill was lukewarm on the Beveridge proposals and this view gained general currency when, after a delay of three months, Parliament was invited merely to welcome the report, with no indication of any proposed government action on the Beveridge plan. The cool reception given by the War Cabinet stemmed from Churchill himself, who was unhappy about the report on two counts. First, he was doubtful whether the Beveridge proposals really were practicable and was anxious to avoid arousing impossible national aspirations. He wrote in a now famous Cabinet note:

A dangerous optimism is growing about the conditions it will be possible to establish here after the war. . . . Ministers should in my view be careful not to raise false hopes as was done last time by speeches about 'Homes for Heroes' etc. . . . It is because I do not wish to deceive the people by false hopes and airy visions of Utopia and Eldorado that I have refrained so far from making promises about the future.[17]

This caution for the future was allied, secondly, to an overriding concern with the present task of winning the war. As was mentioned earlier, Churchill wished to concentrate on fighting for victory while public opinion looked beyond that victory. It seemed to him that this euphoric reconstruction distracted attention from the main immediate problem and was almost indecent in view of the heroic fighting by Britain's ally, Russia, on the Eastern Front.

Behind the scenes there were many influences bearing on Churchill to confirm his scepticism. The Treasury warned about competing claims on the post-war budget, when the restoration of trade would have to take priority and industry not be over-burdened with extra costs. A committee of officials, appointed to review Beveridge's proposals, questioned whether a flat rate scheme could accommodate variations in rent and whether unlimited subsistence benefits could possibly be financed by insurance. Even Bevin argued in cabinet that there would have to be some time limit on benefits and some form of testing to prevent abuse. Churchill was advised in a secret report that the Conservative Party opposed unlimited subsistence benefits and foresaw a continued major role for discretionary means-tested allowances. It should not surprise us therefore to find that in the midst of the euphoria early in 1943 some doubting voices were raised. (Document 9E.)

When the Beveridge Report was debated in February 1943, Labour members moved an amendment in favour of implementing the proposals, and though this was easily defeated it was the nearest the coalition came to falling apart. Of more lasting importance, it confirmed in the public mind that Labour was the party of the Beveridge Report, and James Griffiths, a future Labour Minister in charge of insurance, commented: 'This makes the return of the Labour Party to power at the next election an absolute certainty.'[18] Ironically, where most Prime Ministers have promised the electorate more than was actually delivered, Churchill did the reverse and, though he was popularly regarded as having shelved the report, his government did initiate a great deal of social reform. Attlee did not share Bevin's dislike of Beveridge and he forced Churchill to turn his mind to the future in the latter part of 1943 when, at a Cabinet meeting, Churchill

> elaborated with great dramatic detail, how we should prepare a great book, the Book of the Transition like the War Book, running to perhaps a thousand closely printed pages, or taking the form of a number of reports and precise plans contained in drawers, one above another. . . . All parties in Parliament, the country, our returning soldiers, the whole world, would be filled with admiration if we were able to display a series of neat plans.[19]

Out of this came (in a form not quite as Churchill had anticipated) the so-called 'White Paper chase' of 1944, organised by the new Minister for Reconstruction, Lord Woolton. The White Paper *A National Health Service* of February 1944 indicated how far all-party agreement had come on this issue. Where in 1941 the Government had spoken only of a hospital service, now 'a comprehensive service covering every branch of medical and allied activity' was planned with free treatment financed out of taxation. The proposals were generally popular but were opposed by the British Medical Association (BMA) which, despite a poll of its own members supporting the plans, now began its four-year lobby against a national health service. As one recent researcher has put it, the BMA 'tried frantically to discredit it, finding sinister implications of bureaucratic control lurking everywhere under the idealistic promises of the White Paper... the BMA kept up an unedifying racket until the very eve of the new service's creation'.[20]

The second White Paper in May 1944, *Employment Policy*, marked the belated official acceptance of Keynesian economics, and some have regarded this as more significant than even the full acceptance of Beveridge. The White Paper recommended using public expenditure 'to improve the permanent equipment of society' as a means of avoiding cyclical unemployment. Though unacknowledged, it was an updated version of the 1909 Minority Report. Decaying regions of structural unemployment were to be helped to create new industries along the lines of planned regional development laid out in the 1940 Barlow Report on the location of industry. Despite its importance the employment White Paper received little attention while Beveridge's *Full Employment in a Free Society*, which appeared six months later, was a bestseller.

Popular feeling still acclaimed Beveridge as a hero and denounced tergiversation by the government, whose third White Paper, *Social Insurance*, in September 1944 finally revealed its thinking on the Beveridge Report, much of which was accepted. The coverage of all persons and all risks was included, for this comprehensiveness represented 'the solidarity and unity of the nation which in war have been its bulwark against aggression and in peace will be its guarantee of success in the fight against individual want and mischance'.[21] The major difference between the White Paper and the Beveridge Report was that the former did not accept the subsistence benefits, though it did incorporate flat-rate contributions and benefits. The 1944 White Paper was very much the model on which Labour's 1946 Insurance Act was based. Even before the end of the war the Ministry of National Insurance had been established (in November 1944), and in February 1945 the Coalition Government introduced proposals for family allowances which became law in the summer. Macnicol (1980) has shown that the eventual acceptance of family allowances owed more to a desire to keep down industry's labour costs than to concepts of social justice.

Churchill's War Cabinet had thus laid the plans for tackling three of Beveridge's giants (disease, idleness and want) and furthermore had taken positive legislative action on the other two (squalor and ignorance). Following the Scott Report of July 1942 on the utilisation of land in rural areas and the more controversial Uthwatt Report a month later on redevelopment after the war, a Ministry of Town and Country Planning was set up in 1943. The Uthwatt proposals envisaged the state taking over development rights in the areas outside cities, while within them local authorities should have increased powers of compulsory purchase at 1939 prices. There was party feuding on these ideas and the 1944 Town and Country Planning Act attempted a compromise which increased powers of compulsory purchase in blitzed, slum and overspill areas.

More important was the 1944 Education Act introduced by R. A. Butler. Educational deficiency, like so much else, had been revealed by evacuation which once more generated a desire for improvement on a universal basis. Butler's White Paper, *Educational Reconstruction*, in 1943 was greeted with general acclaim, and *The Times*, which had on its appearance predicted 'the greatest and grandest educational advance since 1870', commented when the White Paper was debated that the Commons 'showed itself of one mind to a degree rare in Parliamentary annals.... Not a single voice was raised in favour of holding up or whittling down any one of the proposals for educational advance.'[22] The White Paper became the basis of the 1944 Act which Butler and his deputy Chuter Ede steered through Parliament. It was a brave attempt to create some system in English education after decades of mere pragmatic evolution.

The Act created the office of Minister of Education and invested him with the duty of providing a comprehensive national educational system The very loaded term 'elementary' was dropped in favour of a definition of the stages of educational development, primary, secondary, further, for which all education authorities (now reduced in number) were to provide. Fee paying was abolished at all local authority secondary schools (though not at direct-grant schools), which thus ensured free education up to the school leaving age, which was to be raised to fifteen in 1945 and to sixteen as soon as possible. The voluntary Church schools were brought under firmer state control, and as a sort of *quid pro quo* an act of religious worship and religious education were made compulsory. The 1944 Act did not in fact legislate for the divisions within secondary education which caused so much later controversy. These lay in the logic of the Hadow and Spens Reports and had been confirmed by the Norwood Committee in 1943 which found three sorts of pupils which fitted in neatly with the three sorts of schools available, grammar, technical and modern. The next twenty years exposed the difficulties of creating 'parity of esteem' and equal opportunity within that state system and between the state and the direct-grant schools. Provisions for nursery schools and county colleges for part-time further education from sixteen to eighteen emphasise the total view of education which was taken in this Act, 'the most important gesture towards democracy made in the twentieth century, a fitting product of the People's War'.[23]

The war was over before most of the provisions of the 1944 Education Act could be implemented, and with peace came a return to the traditional political rivalries. An election was essential, for as Churchill had himself argued in rejecting immediate action on the Beveridge Report, Parliament had to have a renewed mandate, having been sitting for a decade. As early as 1940 J. B. Priestley, whose broadcasts inspired the nation nearly as much as Churchill, had written: 'It is absurd to pretend that this House of Commons brought together by Baldwin in the Stone Age, elected on issues as remote as the Repeal of the Corn Laws, really represents the country.'[24] The British could now turn from the People's War to the people's peace.

II Labour and the creation of the Welfare State

The landslide Labour victory in the 1945 election reputedly surprised both party leaders, Attlee and Churchill, presumably because the euphoria of victory and the achievements of Churchill as a war leader obscured the real concern of the British people for the future. As the dangers of 1940–1 receded, so public apathy about the war had increased and with this came deep-rooted popular fears that ordinary folk would be cheated out of the promised land as had happened in 1918. The nation was expressing an opinion not on the previous five years but on the decade before that. The last election had been in 1935 and this was a belated judgement passed on the depression years of the 1930s, for as one journalist has truly remarked, 'the dole queue was more evocative than El Alamein'.[25] Though Churchill's notorious indiscretion in accusing Labour of wishing to institute a British Gestapo probably had less electoral impact than is usually assumed, nevertheless it served to highlight in Attlee's words 'the difference between Winston Churchill the great leader in war of a united nation and Mr Churchill the great leader of the Conservatives'.[26] Public opinion concurred and Churchill was thanked for his war efforts but discarded for the problems of peace.

In a situation where the declared policies of the two parties were agreed on a large number of pressing issues (as was evident from the White Papers of the Coalition Government in 1944), matters of style and symbolism loomed large. Where the Conservatives adopted the bandwagon technique of the great hero, Labour concentrated more soberly on the proposals for action in its manifesto *Let Us Face the Future*. The underlying tone of this was more convincing than Churchill's hastily concocted package of reforms. While the parties were broadly agreed on the Beveridge Report, the initial reaction to it was still remembered and social security had acquired a symbolic importance for the future. As a Fabian pamphlet had explained in 1943:

> This is becoming a symbol for a society which enables a man to live his life without fear of poverty and family disaster. Other things are as important as freedom from want. But a society that guards its members from want is likely to do its other tasks well. Social security has thus become a touchstone for the future. Herein lies the real significance of the Beveridge Plan.[27]

The electorate held rightly or wrongly that, despite Churchill's wish to bring 'the magic of averages to the rescue of the millions', it was Labour which was more likely to create a new society.

These millennial feelings were shared by incoming Labour MPs, and Dalton spoke of 'walking with destiny', while John Freeman proclaimed the opening of the new Parliament as 'D-Day in the battle for the new Britain'.

With a majority of over 150, Attlee was in a strong position to embark on major legislation, especially since many of his proposals had already been supported by the Conservatives, and in the first year an enormous amount was achieved. Indeed 1945–6 marked the high point in the Labour Government's period of office; after that the severe problems of post-war Britain slowed the pace of reform. Shortages of food and raw materials meant that rationing and controls had to be continued, and the appalling winter of 1946–7, the worst since 1880, led to a major fuel crisis and soaring unemployment. As Britain shivered in the cold and listened to Attlee urging economies in the use of light and heat it appeared that fate had played a cruel trick on a nation which had endured so much in war only to be rewarded with the continued deprivation of the 'age of austerity'. With Britain's factories and shipping crippled by the war and many of her overseas assets sold off to pay for it, even the remarkable increases in production which quickly restored a peace-time economy could not prevent recurring currency crises and in 1949 Britain was forced to devalue, with accompanying cuts in public expenditure. Though the economic problems of post-war Britain would have beset any party in office, the electorate swung back towards the Conservatives, impatient for the end of rationing, controls and a siege economy. In the 1950 election Attlee's divided government had a majority of only five and in a second election in 1951 the Conservatives regained office with a working majority, although Labour actually polled more votes.

Attlee thus learnt, as Churchill had done, that even a remarkable record of achievement in office is no guarantee for future political success, and by any standards Labour's first majority Government had a considerable record. With memories of the 1930s so fresh, most assumed in 1945 that unemployment would be the key issue and someone quipped that idleness through unemployment was the big brother compared to which the rest of Beveridge's five giants were little sisters. Labour's economic policy rested on controls of raw materials in the allocation of scarce resources, accompanied by an extensive programme of nationalisation. The

Bank of England, airways, coal, gas, electricity, railways, canals and ports, and the iron and steel industry were taken into public control during Labour's period of office. In all it represented about a fifth of British industry and not only enabled nationalised industries to be run in the public interest but also gave the Government control over a substantial sector of the economy which aided the direction of the economy at large. It soon turned out that large-scale cyclical unemployment really was a thing of the past, for apart from the exceptional freak 2 million unemployed in early 1947, the two decades following the war rarely witnessed an unemployment rate of above 2 per cent. Assumption (c) of the Beveridge Report had certainly been fulfilled with unemployment below Beveridge's 'irreducible 3 per cent'.

However, full employment brings its own problems, and running the economy at full potential tended to force up wages and costs, hence producing the great post-war bugbear of inflation. Hugh Dalton, Labour's first Chancellor, was often criticised for being ultra-Keynesian in his cheap money policy, but only slowly did he come round to assessing the state of the economy by Keynes's national income and so-called inflationary gap analysis. By 1947 it was clear to many that inflation, not potential depression, was the problem, and so Keynesian deficit spending had to be put into reverse. Just as in times of cyclical depression a budget deficit will put money into the economy and thus stimulate it, so in times of inflation a budget surplus will take money out of the economy and produce 'disinflation'. Dalton used this in 1947 and his successor Sir Stafford Cripps, armed with much wider planning powers in economic affairs, took this further, using Keynesian methods of overall economic planning. Cripps, in the later years of the Labour ministry, faced those two problems which were still taxing the ingenuity of the subsequent Labour Government twenty years later. These were the need to control domestic consumption in order to switch resources into exports, and the search for a means of controlling wages to prevent inflation, the elusive incomes policy.

While most people were relieved to find that full employment went beyond their expectations, they were acutely disappointed in housing. In Beveridge's memo of January 1942 (Document 9B) he had argued that housing was the crucial difference between rich and poor. Labour had promised a massive programme of house-building (4 million houses in a decade), but the construction industry was badly hit by the shortage of materials, despite official controls against inessential building. Though the Government's record of house-building was better than that achieved after the First World War, it did not reach pre-war levels. In 1938 about 350,000 houses were built, while in 1948 the figure was 230,000 and local authority building schemes were limited, especially after the devaluation of 1949. Some help was given by the 1949 Housing Act which enabled local authorities to acquire houses for improvement or conversion with 75 per cent Exchequer subsidies. Alternatively, private owners were offered 50 per cent subsidies from local authorities for improvements in their homes, again with three-quarters of the money coming from central funds. By 1948 over 800,000 families had been rehoused since the war, but despite this, one survey estimated in 1951 that there were 750,000 fewer houses than households. Even when this gap was filled during the 1950s, increased living standards exposed all the more acutely the problems of poor housing which are still with us.

The third of Beveridge's giants, ignorance, was certainly not overcome in the immediate post-war years. In the field of education the heroic phase had been Butler's epoch-making measure, and the Labour Government presided over the working-out of the 1944 Act. By 1947 almost all the education authorities had prepared overall schemes of schooling for their areas, and in 1947 the school leaving age was raised to fifteen. By the time the hopes of the 1944 Act for a school leaving age of sixteen had been realised, very nearly thirty years had passed. Equally forlorn were the aspirations about nursery schools and county colleges. Some of the former were built, but precious few, and the county colleges with compulsory part-time education between sixteen and eighteen were shelved indefinitely. These, together with general school building and proposals for technical education, were the main victims of the cuts in expenditure towards the end of Labour's rule which accompanied first devaluation and then increased defence spending mainly because of the Korean War. The pruning of educational programmes of development after both the wars and the relegation of educational expenditure in order of priority has given rise to queries about how seriously British governments took education in the first half of the twentieth century. The general political crisis at the end of the Labour Government posed for education and the social services generally the question of how sacrosanct this kind of social expenditure ought to be in times of Treasury retrenchment.

Economies in public expenditure did not prevent a determined assault against the other two designated evils, want and disease, and the central components of the British Welfare State have always been the twin pillars of the social security system and national health service which came into operation in July 1948. Of the two, the social security programme was the less controversial since there was broad all-party agreement on the implementation of the Beveridge proposals. The Ministry of National Insurance had already been created in 1944 to take over health insurance, contributory, non-contributory and supplementary pensions from the Ministry of Health, unemployment insurance and assistance from the Ministry of Labour and workmen's compensation from the Home Office. This massive administrative reorganisation was begun in 1945 at the same time as preparations were being made for the introduction of the new family allowances in 1946. It had been the Coalition Government which had introduced the measure implementing Beveridge's assumption (a), though not at the level he recommended, and the 1945 Family Allowances Act established a universal 5s. child allowance, financed from the Exchequer, for second and subsequent children. Thus, as an official report explained, 'The State now accepted the responsibility of making a financial contribution to the cost of bringing up every family of two or more children, regardless of the parents' means'.[28] The Labour Government proposed the payment of these allowances from August 1946, in advance of the other new schemes being passed by Parliament, and a staff of 2,000 were recruited to deal with claims in the new insurance headquarters at Newcastle. Millions of leaflets and claim forms were distributed and by the time the first payments were made some 88 per cent of potential claimants had applied for allowances. By 1949, 4.7 million family allowances were being paid to nearly 3 million families at an annual cost of some £59 million.

The first of Labour's insurance measures was the National Insurance (Industrial Injuries) Act introduced in August 1945 which became law in July 1946. This was broadly in line with the Coalition's proposals of 1944 and there was little opposition during the passage of the Act. Accidents at work were now made the responsibility of the whole society, and the high accident rate of specific industries (e.g. mining and construction) was accommodated by the basic insurance principle of pooling the risks. Despite Beveridge's insistence on comprehensiveness he advised in favour of a separate industrial injuries scheme, partly for historical reasons, and this was accepted, so that within the composite insurance contribution there is an identifiably separate payment on the usual tripartite basis for insurance against accidents at work. Four types of benefit were established: injury benefit payable for the first six months; disablement benefit payable thereafter dependent on the degree of disability; supplementary benefits such as hardship allowances; and death benefits for dependants. It was generally agreed, though on no sound logical basis, that rates of benefit should be higher than the normal insurance payments, and they were set at 45s. per week with 16s. for a wife and 7s. 6d. for a first or only child.

Legislation for a separate industrial injuries scheme enshrined from the beginning a dual inconsistency in a supposedly universal social security system. First, though the Beveridge Report was insistent that all interruptions of earnings should be treated in the same way, the state treats those prevented from earning by industrial accident more generously than the sick or the unemployed. Second, the state identified industrial accident (along with war) as a specific cause of disability deserving of favoured treatment. As Beveridge realised, what was really required was 'a comprehensive scheme covering all casualties, however caused', since 'if a workman loses his leg in an accident his needs are the same whether the accident occurred in a factory or in the street'. He concluded that 'a complete solution is to be found only in a completely unified scheme for disability without demarcation by the cause of disability'.[29] We still await this.

At the time, attention was focused on the new social insurance system itself which was established by the all-embracing National Insurance Act which received the royal assent on 1 August 1946. Again this broadly followed the 1944 White Paper, with some variations in levels of contributions and benefits. The new scheme derived from Beveridge its essential character, its comprehensiveness, covering the whole population and all risks from the cradle to the grave. Within this now universal system with a classified population, an employed man received in return for a single weekly contribution entitlement to seven forms of benefit. These were sickness and unemployment benefit much as before, an old-age (now designated 'retirement') pension, more flexible maternity and widows' benefits, a guardians' allowance for orphans and an entirely new death grant to cover funeral expenses, so long the province of the industrial insurance companies. Again following Beveridge, there were flat-rate benefits in return for flat-rate contributions. The spirit of the 1940s engendered by the war dictated the necessity of the natural justice of a universalism where everyone was treated in the same way, or as Attlee put it, 'equal benefits in exchange for equal payments'.

Even at the time the flat-rate principle had its critics and James Griffiths, the Minister of National Insurance, soon admitted: 'We have reached the limit of what we can do by flat rate of contributions and in future we shall have to give further consideration to see whether some method of financing the insurance scheme other than by flat-rate contributions can be found.'[30] Of course, contributions did vary according to insurance classification (employed, self-employed and non-employed) and by age and sex; equally, the higher total contributions of employees and employers did earn an entitlement to a greater number of benefits than those available to the self-employed or non-employed. However, in 1946 neither contributions nor benefits were related to earnings. It had been Beveridge's aim to provide flat-rate subsistence benefits for all as the national minimum, the floor below which no one would be allowed to fall. Once this was accepted, equity dictated a flat-rate contribution as well.

If the scheme was to be actuarially sound and benefits closely related to contributions, then it followed that the level of benefits would be determined by the level of contributions. Yet because contributions were flat-rate they would have to be fixed at an amount which the lowest-paid worker could afford or, as Griffiths put it, 'The speed of the convoy is that of the slowest ship'. Hence, benefits would have to be pitched very near the margin of subsistence, and though the 1946 benefits were above that recommended by Beveridge there were many who doubted whether they were genuinely at subsistence level. The standard benefit for sickness unemployment and retirement was to be 26s. (with 16s. for a wife and 7s. 6d. for a first child), an increase of 2s. on existing unemployment rates, 8s. on sickness and a full 16s. for pensions. Beveridge had assumed that there would have to be a twenty-year transitional phase for pensions to reach the other levels. Labour decided to incorporate higher pensions from the outset and began paying the new pensions from October 1946. This more generous treatment of pensions than Beveridge had recommended raised fears about its impact upon the insurance scheme, and one social scientist asked: 'Can the community afford retirement pensions on this scale? Should not an attempt be made to lessen the burden of retirement pensions, either by lowering the rate (which would hardly be practicable) or by deferring retirement age?' He warned ominously: 'Higher pensions win votes at elections, but political gestures will not balance the social security budget.'[31] Post-war pensioners crippled by inflation would find this attitude bitterly ironic.

Where insurance benefits did not meet people's needs, supplementary allowances were available on a means-tested basis through the Assistance Board, now renamed the National Assistance Board (NAB). Such a residual relief agency was required not only to bring insurance benefits up to subsistence level but also to cater for those without entitlement to such benefits. Since insurance was the central principle, entitlement to most of the insurance benefits had to be earned by right of contributions, and the National Assistance Board was to deal with those who for one reason or another had not earned or had exhausted their entitlement to benefit. As we have already seen, the old UAB had been set up in 1934 to take over the long-term unemployed and had during the war catered for other categories of destitution. Now by the 1948 National Assistance Act it was to assume national responsibility for those in need still dealt with locally by the Public Assistance Committees. Bevin proclaimed 'At last we have buried the Poor Law', for the Act specifically repealed existing Poor Law legislation and categorically stated that 'the existing Poor Law shall cease to have effect'. Like those other key measures of the 1940s, the 1944 Education Act and the 1946 National Health Service Act, the 1948 National Assistance Act had a simple but universalist tone. (Document 9D.) The NAB was charged with the duty of relieving anyone whose resources did not meet his requirements.

The National Assistance Act provided for an inverted umbrella service covering the whole social security scheme. The NAB was to act as a safety-net catching all those who fell through the strands of the insurance system, and it had to be extraordinarily flexible to meet the variety of need thrown up by a complex society.

Financed and organised nationally, the NAB had at the same time to cater to local needs as the old PACs and the Poor Law Guardians before them had done. By definition it had to discover what resources applicants had before it could decide whether they were sufficient to meet the applicants' needs. The NAB continued the trend from a household to a personal means test and in addition adopted a generous 'disregard' of some capital and income in determining levels of benefit. In fact, with dependent and rent allowances on top of the standard benefit of 40s. for a married couple, some families found themselves better off on national assistance financed out of taxation than on insurance benefit financed by their own contributions.

This anomaly was forced on the Labour Government by the inflation in prices which had already set in during the late 1940s. When Griffiths had established insurance benefit rates in 1946 he believed them to be probably at subsistence level, though subsequent calculations about movements in the cost of living have cast doubt on that. When two years later he had to decide on the national assistance scales to be introduced in 1948, he acknowledged that the cost of living had gone up. The Labour left was highly sensitive about any undermining of the Beveridge proposals which, though non-socialist, the left had espoused because of the guarantee of work or full maintenance. Already in May 1946 left-wing back benchers had voted against the Labour government's limit of 180 days on unemployment benefit and any suggestion in 1948 that national assistance might be below subsistence would have provoked a further Parliamentary row. So Griffiths adopted a scale for national assistance higher than for insurance, relying on the means test to avoid any unnecessary largesse. This was exactly the line taken by Bevin when the 1944 assistance scales were set higher than the rates for contributory pensions:

> while the former [assistance] were designed to cover the maintenance of persons with no other resources and were subject to a test of need, the latter were contractual benefits paid as of right in return for contributions. Benefits under a scheme of contributory insurance had never been designed to meet the needs of all contributors...[we] rejected Sir William Beveridge's argument that benefit rates under the insurance scheme should be related to the cost of maintenance... applicants who proved need would be entitled to obtain higher rates of assistance from the Assistance Board.[32]

The higher level of benefits available through the NAB only confirmed that insurance benefits were not really at subsistence level, and in the next few years the majority of those in receipt of NAB allowances were already receiving some form of insurance benefit.

Four Acts had constructed a social security network which protected everyone against destitution or want: these were the 1945 Family Allowance Act, the 1946 National Insurance and Industrial Injuries Acts and the 1948 National Assistance Act. Furthermore, as Attlee had explained in 1946, the social security system was to be seen in the context of a full employment policy which equally attacked want. Under this universal system the whole population was provided for in times of loss or interruptions of earnings (sickness, unemployment, retirement and industrial injuries benefits), in times of exceptional family expenditure (maternity benefits, child allowances and death grants) and on the death of the breadwinner (widows' and orphans' benefits). Underpinning the social security system, national assistance provided a last-ditch relief agency to guarantee every member of society against destitution. It required a massive administrative exercise to launch the new scheme, for some 25 million people had to be classified, recorded and issued with national insurance numbers. Thousands of staff had to be recruited, many from within the administrative system which had operated since 1911. Insurance records had to be transferred from the 6,000 approved society branches and continuity of health insurance maintained during the winding-up of the societies. Enormous publicity was required to explain the new system to the nation, and 14 million homes received a free copy of a booklet called the *Family Guide to National Insurance*, while a further 50 million leaflets were published by 1949. Cinema, radio, the press and voluntary agencies were all used in the publicity drive. By the appointed day in July 1948 when the whole scheme was to start the nation had to be administratively and psychologically prepared for the new system which of course included Beveridge's assumption (b), a national health service.

We have already noted that the 1944 White Paper had envisaged a free and comprehensive health service available to all without reference to means. It was itself part of that generous universalism which characterised the war years and which suggested a sharp break in the history of medical treatment in England. We noticed how in the nineteenth century the Poor Law medical officer had become a sort of general practitioner and how an embryonic hospital service had evolved under the Poor Law umbrella. National insurance thereafter provided many millions of workers with medical (though not hospital) treatment, and the gaps in coverage had been highlighted many times, creating a build-up of pressure in favour of a comprehensive service. The approved societies had been widely criticised and during the war this criticism had increased. Beveridge had been critical of 'the dissipation of health insurance administration between a thousand approved societies of all sorts and sizes with little if any local attachment, often with no social interest',[33] and it was pretty well inevitable that they would be dispensed with.

Hence the initial problem for Labour's Minister of Health, the fire-brand Aneurin Bevan, was an administrative one, how best to organise a national health service out of the variegated medical and public health elements which already existed. The nineteenth-century pattern of social policy, as we have seen, often combined central direction, supervision and control with local executive and administrative responsibility. There was a good case to be made out for local authorities to run the new health service just as they ran the educational system, now also universal and free. Further-more, either in the public health or welfare fields they already had a long history of providing services and had since 1929 been taking over the public hospitals. Politically the local authorities also had a powerful champion in Herbert Morrison, himself the product of local government in London and an important figure in the Labour Cabinet. Hardly less intractable was the problem of how to finance the health service, through the insurance principle or via the more socialistic general taxation.

The overwhelming argument against the primacy of the local authorities was simply that the medical profession would not wear it. Even before the war was over the doctors had made it clear to Henry Willink, the Coalition Minister of Health, that they were flatly opposed to local authority control, which in the context of the pre-war hospital situation carried with it the implication of inferiority because of the disparity in prestige between the public and the private hospitals. Medical participation in the controlling bodies would be difficult to graft on to the local government structure, and local authorities could not finance a universal health service without massive subvention from central funds. The situation suggested national control through an entirely new and separate set of health authorities, while central financing was to be met partly by insurance but mostly from general taxation. Bevan preserved an element of what was to be called national health insurance by arranging for part of the national insurance contribution to be put towards the cost of the health service. Thus was born the popular myth that the health service is paid for out of insurance contributions, whereas in fact it was never intended that the insurance fund should contribute more than a fraction of the cost. As Bevan explained, 'The nation itself will have to carry the expenditure', and insurance financed only 9 per cent of the cost of the health service in 1949, 10 per cent in 1954 and 14 per cent in 1966.

Bevan's National Health Service Act passed through Parliament quite easily, despite Conservative opposition, and became law in November 1946. In effect the Act established the structure of the new service, while leaving many essential details to be negotiated by the Minister of Health by the time the service was due to begin in July 1948. The basic principle of a universal service available to all was enshrined in the Act, Bevan having rejected any upper income limit as providing a dual standard, 'one below and one above the salt'. As he later explained, there were society-wide benefits to be derived from a universal service available to all, for 'society becomes more wholesome, more serene and spiritually healthier, if it knows that its citizens have at the back of their consciousness the knowledge that not only themselves, but all their fellows, have access, when ill, to the best that medical skill can provide'.[34]

A comprehensive health and rehabilitation service was to be made available to all citizens through a tripartite structure of administration involving hospitals, medical services and local authority health and welfare services. Both local authority and voluntary hospitals were nationalised and put under the control of twenty regional hospital boards whose members were to be appointed by the Minister after due consultation. Individual hospitals within each region were to have their own management committees, and the teaching hospitals were to be separately run by their own boards of governors. Conservatives criticised the appropriation of bequests and the rejection of useful voluntary help, but Bevan replied that overall hospital planning necessitated nationalisation while the voluntary hospitals were too weak financially to do without extra state finance. Furthermore there was, he argued, an increased need for voluntary workers on the new committees.

The hospital boards were quite separate from the local executive councils, in effect an updated version of the Insurance Committees under the 1911 scheme. It was through the executive councils that the main treatment elements were organised, the dental, ophthalmic, pharmaceutical and of course general practitioner (GP) services. The executive councils were to be half professional and half lay and, though voluntary, would employ staff to administer these services. Thus the key figure, the GP, was separate from the hospital system and was also administratively separate from the whole range of local ancillary health and welfare services to be administered by local authorities, for the most part under the Medical Officer of Health (MOH), who retained his public health functions. Thus began that administrative paradox by which GPs and MOHs moved in quite separate spheres of influence.

The local authority health and welfare services included vaccination and immunisation, maternity and child care, domestic help, health visiting, home nursing and ambulances. They also embraced new functions under the National Assistance Act of 1948 which took the financial care of the destitute out of local hands but left the local authorities with responsibility for providing residential accommodation for the destitute, such things as old people's homes and reception centres. Bevan, reporting the passing of the poor-house, explained that 'a system out of keeping with the spirit of the times has now been replaced by a new conception of the community's responsibility towards those unable to fend for themselves either on account of adversity or old age'.[35] In discussing the wider range of local authority welfare services, mention should also be made of the Children Act of 1948 which implemented the Curtis Report on the care of deprived children. Local authorities were instructed to set up Children Committees with professional Children Officers and to concern themselves more with establishing a secure family environment for children in care.

The provision of separate local authority welfare services fragmented the patient's relationship with the channels of treatment. Thus expectant mothers received the aid of a midwife from the local authority, the treatment of a doctor from the executive council and, where a specialist's opinion was sought, a referral to a consultant from the regional hospital board. We are still seeking ways of unifying the health and welfare services available, and the implementation of the Seebohm Report on comprehensive social work departments is part of that process. Bevan hoped that integration would take place in health centres where the whole range of medical and local authority services would be available, but partly through lack of money and partly through the hostility of doctors few health centres were actually established.

No matter how the structure were designed, in the last resort only the doctors could make a health service work, and their mood on the passing of the 1946 Act was intransigent. Indeed within weeks a poll of general practitioners had registered a 64 per cent vote against participating in the new service, and in December a special meeting of the British Medical Association voted by 252 to 17 to break off all discussion with the Minister. Bevan had previously shown a willingness to consult with the doctors though not to negotiate with them, and he was now armed with a Parliamentary Statute which in turn represented the aspirations of the nation. He judged rightly that even the medical profession would not be able to withstand the combined will of Parliament and nation. His mode of attack was to split medical ranks by capitalising on the historic division of interest between the consultants of the Royal Colleges and the medical practitioners. In 1912 Lloyd George had aimed to by-pass the élite to get at the humble working doctor; Bevan used the élite to capture the GP. In effect he bought off ('stuffed their mouths with gold' were his words) the consultants and used them as a counterweight to break down the resistance of the BMA, ably led by Dr Guy Dain, the president, and Dr Charles Hill (the radio doctor), the secretary. Bevan got the support of the upper echelons of the medical profession by a series of concessions with important financial consequences. Consultants were to be allowed to work part-time in the hospitals for high salaries while continuing private practice as well and, more important, were to have their own pay-beds in hospitals for private patients, without limit on the fees that could be charged.

Lord Moran, President of the Royal College of Physicians, was particularly helpful to Bevan in his negotiations with the doctors. First, along with the presidents of the two other Royal Colleges, he persuaded the BMA to rescind its December 1946 decision against negotiation and throughout 1947 detailed discussions took place. However, the two sides were no nearer to a settlement when Bevan met the BMA in December 1947, at a meeting which was particularly acrimonious. The doctors were concerned about four main issues: the sale of private practices, the fear of a salaried medical service, the equity of the dismissal procedures and the possibilities of the direction of labour. Some of the more extreme leaders such as Lord Horder were prepared to stand firm unless all the four points were satisfactorily met and he told the BMA, after another referendum in March 1947 had voted nine to one against the health service, that 'the association regards the points at issue as we regard them, not bargaining points but signs of the doctor being a free man, free to practise his science and art in his patients' best interests...we must not yield on any of the points which collectively or individually spell the doctor's freedom'.[36] Bevan's own denunciation of the doctors' leaders as a 'small body of politically poisoned people' engaged in 'a squalid political conspiracy' hardly conduced to a crisis-breaking atmosphere.

The doctors' case was always based on the 'thin end of the wedge' argument, not what is happening now but what might happen in the future. Direction of doctors was never intended, though a negative control to prevent new practices opening in over-doctored areas was deemed essential to any sort of nationally equal coverage. Disciplinary procedures had many safeguards including a private hearing of an impartial committee, and it was emphasised again and again that doctors and patients would be free to join the NHS or not. In the last resort the two key issues came to be the sale of practices and the question of a state-salaried medical service. Opposition here was really self-defeating, for Bevan would not budge on the first and never intended the second. Sale of the goodwill of practices was expressly forbidden in the 1946 Act on the grounds that it was incompatible with an equal distribution of doctors over the country as a whole and with a patient's freedom of choice. Patients, said Bevan, were being sold like cattle, and he set aside £66 million as compensation for doctors who could draw their share of this on retirement.

As far as a salaried medical service was concerned it was no part of his intention to create this, though the Act did give him power to do so, and it was official Labour policy. Here greater tact and firmer assurances could have allayed medical fears, for he did on one occasion say with reference to a salaried service, 'I do not believe that the medical profession is ripe for it', and when challenged Bevan quipped, 'There is all the difference in the world between plucking fruit when it is ripe and plucking it when it is green'. Medical hostility to a salaried service went back a long time. This had been the gun which Lloyd George had held to the doctors' heads in 1912 when he claimed that opinion was growing in favour of a full-time medical profession, and he warned the doctors 'If they will not accept the terms we offer we shall have to fall back upon the whole time alternative and...once entered upon...there will be no turning back'.[37] Also in 1912, the medical politicians continued to fight while their ranks crumbled as the workaday doctors signed on for the insurance panels.

To some extent this situation repeated itself in 1948 despite Dain's confidence that it could not happen a second time. In fact, opposition to the NHS dwindled rapidly once Bevan announced in April that a salaried service would not be introduced without a further Act of Parliament and that most doctors would be paid solely by capitation fees. This, together with a restatement of assurances on other issues, was enough for Moran to plead immediately in the House of Lords for medical acceptance of the new service. In yet another ballot the 17,000 previously opposed to the health scheme fell to fewer than 10,000. Dain and Hill recognised that the battle had been lost and accepted the advice of the veterans of 1912 that it was better to retreat gracefully but united than to fight on in disunity. They knew that already a quarter of doctors in England (over a third in Wales and Scotland) had signed on for the new service and that the government's publicity campaign was bringing public pressure to bear on doctors from potential NHS patients. At a dramatic meeting of the BMA on 28 May 1948, little over a month before the new service began, the doctors finally, though ruefully, agreed to join the National Health Service, and 18,000 did so in 1948.

So on 5 July 1948, the appointed day, the whole apparatus of what came to be called the Welfare State moved into operation, the National Insurance, Industrial Injuries, National Assistance and National Health Service Acts, while the new family allowances and higher pensions had been paid since 1946. Anxiously the Government watched the administrative and financial implications work themselves out. The insurance scheme worked well and its cost was well below expectations. Indeed in the first year there was a surplus of £95 million, mostly due to savings on expected expenditure and unemployment benefits. The reason was not far to seek, for there were only 243,000 unemployed in July 1949 or 1.2 per cent of the insured labour force. The National Health Service, however, cost far more than anticipated, over £400 million in the first year. By December 1948 some 21 million people had signed acceptance forms for medical treatment in addition to the 19 million insured workers already on doctors' lists. Prescriptions, which had been running at under 7 million a month under the health insurance scheme, rose to 13.5 million in September 1948 and to nearly 19 million a month in 1951. Dental services had been planned for some 4 million cases per year while in fact initial demand was double that. Opticians dispensed 5.25 million pairs of spectacles, and the 1944 estimate of £1 million a year for ophthalmic services was rendered ludicrous by the £22 million spent in the first year of the NHS. Though excessive early demand reflected years of neglect which would soon be treated, even Bevan was frightened by soaring costs and remarked in often-quoted words: 'I shudder to think of the ceaseless cascade of medicine which is pouring down British throats at the present time.' Though Bevan resigned on the issue of NHS charges in 1951, many felt them to be inevitable in view of rising costs.

The incoming Conservatives might introduce prescription charges but they did not dismantle the Welfare State, itself the product of Conservative as well as Labour planning during the war. It is right to see the decade of the 1940s as a whole because of the continuity between war and post-war welfare developments. Yet historians and political analysts have, since Attlee's time, argued about two features of the Labour Government's achievements: how far it simply echoed wartime consensus and how socialist the programme really was. Rab Butler, the leading Conservative politician always argued that Labour policies largely involved merely implementing war-time plans following from the Beveridge Report. Some historians think the consensus has been overstated and in any case the various plans did not necessarily imply action. As one historian puts it, the wartime reports were seen by Labour 'not as blueprints for easy appropriation but as platforms on which to build more radical measures'. Another asserts that the post-war social reform programme, 'owed little or nothing to the notion of a cross party consensus.'[38]

It would be wrong to discount the political imperative arising from the social aspirations generated by the Second World War, which then produced broad agreement between the parties that social policy would be radically changed. Indeed, the Labour Government's policies encouraged further consensus that was to characterise the next decade and was given the title of 'Butskellism'. As one of Attlee's recent biographer explains, 'the success of Labour's efforts undoubtedly helped to deepen the consensus...it made it much easier for progressive Tories to come to the fore in the Conservative Party'.[39]

Such views reinforce the notion that, though radical, the Labour policies were not wholly socialist. The sheer scale of the achievement, in the context of post-war austerity and severe economic dislocation, is surely impressive as Glennester expresses it:

> Here was a society and economy reeling from the most devastating war in its history. Government had to organise and help rebuild a neglected economic infrastructure and housing stock. People had a standard of living and incomes about a third of the level enjoyed by households in the 1990s. Yet government was able to begin to house and educate and care for the health of all its citizens and accept that this was the state's prime duty.[40]

Impressive and radical it may have been, but was Labour's social policy truly socialist?

The official historian of the NHS, Charles Webster, has identified that in some respects Labour retreated from a more socialist position it had adopted by the early 1940s and we have already noted Bevan's compromises on pay beds, private patients and the salaried service. Webster concludes that 'Bevan was noticeably less radical than socialist pressure groups...He thereby sacrificed an opportunity to unify health administration.'[41] In fact, Labour policies were a patchwork quilt – part socialist, part Fabian, part liberal and part pragmatic radicalism. In endorsing the central principle of insurance and tying social benefits to contributions, Labour implicitly rejected more socialistic ideas of the comprehensive rights of citizenship.

At the same time, as in so many other debates, much rests on the definition of the term socialist. Mrs Thatcher was in no doubt that the Attlee Government's socialist credentials were sound. A recent scholar is also in little doubt that Bevan 'consistently injected a specifically socialist element into Labour's social security programme', and he concludes that Labour's agenda in the 1940s 'was one based on the principles of democratic socialism'.[42] However defined, the post-war Labour Government deserves credit. Though its Welfare State 'was a mosaic of reform and conservatism', it had created a 'plausible updated version of a land fit for heroes ... built on the scarred foundation of an ancient, war ravaged community'.[43]

10 The Welfare State – the first half-century

I Welfare consensus, 1951–79

The Welfare State survived the defeat of Attlee's Government in 1951. Indeed over the next quarter of the century the Welfare State became deeply embedded in the British political and social culture, as each party claimed the credit for either creating or developing this enduring institution in Britain. Compared to what had gone before (and what was to follow) this was an age of full employment. It was also the first age of mass affluence for the British people. In such propitious circumstances the Welfare State developed deep roots, which it would be both difficult and electorally dangerous for any party to seek to disturb or prune.

The Conservatives were in office from 1951 to 1964 and again from 1970 to 1974. Labour Governments were in power from 1964 to 1970 and from 1974 to 1979. The welfare consensus forged in war and austerity during the 1940s survived broadly intact until the 1970s. Continuities between party governments were often more evident than dramatic policy changes when one party succeeded another. Two high-profile resignations at the beginning and the end of the 1950s symbolised the consensus that had emerged. In 1951 Bevan and the future Prime Minister Harold Wilson resigned on the matter of health service charges in the face of Gaitskill's draconian budget, which was aimed at increasing military expenditure at the time of the Korean War. Perhaps even more significant was the resignation of Peter Thorneycroft as Chancellor in Macmillan's Government in 1958, when the cabinet refused to support savage welfare cuts at a time of retrenchment. So the Labour resignations demonstrated that the Welfare State could not be immune to the pressures of economic life and government policy, but equally, even the Conservatives would not regard the Welfare State as a sacrificial lamb to be disproportionately savaged at times of economic difficulty. Such parameters of policy development created a broad swathe of common ground, where the parties, whilst not agreeing on everything, certainly shared some common ideals. As Nicholas Timmins explains,

> There was a large degree of consensus of action ... the differences between the parties produced for the Welfare State services an oscillation around a mean rather than any great swing in one direction or another. The trend was in favour of the social democratic ideas embodied by the institutions and services of the Welfare State. In these circumstances and held within pragmatic grounds, the differences between the parties need make no difference to the broad shape of welfare.[1]

It is important not to overstate the idea of consensus of the middle decades of the twentieth century and some historians and social scientists now challenge whether a consensus really existed. It is certainly true that there were some ideological differences in some areas of policy. Education in the case of private schools and housing in the case of the private landlords were areas where the parties were opposed in their political and ideological positions. Yet, in practice, the Conservative and Labour Governments often ended up in similar positions, though starting from a different base and with very different destinations in mind. At election times the Conservatives frequently claimed the credit for improving welfare services and asserted that the Welfare State was safe in their hands.

Conservatives, particularly the so-called 'One-Nation Tories', saw the Welfare State as a necessary part of economic and social cohesion. Yet instinctively the Conservatives favoured individual provision and free market solutions and so the Welfare State became a compensation for the areas of economic and social life where the free market did not deliver. In effect, the Tories supported some elements of welfare as enabling the rest of the social and economic system to operate broadly as a free market. For Conservatives with varying degrees of enthusiasm, at various times, the Welfare State was a necessary expedient and therefore an important feature of British society, which needed to be developed and preserved.

Labour, however, approached the Welfare State from a different political position, although sometimes finishing in a policy position not dissimilar to that adopted by the Conservatives. Labour embraced the Welfare State not just because one of its governments had created it, but because it was a valuable instrument in delivering the wider social and political aspirations of Labour. The Welfare State for Labour was an essential ingredient in creating a fairer society with a more equal distribution of wealth. For Labour, the Welfare State was not a necessary evil but a powerful tool for the protection of the weak and a vital instrument for bringing about the so-called 'new Jerusalem', a land of fair shares and equal opportunity.

Over time the Welfare State came to be debated as an issue between universalism and selectivity. At heart Labour believed in universalism but recognised that for both economic and practical reasons some elements of selectivity would have to exist; the Conservatives, on the other hand, were selectivists at heart but acknowledged the political realities which made some elements of universalism necessary and desirable. Sometimes the party rhetoric exaggerated the differences. This was neatly illustrated around the time of the 1970 election. On Labour's side the Child Poverty Action Group acted as a left-wing pressure group which sought to stiffen the resolve of Wilson's socialist creed. The Conservatives had 'Selsdon Man' the mythical free market inspiration for an incoming Heath Government. These two political influences inhabited quite different points on the political spectrum. In practice, however, there was much continuity between the policies before and after 1970. Even where an ideological welfare consensus had not existed, a practical welfare consensus certainly developed.

For example, both parties introduced NHS charges; both eroded the flat-rate Beveridge principle by the introduction of earnings-related contributions and benefits; both undermined the actuarial basis of the Beveridge scheme by treating National Insurance Contributions as another form of taxation; and both found it necessary to critically review welfare policy in times of economic crisis.

Above all there were two areas in which both Labour and Conservative ministers and policies played a significant role that was to generate challenges and problems that persist up to the present time. The first concerns the so-called poverty trap. Because policies were often targeted at particular areas and because there was no coherent relationship between benefit policy and taxation policy and because the Welfare State became increasingly complex, there were many individuals and social groups for whom the balance of interest between welfare dependency and individual economic survival became problematic. Both parties were to contribute to the widely-held view that the Welfare State reduced incentive and weakened individual motivation to work and to find economic salvation through individual effort. The bizarre and unplanned consequence of what had been individually justifiable policies or benefits came to leave many welfare claimants in a poverty trap in which their effective marginal tax rate could become anything up to 100 per cent.

This did not result from any generalised parsimony on the part of public welfare agencies. Indeed the second significant feature that affected both parties was a relentless growth in social welfare expenditure over the period as a whole. Whether measured in public expenditure terms or as a proportion of the gross domestic product (GDP), from the late 1940s through to the late 1970s welfare state expenditure grew at a more rapid rate than the economy as a whole. Hence, whether there was a Conservative or a Labour government, this was a period when the Welfare State consumed an increasing proportion of national resources. If anything, the rate of expenditure grew more rapidly under the Conservatives than under Labour. It was therefore the governments of both parties that eventually came to be pilloried for allowing the Welfare State to become a burden on the British economy by consuming disproportionate resources and crowding out necessary investment in economic growth.

There are many factors independent of party that explain this relentless growth in social expenditure. The first is a simple matter of demographics. At both ends of the age range there were increased numbers to be dealt with. The baby booms of the late 1940s and again in the 1960s produced more children who needed to be educated and more demand for infant welfare services. As the expectation of life increased so there were more pensioners to be supported, who in turn made disproportionate demands upon the health services. Demographic imperatives could thus be a powerful cause of increased welfare expenditure. Second, the Welfare State was extended to new client groups, some of whom had not even been recognised or who had been inadequately dealt with in the Beveridge-based system. This included groups which emerged from changes in patterns of social behaviour. These included one-parent families, divorced people, women who could no longer be regarded as simply dependent on their husbands, even when they had one, and low wage-earning families. In addition, as we shall see, definitions of poverty broadened into a relative instead of an absolute standard and so this brought more people within the remit of the Welfare State. The third factor that was likely to send expenditure upwards was what might be termed the democratic demand of society. For example, technological changes in health would themselves generate increased expectations that could only be met from increased resources. The democratic process encouraged people to expect – and parties to promise – better standards for all, particularly for those covered by welfare services. Service-led improvements in turn led ministers of spending departments to bid for increased funds so that their favoured policy objective could be delivered.

Finally, many analysts have identified the bureaucratic nature of the British Welfare State as having within it the seeds of further expansion in coverage and expenditure. Professional pride would drive officers towards improving the quality of service and delivery and more senior officers in the government departments central to the Welfare State had an incentive to increase the size of their empires. On this argument there was a built-in momentum towards an increased role for government departments and agencies in the delivery of social welfare services and benefits to the wider British people. Knowing the processes in detail, such officers would naturally wish to remove bottlenecks, to smooth the administration and improve delivery. Such improvements would nearly always involve an increase in resources and thus bureaucracy was a powerful force in support of ministers who wished to enlarge the budgets of their departments. The general issue of continuity, the greater reliance on selectivity and the increased costs of policy development are revealed in a survey on specific policy areas.

The National Health Service was described by one observer as 'the nearest Britain has ever come to institutionalised altruism', by another as 'the greatest improvement in health care ever experienced in the nation's history' and a third ranked it 'next to the monarchy as a unchallenged landmark in the political landscape'.[2]

In such circumstances it was understandable that the NHS was an institution that neither party could afford to dismantle. In the 1950s, health expenditure rose dramatically, as a result of the decades of neglect that had gone before. It appeared to fulfil the fears of those who viewed welfare expenditure as inimical to economic growth, as NHS costs rose relentlessly and apparently out of control. However, in an important counter to such views, the Guillebaud Committee reported in 1955 that, in fact, increased expenditure was largely the result of inflation. The Committee concluded that as a share of GDP, health expenditure had actually fallen and the report promoted the novel approach that social expenditure should be related to both inflation and economic growth and not viewed in simply monetary terms. The Guillebaud Report laid to rest the controversy over health service expenditure and the NHS was largely in a political backwater in the later 1950s and 1960s. This led to a period of consolidation during which both the strengths and the weaknesses of the 1948 settlement were ingrained in practice. In particular, the tripartite structure was not reformed and preventative policies and practices were ignored. So the NHS effectively became a national sickness service, with 70 per cent of the expenditure devoted to hospital (i.e. acute) care.

In the light of this pattern of expenditure some political and policy attention had to be devoted to the distribution and nature of hospital places. In 1962 an ambitious Hospital Plan was developed by Enoch Powell assisted by a new Permanent Secretary at the Ministry and a new Chief Medical Officer. The plan envisaged a national system of large general hospitals where both patients and doctors would have the use of good modern facilities. In fact, the Plan was a failure, partly through the lack of consistent funding, partly through local resistance to hospital closures necessitated by the centralisation of facilities, and partly through failings in the pro-curement of new buildings. The parallel improvements in community support for the elderly and mentally ill simply failed to materialise.

The incoming Wilson Labour Government inherited the hospital building programme which it carried forward. It also committed itself to increasing health service expenditure, a policy broadly fulfilled despite economic crises and retrenchment in the later 1960s. Pre-scription charges neatly illustrate Labour's problem in the 1960s. Introduced by the Conservatives in 1952, prescription charges became a symbol of the Tories' wasted years and the 1964 Labour

Election Manifesto promised their abolition. They were duly abolished in 1965 amidst claims of returning to the free NHS planned by Bevan in 1948. However, the Wilson Government failed to address successfully the problems of economic under-performance and Britain was forced to devalue the pound in 1967. In the wake of this reversal, severe economies in public expenditure were required and prescription charges were re-introduced in 1968.

Labour began the process of institutional changes and health and social security were brought together in a single department under a powerful senior Minister, Richard Crossman. Labour also began to develop ideas for the remodelling of the civil service, local government and the NHS. However, plans for structural reform were not implemented before Labour was surprisingly defeated in the 1970 election. The Conservative Government under Edward Heath took forward many of these ideas and the continuity in large areas of policy before and after 1970 is often cited as the best evidence of a welfare consensus. The one change that Crossman did oversee was the implementation of the 1968 Seebohm Report which recommended the establishment of a united and coherent social services department within local authorities. This also involved a review of professional training and effectively took the personal social services almost wholly into local authority control.

It was Crossman's Tory successor, Keith Joseph, who finally implemented NHS reform in 1974, when a complex new system was introduced which sought to combine professional responsibility with consultative opportunities and which also sought a middle way between central direction and local initiative. New representative regional, area and district committees were established which, in time, were to prove as ineffective and cumbersome as the structure it replaced. As one scholar commented, 'the resulting structure was the most Byzantine ever imposed on a UK public service'.[3] It was a structure that the next Conservative Government would dismantle.

In the mid-1970s the firebrand socialist Barbara Castle tried once more to remove the one Bevan legacy which Labour regretted, pay beds within NHS hospitals. The great fear of doctors in the 1940s had been that Labour would introduce a full-time salaried medical service, eroding the general practitioner's independent status. It will be recalled that Bevan gave the hospital consultants an extremely favourable deal in order to bring pressure to bear on

GPs to join the NHS in 1948. The issue of pay beds and queue jumping recurred again and again in the next thirty years and Barbara Castle was determined to force consultants to choose between working full-time in the private sector or working full-time in the public sector.

A bitter salary and contract dispute ensued, which ended with some progress on the pay beds issue. After a bitter two-year dispute involving both salaries and private beds, there was a compromise agreement that would phase out private beds in NHS hospitals on a planned basis. However, the unintended consequence of Barbara Castle's battle with the doctors was to stimulate a massive growth in private insurance and the provision of new private hospitals outside the NHS. The division between those consultants who did and those who did not see private patients continued into the future.

Housing policy also demonstrated considerable continuity between Labour and Conservative governments, though the rhetoric often suggested otherwise, with Labour seen to favour council housing and the Tories favouring private landlords. In fact, the first great stimulus to council housing building came with the 300,000 per annum target for new house building set by the Conservative Government of 1951. Macmillan established his personal reputation by meeting that target in 1953 and considerably exceeding it in 1954, with the substantial part of this being built by local authorities. The Conservatives felt that it was necessary to restore the rented market which had been subject to rent control since 1939. The 1957 Rent Act gradually deregulated rents with the aim of restoring a healthy private rented market, which would supplement the extensive new house-building programme. This Act gained an unfortunate reputation as allegedly contributing directly to the so-called 'Rachmanism', named after an unscrupulous landlord who terrorised his tenants. Labour made a great deal of political capital out of this scandal and it contributed to the Labour victory of 1964. In order to reverse the position Richard Crossman introduced the 1965 Rent Act which partially restored rent control and introduced rent officers and rent tribunals to adjudicate between landlord and tenant.

The 1960s were characterised by further massive house building and particularly an emphasis on high-rise blocks of flats and massive slum clearance. These policies were later to be criticised both for the unsavoury atmosphere created in the high-rise blocks and by the loss of close-knit communities through slum clearance. Crossman also recognised the desire of the newly discovered 'affluent worker' for personal home ownership and he introduced option mortgages in 1967, which gave mortgage interest relief to those below taxation thresholds and he also exempted house owners from capital gains tax. Both of these stimulated the private housing market which contrasted sharply with some of the poor conditions which still existed in the council house sector. This led to the assertion that there was a contrast between 'public squalor and private affluence'.

The incoming Heath Government also recognised the need to support both private and public housing and introduced the Housing Finance Act of 1972 which gave rent allowances to tenants in both private and public sectors. The Act also permitted increases in council rents, which were bitterly attacked by Labour. When Labour resumed office in 1974 the Government introduced the 1975 Housing, Rent and Subsidies Act which gave local authorities renewed powers to set rent levels and also increase housing subsidies to local authorities. This gave a stimulus to the council house market and nearly 150,000 council houses were built in 1977. However, partly because of the increased financial crisis which led to cuts in Government expenditure and partly through the changes which were to be made by the Thatcher Government, this proved to be the swan song of council house building in the twentieth century.

Education policy was also to display considerable continuity in policy. The 1951 Conservative Government saw itself as taking forward the 1944 Education Act which had, of course, been the work of Rab Butler, now a Conservative Minister. There was no major legislation through the 1950s and 1960s and discretion was given to local authorities to develop their particular schemes of education. There was a considerable amount of school building and also public expenditure increased during these years. The tripartite system envisaged by the 1944 Act never really developed, largely because of a failure to build enough technical schools. In effect, Britain had a binary system of grammar schools and secondary modern schools with selection made at age 11 as a result of an examination. The 11+ came to symbolise the divisions of post-war Britain and the failure to allow pupils from all backgrounds to fulfil their potential.

The new Labour Government of 1964 was committed to abolishing selection at age 11, and the radical socialist Anthony Crosland introduced the famous Circular 10/65 which aimed to 'end selection at 11+ and to eliminate separatism in secondary education'. Local authorities were required to submit plans along comprehensive lines, though they were given a range of models from which to choose. There was much speculation about so-called legislation by circular, since there was no Act of Parliament compelling the introduction of the comprehensive system. There remained great discretion for local authorities and this continued to be a period when the education agenda was largely dominated by education professionals rather than politicians.

There was one issue on which both Conservatives and Labour agreed and that was the need to expand higher education. The Conservatives had appointed the Robbins Committee in 1961, which reported in 1963 recommending a major expansion of higher education opportunities for all those who were qualified to receive it. Several new universities were created in the 1960s and the former colleges of advanced technology were upgraded to universities. The Labour Government wished to continue this expansion of higher education, but decided that no more universities would be created but that the local authority sector would be expanded. In the 1966 White Paper, Crosland proposed the creation of a new institution called a polytechnic which would specialise in applied and professional knowledge in contrast to the traditional universities. The polytechnics, though the creation of a Labour Government, were largely the product of the next Consevative Government between 1970 and 1974.

Similarly, comprehensive school education continued to expand, notwithstanding Circular 10/70 which reversed the previous comprehensive Circular 10/65. It was rather ironic that the education minister who presided over the biggest expansion of comprehensive schools was Margaret Thatcher. As the Tory education minister she began with the draconian economy of removing free school milk which had been a tradition since the 1940s. This earned her the epithet, 'Margaret Thatcher milk snatcher', and re-inforced the notion that the 'Selsdon man' policies were being implemented. However, under Margaret Thatcher, the number of pupils in comprehensive schools doubled from 31 to 62 per cent. She also confirmed the raising of the school leaving age to 16, a measure which had been abandoned by the previous Labour Government at a time of economic crisis. Thatcher also introduced a major expansion of education and wrote the 1972 White Paper, *A Framework for Expansion*. Education was, therefore, another area where there was continuity between the Wilson and the Heath Governments.

When Labour returned to office in 1974 it made the public schools one of its key targets and legislation was made to abolish the direct grant schools, which were forced to either integrate with state schools or become totally independent. Two-thirds of such schools entered the fully independent sector. It was during the Labour Government of the 1970s that public concern about educational standards began to rise significantly. A spectacular case crystallised this concern. An enquiry into the William Tyndale Primary School in Inner London revealed lax local authority control, widespread indiscipline amongst pupils and a radical, child-centred, but ineffective curriculum. The Prime Minister, James Callaghan, initiated in 1976 a 'great debate' about education that went way beyond his own education department and the teaching professionals. The notion of a 'secret garden' in which only those engaged within the profession had legitimate views about education was no longer to be tolerated. In what seemed like an extremely radical idea at the time, Callaghan favoured the introduction of a core curriculum in order to ensure that all pupils achieved a threshold minimum standard of knowledge.

It was in the adaptation of the mainstream social security system that, over time, both parties gradually eroded the strict Beveridge principles of social insurance, because insurance benefits were never really adequate even in 1948. There was a persistent growth in National Assistance mainly to supplement inadequate insurance benefits, particularly pensions. During the 1950s it became increasingly clear that adequate pensions could not be financed from flat-rate contributions. The Labour Party had a major review and developed an earnings-related pensions scheme, which put pressure on the Conservative Government. Though denouncing the Labour scheme, the Conservatives did introduce graduated pensions on earnings-related contributions in 1959. The scheme was fully implemented two years later. It had become apparent that citizens preferred insurance contributions to increased taxation and so it suited governments to preserve the fiction of insurance as an alternative form of taxation. Increasingly insurance contribution increases were related to the needs of the insurance scheme, rather than to the level of benefits that they were intended to finance. So, even the notionally actuarial basis of National Insurance was gradually eroded.

There were other important adaptations of the Beveridge Scheme when Labour entered office in 1964. Labour recognised the wish of workers to have their benefits in times of sickness and unemployment reflect their previous financial commitments. So in 1966 earnings-related supplements were introduced on a means-tested basis which would apply to sickness, employment and widows' benefit. There was a so-called wage stop introduced by which benefit could never be more than 85 per cent of previous earnings. A new Ministry was created, at long last fulfilling Beveridge's ambition, the Ministry of Social Security. Local authorities were empowered to grant rate and rent rebate again on a means-tested basis. Perhaps the most important change was to create the Supplementary Benefits Commission in 1966 to replace the old National Assistance Board. This also meant a change in name from National Assistance to Supplementary Benefit, which was now payable as of right, though still on a means test. It was noted that a third of old-age pensioners who were entitled to National Assistance had not claimed it because of the stigma attached to the benefit. When the benefit was changed well over 300,000 new pensioners claimed Supplementary Benefit.

Despite all these improvements, which also included several upratings of both pensions and insurance, the view gained ground during the 1960s that poverty was increasing rather reducing under the Welfare State. This was largely on the basis of the research of social scientists, who found that there was extensive poverty both amongst those on benefits who refused to claim their full entitlement and among those in work but on low wages and with children. In an important study in 1965 entitled *The Poor and the Poorest*, a new definition of poverty was advanced. This was partly based on a statistical analysis using National Assistance benefit rates and partly by introducing a new concept of relative poverty. This replaced the old subsistence basis (what Rowntree had called the maintenance of physical efficiency) in favour of participatory basis, where those in poverty were those who were unable to participate in the norms of society. This was, of course, an age of affluence with a new consumerism, particularly amongst the young. It was Macmillan who had asserted in 1959 'you have never had it so good'. In such a context there were many social groups who were left behind in the rise of living standards and could not share in the new consumer durables that were becoming commonplace. This participatory poverty line was neatly expressed by one who had professional responsibility to manage it:

> To keep out of poverty people must have an income which enables them to participate in the life of the community. They must be able, for example, to keep themselves reasonably fed, and well enough dressed to maintain their self-respect and to attend job interviews with confidence. Their homes must be reasonably warm; their children should not feel shamed by the quality of their clothing; the family must be able to visit relatives and give them something on their birthdays and at Christmas time; they must be able to read newspapers, and retain their television sets and their membership of trade unions and churches. And they must be able to live in a way which ensures, as far as possible, that public officials, doctors, teachers, landlords and others treat them with the courtesy due to every member of the community.[4]

Out of this academic research came a whole new set of poverty-related charities such as the Child Poverty Action Group and Shelter who pressed the Government strongly to improve the condition of those who were not absolutely in poverty, but relatively in poverty. In the wake of these and other studies it began to be asserted that the poor had got poorer under Labour. Indeed this was claimed in the middle of the 1970 election campaign and may have had some bearing on the defeat of the Labour Government and the success of Edward Heath.

The Heath Government had many elements of continuity, as we have already seen, with the previous Labour Government. However, it took forward the idea of greater selectivity, identifying new social benefits that would be targeted on particular classes of claimants. They extended old-age pensions for the over 80s, who had missed out on the Beveridge scheme and lowered the qualifying age for widows' pensions. More importantly, they introduced a new attendance allowance for disabled people. Much of the Social Security Minister Keith Joseph's time was taken up with developing an earnings-related pension scheme, which in the event was lost once the Government fell in 1974. However, Joseph did introduce a major initiative in the area of child poverty. He noted that the previous family allowance scheme which had operated since 1945 did not cover the first child and he was also influenced by the social science research which showed that low-paid workers with families were continuing to face financial difficulty.

Family Income Supplement (FIS) was introduced by Keith Joseph in 1971 to help those in work, particularly with children, who were on low wages. Their wage levels would be supplemented by an allowance based on a means test. Joseph was taken aback by the vehement opposition to what he saw as a benevolent scheme targeted at the low paid. He was accused of re-introducing the Speenhamland System which had been the bane of the old Poor Law prior to 1834. His critics feared that employers would deliberately reduce wages knowing that the income of the employee would be made up by the Family Income Supplement. In fact, in the complex modern economic system such manipulation was unlikely. What was more important was the unanticipated effect of what came to be called the poverty trap. Because, as we have already seen, the same government introduced rent allowances and housing benefit, whether in the public and the private sector, then a marginal increase in income could lead to the loss of a range of benefits. The effect was that the marginal rate of tax of anyone on FIS and housing benefit could be as high as 85 per cent, and certainly would always be above 50 per cent. So, with the best of intentions, Joseph and his ministerial colleagues had significantly weakened the work incentive. There was also a distinction between short- and long-term benefits, again on the rather old fashioned view that those who were unemployed could by their own efforts redeem their position, while those who were, for example, elderly or long-term sick were less capable of personal salvation. Many argued that this government re-introduced the concept of the deserving and the undeserving poor.

When Wilson won the 1974 election he negotiated the Social Contract with the trade unions, whereby a degree of wage restraint by employees would be compensated by improved social benefits. Barbara Castle was determined to solve the pensions problem once and for all. Her 1975 State Earnings Related Pensions Scheme (SERPS) drew on both the previous Joseph scheme and an earlier scheme developed by Crossman in the 1960s. This essentially provided a basic state pension which would be increased with inflation, together with an earnings-related supplement which would encourage women, particularly, who had a number of years out of the workforce. It was based upon the best 20 years of earnings rather than the full working life. An important new development was the acceptance by Labour of the role that private and occupational pensions could provide. Employees could opt out of SERPS so long as the employer provided a scheme with at least as good benefits as the state scheme. It began a long period when the pensions issue became a genuine partnership between the public and the private sector. Much more controversial was her attempt to deal with family poverty which Joseph's scheme had distorted. Joseph had pointed out that ever since 1945 Family Allowance had not been paid to the first child. Castle proposed to abolish both Family Allowance and Child Tax Allowance and replace them with a child benefit payable for each child, including the first child. However, in order to pay for this new benefit an increase in taxation was required and employees would lose the child tax allowance. This was described as a transfer from the wallet to the purse.

Although the measure was passed Parliament, neither the amount of benefit nor the date of introduction was confirmed. When Callaghan replaced Wilson as Prime Minster in 1976 Barbara Castle left office, and both Callaghan and his Chancellor, Denis Healey, in the midst of an International Monetary Fund (IMF) financial crisis, felt that the measure was not really affordable. So the implementation of Child Benefit was delayed and this was denounced by the poverty lobby as a betrayal. Poverty activists had also been critical of the increased complexity of the Supplementary Benefits regime and Barbara Castle appointed an academic, David Donnison, as full-time chairman of the Supplementary Benefits Commission with a more active brief to advise government on supplementary benefits policy. Donnison used his annual reports to advocate a reduction in the complexity of the benefits regime involving both the Welfare State and local authorities. He argued forcibly that, since means-tested discretionary benefits were now such a large part of the Welfare State, social assistance would have to be adapted to meet this new 'mass role'. In short, the concept of means-tested benefits as a small safety net could no longer be sustained.

By the time of the thirtieth anniversary of the Welfare State in 1978, much of the Beveridge vision had either been distorted or eroded. There were four main areas in which the Beveridge concept of the Welfare State had been changed. First, and perhaps predictably, insurance benefits had never been made adequate and, where individuals had no other source of income, they could not be supported on insurance benefits alone. Second, as a consequence of that, there had been a massive increase in means-tested benefits. Neither National Assistance nor Supplementary Benefit were the simple safety net that Beveridge had envisaged but, as Donnison now argued, were a central plank in the Welfare State itself. It was estimated that there were over forty different means-tested benefits in operation by the late 1970s. Thirdly, the actuarial basis of insurance had been undermined by the introduction of earnings-related contributions and benefits and also by the essentially pay-as-you-go approach in which insurance contributions merely acted as another form of taxation, to balance the current insurance account rather than pay for future benefits.

Finally, the flat-rate principle of treating all insurance risks with the same benefits had been changed, with the distinction between long-term and short-term benefits, thus returning to some extent to old moralistic views on the deserving and undeserving poor. Moreover, the consensus which had characterised the post-war period was certainly now breaking apart and a central plank of the Beveridge vision, namely full employment, could no longer be guaranteed. Faced with the major economic crisis growing from the quadrupling of oil prices in the mid-1970s, the Callaghan Government had to introduce draconian cuts in expenditure as the price for negotiating an IMF loan.

In 1976, Labour supporters were told 'the party is over' and Callaghan himself told his Party 'we used to think you could spend your way out of a recession . . . I tell you in all candour that this option no longer exists'. When forced to go to the country in 1979, Callaghan spoke of 'a shift in what the public wants and what it approves of. I suspect that there is now such a sea change – and it is for Mrs Thatcher'.[5] What historians are now calling the age of the classic Welfare State was clearly coming to a close.

II Thatcherism and the Welfare State in crisis, 1979–97

Callaghan's sea change swept Margaret Thatcher to power in May 1979. In a famous election poster Saatchi & Saatchi depicted a long line of unemployed workers queuing at the unemployment office under the heading 'Labour Isn't Working'. This rising unemployment coupled with the 'winter of discontent' when there were widespread strikes in the public services led to a disillusionment with both Labour and, in some respects, the Welfare State itself. Concerns about the Welfare State simply did not grow overnight and some criticisms had quite a long history. There were five main areas where the Welfare State was criticised and there were complex ideas right across the political spectrum.

The first critique had come from economists who argued that the Welfare State took a disproportionate share of resources and thus crowded out economic investment in more productive areas. This led to the conclusion that the economic performance of Britain since the Second World War had been undermined by a strong commitment to welfare. It could be argued by some that the new Jerusalem of the Welfare State was a false promise that could never be delivered. The second critique concerned the role of welfare benefits in reducing incentives. We have seen how a complex web of means-tested and discretionary benefits had led to a situation where some were clearly better off on welfare than in work. This was harking back to the old Poor Law that had been reformed in 1834. Similarly to that time, the Welfare State had generated demoralisation and an underclass that was dependent on the Welfare State and had lost incentive. As one polemical historian vividly expressed it, the Welfare State was 'a dream turned to a dank reality of segregated, subliterate, unskilled, unhealthy and institutionalised proletariat hanging on the nipple of state maternalism'.[6] The notion of welfare dependency and the social evils which flowed from it were common currency in debates in both Conservative and Labour circles from the 1970s onwards.

The third criticism was concerned with benefit fraud and that the Welfare State was far too generous with certain groups in society. The press began to take up cases (often atypical) where people were 'working and signing on', were abusing the welfare system, in some cases with the invention of aliases, were avoiding taxation through working in the black economy and were thus undermining the basic principles of the Welfare State. Again there were both Labour and Conservative critics of a system which led to fraud on such an apparently extensive scale.

The fourth problem was that the Welfare State needed a massive bureaucracy to administer it, particularly in the NHS and the way employees within the Welfare State created a producer rather than a consumer culture. Health service workers, including doctors, had been on strike and in the 'winter of discontent' a whole range of public employees failed to deliver services which the public expected. It was alleged that in order to regulate the flow of enquiries, Supplementary Benefits officers took the phone off the hook in busy times, or that NHS appointments were arranged to suit the convenience of consultants, rather than patients. Associated with this producer culture was the notion of the expert who knew better than either politicians or the public, about how the service should be delivered. We have already seen how Callaghan introduced the great debate on education, which sought to sidestep the professionals. Elsewhere in the social services there were scandals over social workers and other professionals who had clearly fallen down on the job.

The final criticism came largely from left-wing poverty activists who argued that the Welfare State was not flexible enough to respond to changing patterns of social behaviour – the increase in divorce and in one-parent families; the role of women in a society that created more opportunities; the complexity of modern social living which yielded an infinite variety of social conditions. Within a highly structured Welfare State, notwithstanding its discretionary capabilities, it was argued that it was not possible to meet the variety of need that existed in a modern society. The Beveridge idea of a uniform society based on a traditional family structure was no longer applicable.

This complex web of criticisms, some of which were mutually contradictory, were neatly summed up by Mrs Thatcher herself in her memoirs when she described the situation which greeted her when taking up office.

Welfare benefits, distributed with little or no consideration of their effects on behaviour encouraged illegitimacy, facilitating the break down in families, and replaced incentives favouring work and self-reliance with perverse encouragement for idleness and cheating. The final illusion – that state intervention would promote social harmony or solidarity, or, in Tory language, 'one nation' – collapsed in the 'winter of discontent' when the dead went unburied, critically ill patients were turned away from hospitals by pickets and the prevailing mood was

one of snarling envy and motiveless hostility. To cure the British disease with socialism was like trying to cure leukaemia with
leeches.... They had given up on socialism – the 30-year experiment
had plainly failed and were ready to try something else. That sea
change was our mandate.[7]

Mrs Thatcher saw her mandate as to rein in the role of the state,
reduce public expenditure both absolutely and relatively, to conquer inflation, to reduce personal taxation, to restore incentives
and to address the perceived evils of the Welfare State. This was a
bold and radical agenda and the social revolution came about
relatively slowly, gaining pace after Mrs Thatcher's third election
victory in 1987. Unprecedently, this government used the level
of unemployment as an economic tool to contain inflation.
Unemployment rose from 3 per cent in 1974 to 12 per cent in
the winter of 1982/83. Not since the 1930s had unemployment
been at these levels and it peaked at over three million in the
early 1980s. In this dramatic way Beveridge's assumption of full
employment was well and truly rejected.

There were some important and symbolic changes made during
this administration. These were announced in the budget of
1980 which for the first time in many generations announced
reductions in social security benefits and a host of changes which
would reduce the real income of poorer families. These were
eventually enacted in the 1982 Social Security and Housing Benefit Act. The earnings-related supplements to unemployment and
sickness benefit (introduced in 1965) were abolished and benefits
became taxable. Pensions were up-rated in 1982 in line with
prices rather than earnings. The effect of this was illustrated by
the fact that in 1981 pensions were 23 per cent of average earnings
but by 1995 they had fallen to 15 per cent. Other social welfare
benefits were contained or removed. At the same time the government was introducing major cuts in personal taxation and
offering council house tenants the right to buy their houses with
substantial discounts. David Donnison, the chairman of the Supplementary Benefits Commission, described this period as a major
watershed and he comments that, 'underlying these measures
were far more fundamental shifts in policy... they were proposing quite deliberately to increase a rate of unemployment which
was already rising disastrously... they were cutting the real value
of most of the benefits for working families... whether you

believed in these policies or not, they clearly amounted to a fundamental break with the past.'[8]

These changes were a precursor of a more fundamental review that was then conducted by Norman Fowler in 1986. Still Beveridge exercised an influence over welfare matters and Fowler described his review as the most important since Beveridge, adding that his ambition was to get back to Beveridge. This review, largely of a technical nature, was published in four Green Papers in 1986 and led to the 1986 Social Security Act. This legislation simplified and rationalised some of the complex means-tested schemes and sought to bring them more under defined rules: Family Income Supplement was replaced by Family Credit; Income Support replaced Supplementary Benefit with a simpler administration; the existing Social Fund was changed to a loan rather than a grant.

Fowler also had a close look at the SERPS scheme introduced by Barbara Castle. He was minded to go as far as abolishing it but made some important changes, reducing some of the guarantees in the original scheme, and he also introduced significant tax incentives for people to join private schemes (this was eventually to become Mr Blair's Stakeholder Pension at the end of the century). The effect of the Fowler review was to simplify administration and to reduce the number of claimants for whom their marginal rate of tax was 100 per cent. Some of the more defined benefits were easier to claim, so there were some gainers from this scheme; however, there were also losers. The overall conclusion was that this did not significantly reduce the level of poverty nor did it significantly reduce social expenditure. This was largely due to the high level of unemployment that continued to be a drain on public expenditure. As one scholar commented, 'it was not a brave new world but is was a slightly less idiotic old one'.[9]

It was after the third election victory in 1987 that Mrs Thatcher embarked on an even more radical programme which included further privatisation of utilities, the ill-fated Poll Tax, the break-up of some state bureaucracies moving towards privatisation in the public services and increasing income disparities through changes in taxation policy. The 1988 Education Reform Act was, in a sense, the long-term consequence of the original great debate started by Callaghan in 1976. A ten-subject National Curriculum was to be introduced, supported by a range of tests at different ages. Moreover, local authorities' control over education was loosened, first, by removing polytechnics from local authority control and second, by allowing schools to opt out of local authority control and become grant maintained. These education reforms took several years to be implemented and were further sustained in the Major years through, in effect, the privatisation of school inspection through the creation of OFSTED and the introduction of official school league tables. Local authorities were eventually required to delegate virtually all of their education budget to individual schools, whose Governors now became critically important.

Local authority control over housing was also weakened by the ability of council tenants, in particular districts, to opt out of Local Authority control and become part of Housing Action Trusts. Increasingly, the main provision of social housing was to be provided by Housing Associations rather than by the local authorities themselves. Somewhat against this trend, the Griffith Report on Community Care recommended that Local Authorities should be ultimately responsible for the care of the elderly and infirm, but as enablers rather than providers of services. Community care would, in the future, be provided on a partnership basis between individuals, their families, voluntary associations and the state. Here was a good example of the so-called 'mixed economy of welfare', which was transforming the Welfare State. The spirit of the educational, housing and community care reforms were then to be extended to the jewel of the Welfare State, the National Health Service.

Mrs Thatcher has always been wary about tampering with the National Health Service because she recognised the deep affection the British people had for the NHS and because of its universal application. The NHS was genuinely in the Beveridge mould, since all citizens paid the taxes which funded it and all citizens had free access to health care at the time of need. Despite the massive funding which the NHS received, there were persistent concerns about waiting lists, the unequal geographical distribution of health care that still had a strong social class implication and the need for a more effective and efficient service. The NHS was the biggest employer in Britain and was characterised by many of the producer culture inefficiencies of the state bureaucracies of the Welfare State. The Government now attempted to introduce some elements of consumer pressure to improve performance. The Prime Minister remained nervous about the NHS reforms and it was only the pugnacious tenacity of her Minister, Kenneth Clark, who carried the reforms through against strong opposition from the British Medical Association.

In the White Paper, *Working for Patients* (1989), the Government introduced the idea of the internal market within the NHS through the so-called purchaser/provider split. Health authorities would purchase services from providers, mainly hospitals, and this would introduce an element of competition and an anticipated improvement in service. The great hospitals would become independent through self-governing trust status and general practitioners were able to become fundholders and thus purchase health care for their own patients. Partly because the re-organisation of health care became entangled with an on-going dispute over NHS contracts and partly because this seemed to be creeping privatisation, the proposals were the subject of great controversy within both politics and within the health services themselves. There were times when it appeared the Prime Minister was going to lose her nerve over these reforms but they were, along with the community care changes, legislated in the NHS and Community Care Act of 1990. Though the community care changes were phased in over a longer period and only became fully operational in 1993, the NHS reforms began on time in 1991.

At that time, to the great surprise of political opponents, there were over 300 GP fundholders and some 57 trusts ready to begin operation, including some community and ambulance trusts as well as hospital trusts. A quasi-market had been created within the health service and there had been some dramatic changes in the power and status relationships within the NHS. More and more the managers of trusts were becoming the key figures rather than the senior medical establishment, and the purchasing power of general practitioners altered their relationship with consultants and hospitals who now needed their business. By the time the NHS changes became operational, Mrs Thatcher had resigned and John Major had become Prime Minister. He took these changes further by introducing a broader concept of consumerism through the Citizens Charter of 1991, with the NHS variant, the Patients Charter. This enshrined patients as the key beneficiaries of the NHS and this was further reinforced by a

White Paper, *The Health of the Nation* (1991), which set targets for improvements in health standards with clear expectations on the rate of disease reduction. What these and other reforms demonstrated was an increasing concern about the outputs of the Welfare State rather than simply the financial input. The services in education, local authorities, community care and in health were expected to deliver clear improvements which could then be measured by performance indicators and league tables. This proved John Major's main initiative as the Thatcher revolution was fully implemented during the 1990s.

Rather surprisingly, Major won the 1992 election even though unemployment had risen after the boom of the late 1980s had petered out and public expenditure was growing with an increasing budget deficit in government finances. Yet again, a government needed public expenditure retrenchment and Michael Portillo implemented a review of social expenditure in 1993 which indicated that there would be no sacred cows and all areas of expenditure were under critical review. Portillo and the Social Security Minister, Peter Lilley, were particularly concerned with welfare dependency and the fact that, despite the Thatcherite reforms, social expenditure had continued to grow so that there were, for example, 5.6 million people on Income Support in 1993. This was more than five times greater than the number on National Assistance in 1948. There was a further very public scrutiny on welfare fraud and particular categories of claimants, such as young single mothers, were pilloried and attempts made to reduce social expenditure in these areas. An important symbolic change was that unemployment insurance was renamed the Job Seekers Allowance, was means-tested after six months' benefit and was dependent on a search for a job. This was, in effect, the re-introduction of the 'genuinely seeking work' test of the inter-war years.

The Major Government was beset by accusations of sleaze and corruption and by internal divisions over Europe. As it drifted towards the almost inevitable election defeat which was to occur in 1997, the government was presiding over the final stages of a major change which had taken twenty years to implement fully. The Welfare State was a much more market-based organisation and across whole swathes of public policy the philosophy of 'opt out' was rampant. Schools, council tenants, hospital trusts, GPs could opt out of state control and provide services on a kind of privatised basis within the quasi-market of purchaser and provider that had been created. The universalism so beloved of Beveridge was in retreat. By the 1990s, the Welfare State was a much more residual safety net then the all-embracing concept launched by Beveridge under the image of the five giants. Welfare benefits were much more targeted in a highly selective manner. This was not wholly bad, as the big increases in the 1990s in Disability Benefit shows. However, the language of means testing and stigma reinforced the notion that those who could manage to do so should provide for themselves, whilst the Welfare State existed for the residuum. Self-help ideas were in the air that would have pleased Samuel Smiles in the 1850s. As one scholar comments, 'social policy would never be the same again, the centre of gravity had shifted'. Perhaps the most remarkable aspect of these changes was that the incoming Blair Labour Government would build on and not reverse these trends.

III Postscript: New Labour and the Third Way

When Labour unexpectedly lost the 1992 election there was much soul searching in the party, given four election defeats which had been accompanied by high unemployment, greater disparities between rich and poor, attacks upon trades unions and the weakening of many public services. The Tories had successfully portrayed Labour as still a 'tax and spend' party and had narrowly won the 1992 election. In the wake of this defeat Labour once more went back to the drawing board, but this time for a more fundamental review of its values and policies. Labour set up its own Commission on Social Justice which was charged with developing a 'new Beveridge'. Just as Portillo's review of expenditure was a no-holds-barred exercise, so too the Commission was encouraged to rule nothing out.

When it reported in 1994, it came up with some unpalatable proposals, such as ending the promise to link pensions to earnings, a graduate tax and benefits into work proposals. Labour were still to be committed to the Welfare State but it was to be a different kind of Welfare State:

Instead of a Welfare State designed for old risks, old industries and old family structures, there is a need for an intelligent Welfare State.

... Instead of a safety net to relieve poverty we need a social security system that can help prevent poverty. Instead of a health service designed primarily to treat illness, we need a health policy whose priority is to promote better health. In other words, The Welfare State must not only look after people when they cannot look after themselves, it must enable them to achieve self-improvement and self-support. The Welfare State must offer a hand up rather than a hand out.[10]

Inspired by such language, Blair promised that his Welfare State would be a 'springboard to success not a road to dependency'.

Labour had the ideal politician to translate some of these ideas into new policies. Frank Field had been active in the Poverty Lobby, had been a social policy academic and had studied deeply the ills that beset the Welfare State at the end of the twentieth century. He was particularly concerned about the corroding effect of means-tested benefits and also deplored the way Welfare State policy almost encouraged benefit fraud. Field wanted a total reconstruction of the Welfare State into what he thought of as a stakeholder Welfare State where individual self-interest would be allied to social welfare improvement. His book on this subject concluded:

Britain's present welfare system has the worst of both worlds: it is broken backed, yet its costs escalate. In its efforts to support it actually restrains the citizen offering disincentives rather than incentives, and educating people only about the need to exploit the system . . . [it] proposes a restructuring which brings into central drive position the role of self-interest and self-improvement. Its aim is to help individuals create freer and more fulfilled lives. Fifty years after the efforts of the coalition and post-war Labour governments, it is crucial for Britain to recommence the massive task of welfare reconstruction.[11]

When Labour took office in 1997, Field was given the chance to range widely in the area of social policy and the Green Paper *A New Contract for Welfare* (1998) owed much to Field's ideas. However, Frank Field did not remain long in government, since he was unable to persuade the Cabinet that his plans to restrict the means test and expand contributory insurance were either affordable or electorally deliverable.

Tony Blair's Government promised a new Welfare State from New Labour that would neither be socialist (much to the regret of some old Labour thinkers and supporters) nor would it expose the free market (as the extreme Thatcherites would have wished). It would be a new middle or 'Third Way' – a partnership between public and private. Blair advocated building a Welfare State for the twenty-first century, not dismantling the Welfare State and leaving it as a residual safety net for the destitute.

However, welfare reform was necessary and it would have to be on the basis of a new contract between citizen and the state. The Third Way would promote opportunity and empowerment instead of dependency. This Third Way philosophy is based upon a critical belief that work is the best route out of poverty.

It is indeed the Welfare to Work that marks the central plank in New Labour's Welfare State. Labour introduced the New Deal which had the specific objective of reducing unemployment and encouraging a return to work. For example, 18–24-year-olds were offered four options: subsidised work; full-time education and training; work on an environmental task force; voluntary work. As both Blair and his Chancellor Gordon Brown have said, 'there is no fifth option'. Similarly lone mothers were targeted for advice and support to get them back into the labour market, as were the long-term adult unemployed. Like the Tories before them, New Labour were much influenced by the ideas coming from the USA: partly, the theoretical work of Charles Murray, who advocated withdrawing benefit to increase work incentives, and by the practical policies of the Clinton administration which had a successful record of reducing welfare dependency.

Blair and Brown had an abiding faith in the virtue of work, which would have delighted the Thatcherites. The press noticed a symbolic connection between Brown and Norman Tebbitt. In 1981, Tebbitt had offended the jobless by explaining that when his father had been unemployed in the 1930s, 'he got on his bike and went out looking for work'. This got translated in the popular culture into a 'get on your bike' message to the unemployed. In the Spring of 2000, Gordon Brown issued what *The Economist* called 'on yer bike, part 2'. Brown said, 'we will meet our responsibility to ensure that there are job opportunities and the chance to learn new skills, you must now meet your responsibilities – to earn a wage'.[12] There was a major difference in the two scenarios, since Brown was presiding over a period of reducing unemployment and low inflation – a major contrast to the early 1980s. Brown's own policy of fiscal prudence led him to adopt Conservative spending plans for the first two years of the Labour Government and restrain public expenditure. The Tories ruefully reflected on the fact that the British economy grew steadily from about 1993 and this was the longest lasting economic boom of the whole century and it was Labour, not the Conservatives, who benefited from these propitious economic times.

The financial and economic continuities between Conservative and Labour in the late 1990s were further echoed in the Labour Government's policy on the National Health Service. Blair decided to retain much of the NHS structural reform which was introduced, in particular, retaining the purchaser–provider relationship. GP fundholding was discontinued, but was replaced by something similar in consortia of GP practices that would still have purchasing responsibilities. These then later became the Primary Care Trusts that would have greatly increased resource responsibility and so reflect patient needs in the distribution and delivery of health services. Health authorities were merged to give economies of scale and many Community Mental Health and Ambulance Trusts were also brought together. Overlaying this remodelled NHS was a range of centrally directed bodies that would seek to improve health treatment and health care.

The National Institution for Clinical Excellence (NICE) was given the responsibility of evaluating and authorising particular drugs and treatments. A Commission for Health Improvement was established with renewed targets for reduction in disease and improvements in health conditions. A stronger complaints machinery was introduced and failing doctors could be required to take further training or be disciplined. Strict performance indicators and league tables were also further developed and, as with the example of reducing waiting lists, they had the effect of sometimes distorting performance in order to meet the targets.

The continuity in policy which shows Labour developing policies and activities first initiated under the Major Government should not obscure some radical changes which New Labour introduced. There has been a particularly active policy aimed at the redistribution of wealth. The Blair Government finally honoured the pledge to introduce a national minimum wage, which had been talked about in Labour circles for over a century. Child Benefit was increased in 1998 and 1999 and an income guarantee was introduced for the elderly. Although Gordon Brown fulfilled the manifesto commitment not to increase income tax and indeed reduced the standard rate, there were, none the less, some important tax adjustments which had a redistribution effect. Tax allowances for dividends and mortgage interest relief, which benefited the middle classes, were replaced by targeted help for the poor, particularly those with families. The Prime Minister promised to abolish child poverty within a generation and the Chancellor introduced the rather complex Working Families Tax Credit, which on some calculations would transfer up to £6 billion pounds from the rich to the poor. The distinctive feature of this new policy is that this is a major benefit for those in work and was so calculated to reduce the deterrent effect that had previously created the poverty trap. These tax and benefit changes should also be related to wider policy on social exclusion.

Returning to the policy of the poverty lobby in the 1960s, New Labour wished to attack not only the income levels of the poor but the wider social deprivation that came from exclusion from the mainstream of society. Merely improving the income level of the poor would not itself allow poorer families to participate as full members in an increasingly wealthy society. The policies to attack social exclusion went far beyond the confines of social security and health. In effect, all government departments were expected to contribute as appropriate to the promotion of social inclusion, which was one of the key distinctive messages of the Blair Government. A host of initiatives were launched, such as Employment Zones, Education Action Zones, Health Action Zones and the New Deal for Communities. Although rhetoric was of 'joined-up Government', the practice on the ground often appeared otherwise. In the application of policy on the ground, there appeared to be separate government departments, as ministerial silos each administering their own initiatives independent of others. In order to address this, the Prime Minister set up a special office within 10 Downing Street in order to co-ordinate government policy in a more coherent way. In support of these local initiatives were the newly created Regional Development Agencies, responsible for the promotion of economic development within the regions and a series of enterprise initiatives, which aimed to create social entrepreneurs in socially deprived areas, thus creating self-reliance and employment.

The continuation of a programme which increasingly was creating a mixed economy Welfare State is perhaps illustrated in New

Labour's pension policy. Taking account of the criticism of SERPS, particularly the fear that these guarantees on income would never be delivered and acknowledging that the basic state pension would become increasingly irrelevant, the Labour Government aimed to find a new solution to a problem that was besetting all advanced industrial societies. Greater longevity, combined with declining birth rates in advanced societies, were storing up long-term trouble on pensions, since it was projected that a smaller workforce in the future would be sustaining a larger retired population. In addition, although inflation appeared to be under control, the uncertainties of investment (particularly revealed in the stock market reductions across the world in the first two years of the new century) undermined the long-term position of pension funds. Labour proposed to intro-duce a second state pension that would be targeted on the poor. This was to be further enhanced by the introduction of the so-called Stakeholder Pension in 2001. Generous tax incentives were provided to seek to persuade lower- and middle-income groups to make a greater provision for their future retirement. The pension plans purchased would be from a private provider. Here was the partnership between state compulsion and private enterprise which lay at the heart of Blair's Third Way. It was the Stakeholder Pension that was consistent with the notion that individuals must provide more for themselves and was part of that self-reliance which the government was encouraging in such policies as Welfare to Work. In the same vein of partnership between public and private was the encouragement of more schools to opt out of local authority control and develop their own specialisms and the willingness to use private health care to make up deficiencies within the NHS.

If the outcome of the 1997 election had been clearly predict-able, the same was true of the election of June 2001. Blair was re-elected again with a huge majority although on a much lower turnout and a sense of scepticism about New Labour policies among the electorate. Blair has taken the lesson of the 2001 elec-tion results to re-invigorate the attempts to improve the public services. This will continue the trend in expenditure away from social security and much more towards education and health. The former will focus on the need to improve standards of achievement and boost further the requirements for a highly skilled population to succeed in the global economy. The latter will seek to translate the allocation of increased resources into significantly improved performance. For all the public debate about the soaring costs of the NHS, comparative information produced by some international bodies demonstrates the low proportion of GDP allocated to health care in the UK. Indeed in his public expenditure announcement at the turn of the century, Brown promised to increase NHS expenditure well above the trend for four successive years, simply to reach the European Union average. In particular, observers often compared expenditure on health care in the United States with that in the United Kingdom. On the face of it the United States spent a higher proportion of its resources on health care but this can be taken as misleading. The US may be cited as a very wasteful system, whereas the improved life expectancy and health conditions produced by the NHS is a remarkable example of the efficient use of resources. The second Labour Government is committed both to increasing allocations to health care, but also a rigorous managerialism which will improve the performance of the NHS system.

Blair has stated that the success in delivering improved public services will be a critical element in whether there is a third Labour administration in succession. The Blairite, Third Way, Welfare State is one very different from that planned by the Beveridge Report in 1942.[13] It adopts a strict functionalism in promoting work, independence and self-reliance; it increasingly targets welfare benefits on those in need, thus using more means testing; it addresses the condition of the poor by attacking social exclusion in the round, not just in monetary terms. It has preserved and enhanced the universal state services of health and education; but at the same time it has continued what is sometimes called the privatisation policy of the 1980s and 1990s by developing further the mixed economy, based upon the partnership between the state, the individual, the employer and the voluntary sector. It is an active, not a passive Welfare State promoting the virtue of dignity and independence which Beveridge would have admired. It is sometimes forgotten that the Beveridge Plan itself envisaged a universal minimum below which people would not fall. However, Beveridge always believed the provision above the minimum was the responsibility of the individual.

Modern Britain has created the minimum floor, but has delivered it through means-tested selective benefits, nearer in approach to the Poor Law than to the Beveridge concept. That the Blair Welfare State now seeks to use welfare policy to stimulate a greater sense of self-reliance and self-help, and in so doing brings in the private sector to assist, is an indication of some of the long-term continuities in social policy. As the first half-century of the Welfare State well illustrates, this distinctive and much cherished institution of modern Britain has adapted to meet changed social and political circumstances. It will certainly need to adapt further to retain its central place in British society.

Documentary appendix

1 The factory question

Document 1A: Richard Oastler's letter on 'Yorkshire Slavery', *Leeds Mercury*, 16 October 1830

Let truth speak out, appalling as the statement may appear. The fact is true. Thousands of our fellow-creatures and fellow-subjects, both male and female, the miserable inhabitants of a Yorkshire town (Yorkshire now represented in Parliament by the giant of anti-slavery principles) are this very moment existing in a state of slavery, more horrid than are the victims of that hellish system 'colonial slavery'. These innocent creatures drawl out, unpitied, their short but miserable existence, in a place famed for its profession of religious zeal, whose inhabitants are ever foremost in professing 'temperance' and 'reformation', and are striving to outrun their neighbours in missionary exertions, and would fain send the Bible to the farthest corner of the globe aye, in the very place where the anti-slavery fever rages most furiously, her apparent charity is not more admired on earth, than her real cruelty is abhorred in Heaven. The very streets which receive droppings of an 'Anti-Slavery Society' are every morning wet by the tears of innocent victims at the accursed shrine of avarice, who are compelled (not by the cart-whip of the negro slave-driver) but by the dread of the equally appalling thong or strap of the over-looker, to hasten, half-dressed, but not half-fed, to those magazines of British infantile slavery – the worsted mills in the town and neighbourhood of Bradford!!!

Would that I had Brougham's eloquence, that I might rouse the hearts of the nation, and make every Briton swear, 'These innocents shall be free!'

Thousands of little children, both male and female, but principally female, from seven to fourteen years of age, are daily compelled to labour from six o'clock in the morning to seven in the evening, with only – Britons, blush while you read it! – with only thirty minutes allowed for eating and recreation. Poor infants! ye are indeed sacrificed at the shrine of avarice, without even the solace of the negro slave; ye are no more than he is, free agents; ye are compelled to work as long as the necessity of your needy parents may require, or the cold-blooded avarice of your worse than barbarian masters may demand! Ye live in the boasted land of freedom, and feel and mourn that ye are slaves, and slaves without the only comfort which the negro has. He knows it is his sordid, mercenary master's interest that he should live, be strong and healthy. Not so with you. Ye are doomed to labour from morning to night for one who cares not how soon your weak and tender frames are stretched to breaking! You are not mercifully valued at so much per head; this would assure you at least (even with the worst and most cruel masters) of the mercy shown to their own labouring beasts. No, no! your soft and delicate limbs are tired and fagged, and jaded, at only so much per week, and when your joints can act no longer, your emaciated frames are instantly supplied with other victims, who in this boasted land of liberty are HIRED – not sold – as slaves and daily forced to hear that they are free.

Document 1B: *Report of the Select Committee on Factory Children's Labour*, xv (1831–2), 192, *Minutes of Evidence of Samuel Coulson*

5047.   At what time in the morning, in the brisk time, did those girls go to the mills?

In the brisk time, for about six weeks, they have gone at 3 o'clock in the morning, and ended at 10, or nearly half past at night.

5049.   What intervals were allowed for rest or refreshment during those nineteen hours of labour?

Breakfast a quarter of an hour, and dinner half an hour, and drinking a quarter of an hour.

5051.   Was any of that time taken up in cleaning the machinery?

They generally had to do what they call dry down; sometimes this took the whole of the time at breakfast or drinking, and they were to get their dinner or breakfast as they could; if not, it was brought home.

5054.   Had you not great difficulty in awakening your children to this excessive labour?

Yes, in the early time we had to take them up asleep and shake them, when we got them on the floor to dress them, before we could get them off to their work; but not so in the common hours.

5056.   Supposing they had been a little too late, what would have been the consequence during the long hours?

They were quartered in the longest hours, the same as in the shortest time.

5057.   What do you mean by quartering?

A quarter was taken off.

5059.   What was the length of time they could be in bed during those long hours ?

It was near 11 o'clock before we could get them into bed after getting a little victuals, and then at morning my mistress used to stop up all night, for fear that we could not get them ready for the time; sometimes we have gone to bed, and one of us generally awoke.

5060.   What time did you get them up in the morning?

In general me or my mistress got up at 2 o'clock to dress them.

5061.   So that they had not above four hours' sleep at this time?

No, they had not.

5062.   For how long together was it?

About six weeks it held; it was only when the throng was very much on; it was not often that.

5063.   The common hours of labour were from 6 in the morning till half-past eight at night?

Yes.

5064.   With the same intervals for food?

Yes, just the same.

5056.   Were the children excessively fatigued by this labour?

Many times; we have cried often when we have given them the little victualling we had to give them; we had to shake them, and they have fallen to sleep with the victuals in their mouths many a time.

5066.   Had any of them any accident in consequence of this labour?

Yes, my eldest daughter when she went first there; she had been about five weeks, and used to fettle the frames when they were running, and my eldest girl agreed with one of the others to fettle hers that time, that she would do her work; while she was learning more about the work, the overlooker came by and said, 'Ann, what are you doing there?' she said, 'I am doing it for my companion, in order that I may know more about it.' He said, 'Let go, drop it this minute,' and the cog caught her forefinger nail, and screwed it off below the knuckle, and she was five weeks in Leeds Infirmary.

5067.   Has she lost that finger?

It is cut off at the second joint.

5068.   Were her wages paid during that time?

As soon as the accident happened the wages were totally stopped; indeed, I did not know which way to get her cured, and I do not know how it would have been cured but for the Infirmary.

5069.   Were the wages stopped at the half-day?

She was stopped a quarter of a day; it was done about four o'clock.

5072.   Did this excessive term of labour occasion much cruelty also?

Yes, with being so very much fatigued the strap was very frequently used.

Document 1C: First Report of the Factory Commissioners, xx (1833), 48

1st.   That the children employed in all the principal branches of manufacture throughout the Kingdom work during the same number of hours as the adults.

2nd.   That the effects of labour during such hours are, in a great number of cases:

Permanent deterioration of the physical condition;

The production of disease often wholly irremediable; and

The partial or entire exclusion (by reason of excessive fatigue) from the means of obtaining adequate education and acquiring useful habits, or of profiting from those means when afforded.

3rd.   That at the age when children suffer these injuries from the labour they undergo, they are not free agents, but are let out to hire, the wages they earn being received and appropriated by their parents and guardians.

We are therefore of opinion that a case is made out for the interference of the Legislature in behalf of the children employed in factories.

Document 1D: R. Oastler, *A Well-Seasoned Christmas Pie* (1834)

It is well known to the public that I have for some years rather prominently advocated the necessity of Parliamentary interference for the protection of all children and young persons working in factories, and that I agreed with Mr. Sadler and Lord Ashley in their opinion that 'ten working hours per day ... ' was the utmost extent of time which the law ought to admit for such persons. It is also well known to the public that the labours of Mr. Sadler and Lord Ashley were not successful and that both these honourable gentlemen were defeated in their humane exertions to benefit the industrious classes. It is however true that the excitement throughout the kingdom, arising from a knowledge of the facts which were adduced to prove the necessity of Parliamentary interference, which facts had in no case been disproved, was so great and so well founded, (having been established before a Select Committee of the House of Commons, and also by the reports of a Royal Commission ...) that the Government found itself compelled to pass a Bill, which at the time was declared and proved to be impracticable by the friends of Mr. Sadler's and Lord Ashley's Bill. I may perhaps be allowed to say that every fact of cruelty in the factory system which I have stated, either in speeches letters or conversations, is literally and positively true: and whatever arguments I may have used have been, in my honest opinion, founded upon the soundest policy and the most pure Christian principle.

2 The Poor Law

Document 2A: *Report of the Poor Law Commissioners*, XXVII (1834) 228, 261–2

The first and most essential of all conditions, a principle which we find universally admitted, even by those whose practice is at variance with it, is, that his situation on the whole shall not be made really or apparently so eligible as the situation of the independent labourer of the lowest class. Throughout the evidence it is shown, that in proportion as the condition of any pauper class is elevated above the condition of independent labourers, the condition of the independent class is depressed; their industry is impaired, their employment becomes unsteady, and its remuneration in wages is diminished. Such persons, therefore, are under the strongest inducements to quit the less eligible class of labourers and enter the more eligible class of paupers. The converse is the effect when the pauper class is placed in its proper position, below the condition of the independent labourer. Every penny bestowed, that tends to render the condition of the pauper more eligible than that of the independent labourer, is a bounty on indolence and vice. . . .

We have seen that in every instance in which the able-bodied labourers have been rendered independent of partial relief, or of relief otherwise than in a well-regulated workhouse –

1. Their industry has been restored and improved.
2. Frugal habits have been created or strengthened.
3. The permanent demand for their labour has increased.
4. And the increase has been such, that their wages, so far from being depressed by the increased amount of labour on the market, have in general advanced.
5. The number of improvident and wretched marriages has diminished.
6. Their discontent has been abated, and their moral and social condition in every way improved. . . .

The chief specific measures which we recommend for effecting these purposes, are –

First, that except as to medical attendance, and subject to the exception respecting apprenticeship hereinafter stated, all relief whatever to able-bodied persons or to their families, otherwise than in well-regulated work-houses (i.e. places where they may be set to work according to the spirit and intention of the 43rd of Elizabeth) shall be declared unlawful, and shall cease, in manner and at periods hereafter specified; and that all relief afforded in respect of children under the age of 16, shall be considered as afforded to their parents.

It is true that nothing is necessary to arrest the progress of pauperism, except that all who receive relief from the parish should work for the parish exclusively, as hard and for less wages than independent labourers work for individual employers, and we believe that in most districts useful work, which will not interfere with the ordinary demand for labour, may be obtained in greater quantity than is usually conceived. Cases, however, will occur where such work cannot be obtained in sufficient quantity to meet an immediate demand; and when obtained, the labour, by negligence, connivance, or otherwise, may be made merely formal, and thus the provisions of the legislature may be evaded more easily than in a workhouse. A well-regulated workhouse meets all cases, and appears to be the only means by which the intention of the statute of Elizabeth, that all the able-bodied shall be set to work, can be carried into execution.

Document 2B: *Report of the Poor Law Commissioners,* XXVII (1834) 227

In all extensive communities, circumstances will occur in which an individual, by the failure of his means of subsistence, will be exposed to the danger of perishing. To refuse relief, and at the same time to punish mendicity when it cannot be proved that the offender could have obtained subsistence by labour, is repugnant to the common sentiments of mankind; it is repugnant to them to punish even depredation, apparently committed as the only recourse against want.

In all extensive civilized communities, therefore, the occurrence of extreme necessity is prevented by alms-giving, by public institutions supported by endowments or voluntary contributions, or by a provision partly voluntary and partly compulsory, or by a provision entirely compulsory, which may exclude the pretext of mendicancy.

But in no part of Europe except England has it been thought fit that the provision, whether compulsory or voluntary, should be applied to more than the relief of indigence, the state of a person unable to labour, or unable to obtain, in return for his labour, the means of subsistence. It has never been deemed expedient that the provision should extend to the relief of poverty; that is, the state of one, who, in order to obtain a mere subsistence, is forced to have recourse to labour.

Document 2C: *Report of the Poor Law Commissioners*, XXVII (1834), 263

... although we admit that able-bodied persons in the receipt of out-door allowances and partial relief, may be, and in some cases are, placed in a condition less eligible than that of the independent labourer of the lowest class; yet to persons so situated, relief in a well-regulated workhouse would not be a hardship: and even if it be, in some rare cases, a hardship, it appears from the evidence that it is a hardship to which the good of society requires the applicant to submit. The express or implied ground of his application is, that he is in danger of perishing from want. Requesting to be rescued from that danger out of the property of others, he must accept assistance on the terms, whatever they may be, which the common welfare requires. The bane of all pauper legislation has been the legislating for extreme cases. Every exception, every violation of the general rule to meet a real case of unusual hardship, lets in a whole class of fraudulent cases, by which that rule must in time be destroyed. Where cases of real hardship occur, the remedy must be applied by individual charity, a virtue for which no system of compulsory relief can be or ought to be a substitute.

Document 2D: The aims of the Workhouse – Charles Younge, Chairman of the Sheffield Board of Guardians. *Sheffield Times*, 10 November 1855

The great object of the poor law board is to ensure a constant unvarying and efficient discipline during the entire residence of the pauper within the workhouse. He rises to the minute; he works to the minute; he eats to the minute. He must be clean, respectful, industrious and obedient. In short the habits inculcated in the house are precisely those the possession of which would have prevented his becoming an inmate. The pauper naturally enough concludes that the relief he receives in the workhouse is a very inadequate return for the surrender of his liberty – the full occupa-tion of his time – the value of his labour – the humiliation he must endure in being associated with some of the depraved and abandoned members of the community and the painful consciousness that he has lost all self reliance and self respect. Who can wonder that the honest poor should make every effort to keep out of the workhouse?

Public health

Document 3A: Edwin Chadwick, *Report on the Sanitary Condition of the Labouring Population of Great Britain* (1842) 1965 edn, pp. 219–27

Comparative chances of life in different classes of the community (average age of deceased)

	Professional	Trade	Labourers
Truro	40	33	28
Derby	49	38	21
Manchester	38	20	17
Rutland	52	41	38
Bolton	34	23	18
Bethnal Green	45	26	16
Leeds	44	27	19
Liverpool	35	22	15
Whitechapel	45	27	22
Strand	43	33	24
Kensington	44	29	26
Kendal	45	39	34

Document 3B: Edwin Chadwick, *Report on the Sanitary Condition of the Labouring Population of Great Britain* (1842) 1965 edn, pp. 422–4

First, as to the extent and operation of the evils which are the subject of the enquiry:

That the various forms of epidemic, endemic, and other disease caused, or aggravated, or propagated chiefly amongst the labouring classes by atmospheric impurities produced by decomposing animal and vegetable substances, by damp and filth, and close and overcrowded dwellings prevail amongst the population in every part of the kingdom, whether dwelling in separate houses, in rural villages, in small towns, in the larger towns – as they have been found to prevail in the lowest districts of the metropolis.

That such disease, wherever its attacks are frequent, is always found in connexion with the physical circumstances above specified, and that where those circumstances are removed by drainage, proper cleansing, better ventilation, and other means of diminishing atmospheric impurity, the frequency and intensity of such disease is abated; and where the removal of the noxious agencies appears to be complete, such disease almost entirely disappears.

That high prosperity in respect to employment and wages, and various and abundant food, have afforded to the labouring classes no exemptions from attacks of epidemic disease, which have been as frequent and as fatal in periods of commercial and manufacturing prosperity as in any others.

That the formation of all habits of cleanliness is obstructed by defective supplies of water. That the annual loss of life from filth and bad ventilation are greater than the loss from death or wounds in any wars in which the country has been engaged in modern times.

Secondly, as to the means by which the present sanitary condition of the labouring classes may be improved:

The primary and most important measures, and at the same time the most practicable, and within the recognized province of public administration, are drainage, the removal of all refuse of habitations, streets and roads, and the improvement of the supplies of water.

That the chief obstacles to the immediate removal of decomposing refuse of towns and habitations have been the expense and annoyance of the hand labour and cartage requisite for the purpose.

That this expense may be reduced to one-twentieth or to one-thirtieth, or rendered inconsiderable, by the use of water and self-acting means of removal by improved and cheaper sewers and drains.

That refuse when thus held in suspension in water may be most cheaply and innoxiously conveyed to any distance out of towns, and also in the best form for productive use, and that the loss and injury by the pollution of natural streams may be avoided.

That for all these purposes, as well as for domestic use, better supplies of water are absolutely necessary.

Document 3C: *The Liverpool Sanitary Act*, 1846

And whereas the health of the population, especially of the poorer classes, is frequently injured by the prevalence of epidemical and other disorders, and the virulence and extent of such disorders, is frequently due and owing to the existence of local causes which are capable of removal but which have hitherto frequently escaped detection from the want of some experienced person to examine into and report upon them, it is expedient that power should be given to appoint a duly qualified medical practitioner for that purpose; Be it therefore enacted, that it shall be lawful for the said Council to appoint, subject to the approval of one of her Majesty's principal Secretaries of State, a legally qualified medical practitioner, of skill and experience, to inspect and report periodically on the sanitary condition of the said borough, to ascertain the existence of diseases, more especially epidemics increasing the rates of mortality, and to point out the existence of any nuisances or other local causes which are likely to originate and maintain such diseases and injuriously affect the health of the inhabitants of the said borough, and to take cognisance of the fact of the existence of any contagious disease, and to point out the most efficacious modes for checking or preventing the spread of such diseases, and also to point out the most efficient means for the ventilation of churches, chapels, schools, registered lodging-houses, and other public edifices within the said borough, and to perform any other duties of a like nature which may be required of him; and such person shall be called the 'Medical Officer of Health for the Borough of Liverpool'; and it shall be lawful for the said Council to pay such officer such salary as shall be approved of by one of her Majesty's principal Secretaries of State.

... And be it enacted, that it shall be lawful for the said Council, and they are hereby required to nominate and appoint one or more persons to superintend and enforce the due execution of all duties to be performed by the scavengers appointed under this Act, and to report to the said Council and Health Committee all breaches of the bye-laws, rules and regulations of the said Council and Health Committee and to point out the existence of any nuisances, and such person shall be called 'The Inspector of Nuisances', and the said Council and Health Committee shall require such Inspector to provide and keep a book, in which shall be entered all complaints made by any inhabitant of the said borough of any infringement of the provisions of this Act, or of the bye-laws, rules and regulations made by the said Council for the preservation of due order as may be required by the said Council and Health Committee: and such Inspector shall forthwith inquire into the truth or otherwise of such complaints, and report upon the same to the said Health Committee at their next meeting, and such report, and the order of the said Health Committee thereon shall be entered in the said book, which shall be kept at the office of the said Town Clerk, and shall be open at all reasonable times to the inspection of any inhabitant within the said borough; and it shall be the duty of such Inspector, subject to the direction of the said Council and Health Committee to make complaints before any Justice, and take legal proceedings for the punishment of any person or persons for any offence under this Act, or under any bye-laws made by virtue thereof.

4

Education and welfare

Document 4A: James Kay-Shuttleworth on Education and the Minutes of 1846, quoted by M. Sturt, *The Education of the People* (1967) pp. 178–81

There is little or nothing in the profession of an elementary schoolmaster in this country, to tempt a man having a respectable acquaintance with the elements of even humble learning to exchange the certainty of a respectable livelihood in a subordinate condition in trade or commerce for the mean drudgery of instructing the rude children of the poor in an elementary school as it is now conducted.

For what is the condition of the master of such a school? He has often an income very little greater than that of an agricultural labourer, and very rarely equal to that of a moderately skilful mechanic. Even the income is to a great degree contingent on the weekly pittances paid from the earnings of his poor neighbours, and liable to be reduced by bad harvests, want of employment, strikes, sickness among the children, or, worst of all, by the calamity of his own ill health.

Of late years he may more frequently have a small cottage rent free, but seldom a garden or fuel.

Some portion of his income may be derived from the voluntary subscriptions of the promoters of the school – a precarious source, liable to be dried up by the removal or death of patrons, and the fickleness of friends.

Amid these uncertainties, with the increase of his family his struggles are greater. He tries to eke out his subsistence by keeping accounts and writing letters for his neighbours. He strives to be elected parish clerk, or registrar, or clerk to some benefit club. These additions to his income, if he is successful, barely keep him out of debt, and in old age he has no prospect but hopeless indigence and dependence.

To entrust the education of the labouring classes to men involved in such straits, is to condemn the poor to ignorance and its fatal train of evils. . . .

Every pupil teacher provided with a certificate at the close of his apprenticeship might become a candidate for one of two employments under the patronage of the Government. In each Inspector's district an annual examination will be held to which all apprentices who have obtained the certificate will be admitted to compete for the distinction of an exhibition entitling them to be sent as Queen's scholars to a Normal School under their Lordship's inspection.

A poor man's child may thus at the age of 13 enter a profession at every step in which his mind will expand, and his intellect be stored, and, with the blessing of God, his moral and religious character developed.

In pecuniary rewards, as a pupil teacher, he will earn from £10 the first year to £20 the fifth year; and as a teacher, if he leave college with a certificate of the third class, the best, he will have an augmentation grant of £25 to £30 per annum, on condition that the managers of the school provide him with a house rent free and with a further salary equal to twice the amount of the grant. He may thus have a house and salary of £90 a year, and even if he has only got one of the inferior certificates he still has his house and £60 a year. In addition he also has an income from school pence and some other subsidiary work as clerk to some benefit club....

It cannot be expected that members of the middle class of society will to any great extent choose the vocation of teachers of the poor.... To make every elementary school a scene of exertion from which the highest ranks of teachers may be entered by the humblest scholar, is to render the profession of schoolmaster popular among the poor, and to offer to their children the most powerful incentives to learning.

Document 4B: *Report of the Newcastle Commission*, XXI (1861), I, 243

Even if it were possible, I doubt whether it would be desirable, with a view to the real interests of the peasant boy to keep him at school till he was 14 or 15 years of age. But it is not possible. We must make up our minds to see the last of him, as far as the day school is concerned, at 10 or 11. We must frame our system of education upon this hypothesis; and I venture to maintain that it is quite possible to teach a child soundly and thoroughly, in a way that he shall not forget it, all that is necessary for him to possess in the shape of intellectual attainments, by the time he is 10 years old. If he has been properly looked after in the lower classes, he shall be able to spell correctly the words that he will ordinarily have to use; he shall read a common narrative – the paragraph in the newspaper that he cares to read – with sufficient ease to be a pleasure to himself and to convey information to listeners; if gone to live at a distance from home, he shall write his mother a letter that shall be both legible and intelligible; he knows enough of ciphering to make out, or test the correctness of a common shop bill; if he hears talk of foreign countries he has some notion as to the part of the habitable globe in which they lie; and underlying all, and not without its influence, I trust, upon his life and conversation, he has acquaintance enough with the Holy Scriptures to follow the allusions and the arguments of a plain Saxon sermon and a sufficient recollection of the truths taught him in his catechism, to know what are the duties required of him towards his Maker and his fellow man. I have no brighter view of the future or the possibilities of an English elementary education floating before my eyes than this.

Document 4C: Dr James Kay, Report on Pauper Education, *Fourth Report by the Poor Law Commissioners* (1838), Appendix, p. 140

The pauper children maintained in Union workhouses are dependent, not as a consequence of their errors, but of their misfortunes. They have not necessarily contracted any of the taint of pauperism. They are orphans, or deserted children, or bastards, or children of idiots, or of cripples, or felons, or they are resident in the workhouse with their parents, who seek a brief refuge there.

The dependence of certain of these classes of children cannot be transient. The care of their natural guardians is at an end, or is suspended for so considerable a period that the children have claims on the Board of Guardians, not for food and clothing merely, but for that moral sustenance which may enable them, at the earliest period, to attain independence.

The physical condition of the children who are deprived of the care of natural guardians ought not to be elevated above that of the household of the self-supported labourer. Their clothes, food and lodging should not be better than that which the labourer can provide for his child. But whenever the community encounter the responsibility of providing for the education of children who have no natural guardians, it is impossible to adopt as a standard for the training of such children the average amount of care and skill now bestowed on the moral and religious culture of the children of the labouring classes generally, or to decide that their secular instructions shall be continued within limits confessedly so meagre and inadequate. The privation of such agencies cannot be proposed as a means of preventing undue reliance on the provision created by the law; but on the contrary, education is to be regarded as one of the most important means of eradicating the germs of pauperism from the rising generation, and of securing in the minds and in the morals of the people the best protection for the institutions of society.

5

Laissez-faire and state intervention in the mid-nineteenth century

Document 5A: Adam Smith, *The Wealth of Nations* (1776), Everyman edn (1910) II, pp. 180–1

According to the system of natural liberty, the sovereign has only three duties to attend to; three duties of great importance, indeed, but plain and intelligible to common understandings: first, the duty of protecting the society from the violence and invasion of other independent societies; secondly, the duty of protecting, as far as possible, every member of the society from the injustice or oppression of every other member of it, or the duty of establishing an exact administration of justice; and, thirdly, the duty of erecting and maintaining certain public works and certain public institutions which it can never be for the interest of any individual, or small number of individuals, to erect and maintain; because the profit could never repay the expense to any individual or small number of individuals, though it may frequently do much more than repay it to a great society.

Document 5B: John Stuart Mill, *On Liberty* (1859) pp. 15–16

The object of this Essay is to assert one very simple principle, as entitled to govern absolutely the dealings of society with the individual in the way of compulsion and control, whether the means used be physical force in the form of legal penalties, or the moral coercion of public opinion. The principle is, that the sole end for which mankind are warranted, individually or collectively, in interfering with the liberty of action of any of their number is self-protection. That the only purpose for which power can be rightfully exercised over any member of a civilized community, against his will, is to prevent harm to others. His own good, either physical or moral, is not sufficient warrant. He cannot rightfully be compelled to do or forbear because it will be better for him to do so, because it will make him happier, because, in the opinion of others, to do so would be wise, or even right. These are good reasons for remonstrating with him, or reasoning with him, or persuading him, or entreating him, but not for compelling him, or visiting him with an evil in case he do otherwise. To justify that, the conduct from which it is desired to deter him must be calculated to produce evil to some one else. To only part of the conduct of anyone, for which he is amenable to society, is that which concerns others. In the part which merely concerns himself his independence is, of right, absolute. Over himself, over his own body and mind, the individual is sovereign.

Document 5C: Samuel Smiles, *Self Help* (1859) 1903 edn, pp. 1–3

'Heaven helps those who help themselves' is a well-tried maxim, embodying in a small compass the results of vast human experience. The spirit of self-help is the root of all genuine growth in the individual; and, exhibited in the lives of many, it constitutes the true course of national vigour and strength. Help from without is often enfeebling in its effects, but help from within invariably invigorates. Whatever is done for men or classes, to a certain extent takes away the stimulus and necessity of doing for themselves; and where men are subjected to over-guidance and over-government, the inevitable tendency is to render them comparatively helpless.

Even the best institutions can give a man no active help. Perhaps the most they can do is, to leave him free to develop himself and improve his individual condition. But in all times men have been prone to believe that their happiness and well-being were to be secured by means of institutions rather than by their own conduct. Hence the value of legislation as an agent in human advancement has usually been much over-estimated. To constitute the millionth part of a Legislature, by voting for one or two men once in three or five years, however conscientiously this duty may be performed, can exercise but little active influence upon any man's life and character. Moreover, it is every day becoming more clearly understood, that the function of Government is negative and restrictive, rather than positive and active; being resolvable principally into protection – protection of life, liberty, and property. Laws, wisely administered, will secure men in the enjoyment of the fruits of their labour, whether of mind or body, at a comparatively small personal sacrifice; but no laws, however stringent, can make the idle industrious, the thriftless provident, or the drunken sober. Such reforms can only be effected by means of individual action, economy, and self-denial; by better habits, rather than by greater rights.

It may be of comparatively little consequence how a man is governed from without, whilst everything depends upon how he governs himself from within. The greatest slave is not he who is ruled by a despot, great though that evil be, but he who is the thrall of his own moral ignorance, selfishness and vice. Nations who are thus enslaved at heart cannot be freed by any mere changes of masters or of institutions; and so long as the fatal delusion prevails, that liberty solely depends upon and consists in government, so long will such changes, no matter at what cost they may be affected, have as little practical and lasting result as the shifting of the figures in a phantasmagoria. The solid foundations of liberty must rest upon individual character; which is also the only sure guarantee for social security and national progress. John Stuart Mill truly observes that 'even despotism does not produce its worst effects so long as individuality exists under it; and whatever crushes individuality is despotism, by whatever name it be called').

6

The growing awareness of poverty

Document 6A: *Eighth Annual Report of the Charity Organisation Society* (1876) Appendix IV, pp. 24–5

The principle is, that it is good for the poor that they should meet all the ordinary contingencies of life, relying not upon public or private charity, but upon their own industry and thrift, and upon the powers of self-help that are to be developed by individual and collective effort. Ample room will still be left for the exercise of an abundant charity in dealing with exceptional misfortune, and also in connection with large schemes for the benefit of the working classes which may require, in the first instance of all events, the fostering of wealth and leisure. But it is a hurtful misuse of money to spend it on assisting the labouring classes to meet emergencies which they should themselves have anticipated and provided for. The working man does not require to be told that temporary sickness is likely now and then to visit his household; that times of slackness will occasionally come; that if he marries early and has a large family, his resources will be taxed to the uttermost; that if he lives long enough, old age will render him more or less incapable of toil – all these are the ordinary contingencies of labourer's life, and if he is taught that as they arise they will be met by State relief or private charity, he will assuredly make no effort to meet them himself. A spirit of dependence, fatal to all progress, will be engendered in him, he will not concern himself with the causes of his distress or consider at all how the condition of his class may be improved; the road to idleness and drunkenness will be made easy to him, and it involves no prophesying to say that the last state of a population influenced after such a fashion as this will certainly be worse than the first. One thing there is which true charity does require the working man to be told, and it is the aim of this Society to tell him, not in words merely, but in acts that cannot be confuted. We desire to tell him that those who are born to easier circumstances sympathise with the severe toil and self-denial whch his lot imposes upon him; that many are standing beside him ready and even eager to help if proper occasion should arise; and that if he, or wife, or child should be stricken with protracted sickness, or with some special infirmity, such as we all hope to escape, there are those at hand who will gladly minister to his necessities, and do their best at least to mitigate the suffering which it may be beyond their power to remove.

Document 6B: C. Booth, *Life and Labour of the People in London* (1892) II, pp. 20–1

The inhabitants of every street, and court, and block of buildings in the whole of London, have been estimated in proportion to the numbers of children, and arranged in classes according to the known position and condition of the parents of these children. The streets have been grouped together according to the School Board sub-divisions of 'blocks', and for each of these blocks full particulars are given in the tables of the Appendix. The numbers included in each block vary from less than 2,000 to more than 30,000, and to make a more satisfactory unit of comparison I have arranged them in contiguous groups, 2, 3 or 4 together, so as to make areas having each about 30,000 inhabitants, these areas adding up into the large divisions of the School Board administration. The population is then classified by Registration districts, which are likewise grouped into School Board divisions, each method finally leading up to the total for all London.

The classes into which the population of each of these blocks and districts is divided are the same as were used in describing East London, only somewhat simplified. They may be stated thus:

A.   The lowest class – occasional labourers, loafers and semi-criminals.

B.   The very poor – casual labour, hand-to-mouth existence, chronic want.

C. and D.   The poor – including alike those whose earnings are small, because of irregularity of employment, and those whose work, though regular, is ill-paid.

E. and F.   The regularly employed and fairly paid working class of all grades.

G. and H.   Lower and upper middle class and all above this level.

The Classes C and D, whose poverty is similar in degree but different in kind, can only be properly separated by information as to employment which was obtained for East London, but which, as already explained, the present inquiry does not yield. It is the same with E and F, which cover the various grades of working-class comfort. G and H are given together for convenience.

Outside of, and to be counted in addition to, these classes, are the inmates of institutions whose numbers are specially reported in every census, and finally there are a few who, having no shelter, or no recognised shelter, for the night, elude official enumeration and are not counted at all.

The proportions of the different classes shown for all London are as follows:

A (lowest)	37,610	or	.9 per cent	In poverty, 30.7 per cent
B (very poor)	316,834	"	7.5 per cent	
C and D (poor)	938,293	"	22.3 per cent	
E and F (working class, comfortable)	2,166,503	"	51.5 per cent	In comfort, 69.3 per cent
G and H (middle class and above)	749,930	"	17.8 per cent	
	4,209,170	"	100 per cent	
Inmates of institutions	99,830			
	4,309,000			

Document 6C: B. S. Rowntree, *Poverty: A Study of Town Life* (1901), 2nd edn (1906) pp. 295–8, 300–1

In this chapter it is proposed to briefly summarise the facts set forth in the preceding pages, and to consider what conclusion regarding the problem of poverty may be drawn from them.

Method of Scope of Inquiry. As stated in the second chapter, the information regarding the numbers, occupation, and housing of the working classes was gained by direct inquiry, which practically covered every working-class family in York. In some cases direct information was also obtained regarding earnings, but in the majority of cases these were estimated, the information at the disposal of the writer enabling him to do this with considerable accuracy.

The Poverty Line. Having thus made an estimate, based upon carefully ascertained facts, of the earnings of practically every working-class family in York, the next step was to show the proportion of the total population living in poverty. Families regarded as living in poverty were grouped under two heads:

(a) Families whose total earnings were insufficient to obtain the minimum necessaries for the maintenance of merely physical efficiency. Poverty falling under this head was described as 'primary' poverty.

(b)   Families whose total earnings would have been sufficient for the maintenance of merely physical efficiency were it not that some portion of it was absorbed by other expenditure, either useful of wasteful. Poverty falling under this head was described as 'secondary' poverty.

To ascertain the total number living in 'primary' poverty it was necessary to ascertain the minimum cost upon which families of various sizes could be maintained in a state of physical efficiency. This question was discussed under three heads, viz. the necessary expenditure for (1) food; (2) rent; and (3) all else.

In chapter IV [sc. of Rowntree's study] it was shown that for a family of father, mother, and three children, the minimum weekly expenditure upon which physical efficiency can be maintained in York is 21s. 8d., made up as follows:

	s.	d.
Food	12	9
Rent (say)	4	0
clothing, light, fuel, etc.	4	11
	21	8

The necessary expenditure for families larger or smaller than the above will be correspondingly greater or less. This estimate was based upon the assumptions that the diet is selected with a careful regard to the nutritive values of various food stuffs, and that these are all purchased at the lowest current prices. It only allows for a diet less generous as regard variety than that supplied to able-bodied paupers in workhouses. It further assumes that no clothing is purchased which is not absolutely necessary for health, and assumes too that it is of the plainest and most economical description.

No expenditure of any kind is allowed for beyond that which is absolutely necessary for the maintenance of merely physical efficiency.

The number of persons whose earnings are so low that they cannot meet the expenditure necessary for the above standard of living, stringent to severity though it is, and bare of all creature comforts, was shown to be no less than 7,230, or almost exactly 10 per cent of the total population of the city. These persons, then, represent those who are in 'primary' poverty.

The number of those in 'secondary' poverty was arrived at by ascertaining the total number living in poverty, and subtracting those living in 'primary' poverty. The investigators, in the course of their house-to-house visitation, noted those families who were obviously living in a state of poverty, i.e. in obvious want and squalor. Sometimes they obtained definite information that the bulk of the earnings was spent in drink or otherwise squandered, sometimes the external evidence of poverty in the home was so clear as to make verbal evidence superfluous.

In this way 20,302 persons, or 27.84 per cent of the total population, were returned as living in poverty. Subtracting those whose poverty is 'primary', we arrive at the number living in 'secondary' poverty, viz. 13,072, or 17.93 per cent of the total population.

We have been accustomed to look upon the poverty in London as exceptional, but when the result of careful investigation shows that the proportion of poverty in London is practically equalled in what may be regarded as a typical provincial town, we are faced by the startling probability that from 25 to 30 per cent of the town populations of the United Kingdom are living in poverty.

Document 6D: The Chamberlain Circular (1886)

Pauperism and Distress: Circular Letter to Boards of Guardians
Local Government Board, Whitehall, S.W.
15th March 1886
Sir,

The enquiries which have been recently undertaken by the Local Government Board unfortunately confirm the prevailing impression as to the existence of exceptional distress amongst the working classes. This distress is partial as to its locality, and is no doubt due in some measure to the long continued severity of the weather.

The returns of pauperism show an increase, but it is not yet considerable; and the numbers of persons in receipt of relief are greatly below those of previous periods of exceptional distress.

The Local Government Board have, however, thought it their duty to go beyond the returns of actual pauperism which are all that come under their notice in ordinary times, and they have made some investigation into the condition of the working classes generally.

They are convinced that in the ranks of those who do not ordinarily seek poor law relief there is evidence of much and increasing privation, and if the depression in trade continues it is to be feared that large numbers of persons usually in regular employment will be reduced to the greatest straits. Such a condition of things is a subject for deep regret and very serious consideration.

The spirit of independence which leads so many of the working classes to make great personal sacrifices rather than incur the stigma of pauperism, is one which deserves the greatest sympathy and respect, and which it is the duty and interest of the community to maintain by all the means at its disposal.

Any relaxation of the general rule at present obtaining, which requires as a condition of relief to able-bodied male persons on the ground of their being out of employment, the acceptance of an order for admission to the workhouse, or the performance of an adequate task of work as a labour test, would be most disastrous, as tending directly to restore the condition of things which, before the reform of poor laws destroyed the independence of the labouring classes and increased the poor rate until it became an almost unsupportable burden.

It is not desirable that the working classes should be familiarised with poor law relief, and if once the honourable sentiment which now leads them to avoid it is broken down, it is probable that recourse will be had to this provision on the slightest occasion. . . .

What is required in the endeavour to relieve artisans and others who have hitherto avoided poor law assistance, and who are temporarily deprived of employment is:

1. Work which will not involve the stigma of pauperism;
2. Work which all can perform, whatever may have been their previous avocations;
3. Work which does not compete with that of other labourers at present in employment;

And, lastly, work which is not likely to interfere with the resumption of regular employment in their own trades by those who seek it.

The Board have no power to enforce the adoption of any particular proposals, and the object of this circular is to bring the subject generally under the notice of boards of guardians and other local authorities.

In districts in which exceptional distress prevails, the Board recommend that the guardians should confer with the local authorities, and endeavour to arrange with the latter for the execution of works on which unskilled labour may be immediately employed.

These works may be of the following kinds, among others:

(a) Spade husbandry on sewage farms;
(b) Laying out of open spaces, recreation grounds, new cemeteries, or disused burial grounds;
(c) Cleansing of streets not usually undertaken by local authorities;
(d) Laying out and paving of new streets, etc.
(e) Paving of unpaved streets, and making of footpaths in country roads;
(f) Providing or extending sewerage works and works of water supply.

It may be observed, that spade labour is a class of work which has special advantages in the case of able-bodied persons out of employment. Every able-bodied man can dig, although some can do more than others, and it is work which is in no way degrading, and need not interfere with existing employment.

In all cases in which special works are undertaken to meet exceptional distress, it would appear to be necessary, 1st, that the men employed should be engaged on the recommendation of the guardians as persons whom, owing to previous condition and circumstances, it is undesirable to send to the workhouse, or to treat as subjects for pauper relief, and 2nd, that the wages paid should be something less than the wages ordinarily paid for similar work, in order to prevent imposture, and to leave the strongest temptations to those who avail themselves of this opportunity to return as soon as possible to their previous occupations.

When the works are of such a character that the expenses may properly be defrayed out of borrowed moneys, the local authorities may rely that there will be every desire on the part of the Board to deal promptly with the application for their sanction to a loan.

I shall be much obliged if you will keep me informed of the state of affairs in your district, and if it should be found necessary to make any exceptional provision, I shall be glad to know at once the nature of such provision, and the extent to which those for whom it is intended avail themselves of it.

I am, etc.,

(Signed) J. Chamberlain

Document 6E: Resolutions Agreed by Metropolitan Guardians 1872. *Second Annual Report by the Local Government Board 1872–3*, Appendix, p. 6

1st. That in the opinion of this Conference greater uniformity should prevail in the administration of relief by the Guardians of the several unions and parishes in the Metropolitan district, both as respects the limitations within which out-door relief should, as a rule, be alone afforded, and the scale upon which it should generally be granted.

2nd. That it is desirable to substitute, so far as practicable, in-door for out-door relief to all classes of able bodied poor, whether relief be required on account of sickness, or by alleged want of employment.

3rd. That out-door relief should not, except under special circumstances, be granted to single able-bodied men, nor to single able-bodied women, either with or without illegitimate children.

4th. That out-door relief should not be granted for more than a fortnight to any woman alleging herself to be deserted by her husband, except upon satisfactory proof of such desertion, nor, except in special cases, to any able-bodied widow without children, or with one child only, after the first six months of her widowhood.

5th. That, in special cases of able-bodied widows, with more than one child, it may be desirable to take one or more of the children into the separate or district school of the union, in preference to giving out-door relief.

6th. That out-door relief should invariably be granted for a fixed period only, which should not, in any case, exceed three months.

7th. That all orders to able-bodied men for relief in the labour yard should be given provisionally only by the Relieving Officers until the next meeting of the Guardians, and, if approved, should not be confirmed for more than one month in the first instance.

8th. That out-door relief should not be granted in any case, unless the Relieving Officer has, since the application, visited the home of the applicant, has recorded the date of such visit, and all the particulars required by the Form in the Application and Report Book.

9th. That this Conference recognises the necessity for insisting on increased attention to the frequent and careful visitation of the poor at their own homes, together with a thorough investigation of all applications for relief, as one of the first and most essential steps towards diminishing pauperism.

7

Liberal social policy, 1905–14

Document 7A: Lloyd George and the People's Budget, *The Times*, 11 October 1909, p. 6

But the Lords may decree a revolution which the people will direct. If they begin, issues will be raised that they little dream of, questions will be asked which are now whispered in humble voices, and answers will be demanded then with authority. The question will be asked 'Should 500 men, ordinary men chosen accidentally from among the unemployed, override the judgment – the deliberate judgment – of millions of people who are engaged in the industry which makes the wealth of the country?' That is one question. Another will be, who ordained that a few should have the land of Britain as a perquisite; who made 10,000 people owners of the soil, and the rest of us trespassers in the land of our birth; who is it – who is responsible for the scheme of things whereby one man is engaged through life in grinding labour, to win a bare and precarious subsistence for himself, and when at the end of his days he claims at the hands of the community he served a poor pension of eightpence a day, he can only get it through a revolution; and another man who does not toil receives every hour of the day, every hour of the night, whilst he slumbers, more than his neighbour receives in a whole year of toil? Where did the table of that law come from? Whose finger inscribed it? These are the questions that will be asked. The answers are charged with peril for the order of things the Peers represent; but they are fraught with rare and refreshing fruit for the parched lips of the multitude who have been treading the dusty road along which the people have marched through the dark ages which are now emerging into the light.

Document 7B: Lloyd George's 'Ambulance Wagon' Speech at Birmingham, *The Times*, 12 June 1911, p. 6

I never said this bill was a final solution. I am not putting it forward as a complete remedy. It is one of a series. We are advancing on the road, but it is an essential part of the journey. I have been now some years in politics and I have had, I think, as large a share of contention and strife and warfare as any man in British politics today. This year, this Session, I have joined the Red Cross. I am in the ambulance corps. I am engaged to drive a wagon through the twistings and turnings and ruts of the Parliamentary road. There are men who tell me I have overloaded that wagon. I have taken three years to pack it carefully. I cannot spare a single parcel, for the suffering is very great. There are those who say my wagon is half empty. I say it is as much as I can carry. Now there are some who say I am in a great hurry. I am rather in a hurry, for I can hear the moanings of the wounded, and I want to carry relief to them in the alleys, the homes where they lie stricken, and I ask you, and through you, I ask the millions of good-hearted men and women who constitute the majority of the people of this land – I ask you to help me to set aside hindrances, to overcome obstacles, to avoid the pitfalls that beset my difficult path.

Document 7C: W. Beveridge, *Unemployment: A Problem of Industry* (1909) pp. 208–9

The de-casualisation of employment is thus at one and the same time an extension into the industrial field of the Charity Organisation principle which proscribes casual relief and a development of the trade union principle of the living wage. It may appeal to the Socialist as a part of that industrial organisation in regard to which academic socialism – national ownership of the means of production – is but a means to an end. It may appeal to the individualist, because by diminishing the chances of the labour market it gives more decisive influence to individual merit.

The principle is clear-that every man who cannot be regularly employed by one firm should be engaged only from an Exchange, should be one of a list common to many firms. The definition of the principle is all that lies within the limits of the present discussion. Whether the use of Exchanges should be voluntary or compulsory, whether they themselves should be set up by public authority or by industrial associations, are questions which may for the moment be left on one side. The practical application of the principle involves, no doubt, some system of public Labour Exchanges to cover the large amount of ground which will certainly not be covered in any other way. It admits, however, also of all kinds of private and sectional experiment – of common lists set up by voluntary co-operation of employers, of trade union registration, and much besides. The principle is universal; the practical application of it may be infinitely varied. It must indeed be varied to meet the case. Casual employment is no local disease; it is found in all towns and to some extent in nearly all trades. Nor is it one type of employment rigidly cut off from other types.

Casual employment in all its varieties and its ubiquity is but the acute form of a general phenomenon. So de-casualisation is only a special form of labour market organisation. The under-employment of the dock labourer is paralleled by the constant leakage of employment and earnings affecting substantial minorities in nearly all occupations, skilled and unskilled alike. The excess of individual dock labourers above the number ever required at any one moment is paralleled by the irreducible minimum of unemployment in the trade unions. The problem in the trade unions and even among the skilled men outside them is not as a rule urgent, simply because the wages are as a rule high enough, particularly when spread out through unemployed benefits, to allow for an ample margin of idleness. The problem, however, differs only in degree not in kind. The crowding of the labour market is common to the highest and the lowest ranks of industry, and in all ranks arises from the same central fact – the division of the total demand for labour in fluctuating proportions between different employers and different districts. In all trades there is, just in proportion as the market is unorganised and labour immobile, a possibility and a tendency for fresh men to enter under the influence of local developments at one place though men of the trade are standing idle elsewhere. The dissipation of the demand actually increases its effectiveness in producing a supply. The concentration of the demand at common centres is required in order to bring about the recruiting of trades in accordance with their real growth, not by local accidents, and to give to employment in each occupation as a whole something of the continuity and the orderly progression which characterise employment in a single large undertaking. This is simply the dynamic aspect of the change which has already been considered statically and with reference to one extreme form of overcrowding, under the title of de-casualisation.

Some measure of protection for those within a trade or district against the competition of those outside is an essential, if somewhat paradoxical, consequence of a system of Labour Exchanges. The aim of such a system is, not simply the fluidity, but the organised and intelligent fluidity of labour – the enabling of men to go at once where they are wanted, but at the same time the discouraging of movement to places where men are not wanted.

Document 7D: W. Beveridge, *Unemployment: A Problem of Industry* (1909) pp. 229–30

Insurance against unemployment, therefore, stands in the closest relation to the organisation of the labour market, and forms the second line of attack on the problem of unemployment. It is, indeed, the necessary supplement thereto. The Labour Exchange is required to reduce to a minimum the intervals between successive jobs. Insurance is required to tide over the intervals that will still remain. The Labour Exchange mobilises the reserves of labour for fluctuations and hastens re-absorption after changes of industrial structure. Insurance is needed to provide for the maintenance of the reserves while standing idle and of the displaced men while waiting for re-absorption. No plan other than insurance – whether purely self-supporting or with assistance from other sources – is really adequate. The provision required is one adaptable to an immense variety of individual cases – that is to say, it must be far more flexible than anything to be attained along the lines either of relief works or of elasticity in working hours. The provision required is one made in part by the individual himself; by simple grants of money – whether under the Poor Law or otherwise – his self-respect is endangered. The provision required, however, cannot be made by the individual acting alone: unemployment may never come to him at all, but when it does come, may exceed all possibilities of private saving. The principle of insurance – which is simply that of spreading the wages in a trade so as to provide for the necessary margin of idleness in the trade – is therefore essential. It is at the same time adequate. The spreading of the burden of unemployment over all the men of the trade would make the burden tolerable in all but the most casual occupations. The premiums required for insurance in the principal unions are small relatively to the total wages – smaller indeed in most cases than the amounts added to those wages within recent years. Thre is no reason why the trade unions themselves should not extend the system of unemployed benefits. There is ample warrant in foreign example for giving State encouragement to such extension. There would, according to the opinion of those best qualified to judge – the authors of the German report already quoted – be no impossibility in the State's applying the principle of insurance to the risk of unemployment quite generally and comprehensively, once a test of unemployment had been made available.

Document 7E: W. S. Churchill, 'Notes on Malingering', 6 June 1909, Beveridge Papers, D.026

We seek to substitute for the pressure of the forces of nature, operating by chance on individuals, the pressures of the laws of insurance, operating through averages with modifying and mitigating effects in individual cases. In neither case is correspondence with reality lost. In neither case are pressures removed. In neither case is risk eliminated. In neither case can personal effort be dispensed with. In neither case can inferiority be protected. Chance and average spring from the same family, both are inexorable, both are blind, neither is concerned with the character of individuals or with ethics, or with sentiment. And all deviation into these paths will be disastrous. But the true economic superiority of the new foundations of averages, over the old foundation of chance, arises from the fact that the processes of waste are so much more swift than those of growth and repair, that the prevention of such catastrophes would be worth purchasing by diminution in the sense of personal responsibility; and, further, that as there is no proportion between personal failings and the penalties extracted, or even between personal qualities and those penalties, there is no reason to suppose that a mitigation of the extreme severities will tend in any way to a diminution of personal responsibility, but that on the contrary more will be gained by an increase of ability to fight than will be lost through an abatement of the extreme consequences of defeat.

8 Politics and policy, 1914–39

Document 8A: The Pilgrim Trust, *Men without Work* (1938) pp. 12–14

That the unemployed are grouping themselves everywhere into these two classes, the in-and-out and the long unemployed, can be seen from a study of the six towns in which the present enquiry has been conducted. As we later attempt to show, economic, industrial, social and other conditions varied as widely as six towns can vary. But a comparison of the 1932 and 1936 unemployed register in these six places shows that everywhere the same tendencies could be observed. Total unemployment had fallen to a varying degree. Out of every 100 men and women at the Exchanges in 1932, there have dropped out, by 1936, by finding local employment or employment elsewhere:

In the Borough of Deptford	62
In the City of Leicester	40
In the City of Liverpool	29
In Blackburn C.B.	37
In Crook, Co. Durham	44
In Rhondda U.D.	23

Thus in Deptford nearly three times as many people dropped out of the queue of 100 as did in the Rhondda U.D. But whatever the number of men dropping out, among the remainder there was a higher proportion of long-unemployed men than among the swollen queues of 1932. Among 100 men and women in the queue there were the following long-unemployed:

	1932	1936
Deptford	4	6
Leicester	4	11
Liverpool	19	13
Blackburn	37*	38
Crook	46	56
Rhondda	33	63

* The comparatively high number of long-unemployed men and women in Blackburn for 1932 is explained by the fact that as the depth of the depression was reached much earlier in the cotton industry than elsewhere, the 'last wave' of dismissals had already swollen the long unemployed, whereas this was not so in other industries by September, 1932.

The conclusion to be drawn from this table is inevitable. The reasons or at least some of the reasons, why long unemployment fails to go down to the 1929 level cannot be identified with conditions in certain districts or certain industries, or with differences in the extent of industrial recovery. There is a 'hard core' of long unemployment which will not be resolved by recovery alone, in every town in this country, however prosperous, however diversified its range of industries, or however much its main industry benefits from industrial trends, and wherever it is situated. The problem is of increasing social importance throughout the country and it not entirely bound up with the problem of economic activity and depression. This is one of the main reasons for the inclusion of two prosperous places in the study.

A further conclusion is to be drawn from the table. Everybody knows that there are at present in England prosperous districts and 'depressed areas'. The case of a prosperous district is described by conditions in Deptford, where about 7% of the industrial population were unemployed in November 1936; the Rhondda U.D. is part of a depressed area, and 35% of the industrial population were out of work. The table suggests that this description is inadequate to describe the difference in conditions. Not only are the number unemployed in Deptford very much smaller (in proportion to the working population) than they are in the Rhondda, but they represent entirely different types of unemployment. Only 6% of the Deptford unemployed were long-unemployed, but 63% in the Rhondda. The inclusion of the ins-and-outs in the unemployment figures must produce an entirely false picture of the differences in unemployment conditions in various parts of the country. Between the prosperous and depressed districts there are two differences. The queues in Rhondda are far longer than in Deptford, for example, and at the same time among them the proportion of 'really' unemployed men is far higher. Among every 1,000 workers, 4 in Deptford, but 280 in Rhondda have failed to get a job for at least a year. This gives an idea of the unevenness in the distribution of the long unemployed over the country. The difference between a prosperous and a depressed area is thus not in the neighbourhood of 1:7, but of 1:70. In a depressed community there are 70 long-unemployed men, where in a prosperous community of the same size there is one.

Document 8B: B. S. Rowntree, *Poverty and Progress* (1941) pp. 451, 454, 456–7, 476

In 1899 of the working-class population 15.46 per cent (7,230 persons) were living in primary poverty, i.e. their incomes after paying rent were under 17s. 8d. a week for a family of man, wife and three children, or the equivalent of this for differently constituted families. 17s. 8d. is equal to 30s. 7d. at 1936 prices. In 1936 6.8 per cent of the working class population (3,767 persons) were living in primary poverty. In other words, the proportion of the working-class population living in abject poverty had been reduced by more than one half. It should be pointed out that in 1899 trade in York was booming, and unemployment accounted for only 2.31 per cent of the primary poverty as compared with 44.53 per cent in 1936. Had the level of unemployment in 1936 been the same as in 1899 the proportion of working-class population in primary poverty would have been very much lower.

I suggest that we should probably not be very far wrong if we put the standard of living available to the workers in 1936 at about 30 per cent higher than it was in 1899.

Three causes account for this increase. The first is the reduction in the size of family.... The second is the increase in real wages.... The third cause is the remarkable growth of social services in the period under review.

It will be remembered that I have taken the standard of living attainable by a family of man, wife and three dependent children with an available income of 43s. 6d. a week, after paying rent, as the minimum....

Our inquiry showed that 31.1 per cent of the working-class population were in receipt of insufficient income to enable them to live in accordance with the above standard, and so are classified as living under the poverty line; 18.9 per cent belong to families with incomes of less than 10s. a week above the minimum figure; 13.9 per cent to those with incomes between 10s. and 20s. above it, and 36.1 per cent to families with incomes of not less than 20s. a week above it.

Three quarters of the poverty is due to three causes: 28.6 per cent is due to unemployment, 32.8 per cent to the fact that workers in regular work are not receiving wages sufficiently high to enable them to live above the poverty line, and 14.7 per cent are in poverty on account of old age. Of the income of the families whose poverty is due to unemployment 80 per cent is derived from social service, and 66 per cent is so derived in the case of those whose poverty is due to old age. On the other hand, families whose poverty is due to inadequate wages only derive 1.7 per cent of their total income from social services.

It is gratifying that so much progress has been achieved, but if instead of looking backward we look forward, then we see how far the standard of living of many workers falls short of any standard which could be regarded even for the time being, as satisfactory. Great though the progress made during the last forty years has been there is no cause for satisfaction in the fact that in a country so rich as England, over 30 per cent of the workers in a typical provincial city should have incomes so small that it is beyond their means to live even at the stringently economical level adopted as a minimum in this survey, nor in the fact that almost half the children of working-class parents spend the first five years of their lives in poverty and that almost a third of them live below the poverty line for ten years or more.

We have examined the causes of poverty. Every one is capable of remedy without dislocating industry or our national finances. They can be removed just as the slums, once thought to be inevitable, are being removed today.

War and welfare in the 1940s

Document 9A: Editorial, *The Times*, 1 July 1940

Over the greater part of Western Europe the common values for which we stand are known and prized. We must indeed beware of defining these values in purely 19th century terms. If we speak of democracy we do not mean a democracy which maintains the right to vote but forgets the right to work and the right to live. If we speak of freedom we do not mean a rugged individualism which excludes social organisation and economic planning. If we speak of equality we do not mean a political equality nullified by social and economic privilege. If we speak of economic reconstruction we think less of maximum (though this job too will be required) than of equitable distribution. The attacks of the dictators on 'Pluto democracy' are an effort partly to exploit the impoverishment they have created and partly to conceal its cause. The plea is grotesque enough especially in the conclusions which the dictators seek to draw from it. But the persistence of these attacks and the purpose which they are intended to serve abroad may remind us that the problem of the new order is social as well as international. The European house cannot be put in order unless we put our own house in order first. The new order cannot be based on the preservation of privilege whether the privilege be that of a country, of a class or of an individual.

Document 9B: Papers by W. H. Beveridge to Inter-Departmental Committee on Social Insurance and Allied Service

(i) *Heads of a Scheme for Social Security*, 11 Dec 1941, PRO Cab. 87/76
   1. Assumptions: No satisfactory scheme of social security can be devised, *following assumptions:

---

*Presumably the words 'except on the' were omitted in error [D.F.]

A. A national health service for prevention and comprehensive treatment available to all members of the community.

B. Universal children's allowances for all children up to 14 or if in full-time education up to 16.

C. Full use of powers of the state to maintain employment and to reduce unemployment to seasonal, cyclical and interval unemployment, that is to say to unemployment suitable for treatment by cash allowances.

2. United Social Security: On these three assumptions, a scheme for social security is outlined below, providing for each member of the community basic provision appropriate to all his needs, in return for a single compulsory contribution.

3. Principle of Scheme: The principle of the Social Security Scheme is to ensure for every one income up to subsistence level, in return for compulsory contributions, expecting him to make voluntary provision to ensure income that he desired beyond this. One consequence of this principle is that no means test of any kind can be applied to the benefits of the Scheme. Another is that the Scheme does not guarantee a standard of life beyond subsistence level; men whose powers of earning diminish must adjust themselves to that change.

4. Needs: The needs to be covered are of seven kinds, including as one the composite needs of a married woman.

C. Childhood, provided for by allowances till 14, or if in full-time education till 16.

O. Old Age, including premature old age, met by pension beginning from 65 for man and 60 for woman normally, but beginning earlier for proved permanent invalidity.

D. Disability, that is to say inability through illness or accident to pursue a gainful occupation, met by disability and invalidity benefits.

U. Unemployment, that is to say, inability to obtain paid employment by a person dependent on it and physically fit for it, met by unemployment benefit.

F. Funeral Expenses of self or any person for whom responsible, met by funeral grant

L. Loss in Gainful Occupation other than Employment, e.g. bankruptcy, fire, theft, met by loss grant.

M. Marriage Needs of a Woman, including provision for:

1. Setting up of a home, met by furnishing grant.

2. Maternity met by maternity grant in all cases, and in the case of a married woman also gainfully employed by maternity benefit for a period before and after confinement.

3. Interruption of husband's earning, by his disability or unemployment, met by dependent benefit.
4. Widowhood, met by pension at various rates corresponding to needs and by credit of contributions for unemployment and disability.
5. Separation, i.e. end of husband's maintenance by desertion or legal separation, met by adaptation of widowhood provisions.
6. Old Age, met by pension at 60, with provision for antedating if husband's earning capacity is stopped by old age.
7. Incapacity for household duties, met by grant to meet expenses of paid help in illness.
8. Funeral Grant for self or any person for whom responsible after separation from husband.

(ii) *The Scale of Social Insurance Benefits and the Problem of Poverty,* 16 Jan. 1942, PRO Cab. 87/79
1. *Purpose of Social Insurance.* In paragraph 3 above it is stated that 'the principle of the Social Security Scheme is to ensure for everyone income up to subsistence level in return for compulsory contributions, expecting him to make voluntary provision to ensure income that he desires beyond this'. This principle has two cutting edges. First, it excludes gradation of insurance benefits according to differences of income or standard of living, though it does not exclude, and indeed requires, adjustment of benefit to needs. Second, it excludes reliance on voluntary insurance or savings or help from others as a means of making resources up to the minimum needed for subsistence when the earnings of an insured person are interrupted by any cause. It implies that the benefits provided by the State in return for compulsory contributions should themselves, without any addition made through voluntary insurance, be sufficient for subsistence; it requires the fixing of benefit scales, not arbitrarily, but by reference to reasoned estimates of the cost of providing housing, food, clothing, fuel and other necessaries. The primary purpose of social insurance is to prevent or diminish want due to interruption or loss of earnings through unemployment, sickness, accident, old age, death, widowhood or other causes: with this primary purpose may be associated the making of provision in advance for exceptional expenses such as those connected with death or maternity which cannot readily be met from personal resources. Social insurance pursues its primary aim directly by redistribution of income both between classes and persons and between times of earning and not earning ... no lesser aim should be admitted than the total

abolition of that part of poverty which is due to interruption or loss of earning power....

There is wanted a change of emphasis and direction of effort. The failure in spite of so much general progress to abolish poverty has been due not simply to lack of knowledge but also to undue emphasis upon a simple line of progress namely improvement of wages and working conditions as distinct from living conditions. Health insurance itself for thirty years has remained, on the side of treatment, confined to the paid workers in place of embracing all the unpaid working population of housewives and dependants.... For improvement of the conditions of people it is more important now to concentrate on living conditions than on working conditions; it is necessary to look away from the workman and his wages at the purpose for which these wages are required. To do so, is to see at once that one indispensable step to abolition of poverty is the adjustment of incomes to needs by children's allowances. It is to see, in the second place, that one of the main efforts to follow this war should be directed to improving housing and all this is implied in housing. The difference in the standard of living between those who are wealthy and those who are not wealthy lies not so much in food or clothing as in housing conditions. There is the scope for raising the standard of living and improving health.

Document 9C: *Report on Social Insurance and Allied Services*, Cmd. 6404 (1942) pp. 120–2

300. *Scope of Social Security*: The term 'social security' is used here to denote the securing of an income to take the place of earnings when they are interrupted by unemployment, sickness or accident, to provide for retirement through age, to provide against loss of support by the death of another person, and to meet exceptional expenditures, such as those connected with birth, death and marriage. Primarily social security means security of income up to a minimum, but the provision of an income should be associated with treatment designed to bring the interruption of earnings to an end as soon as possible.

301. *Three Assumptions*: No satisfactory scheme of social security can be devised except on the following assumptions:

(a) Children's allowances for children up to the age of 15 or if in full-time education up to the age of 16;
(b) Comprehensive health and re-habilitation services for prevention and cure of disease and restoration of capacity for work, available to all members of the community;

(c) Maintenance of employment, that is to say avoidance of mass unemployment.

The grounds for making these three assumptions, the method of satisfying them and their relation to the social security scheme are discussed in Part VI. Children's allowances will be added to all the insurance benefits and pensions described below in paras 320–49.

302. *Three Methods of Security*: On these three assumptions, a Plan for Social Security is outlined below, combining three distinct methods: social insurance for basic needs; national assistance for special cases; voluntary insurance for additions to the basic provision. Social insurance means the providing of cash payments conditional upon compulsory contributions previously made by, or on behalf of, the insured persons, irrespective of the resources of the individual at the time of the claim. Social insurance is much the most important of the three methods and is proposed here in a form as comprehensive as possible. But while social insurance can, and should, be the main instrument for guaranteeing income security, it cannot be the only one. It needs to be supplemented both by national assistance and by voluntary insurance. National assistance means the giving of cash payments conditional upon proved need at the time of the claim, irrespective of previous contributions but adjusted by consideration of individual circumstances and paid from the national exchequer. Assistance is an indispensable supplement to social insurance, however the scope of the latter may be widened. In addition to both of these there is place for voluntary insurance. Social insurance and national assistance organised by the State are designed to guarantee, on condition of service, a basic income for subsistence. The actual incomes and by consequence the normal standards of expenditure of different sections of the population differ greatly. Making provision for these higher standards is primarily the function of the individual, that is to say, it is a matter for free choice and voluntary insurance. But the State should make sure that its measures leave room and encouragement for such voluntary insurance. The social insurance scheme is the greater part of the Plan for Social Security and its description occupies most of this part of the report. But the plan includes national assistance and voluntary insurance as well.

303. *Six Principles of Social Insurance*: The social insurance scheme set out below as the chief method of social security embodies six fundamental principles:

Flat rate of subsistence benefit
Flat rate of contribution
Unification of administrative responsibility
Adequacy of benefit

Comprehensiveness
Classification

304. *Flat Rate of Subsistence Benefit*: The first fundamental principle of the social insurance scheme is provision of a flat rate of insurance benefit, irrespective of the amount of the earnings which have been interrupted by unemployment or disability or ended by retirement; exception is made only where prolonged disability has resulted from an industrial accident or disease. This principle follows from the recognition of the place and importance of voluntary insurance in social security and distinguishes the scheme proposed for Britain from the security schemes of Germany, the Soviet Union, the United States and most other countries with the exception of New Zealand. The flat rate is the same for all the principal forms of cessation of earning – unemployment, disability, retirement; for maternity and for widowhood there is a temporary benefit at a higher rate.

305. *Flat Rate of Contribution*: The second fundamental principle of the scheme is that the compulsory contribution required of each insured person or his employer is at a flat rate, irrespective of his means. All insured persons, rich or poor, will pay the same contributions for the same security; those with larger means will pay more only to the extent that as tax-payers they pay more to the National Exchequer and so to the State share of the Social Insurance Fund. This feature distinguishes the scheme proposed for Britain from the scheme recently established in New Zealand under which the contributions are graduated by income, and are in effect an income-tax assigned to a particular service. Subject moreover to one exception, the contribution will be the same irrespective of the assumed degree of risk affecting particular individuals or forms of employment. The exception is the raising of a proportion of the special cost of benefits and pensions for industrial disability in occupations of high risk by a levy on employers proportionate to risk and payroll (paras. 86–90 and 360).

306. *Unification of Administrative Responsiblity*: The third fundamental principle is unification of administrative responsibility in the interests of efficiency and economy. For each insured person there will be a single weekly contribution, in respect of all his benefits. There will be in each locality a Security Office able to deal with claims of every kind and all sides of security. The methods of paying different kinds of cash benefit will be different and will take account of the circumstances of insured persons, providing for payment at the home or elsewhere, as is necessary. All contributions will be paid into a single Social Insurance Fund and all benefits and other insurance payments will be paid from that fund.

307. *Adequacy of Benefit*: The fourth fundamental principle is adequacy of benefit in amount and in time. The flat rate of benefit proposed is intended in itself to be sufficient without further resources to provide the minimum income needed for subsistence in all normal cases. It gives room and a basis for additional voluntary provision, but does not assume that in any case. The benefits are adequate also in time, that is to say except for contingencies of a temporary nature, they will continue indefinitely without means test, so long as the need continues, though subject to any change of conditions and treatment required by prolongation of the interruption in earning and occupation.

308. *Comprehensiveness*: The fifth fundamental principle is that social insurance should be comprehensive, in respect of the persons covered and of their needs. It should not leave either to national assistance or to voluntary insurance any risk so general or so uniform that social insurance can be justified. For national assistance involves a means test which may discourage voluntary insurance or personal saving. And voluntary insurance can never be sure of covering the ground. For any need moreover which, like direct funeral expenses, is so general and so uniform as to be a fit subject for insurance by compulsion, social insurance is much cheaper to administer than voluntary insurance.

309. *Classification*: The sixth fundamental principle is that social insurance, while unified and comprehensive, must take account of the different ways of life of different sections of the community; of those dependent on earnings by employment under contract of service, of those earning in other ways, of those rendering vital unpaid service as housewives, of those not yet of age to earn and of those past earning. The term 'classification' is used here to denote adjustment of insurance to the differing circumstances of each of these classes and to many varieties of need and circumstance within each insurance class. But the insurance classes are not economic or social classes in the ordinary sense; the insurance scheme is one for all citizens irrespective of their means.

Document 9D: Social Legislation, 1944–8

Education Act, 1944

1. (1)   It shall be lawful for His Majesty to appoint a Minister (hereinafter referred to as 'the Minister'), whose duty it shall be to promote the education of the people of England and Wales and the progressive development of institutions devoted to that purpose, and to secure the effective execution by local authorities, under his control and direction, of the national policy

for providing a varied and comprehensive educational service in every area.

National Health Service Act, 1946

1. (1)   It shall be the duty of the Minister of Health (hereinafter in this Act referred to as 'the Minister') to promote the establishment in England and Wales of a comprehensive health service designed to secure improvement in the physical and mental health of the people of England and Wales and the prevention, diagnosis and treatment of illness, and for that purpose to provide or secure the effective provision of services in accordance with the following provisions of this Act.

   (2)   The services so provided shall be free of charge, except where any provision of this Act expressly provides for the making and recovery of charges.

National Assistance Act, 1948

1.   The existing poor law shall cease to have effect and shall be replaced by the provisions of Part II of this Act as to the rendering, out of moneys provided by Parliament, of assistance to persons in need, the provisions of Part III of this Act as to accommodation and other services to be provided by local authorities, and related provisions of Part IV of this Act....

2.   It shall be the duty of the Board in accordance with the following provisions of this Part of this Act to assist persons in Great Britain who are without resources to meet their requirements, or whose resources (including benefits receivable under the National Insurance Acts, 1946) must be supplemented in order to meet their requirements.

Document 9E: C. Clive Saxton, *Beveridge Report Criticised* (1943) p. 31

THE MAIN ISSUES SUMMARISED

1.   There can be no enforceable guarantee of 'Social Security' and it is a false aim unworthy of a great and virile nation.

2.   The Beveridge Plan is cumbrous, and unworkable. It seeks to amalgamate Social Services which are unlike and call for different methods of approach and finance.

3.   The State payment of Children's Allowances is unlikely to fulfil its purpose because it will depress wages and in the result no one will be

better off. There may be something to be said for giving an allowance for the third and succeeding children.

4. A State medical scheme is likely to be unpalatable to most people. It might cause the decline of medical skill and ability. Free choice of doctor would be restricted.

5. The Plan is not sufficiently elastic to meet an unexpected volume of unemployment.

6. An inquiry into the prospects of post-war employment should precede consideration of the Beveridge Plan.

7. Unemployment pay and income needs should be met out of National Taxation each year to the extent that can be afforded when account has been taken of competing claims upon the Budget. The control of 'Assistance' should be in the hands of the Central Government.

8. 'Collective Services' such as Health and Medical needs may be provided as required, by the self-help or contributory insurance principle, founded on 'group' action.

9. Fairness cannot be achieved by a flat rate benefit which takes no account of the wide differences in rents.

Notes and references

Introduction

1 Anon., *A Few Questions on Secular Education*, by the author of 'The Outlines of Social Economy' (1848) p. 23.
2 *Midland Counties Herald*, 22 Apr 1847.

1 The factory question

1 F. Engels, *The Condition of the Working Class in England* (1958 edn, translation) p. 10.
2 *Leicester Journal*, 29 May 1846.
3 Quoted by J. T. Ward, *The Factory Movement* (1962) p. 17.
4 Oastler quoted by C. Creighton, 'Richard Oastler, Factory Legislation and the Working Class Family', *Journal of Historical Sociology*, 5 (1992), p. 301; see also Gray, 'Medical Men, Industrial Labour and the State in Britain, 1830–50', *Social History*, 16 (1991), pp. 19–43; and his 'Factory Legislation and the Gendering of Jobs', *Gender and History*, 5 (1993) pp. 58–80.
5 *Leeds Intelligencer*, 15 Dec 1831.
6 *Leeds Mercury*, 26 Nov 1831.
7 Cavie Richardson, *The Factory System* (1831) p. 12, in Oastler's 'White Slavery' Collection, vol. 4, no. 5.
8 *Leeds Mercury*, 16 June 1832.
9 Ibid.
10 L. Horner, *On the Employment of Children in Factories* (1840), quoted by Ward, *Factory Movement*, p. 214.
11 Select Committee on the Act for the Regulation of Mills and Factories, Q. 1083, *Parliamentary Papers*, 1840 (203) X.
12 Children's Employment Commission, first report, appendix part 11, *Parliamentary Papers*, 1842 (XVII), 195.

13 *Leicestershire Mercury*, 6 Apr 1844.
14 E. Hodder, *The Life and Work of the Seventh Earl of Shaftesbury* (1866) II, p. 199.
15 Quoted by G. B. A. M. Finlayson, *The Seventh Earl of Shaftesbury, 1801–1885* (1981) p. 295.
16 Quoted by P. Smith, *Disraelian Conservatism and Social Reform* (1967) p. 214.
17 Quoted by J. Pellew, *The Home Office, 1848–1914* (1982) p. 130.
18 P. W. J. Bartrip and P. T. Fenn, 'The Administration of Safety: the Enforcement Policy of the Early Factory Inspectorate, 1844–1864', *Public Administration*, LVII (1980) pp. 87–102.
19 A. E. Peacock, 'The Justices of the Peace and the Prosecution of the Factory Acts, 1833–1855' (unpublished Ph.D. thesis, York, 1982).
20 A. E. Peacock, 'The Successful Prosecution of the Factory Acts, 1833–55', *Economic History Review*, lxxxvii (1985) pp. 423–36
21 Quoted by A. H. Yarmi, 'British Employers' Resistance to "Grand-motherly Government"', *Social History* (1984) p. 148.

2 The Poor Law

1 See for example G. R. Boyer, *An Economic History of the English Poor Law 1750–1830*, (1990).
2 *Leicester Journal*, 27 Feb 1807.
3 Sydney Smith, *Edinburgh Review* (1820), quoted by J. R. Poynter, *Society and Pauperism* (1969) p. 330.
4 Quoted ibid., p. 42.
5 For these reforms, see J. D. Marshall, 'The Nottinghamshire Reformers and their Contribution to the New Poor Law', *Economic History Review*, 2nd ser., XIII (1961).
6 M. Blaug, 'The Myth of the Old Poor Law and the Making of the New', and 'The Poor Law Report Re-examined', *Journal of Economic History*, XXIII (1963) and XXIV (1964); D. A. Baugh, 'The Cost of Poor Relief in South-East England', *Economic History Review*, 2nd ser., XXVIII (1975); D. McCloskey, 'New Perspectives on the Old Poor Law', *Explorations in Economic History*, x (1973); J. P. Huzel, 'The Demographic Impact of the Old Poor Law', *Economic History Review*, 2nd ser., XXXIII (1980).
7 G. Himmelfarb, *The Idea of Poverty* (1984), pp. 153–4; D. Englander, *Poverty and Poor Law Reform in 19th Century Britain*, p. 1.
8 Quoted by Poynter, *Society and Pauperism*, p. 125.

9 *Poor Law Report* (1834) p. 261.

10 *Edinburgh Review*, XLVII (1828) pp. 303–29, quoted by Poynter, *Society and Pauperism*, p. 305.

11 S. E. Finer, *The Life and Times of Edwin Chadwick* (1952) p. 94.

12 Quoted by Ward, *Factory Movement*, pp. 184–5.

13 Charles Clements to Secretary of Leeds Board of Guardians, 18 July 1845, PRO, MH, 12/15227.

14 Quoted by A. Brundage, *The Making of the New Poor Law* (1978), p. 159.

15 F. Driver, *Power and Pauperism: The Workhouse System, 1834–1884* (1993).

16 P. Dunkley, 'The "Hungry Forties" and the New Poor Law', *Historical Journal*, XVII (1974) p. 346.

17 W. Rathbone, *Social Duties Considered* (1867) pp. 48–9.

18 L. H. Lees, *The Solidarities of Strangers: The English Poor Laws and the People* (1998) p. 229.

3 Public health

1 R. Baker, *Journal of the Statistical Society*, II (1839) 13.

2 *Leeds Intelligencer*, 21 Aug 1841.

3 Quoted by M. W. Flinn, Introduction to *Chadwick Report* (Edinburgh 1965 edn) p. 25.

4 Quoted by Finer, *Life and Times of Edwin Chadwick*, p. 155.

5 Quoted by R. A. Lewis, *Edwin Chadwick and the Public Health Movement, 1832–1854* (1952) p. 27.

6 Ibid., p. 14.

7 Cf. Flinn, *Chadwick Report*, p. 68: 'Nearly two thirds of these volumes [First Report] are in my handwriting for which I am to get only posthumous credit, if at all.'

8 *Leicester Chronicle*, 17 Oct 1846.

9 *Leeds Mercury*, 29 Mar 1844.

10 Quoted by Lewis, *Chadwick*, p. 108.

11 *Leeds Intelligencer*, 29 Oct 1836.

12 Thoresby Society (Leeds), 22B10, 'Projected Leeds Waterworks', MS note.

13 *Leeds Intelligencer*, 7 July 1838.

14 J. Hole, *The Homes of the Working Classes* (1866) p. 26.

15 *Leeds Intelligencer*, 1 Oct 1836.

16 Lewis, *Chadwick*, p. 110.

17 *Nottingham Review*, 6 Dec 1844.

18 *Birmingham Journal*, 28 July 1849.

19 Quoted by Lewis, *Chadwick*, p. 369.

20 Quoted by A. Brundage, *England's Prussian Minister* (1988), p. 121.

21 S. Szreter, 'The Importance of Social Intervention in Britain's Mortality Decline', *Social History of Medicine*, I (1988), pp. 1–37; also *The GRO and the Public Health Movement in Britain*, idem. 4 (1991) pp. 435–63.

22 M. W. Flinn, 'Introduction' to *The Legal and Medical Aspects of Sanitary Reform* (1969) pp. 14–16.

23 Quoted by R. J. Lambert, *Sir John Simon, 1816–1904* (1963) p. 434.

24 *Leeds Mercury*, 3 Feb 1865.

25 Quoted by Lambert, *Sir John Simon*, p. 370.

26 A. W. W. Dale, *The Life of R. W. Dale* (1899) p. 401.

4 Education and welfare

1 Quoted by M. Sturt, *The Education of the People* (1967) p. 5.

2 Quoted by H. Silver, *The Concept of Popular Education* (1967) p. 45.

3 L. Horner to N. W. Senior, 23 May 1837 in N. W. Senior, *Letters on the Factory Act* (1837) p. 30.

4 Quoted by J. T. Ward and J. H. Treble, 'Religion and Education in 1843', *Journal of Ecclesiastical History*, XX (1969) p. 109.

5 Quoted by C. M. Brown, 'Leonard Horner 1785–1864: His Contribution to Education', *Journal of Educational Administration and History*, xvii (1985) p. 9.

6 W. F. Hook, *A Letter to the Lord Bishop of St Davids* (1846) p. 38.

7 *Nonconformist Elector*, 9 July 1847.

8 *Quarterly Review*, Sep 1846.

9 *Hansard*, 13 Feb 1862, CLXV 229.

10 E. Baines to J. Kay-Shuttleworth, 19 Oct 1867, Baines Papers (Leeds City Archives).

11 G. Sutherland, *Elementary Education in the Nineteenth Century* (1971) p. 28.

12 Smith, *Disraelian Conservatism and Social Reform*, pp. 246–7.

13 Local Government Board, *Third Annual Report* (1873–4), Appendix p. 247.

14 Quoted by F. Smith, *A History of English Elementary Education* (1931) p. 331; *Schoolmaster*, 21 Mar 1891, quoted by Sturt, *Education of the People*, p. 381.

15 *Seventh Annual Report of the Poor Law Commissioners* (1841), quoted by R. G. Hodgkinson, *The Origins of the National Health Service* (1967) p. 60.

16 Lambert, *Sir John Simon*, p. 250.
17 K. Jones, *Asylums and After* (1993), p. 91.
18 R. Pinker, *English Hospital Statistics, 1861–1938* (1966) p. 49.
19 Quoted by Hodgkinson, *Origins of the National Health Service*, p. 521.
20 *Hansard*, 8 Feb 1867, CLXXXV 163.
21 *Bradford Observer*, 21 January 1869; J. Leeson to Poor Law Board, 31 March 1869, PRO MH12/14737.
22 Quoted by B. Abel-Smith, *The Hospitals, 1800–1948* (1964) p. 64.
23 Thorold Rogers (1870), quoted by Hodgkinson, *Origins of the National Health Service*, p. 695.
24 J. Harris, *Private Lives: Public Spirit* (1994), p. 191.
25 Grey to Russell, 27 Dec 1850, quoted by H. Parris, *Constitutional Bureaucracy* (1969) p. 208.
26 *Second Report of the Surveyor-General of Prisons* (1847) p. 56, quoted by J. Carlbach, *Caring for Children in Trouble* (1970) p. 50.
27 Quoted ibid., p. 51.
28 Quoted by D. Owen, *English Philanthropy, 1660–1960* (1965) p. 155.

5 *Laissez-faire* and state intervention in the mid-nineteenth century

1 Adam Smith, *An Inquiry into the Nature and Causes of the Wealth of Nations* (Everyman edn) I, p. 398.
2 Quoted by D. and R. Porter, 'The Politics of Prevention: Anti-Vaccinationism and Public Health in Nineteenth-century England', *Medical History*, 32(1988) p. 241.
3 *Leeds Mercury*, 14 Sep 1850.
4 Quoted by H. Perkin, *The Origins of Modern English Society, 1780–1880* (1969) p. 227.
5 *Cambridge Independent Press*, 5 Sep 1850.
6 W. L. Burn, *The Age of Equipoise* (1964) p. 8.
7 *Leeds Times*, 23 Sep 1837.
8 *Life and Struggles of William Lovett* (1967 edn) p. 204.
9 *Leeds Times*, 25 Oct 1845.
10 The Co-operator (1866–7), quoted by Perkin, *Modern English Society*, p. 387.
11 J. Morley, *Life of Gladstone* (1905) I, p. 758.
12 Quoted by F. B. Smith, *The Making of the Second Reform Bill* (1966) p. 11.
13 *The Times*, 4 May 1847.
14 Parris, *Constitutional Bureaucracy*, p. 281.

15 Burn, *Age of Equipoise*, pp. 135–6.
16 S. Webb, *Socialism in England* (1889) pp. 116–17.
17 E. Halévy, *The Growth of Philosophical Radicalism* (1928).
18 *Hansard*, 22 May 1846, LXXXVI, 1031, 1034.
19 J. B. Brebner, 'Laissez-faire and State Intervention in Nineteenth-Century Britain', *Journal of Economic History*, supplement, VIII (1948) pp. 59–73.
20 O. MacDonagh, 'The Nineteenth-Century Revolution in Government: a Reappraisal', *Historical Journal*, I (1958) pp. 52–67; *The Passenger Acts: A Pattern of Governmental Growth* (1961).
21 D. Roberts, *Victorian Origins of the British Welfare State* (New Haven, 1968).
22 H. Parris, 'The Nineteenth-Century Revolution in Government: a Reappraisal Reappraised', *Historical Journal*, III (1960) pp. 17–37.
23 W. C. Lubenow, *The Politics of Government Growth* (1971).
24 Charles Dickens, *Hard Times* (1902 edn) p. 3.
25 *Leeds Mercury*, 26 Feb 1848.
26 Wood to Lord John Russell, 31 Dec 1850, quoted by Parris, *Constitutional Bureaucracy*, p. 208.
27 J. S. Mill, *Considerations on Representative Government* (1912 edn) p. 377.
28 *Nonconformist*, 30 Sep 1846.
29 Quoted by Hodgkinson, *Origins of the National Health Service*, p. 213.
30 Quoted by Lubenow, *Politics of Government Growth*, pp. 27–8.
31 L. Goldman, 'The Social Science Association, 1857–1886', *English Historical Review*, CI (1986), p. 97.
32 *Hansard*, 13 Feb 1862, CLXV 211.

6 The growing awareness of poverty

1 G. Levine (ed.), *The Emergence of Victorian Consciousness* (New York, 1967) p. 11 [my italics].
2 Morley, *Life of Gladstone*, 1767.
3 Quoted by K. Woodroffe, *From Charity to Social Work in England and the United States* (1962) p. 21.
4 Quoted by B. Harrison, 'Philanthropy and the Victorians', *Victorian Studies*, IX (1966) p. 360.
5 *Porcupine*, 1 June 1861.
6 Owen, *English Philanthropy*, pp. 141, 390; *Charity Organisation Reporter*, 27 Sep 1884, quoted by Woodroffe, *From Charity to Social Work*, p. 23.

7 H. Fawcett, *Pauperism: Its Causes and Remedies* (1871) p. 56.

8 Quoted by K. de Schweinitz, *England's Road to Social Security* (New York, 1946) p. 142.

9 Quoted by N. McCord, *The Anti-Corn Law League* (1958) p. 27.

10 *Life and Struggles of William Lovett*, p. 115.

11 *Charity Organisation Reporter*, 13 July 1882, quoted by Woodroffe, *From Charity to Social Work*, p. 23.

12 C.O.S. *Annual Report* (1883), quoted by C. L. Mowat, *The Charity Organisation Society, 1869–1913* (1961) p. 35.

13 J. Lewis, *The Voluntary Sector, The State and Social Work in Britain* (1995) p. 11.

14 Quoted by A. S. Wohl, Introduction to A. Mearns, *Bitter Cry of Outcast London* (1970 ed.) p. 9.

15 W. Booth, *In Darkest England and the Way Out* (1890) p. 47.

16 A. Toynbee, '*Progress and Poverty*': *A Criticism...*(1883).

17 A. Sykes, *The Rise and Fall of British Liberalism* (1997) p. 174.

18 Quoted by T. S. and M. B. Simey, *Charles Booth: Social Scientist* (1960) p. 64.

19 Hyndman, 24 June 1884, quoted by H. Ausubel, *In Hard Times* (1960) p. 149.

20 Arthur Balfour at Manchester, 16 Jan 1895, quoted by E. Halévy, *Imperialism and the Rise of Labour* (1951) p. 231.

21 Quoted by R. C. K. Ensor, *England, 1870–1914* (1936) p. 87.

22 J. Harris, *Private Lives, Public Spirit: Britain, 1870–1914* (1994) p. 239.

23 Quoted by A. M. McBriar, *Fabian Socialism and English Politics, 1884–1918* (1962) p. 241.

24 R. Muir, *A History of Liverpool (1907)*, reprinted 1970, p. 337.

25 *Hansard*, 22 Feb 1884, CCLXXXIV, 1703.

26 M. E. Rose, 'The Crisis of Poor Relief in England', in W. Mommsen (ed.), *The Emergence of the Welfare State in Britain and Germany* (1981) pp. 50–70.

7 Liberal social policy, 1905–14

1 *The Times*, 30 Jan 1906.

2 Quoted by A. Wilson and G. S. Mackay, *Old Age Pensions* (1941) p. 28.

3 W. George, *My Brother and I* (1958) p. 220.

4 Glasgow Speech October 1906, quoted by M. Bentley, *The Climax of Liberal Politics*, (1987) p. 112.

5 Churchill to Lloyd George, 6 Oct 1910, Lloyd George Papers, C/3/15/1, Lloyd George speech at Cardiff, 11 Oct 1906, published in D. Lloyd George, *Better Times* (1910) p. 36.

6 W. S. Churchill, *The People's Rights* (1909), reprinted 1970, pp. 118–19.

7 *Hansard*, 29 Apr 1909.

8 B. Webb, *Our Partnership* (1948) p. 322.

9 *Report of the Royal Commission on the Poor Law and Relief of Distress*, XXXVII (1909) Appendix, vol. I: Minutes of Evidence, Q. 2230.

10 Evidence of Dr Fuller, quoted in M. Cole, *Beatrice Webb* (1945) p. 97.

11 *Poor Law Report* (1909) pp. 643–4.

12 'Memorandum on Coalition', 17 Aug 1910, *Lloyd George Papers*, C/3/14/8.

13 Bunbury, *Lloyd George's Ambulance Wagon*, p. 80.

14 Churchill to H. Llewellyn Smith, 'Notes on Malingering', 6 June 1909, *Beveridge Papers*, D.026.

15 Lloyd George to Braithwaite, 24 and 27 Mar 1911, *Braithwaite Collection*, II 46.

16 Diary, 28 Feb 1911, *Braithwaite Collection*, I.

17 C. Petrie, *The Life and Letters of the Right Hon. Sir Austen Chamberlain* (1939) I, 277.

18 Bunbury, *Lloyd George's Ambulance Wagon*, p. 140.

19 R. S. Churchill, *Winston S. Churchill*, vol. II (1967) p. 263.

20 E. Hughes, *Keir Hardie* (1956) p. 200.

21 R. S. Churchill, *Winston S. Churchill: Companion*, vol. II, pt 2 (1969) p. 863.

22 H. Spender, *Contemporary Review*, Jan 1909, quoted by B. B. Gilbert, *The Evolution of National Insurance in Great Britain* (1966) p. 257.

23 E. P. Hennock, *British Social Reform and German Precedent* (1987), pp. 206–9; see also G. A. Ritter, *Social Welfare in Germany and Britain* (1986), pp. 179–86.

24 *Minority Report*, p. 921.

25 Gilbert, *Evolution of National Insurance*, Ch. vi.

26 'Memo on Coalition', 17 Aug 1910, pp. 5–6; *Lloyd George Papers*, C/3/14/8.

27 Ibid.

28 Quoted by Gilbert, *Evolution of National Insurance*, p. 315.

29 Hennock, op. cit.

30 Bunbury, *Lloyd George's Ambulance Wagon*, p. 116.

31 *Lloyd George Papers*, C/26/2.

32 Bunbury, *Lloyd George's Ambulance Wagon*, pp. 121–2.

33 Memo to Local Government Board (*c.* 1907), *Beveridge Papers*, D.025.

34 Churchill, 'Notes on Malingering', 6 June 1909, p. 2, *Beveridge Papers*, D.026.

35 Gilbert, *Evolution of National Insurance*, p. 272.

36 'Proportioning of Benefits to Contributions, Further Memo', 1 Sept 1909, *Beveridge Papers*, D.026.
37 A. Marwick, *Britain in the Century of Total War* (1968) p. 33.
38 R. S. Churchill, *Winston S. Churchill: Companion*, vol. II, pt 2, pp. 861, 863.
39 Ibid.
40 G. Ritter, op. cit., p. 185.

8 Politics and policy, 1914–39

1 *The Elements of Reconstruction* (1916) p. 48.
2 Quoted by B. B. Gilbert, *British Social Policy, 1914–1939* (1970) p. 5.
3 Viscountess Rhondda *et al.*, *D. A. Thomas, Viscount Rhondda* (1921) p. 267.
4 K. Middlemas (ed.), *Thomas Jones: Whitehall Diary*, vol. I (1969) pp. 73–4.
5 Quoted by M. Swenarton, *Homes Fit for Heroes* (1981) p. 78.
6 Quoted by A. Marwick, *The Deluge* (1967 edn) p. 262.
7 *Report of the Insurance Sub Committee*, Ministry of Reconstruction, 12 Feb 1918, copy in *Beveridge Papers*, D.030.
8 'The Past and Present of Unemployment Insurance', a lecture at Oxford, 7 Feb 1930, *Beveridge Papers*, D.040.
9 'General Memo for Guidance of Local Committees and Officers of the Ministry of Labour' (1923/4), *Beveridge Papers*, D.030.
10 *Report of the Unemployment Insurance Committee* (1927) I, para 81.
11 W. H. Beveridge, *Unemployment: A Problem of Industry* (1930 edn) p. 420.
12 J. M. Keynes and H. Henderson, *Can Lloyd George Do It?* (1929) p. 25.
13 R. Skidelsky, *Politicians and the Slump* (1967) p. xi.
14 Lord Bradbury, in *Report of the Macmillan Committee on Finance and Industry*, quoted by D. Winch, *Economics and Policy* (1969) p. 131.
15 *Hansard*, 5th ser., CLXLX, 12 Feb 1924, col. 760.
16 Beveridge to Churchill, 5 Feb 1930, *Beveridge Papers*, L. II 218.
17 K. Feiling, *The Life of Neville Chamberlain* (1946) p. 191.
18 Quoted by Skidelsky, *Politicians and the Slump*, p. 363.
19 *Daily Telegraph*, 21 Aug 1931.
20 D. Vincent, *Poor Citizens* (1991), p. 101.
21 W. Hannington, *The Problem of the Distressed Areas* (1937) p. 252.
22 C. L. Mowat, *Britain between the Wars* (1955) p. 471.
23 PEP, *Report on the British Social Services* (1937) p. 145.
24 J. M. Keynes, *The General Theory of Employment, Interest and Money* (1936) p. 381.

25 PEP, *British Social Services*, p. 108.

26 Quoted by Gilbert, *British Social Policy*, p. 283.

27 J. S. Clarke, 'National Health Insurance', in W. A. Robson (ed.), *Social Security* (1943) p. 112.

28 PEP, *Report on the British Health Services* (1937) p. 414.

29 Gilbert, *British Social Policy*, p. 195

30 Hoare to Chamberlain, quoted by J. Macnicol, *The Politics of Retirement in Britain* (1998) p. 207.

31 P. Addison, *Churchill on the Home Front* (1992) p. 241.

32 Macnicol, op. cit., p. 216.

33 C. Webster, 'Health, Welfare and Unemployment During the Depression', *Past and Present*, 109 (1985) pp. 204–30 and 'Health or Hungry Thirties', *History Workshop Journal*, 13 (1992) pp. 110–29. See also N. Whiteside, 'Counting the Cost: Sickness and Disability, 1920–39', *Economic History Review*, XL (1987) pp. 228–46; K. Laybourn, *Britain on the Breadline* (1990).

34 Vincent, op. cit., pp. 51–102; N. Whiteside, 'Private Provision and Public Welfare' in D. Gladstone (ed.), *Before Beveridge* (1999) pp. 26–42.

35 PEP, *British Social Services*, pp. 167–8.

36 J. Stevenson, *British Society, 1914–45* (1984) p. 60.

9 War and welfare in the 1940s

1 W. H. Beveridge, *The Pillars of Security* (1943) pp. 107–8.

2 *The Economist*, 1 May 1943, quoted by R. M. Titmuss, *Problems of Social Policy* (1950) p. 516.

3 P. Addison, *The Road to 1945* (1975); cf. J. Harris, 'Some Aspects of Social Policy in Britain during the Second World War', in Mommsen (ed.), *Welfare State in Britain and Germany* (1981) pp. 247–62.

4 Quoted by Titmuss, *Problems of Social Policy*, p. 511.

5 Sir John Boyd Orr, *Food, Health and Income* (1936) p. 21.

6 A. Briggs, *Social Thought and Social Action: A Study of the Work of Seebohm Rowntree* (1961) p. 303.

7 Memorandum dated 16 Jan 1942, *Beveridge Papers*, D.026 (see Document 9B, ii).

8 Beveridge Note, 2 June 1942, *Beveridge Papers*, H.A. 144.

9 W. H. Beveridge, *Social Insurance and Allied Services* (1942) p. 17.

10 Beveridge, *Pillars of Security*, pp. 55, 132.

11 Quoted by V. George, *Social Security* (1968) p. 42.

12 *Daily Mirror*, 2 Dec 1942, quoted by N. Timmins, *The Five Giants* (1995) p. 7.

13 A. Digby, *British Welfare Policy* (1989), p. 100; H. Fawcett and R. Lowe (eds), *Welfare Policy in Britain* (1999) p. 5, B. Abel-Smith, in J. Hills, J. Ditch and H. Glennester (eds), *Beveridge and Social Security* (1994) p. 10; H. Glennester, *British Social Policy since 1945* (2nd edn, 2000) p. 38.

14 S. Ball (ed.), *Parliament and Politics in the Age of Churchill and Attlee* (1999) p. 344.

15 C. Barnett, *The Lost Victory* (1995) p. 128.

16 *Manchester Guardian*, 15 Feb 1943.

17 W. S. Churchill, *The Second World War*, vol. IV (1954) p. 861.

18 J. Beveridge, *Beveridge and His Plan* (1954) p. 146.

19 Hugh Dalton's Diary, 23 Oct 1943, quoted by H. Pelling, *Britain and the Second World War* (1970) p. 182.

20 A. Calder, *The People's War* (1969) p. 540.

21 *Social Insurance*, pt I, Cmd 6550 (1944) p. 6.

22 *The Times*, 24 and 31 July 1943.

23 Calder, *People's War*, p. 545.

24 *News Chronicle*, 11 Nov 1940.

25 A. Howard, 'We Are the Masters Now', in M. Sissons and P. French (eds), *The Age of Austerity* (1963) p. 16.

26 *The Listener*, 14 June 1945.

27 R. W. B. Clarke, 'The Beveridge Report and After', in Robson, *Social Security*, p. 272.

28 *Report of the Ministry of National Insurance, 1944–1949*, Cmd 7955 (1950) p. 5.

29 Beveridge, *Social Insurance and Allied Services*, pp. 38–9.

30 *Hansard*, 16 June 1948.

31 D. C. Marsh, *National Insurance and Assistance in Great Britain* (1950) pp. 110–11.

32 Bevin Memorandum to Cabinet, 17 Nov 1943, *Prime Minister's Papers*, PRO PREM, pp. 110–11.

33 Beveridge Memo, 16 Jan 1942, *Beveridge Papers*, D.026; Robson, *Social Security*, and H. Levy, *National Health Insurance: A Critical Study* (1944).

34 A. Bevan, *In Place of Fear* (1952) p. 100.

35 *Report of the Ministry of Health*, 1949, Cmd 7910 (1950) p. iii.

36 Quoted by A. Lindsey, *Socialised Medicine in England and Wales* (Chapel Hill, NC, 1962) p. 59.

37 Notes for speech, 23 Oct 1912, *Lloyd George Papers*, C/18/8/2.

38 S. J. Brooke, *Labour's War* (1992), p. 110; M. Francis, *Ideas and Politics under Labour, 1945–1951* (1997) p. 226. See also K. Jeffreys, *The Churchill Coalition and Wartime Politics* (1991).

39 R. Pearce, *Attlee* (1997) p. 157.

40 H. Glennester, *British Social Policy Since 1945* (2nd edn, 2000), p. 63.
41 C. Webster, *The Health Services Since the War*, vol. I (1988), p. 83.
42 M. Thatcher, *Downing Street Years*, (1993) p. 6 and *The Path to Power* (1995) p. 69; Francis, op. cit., pp. 132, 226.
43 K. O. Morgan, *Labour in Power, 1945–1951* (1984) p. 179–87.

10   The Welfare State – the first half-century

1 N. Timmins, *The Five Giants* (1995), p. 170.
2 P. Hennessey, *Never Again* (1993), p. 132; C. Webster, *The National Health Service: A Political History* (1998), p. 2; R. Klein, *The Politics of the NHS* (1989) p. 32.
3 H. Glennester, *British Social Policy Since 1945* (2nd edn, 2000) p. 120.
4 D. Donnison, *The Politics of Poverty* (1982) p. 8.
5 Quoted by Timmins, op. cit., p. 355.
6 C. Barnett, *The Audit of War* (1986) p. 304.
7 M. Thatcher, *The Downing Street Years* (1993) p. 8.
8 Donnison, op. cit., pp. 206–7.
9 Glennester op. cit., p. 170.
10 *Report of the Commission on Social Justice* (1994) pp. 223–4.
11 F. Field, *Making Welfare Work* (1995) p. 192.
12 *The Economist*, 4 March 2000, p. 30.
13 For a critical review of the 'third way', see M. Powell (ed.), *New Labour, New Welfare State?* (1999).

Select bibliography

Place of publication is not given for works published in the United Kingdom. An asterisk denotes a work of central importance in the history of social policy. In each section group A comprises books and group B articles and essays.

IA. General surveys on the development of social policy

Ashford, D. E., *The Emergence of the Welfare State in Britain* (1994).
Bruce, M., *The Coming of the Welfare State* (1968).
Checkland, S. G., *British Public Policy, 1776–1939* (1983).
Digby, A., *British Welfare Policy: Workhouse to Workfare* (1989).
Finlayson, G., *Citizen State and Social Welfare in Britain, 1830–1990* (1994).
Fraser, D., *The Welfare State* (2000).
Heclo, H., *Modern Social Politics in Britain and Sweden* (1974).
Henriques, U., *Before the Welfare State* (1977).
*Kohler, P. A. and Zacher, H. E. (eds), *The Evolution of Social Insurance, 1881–1981* (1982).
Laybourn, K., *The Evolution of Social Policy and the Welfare State* (1995).
*Marshall, T. H., *Social Policy* (1975).
Mencher, S., *Poor Law to Poverty Programme* (Pittsburgh, 1968).
Midwinter, E., *The Development of Social Welfare in Britain* (1994).
Rimlinger, G. V., *Welfare Policy and Industrialisation in Europe, America and Russia* (1971).
Rodgers, B., *The Battle Against Poverty*, 2 vols (1968).
Schweinitz, K. de, *England's Road to Social Security* (1943; reprinted New York, 1961).
Thane, P., *The Foundations of the Welfare State* (1982).
Williams, G., *The Coming of the Welfare State* (1967).

IB

Briggs, A., 'The Welfare State in Historical Perspective', *European Archives of Sociology*, XI (1961).

Goldthorpe, J., 'The Development of Social Policy in England, 1800–1914', *Transactions of the Fifth World Congress of Sociology*, 4 (1962).

Rimlinger, G., 'Welfare Policy and Economic Development: a Comparative Historical Perspective', *Journal of Economic History*, 26 (1966).

Saville, J., 'The Welfare State: an Historical Approach', *New Reasoner*, 3 (1957).

Woodroffe, K., 'The Making of the Welfare State: a Summary of its Origins and Development' in H. R. Winkler (ed.), *Twentieth-Century Britain* (1976).

II. Collections of documents

Birch, R. C., *The Shaping of the Welfare State* (1969).

Bruce, M., *The Rise of the Welfare State* (1973).

*Evans, E. J., *Social Policy 1830–1914* (1978).

*Hay, J. R., *The Development of the British Welfare State 1880–1975* (1978).

Pierson, C. and Castle, F. C. (ed.), *The Welfare State Reader* (2000).

Pope, A., Pratt, A. and Hoyle, B. (eds), *Social Welfare in Britain 1885–1985* (1986).

Watkin, B., *Documents on Health and Social Services* (1975).

III. Social consequences of industrialisation

Briggs, A., *Victorian Cities* (1963).

Checkland, S. G., *The Rise of Industrial Society in England* (1964).

Cole, G. D. H. and Postgate, R., *The Common People, 1746–1946* (1961).

Dyos, H. J., and Wolff, M., *Victorian City: Images and Realities*, 2 vols (1973).

*Engels, F., *The Condition of the Working Class in England*, trans. and ed. W. O. Henderson and W. H. Chaloner (1971).

Hammond, J. L. and B., *The Age of the Chartists, 1832–1854* (1930).

* Perkin, H., *The Origins of Modern English Society, 1780–1880* (1969).

Pike, E. R., *Human Documents of the Industrial Revolution* (1966).

Ryder, J. and Silver, H., *Modern English Society: History and Structure, 1850–1970* (1970).

Thommis, M. I., *The Town Labourer and the Industrial Revolution* (1974).

——, *Responses to Industrialisation* (1976).

*Thompson, E. P., *The Making of the English Working Class* (1963).

IVA. The factory question

Bartrip, P. W. J., *Workmen's Compensations in Twentieth Century Britain: History and Social Policy* (1987).

Bartrip, P. W. J. and Burman, S. J., *The Wounded Soldiers of Industry: Industrial Compensation Policy 1833–1897* (1983).

Best, G. F. A., *Lord Shaftesbury* (1965).

Cruikshank, M., *Children and Industry* (1981).

*Driver, C., *Tory-Radical: The Life of Richard Oastler* (New York, 1946).

*Finlayson, G. B. A. M., *The Seventh Earl of Shaftesbury* (1981).

Fitzgerald, R., *British Labour Management and Industrial Welfare, 1846–1939* (1988).

*Gray, R., *The Factory Question and Industrial England, 1830–1860* (1996).

Henriques, U., *The Early Factory Acts and their Enforcement* (1971).

Hodder, E., *The Life and Work of the Seventh Earl of Shaftesbury* (1886).

Hutchings, B. L. and Harrison, A., *A History of Factory Legislation* (1926).

Thomas, M. W., *The Early Factory Legislation* (1948).

*Ward, J. T., *The Factory Movement* (1962).

——(ed.), *The Factory System* (1970).

IVB

Bartrip, P. W. J., and Fenn, P. T., 'The Administration of Safety: the Enforcement Policy of the Early Factory Inspectorate 1844–1864', *Public Administration*, LVIII (1980).

——, 'British Government Inspection, 1832–1875: Some Observations', *Historical Journal*, 25 (1980).

Bartrip, P. W. J, 'State Intervention in Mid-Nineteenth Century Britain: Fact or Fiction', *Journal of British Studies* (1984).

Bartrip, P. W. J and Fenn, P. T., 'Factory Fatalities and Regulations in Britain 1878–1913', *Explorations in Economic History*, 25 (1988).

Blaug, M., 'The Classical Economists and the Factory Acts: a Re-Examination', *Quarterly Journal of Economics*, LXIII (1958).

Bolin Hort, P., 'A Decided Failure? The Enforcement of Factory Acts in the Glasgow District, 1834–1870', *Scottish Labour History Society Journal*, 26 (1991).

Creighton, C. 'Richard Oastler, Factory Legislation and the Working-Class Family', *Journal of Historical Sociology* (1992).

Gray, R. 'Medical Men, Industrial Labour and the State in Britain 1830–1850', *Social History*, 16 (1991).

Gray, R. 'Factory Legislation and the Gendering of Jobs in the North of England 1830–1860', *Gender and History* 5 (1993).

Heesom, A., 'The Coal Mines Act of 1842', *Historical Journal*, 24 (1981).

MacDonagh, O. O. G. M., 'Coal Mines Regulation: The First Decade, 1842–1852', in R. Robson (ed.), *Ideas and Institutions of Victorian Britain* (1967).

Mandler, P., 'Cain and Abel: Two Aristocrats and the Early Victorian Factory Acts' *Historical Journal*, 27 (1984).

Martin, B., 'Leonard Horner: a Portrait of an Inspector of Factories', *International Review of Social History*, XIV (1969).

Marvel, H. P., 'Factory Regulation: A Re-interpretation of Early English Experience', *Journal of Law and Economics*, XX (1977).

Melling, J., 'Employers, Industrial Housing and the Development of Company Welfare Policies', *International Review of Social History*, XXXVI (1981).

Nardinelli, C., 'Child Labour and the Factory Acts', *Journal of Economic History*, XV (1980).

Webb, R. K., 'A Whig Inspector', *Journal of Modern History*, XXVII (1955).

Peacock, A. E., 'The Successful Prosecution of the Factory Acts, 1833–1855', *Economic History Review*, XXXVII (1984).

Rose, S., 'From Behind the Women's Petticoats: the English Factory Acts of 1878 as a Social production', *Journal of Historical Sociology*, 4 (1991).

Ward, J. T., 'Richard Oastler, Politics and Factory Reform, 1832–1833', *Northern History*, 24 (1988).

Yarmie, A. H., 'British Employers' Resistance to "Grandmotherly Government" 1850–1880', *Social History*, 9 (1984).

VA. The old Poor Law

*Boyer, G. R., *An Economic History of the English Poor Law, 1750–1850* (1990).

Cowherd, R., *Political Economists and the English Poor Law* (Athens, Ohio, 1977).

Dunkley, P., *The Crisis of the Old Poor Law in England 1795–1834* (1982).

Hampson, E. M., *The Treatment of Poverty in Cambridgeshire* (1934).

Hindle, G. B., *Provision for the Relief of the Poor in Manchester 1754–1826* (1975).

Marshall, D., *The English Poor in the Eighteenth Century* (1926).

*Marshall, J. D., *The Old Poor Law, 1795–1834* (1968).

Mitchelson, N., *The Old Poor Law in East Yorkshire* (1953).

Neuman, M., *The Speenhamland County* (1982).

Nicholls, G. and Mackay, T., *History of the English Poor Law* (1904).

Oxley, G. W., *Poor Relief in England and Wales 1601–1834* (1974).

*Poynter, J. R., *Society and Pauperism* (1969).

*Rose, M. E. (ed.), *The English Poor Law, 1870–1930* (1971).

Slack, P., *The English Poor Law 1531–1782* (1990).

*Webb, S. and B., *History of English Local Government*, vol. VII: *The Old Poor Law* (1927, reprinted in 1963).

VB

Baugh, D. A., 'The Cost of Poor Relief in South East England', *Economic History Review*, 2nd ser., XXVIII (1975).

Blaug, M., 'The Myth of the Old Poor Law and the Making of the New', *Journal of Economic History*, XXIII (1963).

——, 'The Poor Law Report Re-examined', *Journal of Economic History*, XXIV (1964).

Boyer, G. R., 'An Economic Model of the English Poor Law *c*. 1780–1834', *Explorations in Economic History*, XXII (1985).

Coats, A. W., 'Economic Thought and Poor Law Policy in the Eighteenth Century', *Economic History Review*, 2nd ser., XXIII (1960).

Huzel, J. P., 'The Demographic Impact of the Old Poor Law', *Economic History Review*, 2nd ser., XXXIII (1980).

Mandler, P., 'Jones and Paupers: Christian Political Economy and the Making of the New Poor Law', *Historical Journal*, 33 (1990).

Mandler, P., 'The Making of the New Poor Law Redivivus', *Past and Present*, 117 (1987).

McCloskey, D., 'New Perspectives in the Old Poor Law', *Explorations in Economic History*, X (1973).

Rose, M., 'Social Policy and Business: Parish Apprenticeship and the Early Factory System, 1750–1834', *Business History*, XXXI (1989).

Solar, P. M., 'Poor Relief and English Economic Development before the Industrial Revolution', *Economic History Review*, XLVIII (1995).

Taylor, J. S., 'The Impact of Pauper Settlement, 1691–1834', *Past and Present*, 73 (1976).

Wells, R., 'Migration, the Law and Parochial Policy', *Southern History*, 15 (1993).

VIA. The new Poor Law

Brundage, A., *The Making of the New Poor Law* (1978).

*Checkland, S. G. and E. (eds), *The Poor Law Report of 1834* (1974).

*Crowther, A., *The Workhouse System 1834–1929* (1981).

Digby, A., *Pauper Palaces* (1978).

——, *The Poor Law in Nineteenth-Century England and Wales* (1982).

Driver, F., *Power and Pauperism: The Workhouse System 1834–1884* (1993).

Edsall, N. C., *The Anti-Poor Law Movement* (1971).

*Englander, D., *Poverty and Poor Law Reform in 19th Century Britain, 1834–1914* (1998).

*Finer, S. E., *The Life and Times of Edwin Chadwick* (1952).

Fraser, D. (ed.), *The New Poor Law in the Nineteenth Century* (1976).

Himmelfarb, G., *The Idea of Poverty*, (New York, 1984).

Knott, J., *Popular Opposition to the Poor Law* (1986).

*Lees, L. H., *The Solidarities of Strangers: The English Poor Laws and the People, 1700–1948* (1998).

Longmate, N., *The Workhouse* (1974).

Martin, E. W. (ed.), *Comparative Developments in Social Welfare* (1972).

Midwinter, E. C., *Social Administration in Lancashire* (1969).

*Rose, M. E., *The Relief of Poverty 1834–1914* (1972).

Rose, M. E. (ed.), *The Poor and the City: The English Poor Law in its Urban Context 1834–1914* (1985).

Treble, J. H., *Urban Poverty in Britain 1830–1914* (1979).

Weaver, S. A., *John Fielden and the Politics of Popular Radicalism 1832–1847* (1991).

*Webb, S. and B., *English Poor Law History*, 3 vols (1929, reprinted 1963).

Williams, K., *From Pauperism to Poverty* (1981).

Wood, P., *Poverty and the Workhouse in Victorian Britain* (1991).

VIB

Appel, W. and Dunkley, P., 'English Rural Society and the New Poor Law: Bedfordshire, 1834–1847', *Social History*, 10 (1985).

Boot, H. M., 'Unemployment and Poor Relief in Manchester, 1845–50', *Social History*, 15 (1990).

Boyson, R., 'The Poor Law in North East Lancashire, 1834–71', *Transactions of the Lancashire and Cheshire Antiquarian Society*, LXX (1960).

Caplan, M., 'Settlement Chargeability and the New Poor Law', *International Review of Social History*, 23 (1978).

Crocker, R. H., 'The Victorian Poor Law in Crisis and Change: Southampton 1870–1895', *Albion*, 19 (1987).

Digby, A., 'The Labour Market and the Continuity of Social Policy after 1834', *Economic History Review*, 2nd ser., XXVIII (1975).

——, 'The Relief of Poverty in Victorian York' in C. H. Feinstein (ed.), *York 1831–1981* (1981).

Dunkley, P., 'The "Hungry Forties" and the New Poor Law: a Case Study', *Historical Journal*, XVII (1974).

Driver, F., 'The Historical Geography of the Workhouse System in England and Wales, 1934–1883', *Journal of Historical Geography*, 15 (1989).

Fraser, D., 'The English Poor Law and the Origins of the British Welfare State', in W. Mommsen (ed.), *The Emergence of the Welfare State in Britain and Germany, 1850–1950* (1981).

——, 'Poor Law Politics in Leeds, 1833–1855', *Publications of the Thoresby Society*, LIII (1970).

Harling, P., 'The Power of Persuasion, Central Authority, Local Bureaucracy and the New Poor Law', *English Historical Review*, CVII (1992).

Henriques, U., 'Bastardy and the New Poor Law', *Past and Present*, XXXVII (1967).

——, 'How Cruel was the Victorian Poor Law?', *Historical Journal*, XI (1968).

Lewis, R. A., 'William Day and the Poor Law Commissioners', University of Birmingham *Historical Journal*, IX (1964).

Lindert, P. H., 'Poor Relief before the Welfare State', *European Review of Economic History*, 2 (1998).

McCord, N., 'The 1834 Poor Law Amendment Act on Tyneside', *International Review of Social History*, XIV (1969).

Marshall, J. D., 'The Nottinghamshire Reformers and their Contribution to the New Poor Law', *Economic History Review*, 2nd ser., XIII (1961).

Mackinnon, M., 'Poor Law Policy, Unemployment and Pauperism', *Explorations in Economic History*, 23 (1986).

Mackinnon, M., 'English Poor Law Policy and the Crusade Against Out Relief', *Journal of Economic History*, 47 (1987).

Metz, K. H., 'From Pauperism to Social Policy: Towards a Historical Theory of Social Policy', *International Review of Social History*, 37 (1992).

Roberts, D., 'How Cruel was the Victorian Poor Law?', *Historical Journal*, VI (1963).

Rose, M. E., 'The Allowance System under the New Poor Law', *Economic History Review*, 2nd ser., XIX (1966).

——, 'The Anti-Poor Law Movement in the North of England', *Northern History*, (1966).

——, 'The Poor Law in an Industrial Area' in R. M. Hartwell (ed.), *The Industrial Revolution* (1970).

Searby, P., 'The Relief of the Poor in Coventry 1830–1863', *Historical Journal*, 20 (1977).

Smith, R., Walsh, V. J. and Griffin, C. P., 'Poor Law and Poor Relief in the 19th Century Midlands', *Midland History*, II (1974).

VIIA. Public health and local government (see also Sections IX and XI)

Boyd, N., *Josephine Butler, Octavia Hill, Florence Nightingale: Three Victorian Women who Changed the World* (1982).

Brockington, C. F., *Public Health in the Nineteenth Century* (1965).

*Chadwick, E., *Report on the Sanitary Condition of the Labouring Population* (1842), ed. M. W. Flinn (1965).

Dennis, R. J., *English Industrial Cities of the Nineteenth Century* (1984).

Durey, M., *The Return of the Plague: British Society and the Cholera* (Dublin, 1979).

Fraser, D., *Power and Authority in the Victorian City* (1979).

Frazer, W. M., *The History of English Public Health* (1950).

Frazer, W. M., *Duncan of Liverpool* (1947).

Hennock, E. P., *Fit and Proper Persons* (1973).

*Lambert, W. R. J., *Sir John Simon 1816–1904* (1963).

*Lewis, R. A., *Edwin Chadwick and the Public Health Movement* (1952).

Longmate, N., *King Cholera* (1966).

Morris, R. J., *Cholera 1832* (1976).

Pelling, M., *Cholera Fever and English Medicine* (1978).

Simon, J., *English Sanitary Institutions* (1890).

Stewart, A. P. and Jenkins, E., *The Medical and Legal Aspects of Sanitary Reform* (1866), ed. M. W. Flim (1969).

Walvin, J., *English Urban Life 1776–1851* (1984).

*Wohl, A. S., *Endangered Lives: Public Health in Victorian Britain* (1983).

Woods, R. and Shelton, N., *An Atlas of Victorian Mortality* (1997).

VIIB

Briggs, A., 'Cholera and Society', *Past and Present*, XLX (1961).

Calcott, M., 'The Challenge of Cholera: The Last Epidemic at Newcastle upon Tyne', *Northern History*, 20 (1984).

Davies, C., 'The Health Visitor as Mother's Friend: A Women's Place in Public Health', *Social History of Medicine*, 20 (1988).

Fraser, D., 'The Politics of Leeds Water', *Publications of the Thoresby Society*, LIII (1970).

——, 'Improvement in Early Victorian Leeds', *Publications of the Thoresby Society*, LIII (1970).

Gill, C., 'Birmingham under the Street Commissioners', *University of Birmingham Historical Journal*, I (1948).

Grant, P. K. J., 'Merthyr Tydfil in the Mid Nineteenth Century: The Struggle for Public Health', *Welsh Historical Review*, 14 (1989).

Gutchen, R., 'Local Improvements and Centralisation in Nineteenth-Century England', *Historical Journal*, IV (1961).

Hamlin, C., 'Muddling in Bumbledon', *Victorian Studies*, 32 (1988).

Hennock, E. P., 'Urban Sanitary Reform a Generation before Chadwick?', *Economic History Review*, X (1957).

——, 'Finance and Politics in Urban Local Government', *Historical Journal*, VI (1963).

Keith-Lucas, B., 'Some Influences Affecting the Development of Sanitary Legislation in England', *Economic History Review*, 2nd ser., VI (1954).

Lambert, R. J., 'Central and Local Relations in Mid-Victorian England', *Victorian Studies*, VI (1962).

MacLeod, R. M., 'The Alkali Acts Administration, 1863–84', *Victorian Studies*, LX (1965).

Mattossian, M. K., 'Death in London, 1750–1909', *Journal of Interdisciplinary History*, XVI (1985).

Porter, R. and Porter, D., 'The Politics of Prevention: Anti-Vaccination and Public Health in Nineteenth Century England', *Medical History*, 32 (1988).

Szreter, S., 'The Importance of Social Intervention in Britain's Mortality Decline, 1850–1914: A Reinterpretation of the Role of Public Health', *Social History of Medicine*, 4 (1988).

Szreter, S., 'The GRO and the Public Health Movement in Britain 1837–1914', *Social History of Medicine*, 1 (1988).

VIIIA. Education

Adamson, J. W., *English Education, 1889–1902* (1964).

Ball, N., *Educating the People: A Documentary History of Elementary Schooling in England, 1840–1870* (1983).

Barnard, H. C., *A History of English Education from 1760* (1961).

Boyd, N. and Cowherd, R. G., *The Politics of English Dissent* (1959).

Cruikshank, M., *Church and State in English Education* (1963).

Curtis, S. J., *History of Education in Great Britain* (1963).

Digby, A. and Searby, P., *Children School and Society in Nineteenth-Century England* (1981).

Ellis, A., *Educating the Masters: Influences on the Growth of Literacy in Victorian Working-Class Children* (1984).

Hunt, F., (ed.), *Lessons for Life – The Schooling of Girls and Women, 1850–1950* (1987).

Hurt, J. S., *Education in Evolution* (1971).

*——, *Elementary Schooling in the Working Classes, 1860–1918* (1979).

Laquer, T. W., *Religion and Respectability: Sunday Schools and Working-Class Culture 1780–1850* (1976).

Lawson, J. and Silver, H., *A Social History of Education in England* (1973).

McCann, P. (ed.), *Popular Education and Socialization in the Nineteenth Century* (1977).

Machin, G. I. T., *Politics and the Churches in Great Britain 1832–1868* (1977).

Musgrave, P. W., *Society and Education Since 1800* (1968).

Paz, D. G., *The Politics of Working Class Education in Britain* (1980).

Purvis, J., *Hard Lessons: The Lives and Education of Working Class Women in Nineteenth Century England* (1989).

——, *A History of Women's Education* (1991).

Roach, J., *A History of Secondary Education in England 1800–1870*, Longman (1987).

——, *Secondary Education in England 1870–1902: Public Activity and Private Enterprise* (1991).

Reeder, D. E. (ed.), *Urban Education in the Nineteenth Century* (1977).

Rich, E. E., *The 1870 Education Act* (1971).

*Sanderson, M., *Education, Economic Change and Society in England, 1780–1870* (1983).

Silver, H., *The Concept of Popular Education* (1965).

Smith, F., *Life and Work of Sir James Kay-Shuttleworth* (1932).

——, *A History of English Elementary Education* (1931).

Stephens, W. B., *Education, Literacy and Society, 1830–1870* (1987).

Stewart, W. A. C. and McCann, W. P., *The Educational Innovators, 1750–1880* (1967).

*Sturt, M., *The Education of the People* (1967).

Sutherland, G., *Elementary Education in the Nineteenth Century* (1971).

*——, *Policy Making in Elementary Education 1870–1895* (1973).

Wardle, D., *English Popular Education, 1780–1970* (1970).

VIIIB

Alexander, J. L., 'Lord John Russell and the Origins of the Committee of the Council in Education', *Historical Journal*, 20 (1977).

Brown, C. M., 'Leonard Horner, 1785–1864: his Contribution to Education', *Journal of Educational and Admin History*, 17 (1985).

Gomersall, M., 'Ideals and Realities: The Education of Working Class Girls 1800–1870', *History of Education*, 17 (1988).

Horn, P., 'The Education and Employment of Working Class Girls 1870–1914', *History of Education*, 17 (1988).

Johnson, R., 'Educational Policy and Social Control in Early Victorian England', *Past and Present*, 49 (1970).

Paz, D. G., 'Sir James Kay-Shuttleworth: The Man Behind the Myth', *History of Education*, 14 (1985).

Phillips, R. J., 'E. C. Tufnell, Inspector of Poor Law Schools 1847–1874', *History of Education*, 5 (1976).

Richards, N. J., 'Religious Controversy and the School Boards 1870–1902', *British Journal of Educational Studies*, XVIII (1970).

Sanderson, M., 'Education and the Factory in Industrial Lancashire, 1780–1840', *Economic History Review*, 2nd ser., XX (1967).

——, 'Social Change and Elementary Education in Industrial Lancashire, 1780–1840', *Northern History*, III (1968).

Selleck, R. W. J, 'Mary Carpenter: a Confident and Contradictory Reformer', *History of Education*, 14 (1985).

Ward, J. T., 'A Lost Opportunity in Education', *Researches and Studies*, XX (1959).

Ward, J. T. and Treble, J. H., 'Religion and Education in 1843', *Journal of Ecclesiastical History*, XX (1969).

IXA. Medical services

*Abel-Smith, B., *The Hospitals 1800–1948* (1964).

Brand, J. L., *Doctors and the State* (Baltimore, 1965).

Cartwright, F. F., *A Social History of Medicine* (1977).

Checkland, O. and Lamb, M. (eds), *Health Care as Social History: The Glasgow Case* (1982).

Cherry, S., *Medical Services and the Hospitals in Britain, 1860–1939* (1996).

Digby, A. *The Evolution of British General Practice, 1830–1948* (2000).

Jones, K., *Lunacy Law and Conscience, 1744–1845* (1955).

——, *Mental Health and Social Policy, 1845–1959* (1961).

——, *Asylums and After* (1993).

Leff, S., *Social Medicine* (1953).

Pinker, R., *English Hospital Statistics, 1861–1938* (1966).

Scull, A., *Museums of Madness* (1979).

——, *The Most Solitary of Afflictions: Madness and Society in Britain 1700–1900* (1993).

*Smith, F. B., *The People's Health, 1830–1910* (1979).

Webster, C. (ed.), *Biology, Medicine and Society, 1840–1940* (1982).

Woodward, J., *To Do the Sick No Harm* (1974).

Woodward, J. and Richards, D. (eds), *Health Care and Popular Medicine in England in the Nineteenth Century* (1977).

Youngson, A. J., *The Scientific Revolution in Victorian Medicine* (1979).

IXB

Brand, J. L., 'The Parish Doctor: England's Poor Law Medical Officers and Medical Reform, 1870–1900', *Bulletin of the History of Medicine*, XXXV (1961).

Holloway, S. W. F., 'Medical Education in England, 1830–1858', *History*, XLIX (1964).

Lambert, R. J., 'A Victorian National Health Service', *Historical Journal*, V (1962).

MacLeod, R. M., 'The Frustration of State Medicine, 1880–1899', *Medical History*, XI (1967).

O'Neill, J. E., 'Finding a Policy for the Sick Poor', *Victorian Studies*, VII (1964).

Walton, J. K., 'The Treatment of Pauper Lunatics in Victorian England', in A. Scull (ed.), *Madhouses, Mad-Doctors, and Madmen* (Philadelphia, 1981).

XA. Law and order

Bailey, V. (ed.), *Policing and Punishment in Nineteenth-Century Britain* (1981).

Carlebach, J., *Caring for Children in Trouble* (1970).

Carpenter, M., *Preparatory School* (1851); reprinted New York (1969).

*Donajgrodzki, A. P. (ed.), *Social Control in Nineteenth-Century Britain* (1977).

Elmsely, C., *The English Police: A Political and Social History* (1991).

Hart, J. M., *The British Police* (1951).

Hay, D. and Snyder, F., *Policing and Prosecution in Britain, 1750–1850* (1989).

Howard, D. L., *The English Prisons* (1960).

Mather, F. C., *Public Order in the Age of the Chartists* (1958).

Palmer, S. H., *Police and Protest in England and Ireland, 1780–1850* (1988).

*Parris, H., *Constitutional Bureaucracy* (1969).

Pellew, J., *The Home Office, 1848–1914* (1982).

Phillips, D. and Storch, R. D., *Policing Provincial England, 1829–1856* (1999).

Radzinowicz, L., *A History of English Criminal Law*, vol. III (1956); vol. IV (1968).

Steedman, C., *Policing the Victorian Community* (1984).

*Taylor, D., *The New Police in Nineteenth-Century England* (1997).

Tobias, J. J., *Crime and Industrial Society in the Nineteenth Century* (1967).

XB

Gatrell, V. A. C., 'Crime, Authority and the Policeman State' in F. M. L. Thompson (ed.), *Cambridge Social History*, vol. 3 (1990).

Hart, J. M., 'Reform of the Borough Police, 1833–56', *English Historical Review*, LXX (1955).

——, 'The County and Borough Police Act, 1956', *Public Administration*, XXXVI (1956).

Jones, D. J. V., 'The New Police, Crime and People in England and Wales 1829–88', *Transactions of the Royal Historical Society*, 33 (1993).

Parris, H., 'The Home Office and the Provincial Police in England and Wales, 1856–1870', *Public Law* (1961).

Swift, R., 'Urban Policing in Early Victorian England 1835–1856: A Reappraisal', *History*, 73 (1988).

XI A Housing

*Ashworth, W., *The Genesis of Modern British Town Planning* (1954).

Beevers, R., *The Garden City Utopia: A Critical Biography of Ebenezer Howard* (1988).

Burnett, J., *A Social History of Housing, 1815–1985* (2nd edn) (1986).

Chapman, S. D. (ed.), *The History of Working-Class Housing* (1971).

Cherry, G. E., *The Evolution of British Town Planning* (1974).

*Daunton, M. J., *House and Home in the Victorian City: Working Class Housing, 1850–1914* (1983).

Daunton, M. J., *Councillors and Tenants* (1984).

Englander, D., *Landlord and Tenant in Urban Britain, 1838–1918* (1983).

Gauldie, E., *Cruel Habitations* (1974).
*Stedman Jones G., *Outcast London* (1971).
Tarn, J. N., *Five Per Cent Philanthropy* (1974).
Wohl, A. S., *The Eternal Slum* (1977).

XIB

Dennis, R., 'The Geography of Victorian Values: Philanthropic Housing in London 1840–1900', *Journal of Historical Geography*, 15 (1989).
Hopkins, E., 'Working Class Housing in Birmingham During Industrial Revolution', *International Review of Social History*, XXXI (1986).
Rodger, R., 'Political Economy, Ideology and the Persistence of Working-Class Housing Problems in Britain 1850–1914', *International Review of Social History*, 32 (1987).

XII. Social ideas

Bahmueller, C. F., *The National Charity Company: Jeremy Bentham's Silent Revolution* (1981).
Bradley, I., *The Call to Seriousness* (1976).
Briggs, A., *Victorian People* (1954).
Burn, W. L., *The Age of Equipoise* (1964).
Clark, G. Kitson, *The Making of Victorian England* (1962).
——, *Churchmen and the Condition of England Question* (1973).
Gosden, P. H. J. H., *The Friendly Societies in England, 1815–1875* (1961).
——, *Self-Help* (1973).
*Halévy, E., *The Growth of Philosophic Radicalism* (1928).
Harrison, B. and Hollis, P., *Robert Lowery, Radical and Chartist* (1979).
Harrison, B., *Peaceable Kingdom: Stability and Change in Modern Britain* (1982).
Harrison, R., *Before the Socialists* (1965).
Hilton, B., *The Age of Atonement: The Influence of Evangelicalism in Social and Economic Thought 1795–1865* (1988).
*Hopkins, E., *Working-Class Self Help in Nineteenth-Century England* (1995).
Houghton, W. E., *The Victorian Frame of Mind* (1957).
Howe, A., *Free Trade and Liberal England* (1997).
Kirk, N., *The Growth of Working Class Reformism in Mid-Victorian England* (1985).

Leventhal, F. M., *Respectable Radical: George Howell and Victorian Working-Class Politics* (1970).

Levine, G. (ed.), *The Emergence of Victorian Consciousness* (New York, 1967).

Marsden, G., (ed.), *Victorian Values* (1990).

Pearson, R. A. and Williams, G. L., *Political Thought and Public Policy in the Nineteenth Century* (1984).

Roberts, D., *Paternalism in Early Victorian England* (1978).

Tholfsen, T. R., *Working-Class Radicalism in Mid-Victorian England* (1976).

Thomas, W. E. S., *The Philosophic Radicals* (1979).

*Thompson, F. M. L., *The Rise of Respectable Society* (1988).

Tyrell, A., *Joseph Sturge and the Moral Radical Party in Early Victorian Britain* (1987).

Young, G. M., *Victorian England: Portrait of an Age* (1953).

XIIIA. *Laissez-faire* and state intervention

Chester, N., *The English Administrative System, 1780–1870* (1981).

Cromwell, V., *Revolution or Evolution* (1977).

*Dicey, A. V., *Law and Public Opinion during the Nineteenth Century* (1914; reprinted 1962).

Lubenow, W. C., *The Politics of Government Growth* (1971).

MacDonagh, O., *The Passenger Acts: A Pattern of Government Growth* (1961).

——, *Early Victorian Government* (1977).

Macleod, R. (ed.), *Government and Experts: Specialists, Administrators and Professional, 1860–1919* (1988).

*Parris, H., *Constitutional Bureaucracy* (1969).

Perkins, H., *The Rise of Professional Society: England Since 1880* (1989).

Prest, J., *Liberty and Locality* (1990).

*Roberts, D., *Victorian Origins of the British Welfare State* (New Haven, 1968).

Stansky, P. (ed.), *The Victorian Revolution: Government and Society in Victorian Britain* (New York, 1973).

Sutherland, G. (ed.), *Studies in the Growth of Nineteenth-Century Government* (1972).

*Taylor, A. J., *Laissez Faire and State Intervention in Nineteenth-Century Britain* (1972).

XIIIB

Aydelotte, W. O., 'Conservative and Radical Interpretations of Early Victorian Social Legislation', *Victorian Studies*, XI (1967).

Brebner, J. B., 'Laissez-faire and State Intervention in Nineteenth-Century Britain', *Journal of Economic History*, VIII (1948).

Crouch, R. L., 'Laissez-faire in Nineteenth-Century Britain: Myth or Reality?', *Manchester School of Economic and Social Studies*, XXXV (1967).

Dinwiddy, J. R., 'Early Nineteenth-Century Reaction to Benthanism', *Transactions of the Royal Historical Society*, 34 (1984).

Hart, J., 'Nineteenth-Century Social Reform: A Tory Interpretation of History', *Past and Present*, XXXI (1965).

Goldman, L., 'The Social Science Association, 1857–1886: The Context for Mid-Victorian Liberalism', *English Historical Review*, CI (1986).

Henriques, U., 'Jeremy Bentham and the Machinery of Social Reform', in H. Hearder and H. R. Loyn (eds), *British Government and Administration* (1974).

Holmes, C. J., 'Laissez-faire in Theory and Practice, Britain, 1800–1875', *Journal of European Economic History*, 5 (1976).

Hume, K. J., 'Jeremy Bentham and the Nineteenth-Century Revolution in Government', *Historical Journal*, X (1967).

Kitson Clark, G., 'Statesmen in Disguise', *Historical Journal*, II (1959).

MacDonagh, O. O. G. M., 'The Nineteenth-Century Revolution in Government: a Reappraisal', *Historical Journal*, I (1958).

Parris, H., 'The Nineteenth-Century Revolution in Government: a Reappraisal Reappraised', *Historical Journal*, III (1960).

Perkin, H., 'Individualism Versus Collectivism in Nineteenth-Century Britain: a False Antithesis', *Journal of British Studies*, XVII (1977).

Roberts, D., 'Jeremy Bentham and the Victorian Administrative State', *Victorian Studies*, II (1959).

XIVA. Philanthropy

Bosanquet, H., *Social Work in London* (1914).

Daunton, M. J. (ed.), *Charity, Self-Interest and Welfare in the English Past* (1996).

Jones, C. and Barry, J., *Medicine and Charity Before the Welfare State* (1991).

Kirkman Gray, B., *A History of English Philanthropy* (1905; reprinted 1967).

Lewis, J., *The Voluntary Sector, the State and Social Work in Britain* (1995).

Mandler, P. (ed.), *The Uses of Charity* (1990).

McCarthy, D. (ed.), *Lady Bountiful Revisited: Women, Philanthropy Power* (New Jersey, 1990).

*Mowat, C. L., *The Charity Organisation Society, 1869–1913: Its Ideas and Work* (1961).

*Owen, D., *English Philanthropy, 1660–1960* (1965).

Prochaska, F. K., *Women and Philanthropy in Nineteenth-Century England* (1980).

Prochaska, F. K., *The Voluntary Impulse: Philanthropy in Modern Britain* (1988).

Simey, M. B., *Charitable Effort in Liverpool in the Nineteenth Century* (1951).

*Woodroffe, K., *From Charity to Social Work in England and the United States* (1962).

Young, A. F. and Ashton, E. T., *British Social Work in the Nineteenth Century* (1956).

XIVB

Cahill, M. and Jowitt, T., 'The New Philanthropy: the Emergence of the Bradford City Guild of Help', *Journal of Social Policy*, 9 (1980).

Gerard, J., 'Lady Bountiful: Women of the Landed Classes and Rural Philanthropy', *Victorian Studies*, 30, (1986/7).

Harrison, B., 'Philanthropy and the Victorians', *Victorian Studies*, IX (1966).

Kidd, A. J., 'Charity Organisation and Unemployed in Manchester c. 1870–1914', *Social History*, XI (1984).

Kidd, A. J., 'Philanthropy and the "Socialist Paradigm" ', *Social History*, 21 (1996).

Laybourn, K., 'The Guild of Help and the Changing Face of Edwardian Philanthropy', *Urban History*, 30 (1993).

Moore, M. J., 'Social Work and Social Welfare', *Journal of British Studies*, XVI (1977).

Morris, R. J., 'Voluntary Services and British Urban Elites, 1780–1850', *Historical Journal*, 26 (1983).

XVA. Ideology and poverty c.1870–c.1914

Ausubel, H., *In Hard Times* (1960).

*Booth, Charles, *Life and Labour of the People in London*, 17 vols (1889–1903).

Bradley, J. L. (ed.), *London Labour and the London Poor: Selections* (1965).

*Briggs, A., *Social Thought and Social Action: A Study of the Work of Seebohm Rowntree* (1961).

Brown, K. D. (ed.), *Essays in Anti-Labour History* (1974).

Clarke, P. F., *Liberals and Social Democrats* (1978).

Collini, S., *Liberalism and Sociology* (1978).

Court, W. H. B., *British Economic History, 1870–1914* (1965).

Englander, D. and O'Day, R. (eds), *Retrieved Riches: Social Investigation in Britain 1840–1914* (1995).

*Freeden, M., *The New Liberalism* (1978).

*Harris, J., *Private Lives, Public Spirit: A Social History of Britain, 1870–1914* (1993).

Himmelfarb, G., *Poverty and Compassion: The Moral Imagination of the Late Victorians* (New York, 1991).

Jones, P. A., *The Christian Socialist Revival, 1877–1914* (1968).

Keating, P. (ed.), *Into Unknown England* (1976).

Langan, M. and Schwartz, B. (eds), *Crises in the British State, 1880–1930* (1985).

Lynd, H. M., *England in the Eighteen-Eighties* (1954).

McBriar, A. M., *Fabian Socialism and English Politics, 1884–1918* (1962).

Mayhew, H., *London Labour and the London Poor* (1862; reprinted 1968).

*Mearns, A., *The Bitter Cry of Outcast London* (1883; reprinted 1970, ed. A. S. Wohl).

Richter, M., *The Politics of Conscience: T. H. Green and His Age* (1966).

*Seebohm Rowntree, H., *Poverty: A Study of Town Life* (1901).

Simey, T. S. and M. B., *Charles Booth: Social Scientist* (1960).

Soffer, R., *Ethics and Society in England* (Berkeley, 1978).

*Stedman Jones, G., *Outcast London* (1971).

Thompson, E. P. and Yeo, E. (eds), *The Unknown Mayhew* (1971).

Vincent, A. and Plant, R., *Philosophy, Politics and Citizenship: The Life and Thought of the British Idealists* (1984).

*Webb, B., *My Apprenticeship* (1962).

*——, *Our Partnership* (1948).

XVB

Clarke, P. F., 'The Progressive Movement in England', *Transactions of the Royal Historical Society*, 5th ser., 24 (1974).

Freeden, M., 'J. A. Hobson as a New Liberal Theorist', *Journal of the History of Ideas*, 24 (1973).

——, 'Eugenics and Progressive Thought', *Historical Journal*, 22 (1979).

Harris, J., 'Political Thought and the Welfare State 1870–1914', *Past and Present*, 135 (1992).

Hennock, E. P., 'Poverty and Social Theory in England', *Social History*, I (1976).

Mason, J. W., 'Political Economy and the Response to Socialism in Great Britain 1870–1914', *Historical Journal*, 23 (1980).

Weiler, P., 'The New Liberalism of L. T. Hobhouse', *Victorian Studies*, 16 (1972).

Wohl, A. S., 'The Bitter Cry of Outcast London', *International Review of Social History*, XIII (1968).

XVIA. Late Victorian politics and social policy

Ausubel, H., *The Late Victorians* (New York, 1955).

Fraser, P., *Joseph Chamberlain* (1966).

Garvin, J. L., *The Life of Joseph Chamberlain*, vols I–IV (1932–6).

Halévy, E., *History of the English People in the Nineteenth Century*, vol. V: *Imperialism and the Rise of Labour* (1951).

Hanes, D. G., *The First British Workmen's Compensation Act, 1897* (New Haven, 1968).

*Harris, J., *Unemployment and Politics* (1972).

Jay, R., *Joseph Chamberlain* (1981).

Judd, D., *Radical Joe* (1977).

Marsh, P., *The Discipline of Popular Government* (1978).

McBrier, A. H., *An Edwardian Mixed Doubles: The Bosanquets and the Webbs. A Study in British Social Policy (1890–1929)* (1987).

Meller, H. E., *Leisure and the Changing City* (1976).

Pelling, H., *Popular Politics and Society in Late Victorian Britain* (1968).

Petrie, C., *Walter Long and His Times* (1936).

Rhodes, James R., *Lord Randolph Churchill* (1959).

Searle, G. R., *The Quest for National Efficiency* (1970).

Semmel, B., *Imperialism and Social Reform* (1960).

*Smith, P., *Disraelian Conservatism and Social Reform* (1967).

Young, K., *Arthur James Balfour* (1963).

XVIB

Rose, M. E., 'The Crisis of Poor Relief in England 1860–1890', in W. Mommsen (ed.), *The Emergence of the Welfare State in Britain and Germany 1850–1950* (1981).

Thane, P., 'Women and the Poor Law in Victorian and Edwardian England', *History Workshop*, 6 (1978).

Vorspan, R., 'Vagrancy and the New Poor Law in late Victorian and Edwardian England', *English Historical Review*, XCII (1977).

XVIIA. Liberal social policy

Beveridge, W. H., *Unemployment a Problem of Industry* (1909).
Bentley, M., *The Climax of Liberal Politics* (1987).
Brown, K. D., *Labour and Unemployment* (1971).
Brooks, D., *The Age of Upheaval. Edwardian Politics, 1899–1914* (1995).
*Bunbury, H. N. (ed.), *Lloyd George's Ambulance Wagon* (1957).
Brown, K. D., *Labour and Unemployment* (1971).
Churchill, R. S., *Winston S. Churchill*, vol. II: *1901–1914* (1967); Companion to vol. II, pt 2: *1907–1911* (1969).
Cockmack, U., *The Royal Commission on the Poor Laws and the Welfare State* (1953).
Emy, H. V., *Liberal Radicals and Social Politics* (1973).
*Gilbert, B. B., *The Evolution of National Insurance in Great Britain* (1966).
Grigg, J., *Lloyd George, The People's Champion* (1978).
Halévy, E., *History of the English People in the Nineteenth Century*, vol. VI: *The Rule of Democracy* (1951).
*Hay, J. R., *The Origins of the Liberal Welfare Reforms* (1975).
Hendrick, H., *Child Welfare, England 1872–1989* (1994).
Hennock, E. P., *British Social Reform and German Precedents* (1987).
Hughes, E., *Keir Hardie* (1956).
Jenkins, R., *Mr. Balfour's Poodle* (1954).
——, *Asquith* (1964).
Jones, T., *Lloyd George* (1951).
Koss, S., *Asquith* (1976).
*Masterman, C. F. G., *The Condition of England* (1909).
Masterman, L., *C. F. G. Masterman* (1939).
*Macnicol, J., *The Politics of Retirement in Britain 1878–1948* (1998).
Morris, A. J., *Edwardian Radicalism* (1974).
Murray, B. K., *The People's Budget* (1980).
Nowell-Smith, S., *Edwardian England, 1901–1914* (1964).
Petrie, C., *The Life and Letters of the Right Hon. Sir Austen Chamberlain*, vol. I (1939).
Powell, D., *The Edwardian Crisis: Britain, 1901–1914* (1996).
Read, D., *Edwardian England* (1972).
——, *Documents from Edwardian England* (1973).
Ritter, G. A., *Social Welfare in Germany and Britain* (1986).
Rowland, P., *The Last Liberal Government*, 2 vols: *The Promised Land, 1906–10* (1968); *Unfinished Business, 1911–1914* (1970).

* *Royal Commission on the Poor Laws, Majority and Minority Reports* (1909).

Sykes, A., *The Rise and Fall of British Liberalism* (1997).

Thane, P. (ed.), *The Origins of Social Policy* (1978).

Thomas, M., *David Lloyd George* (1948).

*Webb, B., *Our Partnership* (1948).

Webb, S. and B., *English Poor Law Policy* (1909; reprinted 1963).

XVIIB

Arnstein, W., 'Edwardian Politics' in A. O'Day (ed.), *The Edwardian Age* (1979).

Brown, J., 'The Appointment of the 1905 Poor Law Commission', *Bulletin of the Institute of Historical Research*, 42 (1969).

Dutton, D. J., 'The Unionist Party and Social Policy 1906–1914', *Historical Journal*, 24 (1981).

Gilbert, B. B., 'David Lloyd George: Land, the Budget and Social Reform', *American Historical Review*, LXXXI (1976).

——, 'David Lloyd George: the Reform of British Landholding and the Budget of 1914', *Historical Journal*, XXI (1978).

Hay, J. R., 'Employers and Social Policy in Britain, 1905–14', *Social History*, 2 (1977).

Hennock, E. P., 'The Origins of National Insurance and the German Precedent', in Mommsen, cited above XVIB.

Howkins, A., 'Edwardian Liberalism and Industrial Unrest', *History Workshop*, 4 (1977).

Thane, P., 'The Working Class and State Welfare in Britain 1880–1914', *Historical Journal*, 27 (1984).

Vincent, A. W., 'The Poor Law Reports in 1909 and the Social Theory of the Charity Organisation Society', *Victorian Studies*, 27 (1984).

Vinson, A., 'The Edwardians and Poverty: Towards a Minimum Wage?', in D. Read (ed.), *Edwardian England* (1982).

Woodruffe, K., 'The Royal Commission on the Poor Laws, 1905–9', *International Review of Social History*, XXII (1977).

XVIIIA. War and post-war 1914–22

Addison, C., *Politics from Within, 1911–1918* (1924).

Beaverbrook, Lord, *The Decline and Fall of Lloyd George* (1963).

Burk, K. (ed.), *War and the State: The Transformation of British Government, 1914–19* (1982).

Cowling, M., *The Impact of Labour, 1920–1924* (1971).

*Gilbert, B. B., *British Social Policy, 1914–1924* (1971).
Graves, R. and Hodge, A., *The Long Weekend* (1961).
Harris, J., *William Beveridge* (1977).
Honigsbaum, F., *The Battle for the Ministry of Health* (1972).
Johnson, P. B., *Land Fit for Heroes: the Planning of British Reconstruction, 1916–1919* (Chicago, 1968).
Marwick, A., *Women at War, 1914–1918* (1979).
*——, *The Deluge* (1964; Penguin edn 1967).
Morgan, K. O., *Consensus and Disunity: The Lloyd George Coalition Government, 1918–1922* (1979).
Morgan, K. O. and J., *Portrait of a Progressive...(Addison,* 1980).
Orbach, L. F., *Homes for Heroes* (1977).
Swenarton, M., *Homes Fit for Heroes* (1981).
Wall, R. and Winters, J. (eds), *The Upheaval of War, Family Work and Welfare in Europe, 1914–1918* (1988).
Wilson, T., *The Downfall of the Liberal Party, 1914–1935* (1966).

XVIIIB

Abrams, P., 'The Failure of Social Reform 1918–20', *Past and Present,* XXIV (1963).
Lowe, R., 'The Ministry of Labour 1916–1924: a Graveyard of Social Reform?', *Public Administration,* 52 (1974).
——, 'The Erosion of State Intervention in Britain 1917–24', *Economic History Review,* XXXI (1978).
Pederson, S., 'Gender, Welfare and Citizenship in Britain during the Great War', *American Historical Review,* 95 (1990).
Whiteside, N., 'Welfare Legislation and the Unions During the First World War', *Historical Journal,* 23 (1980).
Wilding, P., 'The Genesis of the Ministry of Health', *Public Administration,* 45 (1967).
——, 'The Housing and Town Planning Act 1919', *Journal of Social Policy,* 2 (1973).
Winter, J. M., 'The Impact of the First World War on Civilian Health in Britain', *Economic History Review,* XXX (1977).

XIXA. Unemployment between the wars

Aldcroft, D. H., *The Inter-War Economy; Britain, 1919–1939* (1970).
Alford, B. W. E., *Depression and Recovery: British Economic Growth, 1918–1939* (1972).

Bassett, R., *1931: Political Crisis* (1958).

*Beveridge, W. H., *Unemployment: A Problem of Industry, 1909 and 1930* (1930).

Blaxland, G., *J. H. Thomas: A Life for Unity* (1964).

Bullock, A., *Life and Times of Ernest Bevin*, vol. I: *1881–1940* (1960).

Carnegie Trust, *Disinherited Youth* (1943).

Citrine, W. (Lord Citrine), *Men at Work* (1964).

Cole, M. I., *The Condition of Britain* (1937).

——, (ed.), *Beatrice Webb's Diaries, 1924–1932* (1956).

Constantine, S., *Social Conditions in Britain, 1918–1939* (1983).

Dalton, H., *Call Back Yesterday* (1953).

Davison, R. C., *The Unemployed: Old Policies and New* (1929).

——, *British Unemployment Policy: The Modern Phase since 1930* (1938).

*Deacon, A., *The Search for the Scrounger* (1976).

Gladstone, D. (ed.), *Before Beveridge: Welfare Before the Welfare State* (1999).

Hamilton, M. A., *Arthur Henderson* (1938).

*Hannington, W., *The Problem of the Distressed Areas* (1937).

Laybourn, K., *Britain on the Breadline* (1990).

Lowe, R., *Adjusting to Democracy: The Role of the Ministry of Labour in British Politics, 1916–1939* (1986).

Marquand, D., *Ramsay MacDonald* (1977).

*Millet, J. D., *The Unemployment Assistance Board* (1940).

*Mowat, C. L., *Britain Between the Wars* (1955).

Nicolson, H., *King George the Fifth* (1952).

*Orwell, G., *The Road to Wigan Pier* (1937; reprinted 1971).

Page, N., *The Thirties in Britain* (1991).

*Pilgrim Trust, *Men without Work* (1938).

Pollard, S., *The Development of the British Economy, 1914–1960* (1962).

Richardson, H. W., *Economic Recovery in Britain, 1932–1939* (1967).

Samuel, H. (Lord Samuel), *Memoirs* (1954).

Skidelsky, R., *Politicians and the Slump* (1967).

Snowden, P., *Autobiography* (1934).

Stevenson, J. and Cook, C., *The Slump: Society and Politics During the Depression* (1977).

Taylor, A. J. P., *English History 1914–45* (1965).

Tout, H., *The Standard of Living in Bristol* (1938).

*Vincent, D., *Poor Citizens: The State and the Poor in the Twentieth Century* (1991).

*Winch, D., *Economics and Policy* (1969).

Whiteside, N., *Bad Times* (1991).

XIXB

Benjamin, D. and Kochin, L., 'Searching for an Explanation of Unemployment in Inter-War Britain', *Journal of Political Economy*, 87 (1979).

Briggs, E. and Deacon, A., 'The Creation of the Unemployment Assistance Board', *Policy and Politics*, 2 (1973).

Deacon, A., 'Concession and Coercion: The Politics of Unemployment Insurance', in A. Briggs and J. Saville (eds), *Essays in Labour History, 1918–1939* (1977).

Garside, W., 'Juvenile Unemployment and Public Policy Between the Wars', *Economic History Review*, 2nd ser., XXX (1977).

Linsley, C. A. and C. L., 'Booth, Rowntree and Llewellyn Smith: a Reassessment of Inter War Poverty', *Economic History Review*, XLVI (1993).

McKibbin, R., 'The Economic Policy of the Second Labour Government, 1929–31', *Past and Present*, 68 (1975).

Miller, F. M., 'National Assistance or Unemployment Assistance: the British Cabinet and Relief Policy 1932–33', *Journal of Contemporary History*, 9 (1974); 14 (1979).

——, 'The Unemployment Policy of the National Government 1931–1936', *Historical Journal*, 19 (1976).

Skidelsky, R., 'Keynes and the Treasury View: the Case For and Against an Active Unemployment Policy in Britain 1920–1939' in W. J. Mommsen (ed.), *The Emergence of the Welfare State in Britain and Germany* (1981).

Wolcott, S., 'Keynes versus Chruchill: Revolution and British Unemployment in the 1920s', *Journal of Economic History*, 53 (1993).

Webster, C., 'Healthy or Hungry Thirties', *History Workshop*, 13 (1982).

——, 'Health Welfare and Unemployment during the Depression', *Past and Present*, 109 (1985).

XXA. Pensions, health and other areas of social policy

*Bowley, M., *Housing and the State, 1919–1944* (1945).

Branson, N. and Heinemann, M., *Britain in the Nineteen Thirties* (1971).

Crowther, A., *Social Policy in Britain, 1914–39* (1988).

Daunton, M. J., *Councillors and Tenants: Local Authority Housing in English Cities, 1914–39* (1983).

Eder, N. R., *National Health Insurance and the Medical Profession in Britain, 1913–39* (1982).

Grant, M., *Propoganda and the Role of the State in Inter-War Britain* (1994).

Harris, R. S., *National Health Insurance in Great Britain, 1911–1946* (1946).

*Levy, H., *National Health Insurance: A Critical Study* (1944).

Mann, K., *The Making of an English 'Underclass'* (1992).

Melling, J. (ed.), *Housing Social Policy and the State* (1980).

Newsholme, A., *Fifty Years in Public Health* (1935).

Pederson, S., *Family, Dependence and the Origins of the Welfare State* (1993).

Peden, G. C., *British Economic and Social Policy: Lloyd George to Margaret Thatcher* (1985).

*PEP, *Report on the British Health Services* (1937); *Report on the British Social Services* (1937).

*Robson, W. A. (ed.), *Social Security* (1943).

Seebohm Rowntree, B., *Poverty and Progress* (1941).

Stevenson, J., *Social Conditions in Britain Between the Wars* (1977).

——, *British Society, 1914–1945* (1984).

Wilson, A. and Mackay, G. S., *Old Age Pensions* (1941).

XXB

Cherry, S., 'Before the National Health Service: financing the voluntary hospitals, 1900–1939', *Economic History Review*, L (1997).

Crowther, M. A., 'Family Responsibility and State Responsibility in Britain Before the Welfare State', *Historical Journal*, 25 (1982).

Ryan, P., 'The Poor Law in 1926' in M. Morris (ed.), *The General Strike* (1976).

Whiteside, M., 'Unemployment and Health: a Historical Perspective', *Journal of Social Policy*, 17 (1988).

——, 'Regulating Markets in the National Health Insurance Scheme 1914–46', *Public Administration*, 75 (1997).

XXIA. The Second World War

Addison, P., *The Road to 1945* (1975).

Barnett, C., *The Audit of War* (1986)

Beveridge, J. (Lady Beveridge), *Beveridge and His Plan* (1954).

*Beveridge, W. H. (Lord Beveridge), *Pillars of Security* (1943).

*——, *Full Employment in a Free Society* (1944).

*——, *Power and Influence* (1953).

*Beveridge Report, *Social Insurance and Allied Services* (1942).

Bourdillon, A. F. C. (ed.), *Voluntary Social Services* (1945).

Brown, J., *The British Welfare State: A Critical History* (1995).

Brooke, S., *Labour's War: The Labour Party During the Second World War* (1992).

Bullock, A., *Life and Times of Ernest Bevin*, vol. II (1966).

*Calder, A., *The People's War* (1969).

Ferguson, S. and Fitzgerald, H., *Studies in the Social Services* (1954).

Gosden, P. H. J. H., *Education in the Second World War* (1976).

Government White Papers: *Insurance* (1944); *Health* (1944); *Full Employment* (1944).

Harrington, W. and Young, P., *The 1945 Revolution* (1978).

*Harris, J., *William Beveridge: A Biography* (2nd edn, 1997).

Harrison, T., *Living Through the Blitz* (1976).

*Hills, J., Ditch, J., and Glennister, H. (eds), *Beveridge and Social Security* (1994).

Jeffreys, K., *The Churchill Coalition and Wartime Politics 1940–1945* (1991).

Lee, J. M., *The Churchill Coalition, 1940–1945* (1980).

Levy, H., *National Health Insurance: A Critical Study* (1944).

*Macnicol, J., *The Movement for Family Allowances 1918–45* (1980).

McLaine, I., *Ministry of Morale* (1979).

Marwick, A., *Home Front: The British and the Second World War* (1976).

Milward, A. S., *The Economic Effects of the World War on Britain* (1970).

——, *War Economy and Society 1939–1945* (1977).

Morrison, H. (Lord Morrison), *Autobiography* (1960).

Peden, G. C., *Keynes, The Treasury and British Economic Policy* (1998).

Pelling, H., *Britain and the Second World War* (1970).

*Robson, W. A. (ed.), *Social Security* (1943).

Smith, H. L. (ed.), *War and Social Change* (1986).

Smith, H. L., *Britain and the Second World War: A Social History* (1996).

*Titmuss, R. M., *Problems of Social Policy* (1950).

Williams, K. and Williams, J. (eds), *A Beveridge Reader* (1997).

Woolton, Lord, *Memoirs* (1959).

XXIB

Harris, J., 'Social Planning in Wartime' in J. M. Winter (ed.), *War and Economic Development* (1976).

——, 'Some Aspects of Social Policy in Britain During the Second World War', in Mommsen (ed.), cited in XIXB.

——, 'Did British Workers Want the Welfare State?' in J. Winter (ed.), *The Working Class in Modern British History* (1983).

Jeffreys, K., 'British Politics and Social Policy during the Second World War' *Historical Journal*, 30 (1987).

Leaper, R., 'The Beveridge report in its Contemporary Setting', *International Social Security Review*, 45 (1992) (see also articles by B. Abel-Smith and G. Perrin in the same issue).

Lowe, R., 'The Second World War, Consensus and the Foundation of the Welfare State', *20th-Century British History*, 1 (1990).

Pelling, H., 'The 1945 General Election Reconsidered', *Historical Journal*, 23 (1980).

Welshman, J., 'Evacuation and Social Policy during the Second World War Myth and Reality', *20th-Century British History*, 9 (1998).

XXIIA. Labour Government, 1945–51

Addison, P., *Now the War is Over* (1985).

Annual Government Reports: *Report of the Ministry of Health*, 1949, Cmd 7910 (1950); *Report of the Ministry of National Insurance*, 1944–49, Cmd 7955 (1950).

Attlee, C. R. (Lord Attlee), *As It Happened* (1954).

*Bevan, A., *In Place of Fear* (1952).

Chester, D. N., *The Nationalisation of British Industry 1945–1951* (1975).

Cullingworth, J. B., *Housing Needs and Planning Policy* (1960).

Donoughue, B. and Jones, G. W., *Herbert Morrison* (1973).

Dunleavy, P., *The Politics of Mass Housing in Britain, 1945–75* (1981).

Eatwell, R., *The 1945–1951 Labour Governments* (1979).

Eckstein, H., *The English Health Service* (Cambridge, MA, 1958).

Fielding, S., Thompson, R. and Tiratsoo, N., *England Arise!* (1995).

Francis, M., *Ideas and Policies under Labour, 1945–1951* (1997).

*Foot, M., *Aneurin Bevan, 1945–1960* (1973).

Forsyth, G., *Doctors and State Medicine* (1966).

George, V., *Social Security* (1968).

*Gregg, P., *The Welfare State* (1967).

*Hall, P., *The Social Services of Modern England* (1955).

Harris, K., *Attlee* (1982).

Henessey, P., *Never Again* (1993)

Hopkins, H., *The New Look* (1963).

*Lindsey, A., *Socialised Medicine in England and Wales* (Chapel Hill, NC, 1962).

Marsh, D. C., *National Insurance and Assistance in Great Britain* (1950).

Marwick, A., *British Society Since 1945* (1982).
*Morgan, K. O., *The People's Peace* (1992).
Pearce, R., *Attlee* (1997).
Pritt, D. N., *The Labour Government, 1945–1951* (1963).
Ross, J. S., *The National Health Service in Great Britain* (1952).
Sissons, M. and French, P. (eds), *The Age of Austerity* (1963).
Stark Murray, D., *Why a National Health Service?* (1971).
Tiratsoo, N., *The Attlee Years* (1993).
*Webster, C., *The Health Services Since the War I* (1988).
Willcocks, A. J., *The Creation of the National Health Service* (1967).
Williams, P., *Hugh Gaitskell* (1979).
Worswick, G. D. N. and Ady, P. H. (eds), *The British Economy, 1945–1950* (1952).

XXIIB

Atkinson, A. B., Maynard, A. K. and Trinder, C. G., 'National Assistance and Low Incomes in 1950', *Social Policy and Administration*, 15 (1981).
Deacon, A., 'An End to the Means Test: Social Security and the Attlee Government', *Journal of Social Policy*, 11 (1982).
Hess, J. C., 'The Social Policy of the Attlee Government', in Mommsen (ed.), cited in XIXB.
Marwick, A., 'The Labour Party and the Welfare State in Britain' in H. Winkler (ed.), *Twentieth Century Britain* (1976).
Rubinstein, D., 'Socialism and the Labour Party: The Labour Left and Domestic Policy 1945–1950', in D. E. Martin and D. Rubinstein (eds), *Ideology and the Labour Movement* (1979).
Tomlinson, J. D., 'Why so Austere? The British Welfare State in the 1940s', *Journal of Social Policy*, 27 (1998).
Whiteside, N., 'Creating the Welfare State in Britain', *Journal of Social Policy*, 25 (1996).

XXIII. Social policy since 1948

Abel-Smith, B. and Townsend, P., *The Poor and the Poorest* (1966).
*Atkinson, A. B., *Poverty in Britain and the Reform of Social Security* (1967).
Banting, K., *Poverty Politics and Policy* (1979).
Barr, N., *The Economics of the Welfare State* (1987)
Blackburn, R., *Banking on Death: The History and Future of Pensions* (2002).

Butterworth, E. and Holman, R., *Social Welfare in Modern Britain* (1975).

Commission for Social Justice, *Social Justice Strategies for Renewal* (1994).

*Deacon, A. and Bradshaw, A., *Reserved for the Poor: The Means Test in British Social Policy* (1983).

*Donnison, D., *The Politics of Poverty* (1982).

*Field, F., *Making Welfare Work* (1995).

George, V. and Page, R. (eds), *Modern Thinkers on Welfare* (1995).

George, V. and Wilding, P., *Ideology and Social Welfare* (1976).

Esping-Anderson, G., *The Three Worlds of Welfare Capitalism* (1990).

Fawcett, H., and Lowe, R. (eds), *Welfare Policy in Britain* (1998).

Giddens, A., *The Third Way and its Critics* (2000).

Ginsburg, N., *Class Capital and Social Policy* (1979).

Gladstone, D., (ed), *British Social Welfare* (1995).

*Glennester, H., *British Social Policy Since 1945* (2nd edn, 2000).

Gough, I., *The Political Economy of the Welfare State* (1979).

*Higgins, J., *States of Welfare* (1981).

Hill, M., *The Welfare State in Britain* (1993).

Jones, H. and Kandlish, M (eds), *The Myth of Consensus: New Views on British History, 1945–64* (1996).

Jordan, B., *Freedom and the Welfare State* (1976).

King, D., *Actively Seeking Work, The Politics of Unemployment and Welfare Policy* (1995).

*Lowe, R., *The Welfare State in Britain Since 1945* (2nd edn, 1999).

Marsh, D. C., *The Future of the Welfare State* (1964).

Mishra, R., *Society and Social Policy* (1977).

Page, R. N. and Silburn, R., *British Social Welfare in the Twentieth Century* (1999).

Parry, N., Rustin, M. and Satyamurti, C., *Social Work Welfare and The State* (1979).

Pinker, R., *Social Theory and Social Policy* (1971).

——, *The Idea of Welfare* (1979).

Powell, M., *New Labour, New Welfare State?*(1999).

Robson, W. A., *Welfare State and Welfare Society* (1976).

Runciman, W. G., *Relative Deprivation and Social Justice* (1966).

Seebohm Rowntree, B., *Poverty and the Welfare State* (1951).

Sullivan, N., *The Development of the British Welfare State* (1996).

Timmins, N., *The Five Giants. The Biography of the Welfare State* (1995).

*Titmuss, R. M., *Essays on 'The Welfare State'* (1958).

*——, *Commitment to Welfare* (1968).

Townsend, P. (ed.), *The Concept of Poverty* (1970).
Watkin, B., *The National Health Service: The First Phase* (1978).
*Webster, C., *The National Health Service: A Political History* (1998).
——, *The Health Services Since the War*, vol. II (1996).

Index